Ending Human Trafficking and Modern-Day Slavery

Dedication

This book is dedicated to my family for their unwavering support

and to the girls of the world, especially those in mine—

Harley, Anielly, Adri, Mischa, Cassie, Jewel, Nikki, Trinity, Aoife, Penny, Mia, Malia, Koa, Lily, Karessa, Sierra, Alana, Jazlyn, Rhianne, Mahliya, Genevie, Ligaya, Chayce, Roxy, Faith, Sophia, Sarissa, Adele, and Stella

May you grow to be fierce, brave, curious, and entirely in control of your own destiny.

Ending Human Trafficking and Modern-Day Slavery: Freedom's Journey

Annalisa Enrile, Ph.D.

Los Angeles | London | New Delhi
Singapore | Washington DC | Melbourne

FOR INFORMATION:

SAGE Publications, Inc.
2455 Teller Road
Thousand Oaks, California 91320
E-mail: order@sagepub.com

SAGE Publications Ltd.
1 Oliver's Yard
55 City Road
London EC1Y 1SP
United Kingdom

SAGE Publications India Pvt. Ltd.
B 1/I 1 Mohan Cooperative Industrial Area
Mathura Road, New Delhi 110 044
India

SAGE Publications Asia-Pacific Pte. Ltd.
3 Church Street
#10-04 Samsung Hub
Singapore 049483

Acquisitions Editor: Joshua Perigo
Editorial Assistant: Alissa Nance
Production Editor: Kimaya Khashnobish
Copy Editor: Kimberly Cody
Typesetter: C&M Digitals (P) Ltd.
Proofreader: Alison Syring
Indexer: Diggs Publication Services
Cover Designer: Gail Buschman
Marketing Manager: Jenna Retana

Copyright © 2018 by SAGE Publications, Inc.

Printed in the United States of America

ISBN: 9781506316734

Library of Congress Cataloging-in-Publication Data

Names: Enrile, Annalisa V., author.

Title: Ending human trafficking and modern-day slavery : freedom's journey / Annalisa V. Enrile.

Description: First Edition. | Thousand Oaks : SAGE Publications, [2017] | Includes bibliographical references and index.

Identifiers: LCCN 2017013960 | ISBN 9781506316734 (pbk. : alk. paper)

Subjects: LCSH: Human trafficking. | Slave trade. | Prostitution. | Women—Crimes against—Prevention.

Classification: LCC HT985 .E57 2017 | DDC 306.3/62—dc23
LC record available at https://lccn.loc.gov/2017013960

This book is printed on acid-free paper.

17 18 19 20 21 10 9 8 7 6 5 4 3 2 1

Contents

12   Faith-Based Organizations   251

13   Prevention   269

About the Author

ANNALISA ENRILE, PhD, MSW is one of the few Filipina PhDs in social work, having chosen the field as a way to bring to light important social issues in the Filipino-American community, the fastest-growing Asian immigrant population in the United States. She frequently speaks out against sex trafficking, militarization, and exploitative migrant labor. A voice for equity, human rights, and global justice, Annalisa has been recognized as one of the 100 Most Influential Filipinas in the World (FWN Global 100) for her efforts to stop violence against women. She has worked with students, communities, and academic partners to create social change and impact through innovation and collaboration.

Annalisa is a Clinical Associate Professor at the USC Suzanne Dworak-Peck School of Social Work. She teaches human behavior, management, social innovation, social change, global violence against women, and global social work. Annalisa develops curriculum and creates unique learning experiences and opportunities for students. She leads one of the school's original global immersion programs to the Philippines and Europe, in the areas of diversity, human rights, gender violence, trafficking, and change. Annalisa also coordinates the school's Doctorate in Social Work (DSW) Residency program. Annalisa is active in community organizations, including serving on several anti-trafficking task forces, and is on the board of the Mariposa Center for Change, an organization that serves women and children of color. She consults with organizations such as the Coalition to Abolish Slavery and Trafficking (CAST), Covenant House, Inc., YWCA Greater Los Angeles, and Search to Involve Pilipino Americans (SIPA). She practices transnational social work, having been an activist and advocate for vulnerable populations around the world since 1993. Annalisa would like to personally thank her family for all their support and her *kasamas* who taught her what it means to fight for women's genuine liberation, to stand in your truth and remind her every day just what is at stake if we do not struggle.

About the Contributors

Gabrielle Aquino, MSW is a Filipina-American social worker who received her Bachelor's degree in Psychology from Azusa Pacific University and her Master's degree in Social Work from University of Southern California. She has worked in the educational setting since 2009 because she believes that education plays a pivotal role in the lives of the youth she serves. In 2016, Gabrielle served on a mission's trip with her church, Fellowship Monrovia, to help a sex trafficking survivor achieve her dream of owning a cake shop. She also empowered at-risk youth by equipping them with skills so they can pursue a higher education, disrupting the common cycle of sex trafficking in Thailand. She is currently working as a school social worker at Monseñor Oscar Romero Charter School in Los Angeles to help promote Positive Behavior Interventions in the school and provide support for students so they can achieve their dreams. Gabrielle would like to thank God, her family, bible study, lifegroup, and sisters who constantly fuel her with the courage and hope to follow her dreams.

Wilhelmina De Castro, MSW, LCSW is a practicing clinical social worker and an adjunct faculty member of the USC Suzanne Dworak-Peck School of Social Work. Wilhelmina received her Bachelor's degree in Sociology from the University of California Riverside and pursued her Master's degree in Social Work at the University of Southern California. Wilhelmina has trained and practiced international social work in Southeast Asia and Central and South America. Her domestic and international work has focused on addressing and eradicating forces that contribute to human trafficking and more specifically the trafficking of girls and women. Wilhelmina has partnered with a number of nonprofits and in developing multidimensional programs to address the complex nature of domestic and international trafficking. Operating from an empowerment framework, Wilhelmina's clinical training also includes evidence-based practices that address complex trauma, domestic violence, substance abuse, depression, and psychosis. Wilhelmina would like to dedicate her work to her family, her partner, and the liberation of all women.

Charisma De Los Reyes, MSW is a Policy Analyst and Human Trafficking & Commercial Sexual Exploitation of Children (CSEC) Liaison for Child Welfare Services in San Diego County. She has over 14 years of experience in social services. She is recognized as San Diego's child welfare Agency's human trafficking and CSEC subject matter expert providing trainings, policy advisement, consultation and technical assistance to social workers and community partners across the county who encounter victims of human trafficking or children at risk for commercial sexual exploitation. Her child welfare experience also includes investigations, family preservation and engagement, placement and congregate care as well as community child maltreatment prevention projects. Charisma is a community organizer and activist with over 20 year's experience engaging in social justice and advocacy work around women's and girls' issues, both locally and internationally. Her international work includes working with communities impacted by trafficking in Southeast Asian region.

Melanie G. Ferrer-Vaughn, MSW is originally from the Bay Area, started her career as a social worker in Los Angeles, and is dedicated to combating violence against women. She has worked as a clinician helping children and families heal from sexual abuse, served overseas in the Philippines working with survivors of sex trafficking, managed a domestic violence shelter in WA, and currently works with organizations and schools to build capacity on how to identify and engage youth who are commercially sexually exploited. Melanie reenergizes herself by being with loved ones and having quality conversation around a table of great food, taking on her next DIY project, and tending to her many plants. Melanie would like to say: Annalisa, thank you for allowing me this opportunity and believing in me. Dad, Mom, and Sissy, thank you for allowing me to follow my heart and dreams, even when that meant moving away from home. My best friend and partner, Eric, your unceasing support and encouragement have continuously propelled me forward. Grandma, everything is always for you — still missing you.

Megan Healy, MSW is a Los Angeles native who received her Bachelor's degree from Loyola Marymount University and her MSW from the USC Suzanne Dworak-Peck School of Social Work. Megan is currently a social worker for the Department of Children and Family Services in Los Angeles where she specifically works with trafficked youth and CSEC. Megan is passionate about international human rights and child welfare. Megan would like to thank her family and friends for all their love and unwavering support.

Renée Smith-Maddox, PhD is a Clinical Associate Professor and Vice Chair of the Department of Social Change and Innovation at the University of Southern California Suzanne Dworak-Peck School of Social Work. She teaches policy advocacy, management, social innovation, and program evaluation courses and designs experiential learning opportunities for the Master of Social Work program and the Virtual Academic Center. As Vice Chair, Dr. Smith-Maddox provides leadership and oversight for curriculum development and instructional design. She is a member of the University's Diversity and Inclusion Council and Campus Climate Committee. Her professional and research interests include cultivating social change through social labs, teaching diversity as well as issues relating to diversity, inclusion, and equity in higher education. Renee is grateful for our diverse group of contributors who were enthusiastic in sharing ideas from their diverse interests and experiences. "Each person acted as a critical friend in reading and commenting on each other's work before finalizing—a truly collaborative project."

Acknowledgments

No one tells you when you begin to write a book that it will take more than a village. It will take a microcosm of coauthors, subject matter experts, stakeholders, other researchers, and muses. We were blessed with an outpouring of organizational support but have selected to list individuals. If by chance we have not included your name, know that you are appreciated and valued; your impact was felt. Our deepest gratitude to the valuable hands, hearts, spirits, and minds that touched this endeavor.

SPECIAL THANKS:

Liza Largoza Maza

Keavy Vicente

GreenHouse: The Center of Social Innovation

All the courageous women and men who told us their stories

WITH APPRECIATION:

Robert Acker

Hortensia Amaro, PhD

Rafael Angulo, MSW

Judith Anxonovich, MS

Maria Aranda, PhD

Ron Avi Astor, PhD

Agnes Bartolome, BSN, RN

Congresswoman Karen Bass, MSW

Liberato Bautista

William Bedroissian, MSW

Andrew Benedict-Nelson

Karra Bikson, PhD

Devon Brooks, PhD

Kat Carrido, MBA

Dina Cerezo

Anna Cho Fenly, MSW

Chrissie Deguzman

Laylani De La Vega

Greg Derelian

Tina DeZuniga

Monica Ellis, MA

Winston Emano

Amy Enrile

Eliza Enrile

Leonilo Enrile	Doris Mendoza
Dennis Garcia	Judith Mirkinson, JD
Katie Feifer	Sam Mistrano, JD
Enika Fluellen	Jacqueline Mondros, Ph.D.
Dean Marilyn Flynn, PhD	Obeth Montes
Matt Friesch	Sandra Morgan, PhD
Nancy Giordino	Mr. Del Mundo
Grace Grande	Alissa Nance
Edwin Habacon	Julia Ormond
Daniel Heimpel	Cristina Palabay
Johanna Herr	Nes Parker
Daniel Hester	Tyan Parker-Dominguez, PhD
Aldina Hovde, MSW	Alexa Pham
Asha Jayasinghe	Olivia Quinto, JD
Maheen Kaleem	Milady Quito, MA
Charlie Kaplan, PhD	Oliver Ritchie
Peter Katona	Sasha Rodovich
James Kelly	Faith Santilla
Jorja Leap, PhD	William Sarni
Maitet Ledesma	Rhonda Sciortino
Jeff Leitner	Dorothy Scott
Jollene Levid, MSW	Shah Shelbe, MS
Carrie Lew, PhD	Sharon Shelton
Caroline Lim, PhD	Grace Shiba
Rachel Lloyd	Cherrie Short, MSC
Susan Lubi	Rona Smith
Martha Lyon-Levine, PhD	Wendy Smith, PhD
Saskia Maarsen	Aquilina Soriano
Anthony Maddox, PhD	Elizabeth Swart, PhD
Paul Maiden, PhD	Lynn Tamayo
Howell Malham	Wilfred Uytengsu
Natalie Manzo	Lalee Vicedo, LCSW

Melanie Vicedo

Christopher Vicente

Vivien Villaverde, MSW

Stephanie Wander

Faye Washington

Sara Watanabe

Eugenia Weiss, PhD

Doni Whitsett, PhD

(Doña) Marleen Wong, PhD

Kristen Zaleski, PhD

A special thank you to those who literally sheltered our writing with rooms, rest houses, and even resorts of our own.

Julia Ormond, Paradise Cove

Noy DelMundo, Anilao, Batangas

The Farm at San Benito

SAGE WOULD LIKE TO THANK THE FOLLOWING REVIEWERS:

Roksana Alavi
University of Oklahoma

Jane H. Bayes
California State University, Northridge

Julie V. Brown
University of North Carolina at Greensboro

N. Chubbock
Nottingham Trent University

Maria A. Conn
Chestnut Hill College

Jan Bourne-Day
Manchester Metropolitan University Cheshire

Michelle Dietert
Texas A & M University – Central Texas

Nancy Janus
Eckerd College

Suman Kakar
Florida International University

Marleen Milner
Southeastern University

Tatyana Nestorova
Ohio State University

David Porteous
Middlesex University

Tazreena Sajjad
American University

Nadia Shapkina
Kansas State University

Kali Wright-Smith
Westminster College

Simon T. Sneddon
University of Northampton

Laura L. Starzynski
Wayne State University

Wendy Stickle
University of Maryland

Nelseta Walters-Jones
University of Maryland Eastern Shore

Ralph Weisheit
Illinois State University

Manuel F. Zamora
Angelo State University

Preface: A Different Kind of Textbook

I was 19 years old when I first met survivors of trafficking. I was attending a women's conference in Santa Barbara, California, convened by GABRIELA Philippines and Gabriela Network. It was 1995 and the conference was held in preparation for what would become a landmark event in the international women's movement—the UN's Fourth World Conference on Women in Beijing, China. In this sleepy, oceanside college town, I met factory workers from Saipan who had their lives threatened for speaking out about what was happening in export processing zones, children who were sold for sex and labor in the Philippines, and mail-order brides who had been sex trafficked and held against their will throughout Canada. This event was the catalyst to what would become my life's work in the women's movement and in my professional career.

I have now spent over 20 years in the field of human trafficking and modern day slavery. I've worked in all aspects of it—from prevention to protection; rescue to healing; and from activism to academia. When the public began being more aware of this issue, I was often told that I should write a book. I always demurred, not feeling that I was a *traditional* academic (whatever that means) and opting to focus my expression to my work in the field. And, then I began to notice the deluge of literature that was being produced—some of it spot on and some of them pure works of fiction. I also started teaching a course on global violence against women and I realized that despite the millions of pages that had been written, there was nothing that quite addressed the continuum of services that providers are responsible for. I knew that I had the background to draw from, but I still was hesitant to undertake such a daunting task. Then, in another moment of serendipity, I found myself at yet another conference where the recurring theme was the lack of knowledge of best practices around human trafficking and modern-day slavery. There was also a huge shift happening in the anti-trafficking movement from a human rights frameworks to a reliance on security and law enforcement. Finally, there was an explosion in the glamorizing of pimp culture, commodification of women's bodies, the cheapening of human lives, and the rise of migrant movement either through the push-pull of labor or as the result of conflict or natural disaster. I could keep going on and on, but the point is very few people were talking about these things. It felt like it was time to put my thoughts, experiences, and perspective onto paper.

I decided if I was going to write this book, it could not just be about human trafficking and modern-day slavery as an academic subject: I wanted to bring to life the issue's complex relationship to the helping profession and other disciplines such as business, policy, technology, and even religion. I wanted to bring to the forefront the voices of survivors and allies. I wanted this to be not only a handbook of practical information but also a call to action to abolish this system all together. I wanted to make sure that the process of writing the book honored the transnational women's movement and began to redefine the way we think about the *creation of scholarship*. I wanted a lot of things.

The first step was redefining our notions of scholarship. Along the way, I have met some incredible women who have been engaged in the field and whose commitment and passion have fueled genuine change. How could the traditional paradigm of research and the scientific method express their real-world and hands-on history as well as have them inform this book the way they have informed the field? In academia, we value the author of the words and the tester of hypothesis and theory. We don't give credit to the convener of thoughts, the gatherer of stories, the community mentors, or the on-the-spot responders. There is no byline for those activities to share. This book aims to change that. I have brought together a group of *Anti-Trafficking Warriors*, gladiators in the fight to stop trafficking. Each of these women have made significant contributions in the realm of human rights and trafficking. Not all of them are researchers or writers, but each one has contributed to the formation of the book whether this was through the sharing of their insights, creating dialogues in the community to test our ideas, relationships with survivors, growing of networks of providers and other stakeholders . . . as you can see, more than the list of what we wanted to do, the list of the talents that we brought together in the project was endless. I wanted to value the process of cocreation. So the book became a process of *we*. Each chapter begins with a personal vignette of one of our warriors and an instance of her work that also addresses the theme or content of the chapter. We wanted readers to be able to get a view from the frontlines. It's been an honor to bring all our collective knowledge together.

Once we assembled our team of anti-trafficking warriors, we addressed the issue of *how* we would talk about human trafficking and modern-day slavery. From the beginning, just as we come from diverse backgrounds of circumstance and experience, we knew that we had to approach the issue through a diversity of fields and so as much as possible we have tried to do just that—examination and analysis from a multidisciplinary perspective. In line with this type of intersectional thinking, we decided that we would attempt to provide a global perspective to the book. There are more things about the world that are the same than different, but it is important to note the cultural, and historical nuances that each country specifically faces. Where we have been able to, we have included international discussions and examples. It is important to note that we don't claim to give a comprehensive global scope, nor do any of the countries we mention serve as templates for universalizing phenomena, but we did feel it was imperative to provide a real view of what is occurring at the regional level and within individual countries.

Each chapter is constructed as a practical guide and not just a conceptual discourse that waxes on and on about the topic. Other people could *talk* about trafficking. We want readers to "do" and take action. Often, books on trafficking straddle the edge of actual action planning. We want people to walk away with actual methodologies they can put into practice, or at least think about in terms of how to prevent, intervene, and advocate for. To accomplish this, each chapter ends with a "call to action," or a challenge of how to continue to build the anti-trafficking and abolitionist movements.

Finally, we wanted to put the voices of the survivors and their closest allies at the forefront of the book. This has been the most gratifying, humbling, and inspiring experience we've ever had. Again, we didn't want to just narrowly define survivor's participation as sharing of their stories. We also turned to groups of survivors for every chapter we wrote to make sure that our words were relevant and had impact. We met with key informants as we got stuck in the process not knowing if we were going in the right direction, or just regurgitating old ideas. We have included the paths survivors have gone through in our case vignettes and examples. All cases and examples presented here are based on our interactions and communication with survivors and at times their allies (as in the case of the discussion of Women's Human Rights' Defenders). And, of course, we listened to what they dreamed of and envisioned when we asked what the end of human trafficking and modern-day slavery would look like.

Human trafficking and modern-day slavery is gaining momentum in our social consciousness. More and more people are beginning to understand the scope and scale of this horrific phenomenon. Governments are now engaged and companies working to create immediate solutions. But, this hasn't always been the case. This book was written to honor the process of what has gotten us to this point and hopefully provide steps to moving forward.

Historical Contexts, Definitions, and Root Causes of Human Trafficking and Modern-Day Slavery

It is difficult to figure out where to begin when discussing human trafficking and modern-day slavery. We could open with random references to the United Nations' treaties or conventions or even when the United States first began to create policies, dedicate offices, and allocate funds to the issues. Isn't this the starting point, here at the turn of the 21st century, making this a wicked problem of our time? Yes, it would be easy to make this the starting point, but the truth about trafficking came to light long before. The International Women's Movement already had human trafficking and modern-day slavery on its agenda as early as the 1970s. From the beginning, this issue was multilayered and multidimensional. To fully understand human trafficking and modern-day slavery, we must begin to unravel the myths and misinformation surrounding it, as well as provide basic understanding for how to address it.

Most texts have ignored the full historical context and root causes of human trafficking and modern-day slavery or have chosen to just focus on incidences and prevalence. By doing so, the implication for the helping professions and the interventions that we use are severely limited. We must begin to understand not only the full scope of the issue but also how this issue originates and what the various push-pull factors and social determinants are. Our definition of the problem will also define our solution set in terms of how we treat and eventually prevent it. Therefore, this first part of the book provides a space where we examine root causes of how human trafficking and modern-day slavery evolved and how it continues to occur across and within borders.

In chapter 1, we will first define and understand trafficking from a number of conceptual angles. In addition to creating a common taxonomy, we will highlight several approaches that we might take in understanding the issue. In chapter 2, we will offer a look at the business of slavery, primarily from the economic model of supply and demand because the arguments have been laid out by leading economists in the field. In chapter 3, we will take you through identified root causes and social determinants that go beyond anecdotal viewpoints on this issue. Some of these may be controversial, such as the role of the police, military, and even of the state as perpetrators. Some of them may even seem archaic such as patriarchy. But, we assure you, all these root causes and determinants are not only pivotal to understanding but relevant to current circumstances.

For the purposes of this book, we will be operating from several theoretical lenses. These include empowerment theory and a critical feminist perspective. Empowerment theory is predicated on the premise of agency and action. Wherever possible, we will look at perspectives from those who are engaged in the topics we present and from the perspective of those who are trafficked as well as others who may be affected. Empowerment theory is also concerned with understanding ecosystemic contexts, including multiple perspectives such as historical, political, scientific, sociocultural, and economic concerns and the systems, subsystems, and suprasystems contained within. This theoretical vantage point also challenges the reader to expressions of action with a large component of this theory based on being able to *act* on the knowledge that is generated.

The feminist perspective will center around theories of transnational feminism, radical, and materialist feminisms. Transnational feminism (which has its roots in radical and materialist feminism) is a developing perspective that also takes into account intersections of nationhood, ethnicity, race, gender, sexuality, religion, politics, and socioeconomics within the context of globalization and colonialization. Transnational feminism examines how these things have redefined (or removed) borders, realigned migration patterns, and as such re-created power differentials. This perspective upholds the definition of sisterhood and solidarity based on equity, understanding, and mutual experiences. It is important to note there is a lot of variability in the women's movement and within feminist ideologies overall. Historically, feminists have had contrasting viewpoints toward trafficking and modern-day slavery and therefore, have had clashing solutions sets. For instance, liberal feminists focus on decriminalization and many times legalization of the prostitution industry. Transnational, radical, and materialist feminists tend to have the view of abolitionist tactics. But prostitution is only one aspect of trafficking, and we will not let ourselves get stuck in that debate at the detriment of other aspects and forms of trafficking, especially the migration and exploitation of global labor. Though we have no wish to oversimplify, the book will adhere to the global definition of the United Nation's "Palermo Protocol," the backbone of trafficking policies and legislation. Chapter 1 goes into depth about this particular definition and how we will continue to define and describe issues in this text.

Each chapter will have a set of learning objectives, discussion questions, and important points highlighted either through place-specific examples or overall trends in the field. You will also be provided with challenge-based activities in each section to put into practice the skill sets you are acquiring. A glossary of vocabulary words will be provided at each section introduction. The list is not exhaustive but meant to provide a foundation for a common language of human trafficking and modern-day slavery. At the end of each section, we will also supplement with case vignettes or a long, complex case example. By understanding and giving you exposure to these types of cases, you will be able to then begin to gain practical understandings about human trafficking and modern-day slavery. There is nothing more powerful that the stories survivors are sharing, so we will also tell their stories throughout this text.

GLOSSARY OF TERMS

Amerasian—the term used to commonly refer to a person born of a U.S. military father and an Asian mother (particularly, this term colloquially refers to the phenomenon of the Asian women who are prostituted). Often, this person is the subject of discrimination based on their parentage.

APEC—the Asia-Pacific Economic Cooperation was created in 1989. Twenty-one countries make up this forum. The United States is one of the members of the economic community.

Caste—system of dividing society into hereditary classes. Some groups inherit specific perks while others specific detriments are due to parentage.

Chattel Slavery—often referred to as "traditional slavery" because of the person being owned as personal property.

Contractualization—replacing of regular workers with temporary workers who receive lower wages with no or less benefits.

Deregulation—reduction or elimination of government power in a particular industry in favor of privatization. Deregulation is usually enacted to create more competition within the industry.

EU—the European Union, formerly known as the European Economic Community, was begun in the aftermath of World War II but formalized into the organization in 1993. Twenty-eight countries make up this union. The EU abolished formal "borders" between countries, allowing citizens to travel throughout the participating countries to access better jobs and living conditions. In 2016, the United Kingdom exited from the EU opting to be independent, which caused economic instability in the region.

Export Processing Zone—areas within developing countries that offer incentives and a barrier-free environment to promote economic growth by attracting foreign investment for export-oriented production.

GDP—Gross Domestic Product is the monetary value of all the finished goods and services produced within a country's borders in a specific time period.

Globalization—the development of an increasingly integrated *global* economy marked especially by free trade, free flow of capital, and the tapping of cheaper foreign labor markets.

Human Rights—legal, ethical, or social principles sometimes expressed as policies or legislation that describe and/or protect rights that are understood to be inalienable, fundamental, and inherent to all human beings regardless of their status. Human rights are considered to be universal invariants such as the right to life, health and well-being, food, and shelter. Further, rights such as education, freedom from enslavement, and political freedom are also considered by many (though not all) to be human rights.

IMF—according to the website, the International Monetary Fund is an organization of 189 countries, working to foster global monetary cooperation, secure financial stability, facilitate international trade, promote high employment and sustainable economic growth, and reduce poverty around the world.

Labor Migration—the movement of people for the purpose of employment, often in the informal sector or sectors vulnerable to abuse and exploitation.

Liberalization—process of relaxing government restrictions. These relaxations of policies can be in social, political, or economic forums.

Mail-Order Brides—a woman brought from another country to be married, usually in return for a payment to a company that makes such arrangements.

Militarization—the process by which a society organizes itself for military conflict and violence.

Military-Industrial Complex—network of individuals and institutions involved in the production of weapons and military technologies. The military-industrial complex in a country typically attempts to marshal political support for continued or increased military spending by the national government.

Modern-Day Slavery—refers to the current phenomena of slavery after the 20th century.

Multinational Corporation—a company that is operating in several different countries but usually manages in one "home" country. The corporation usually makes a large amount of its profits from business in various outside countries.

NAFTA—North American Free Trade Agreement refers to the trade agreement between the United States, Mexico, and Canada signed on January 1, 1994.

Non-Personage—no longer having qualities that would define a human being.

Patriarchy—system of government, society, and culture where men hold all power and decision making (and women are largely excluded). The ideology that men inherently should hold all the power. In patriarchal cultures, familial lines are traced through the male line.

Price Elasticity of Demand—the measure of the change in demand of a product because of the change in price.

Push and Pull Factors—socioeconomic, political, cultural, or other forces that force people to migrate to a new location. Push factors are those that drive people to leave their homelands (usually conflict, poverty, natural disaster, etc.). Pull factors are those that attract people to a new location (such as job opportunities, education, quality of living).

ROI—return on investment is a ratio designed to understand the profitability of a commodity.

Social Determinants—conditions and contexts into which people live, such as where they are born, grow, live, health, class, culture, religion. Social determinants may shape situations and affect distribution or access to resources.

Supply and Demand—amount of a commodity, product, or service available and the desire of buyers for it, considered as factors regulating its price.

Supply Chain—a network between a company and its suppliers to produce and distribute a specific product, and the supply chain represents the steps it takes to get the product or service to the customer.

Structural Adjustment Loan—type of loan provided to developing countries. This loan often creates dependency of developing nations on developed nations and has been widely criticized as creating more poverty instead of alleviating poverty.

Structural Adjustment Program—loans provided by the IMF and the World Bank to countries and regions that are experiencing economic crisis.

TIP Report—The Trafficking in Persons (TIP) Report is the U.S. Government's principal diplomatic tool to engage foreign governments on human trafficking.

Trafficking—the recruitment, transportation, transfer, harboring, or receipt of persons, by means of the threat or use of force or other forms of coercion, of abduction, of fraud, of deception, of the abuse of power or of a position of vulnerability or of the giving or receiving of payments or benefits to achieve the consent of a person having control over another person for the purpose of exploitation. Exploitation shall include, at a minimum, the exploitation of the prostitution of others or other forms of sexual exploitation, forced labor or services, slavery or practices similar to slavery, servitude, or the removal of organs. *Important notation: Trafficking is not limited to physical coercion, "grab and go" kidnapping, or moving across borders or locations.*

Transnational (Corporations)—operating in or involving more than one country. Unlike other companies that operate in multiple countries, a transnational corporation does not identify any one country as its home base.

Transnational Social Movements—a group of organizations or single organization in multiple countries that are united in fighting for a similar goal or cause. They are committed to consistent and sustained action, usually against social injustice.

World Bank—international financing group that works to promote developing nations. The organization offers loans to developing countries to promote the goal of ending extreme poverty. However, there is much criticism of the World Bank because of its use of structural adjustment plans that are often the basis of loans as well as how the bank is governed. The World Bank is part of the World Bank Group, which is part of the United Nations.

Introduction and History of Human Trafficking and Modern-Day Slavery

Chapter Objectives

1. Readers will recognize and label definitions of trafficking.

2. Readers will be able to identify, describe, and classify different types of trafficking.

3. Readers will demonstrate understanding of the scope and prevalence of trafficking domestically and globally.

4. Readers will develop conceptual approaches to human trafficking.

I was only 19 years old, a sophomore in college. I'd barely been in love, much less understood the negotiations of sexual politics, and had yet to learn that one had nothing to do with the other. Sexual assault was an urban bogeyman, told to me by parents who did not want me to drink too much at some fraternity house and end up a statistic. Women who sold their bodies were encapsulated into stories a la Pretty Women, where "hookers" with a heart of gold could find billionaires and be saved. In other words, I knew nothing about nothing.

I went to my first international women's conference on a lark. I saw a poster on a bulletin board that it was being held in Santa Barbara, California, and went on a road trip with a group of friends. That was when I met Carmen, who shared her experience of being sexually exploited. As a half African American and Filipina "Amerasian" street child born in Olongapo, Philippines (home of the former U.S. Subic Bay Military Base), she was ridiculed for her darkness and lack of a father. Everyone

(Continued)

(Continued)

called her mother a prostitute, and it was not long before she was brought into a club and forced to dance and eventually perform sexual acts. Her mother had died a year earlier of what looked like AIDS, but what the hospital said was nothing more than acute pneumonia. Carmen was only 14. When she turned 17, a man from Australia began to write her letters through an ad that her pimp placed on a website. Eventually, this man said he loved her and paid a fee to the pimp and bar owner to release her as his fiance. Carmen became one of thousands of "mail-order brides" who would leave the Philippines. She said to us, "I left with so much hope that my life was going to be better." It wasn't. Carmen moved to the Australian outback, where she was alone and isolated with only her husband to support her. At first, he was kind, but he started to control all her actions and then started to beat her. Three years later, at the age of 20, she ran away by hiding in a supply van that went to the city. Once there, she slept on the street until she found a couple traveling to the United States who were looking for a nanny. She agreed to work for them and they liked her because she spoke English. Carmen said, "I remember getting on the plane and thinking, now my life will get better." It didn't. Once they arrived in the United States, her new "employers" took away her passport and locked her in their condo where she was forced to work 20 hour days and be at their beck and call. She slept on the floor of a small room and escaped only when one of her traffickers forgot to lock the door one day. By this time, she was 22 years old. She was alone on the streets of Los Angeles and looked for help. She found a women's shelter, but they could not help her because they didn't understand what happened to her and moreover, didn't seem to believe or understand her story. Again, she lived on the street until she found an organization that provided transitional housing who agreed to let her stay the night. After hearing her story, they began to help her get her life back together. Carmen ended her talk, "I still have hope. My life got better."

Carmen was 22—only a few years older than me, but we were a universe apart. Her story was compelling, but it wasn't the only story I heard during that conference. It was 1995—a week before the historic Fourth World Conference on Women that would be held in Beijing. The word "trafficking" was used, but not widely. It was still a human rights phenomenon that feminists and other activists were trying to interject into the mainstream. I would understand that later, when I became part of the "movement." But, at this moment, there was only the words of women who shared experiences I never imagined existed and the blossoming of the idea that I could do something to help create change. To this day, more than twenty years later, I still like to think of that something as "Carmen's hope."

—Annalisa Enrile

Beaten, bound, and broken. These are the images of trafficking that dominate the media and public imagination. Equally prevalent is the idea of a shadowy underworld where clandestine deals are made selling human beings, usually children and women.

Of course, some of these images are hyperboles and stereotypes, but they are rooted in truth. Trafficking *is* criminal, illegal activity, occurring under the radar. Yet, it is also true that trafficking happens not only out in the open but also within established institutions. For example, in the United States, child welfare agencies are challenged with traffickers and procurers purposefully entering foster homes, camps, and group homes to recruit girls into commercial sexual exploitation of children (CSEC) situations (Fong & Cardoso, 2010). In the Philippines, labor migration has long been an official policy of the government, encouraging women's migrant labor in exchange for the high remittances that are keeping the country's GDP afloat. Philippine government officials often turn a blind eye to the vulnerabilities of labor trafficking and modern-day slavery that many women find themselves in. Even in areas where there is legalization of prostitution, it is often a front for the exploitation of other classes and populations of women who are being trafficked literally behind storefronts, as evidenced in Amsterdam and Belgium. It is not surprising, then, that one of the most globally complicated issues is trafficking and modern-day slavery. Thousands of nonprofit organizations, nongovernmental spaces, and mixed enterprises have risen to the challenge in the efforts of prevention, education, and clinical interventions to address and end trafficking. The movement against trafficking and modern-day slavery has reached a crescendo, building on a groundswell of support. However, this has been a painstaking, community-mobilizing process. To understand both the issue and the fight against it, one must examine and understand the trajectory of building these pathways to freedom.

There has never been a lull in the commodification of women (and children) in the flesh trade for either sex or labor. In the last twenty-five years, we have seen a greater demand for modern-day slavery. The push of globalization and the drive for cheaper labor and super-profits have made it so that businesses believe that they have almost no options but to exploit slave or slavelike conditions in parts (or whole) of their supply chain if they want to generate a profit. Further, globalization, which moves goods and peoples in newer and more frequent migration patterns, reveals some aspects of how trafficking is actually expanding instead of retracting. This is despite the amount of education, awareness, and prevention work that is being done (Jani & Anstadt, 2013).

HISTORY OF SLAVERY

Slavery, as we know from our history lessons, is a legacy in colonialism and imperialism, serving as the fuel to agricultural industries up until the end of the 19th century. Freeing slaves took political acts by government (first in Europe and then in the Americas), but these acts had to be followed up by social, economic, and psychological supports. In many cases, this did not happen and slavelike conditions and mentalities persisted (Craig, 2013). In fact, more than 200,000 adult slaves remained in former French colonies in Africa's Sahel until the 1960s (*The Economist,* October 30, 2016). The repercussions of slavery are apparent when one looks at the uneven economic and social development of nations that were suppliers of slave labor, which informed the construction of notions of the world as *first* and *third; north* and *south;* and *developed* and *undeveloped.* A better way to understand the true status of countries are categories of *rich* and *poor* (countries that are generally defined as having poverty levels of 50% or more). Slavery, in all its forms has consistently existed in modern societies long after the 19th century. In fact, we are living in a time when there are more slaves than any other point in history (Skinner, 2008).

Two disciplinary lenses best equipped to discuss the timeline of slavery are that of history and anthropology. The historical lens provides a perspective that includes the political economy of context. Anthropologists account for almost 10% of all slavery studies. In a review of studies, very little of the content covered slavery in the New World. Similarly, ancient slavery was treated as a consequence of necessity, of social and human development. At most, it was examined as a by-product of spoils of war. It is not until the phenomenon of *chattel slavery* that anthropologists begin to analyze the institution as its own whole system of economy.

It is impossible to dispute the fact that slavery has been in existence from some of our earliest records of humanity. In 1720 BC, the Code of Hammurabi is the first to document the law as it pertains to slavery and around that same time, there are biblical accounts. In 700 BC, there is evidence of the African slave trade that operated internally within the Sahara Desert and required places that served as "trading posts," which are the first signs of the selling of humans we have historically (History World, n.d.). In 416 BC, slavery is prominent in the wars between the Greeks and the Turks. Slavery becomes a feature of societal hierarchies throughout the ancient world. Egyptian and Roman armies and governments make slavery not only a spoil of warfare but also a key component in the development of their empires.

In 1446, "new world" chattel slavery as we know it begins with Portugal claiming ownership of Guinea, which will become the center of the African slave trade. The key features of "chattel slavery" is the coercion into slavery, often in the form of kidnapping. Slaves are usually transported and kept through a series of violent beatings and threats to their loved ones. Chattel slavery is complete ownership of a slave so that they are thought of and treated as property that is owned in perpetuity. This includes any offspring so that their children are born enslaved and may also be sold. In 1793, the Fugitive Slave Laws passes in the United States, which allows slave owners to go after runaway slaves who had escaped to the North. The Underground Railroad begins with a group of abolitionists in the northern states who transport, hide, and shuttle slaves into freedom.

The world begins to move toward antislavery legislation in the mid-1800s. In 1850, Brazil, who at the time was the second largest importer of African slaves, bans the slave trade. In the United States, it will take a Civil War and fifteen more years to pass the 13th Amendment to the U.S. Constitution in 1865 that will outlaw any "involuntary servitude." Ten years later, in 1875, Portugal made slavery illegal. However, it was not until 1981 that the last of chattel slavery in the world was obliterated from the West African nation of Mauritania, where there was anywhere from 350,000 to 680,000 slaves (Sutter, 2012). Although chattel slavery ended, it did not mean that slavery in the world was eliminated. Instead, it took on a different form now referred to as "modern-day slavery."

The defining feature of modern-day slavery is the move from a master-slave relationship (i.e., legal ownership) to one where illegal control and forced labor are enforced. In some ways, this is a slight nuance, or even semantics, but in the world of trafficking it is a distinction that poses questions of human rights, legality, labor laws, immigration/migration, and political economy (Manzo, 2005). For anti-trafficking practitioners, it is maddening splitting of hairs because whether slavery takes an old or modern form, it continues to rely on a system of exploitation, violence, and loss of free will (Bales, 1999).

According to Bales (2007), there was resurgence of slavery from 1945 onward because of an increase in the world's population and massive economic changes that widened the gap between the rich and the poor, and this was accompanied by police and military corruption. The poorest places were the ones with the highest incidences of slavery. This grew into post–World War II tensions and conflict. After the tumult of the 1970s, particularly in Vietnam and other parts in Southeast Asia, military and political conflict occurred within the backdrop of the rest and recreation industry. The fall of the Soviet Union in 1991 also set off a wave of mail-order brides from former Soviet-block countries especially the Ukraine, Russia, Belarus, and Moldova (Jackson, 2007). This moved the center of the sex trafficking trade from Asia to Europe, especially from the Ukraine, the second largest country in Europe (Hughes, 2000). Marriage agencies were created, but a major way that recruitment occurred was actually through other women who were trafficked and victimized. Although technically not included of the official definition of "trafficking," the vulnerability to abuse that (mostly) women find themselves in as a mail-order bride intersects with more traditional notions of sex trafficking. This, coupled with the prostitution of hundreds of thousands of women from the former Soviet Union, including Russia, to over 50 countries in the world, became known as the "Natasha" trade (Vandenberg, 1997).

The 1990s were rife with international trade agreements that were, for the most part, favorable only for already rich countries such as NAFTA and APEC. These agreements were based on deregulation and liberalization of industry, which turned already poor or poorer countries into slavery zones or countries where a large portion of its labor force is involved in slave-like labor. Labor trafficking and modern-day slavery compose the largest portion of trafficking, though it is eclipsed by sex trafficking. The International Labor Organization finds a parallel between where the largest number of forced laborers are found and the degree of development (paralleled by these economic agreements). For instance, the Asia-Pacific region accounts for the largest numbers (56% of the global totals), followed by Africa (18%), and Latin America (9%) (ILO, 2014). Men and boys compose a larger number of those who are labor trafficked, particularly in the industries of agriculture, fishing, construction, and mining. Domestic workers were separated from these overall numbers because they represent a distinct proportion to those of forced labor and second, because a profit estimate could not be generated due to the totally informal nature of this sector (ILO, 2013). From these historical events and phases, growing vulnerabilities to what is considered the current state of trafficking, the foundation of exploitation, commodification, and resistance are found (see Figure 1.1)

Figure 1.1   Human Trafficking Data, 2012

WHAT IS HUMAN TRAFFICKING?

The terms "human trafficking" and "trafficking in persons" describe the acts associated with recruiting, harboring, transporting, providing, or obtaining a person for the purposes of forced labor or prostitution. This brutal crime can take many nuanced forms, but the common thread among them is a person, or group of people, being held against their will and forced to either work or perform sex acts for the benefit of their captor and often with little or no benefit of any kind to themselves.

It is important to differentiate between human trafficking and the act of migrant smuggling. There are four key differences. First, smuggling always involves consent, while trafficking does not. Second, smuggling ends with the migrants' arrival at their destination, while trafficking involves the ongoing exploitation of the victim. Third, smuggling is always transnational, whereas trafficking does not have to involve transporting the victim. Finally, income from smuggling is derived from the transportation or facilitation of an illegal border crossing, while income from trafficking is derived from continued exploitation of the victim.

The Act

| Recruitment |
| Transport |
| Transfer |
| Harboring |
| Receipts of persons |

+

The Means

Threat/use of force	Abuse of power
Coercion	Giving payments
Abduction	Giving benefits
Fraud	Deception

+

The Purpose

Prostitution of others	Removal of organs
Sexual exploitation	Slavery
Forced labor	Other exploitation

The **three primary elements** of human trafficking, the act of trafficking, the means of trafficking, and the purpose of trafficking, are listed in this chart.

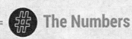 The Numbers

800K   The number of people trafficked across international borders every year is approximately 800,000.

2.5M   It is estimated that the number of total human trafficking victims in the world is 2.5 million at any given time.

$32B   The global human trafficking industry generates $32 billion a year in profits.

76%   In 2009, 76 percent of all global human trafficking victims were female.

Trafficking Across the Globe

According to the United Nations 2012 Global Report on Trafficking in Persons, exploitation may take many forms. For the UN report, 81 countries reported information about the forms of exploitation for a total of 34,800 victims detected between 2007 and 2010 in those countries. The data show that in Europe, Central Asia, and the Americas, more than half of all human trafficking cases involved sex trafficking. And while sex trafficking crimes make up a smaller percentage of cases of human trafficking in Africa, the Middle East, Asia, and the South Pacific, they still make up a significant portion of the total cases of human trafficking in those regions.

Sexual exploitation   Forced labor   Organ removal & other forms

EUROPE & CENTRAL ASIA
- 62%
- 31%
- 7%

AMERICAS
- 51%
- 44%
- 5%

SOUTH ASIA, EAST ASIA, & PACIFIC
- 44%
- 47%
- 9%

AFRICA & THE MIDDLE EAST
- 36%
- 49%
- 15%

Sex Trafficking

According to the U.S. State Department, when an adult or child is coerced, forced, or deceived into prostitution through one of these means after initially consenting — that person is a victim of sex trafficking. Under these circumstances, the perpetrators involved in recruiting, harboring, transporting, providing, or obtaining a person for that purpose are responsible for trafficking crimes. The State Department says sex trafficking also may occur within debt bondage, as women and girls are forced to continue in prostitution through the use of unlawful "debt" purportedly incurred through their transportation, recruitment, or even their crude "sale" — which exploiters insist they must pay off before they can be free.

79% Of all of the types of exploitation, sex trafficking is identified 79 percent of the time, making it the most commonly identified form.

1M Approximately one million children are exploited by the global sex trafficking industry each year.

12-14 The average age of entry into sex trafficking in the United States, Canada, and Mexico.

Source: Grayson Mendenhall and Kristi Walker

DEFINING TRAFFICKING

One hundred sixteen countries signed the United Nations Convention against Transnational Organized Crime in Palermo, Italy, in 2000. Since then, the protocol has been ratified several times. The protocol has been referred to since then as the "Palermo Protocol" and focuses on the three P's: prevention, prosecution, and protection. The United Nations, through the Palermo Protocol, developed a widely accepted definition of trafficking as: trafficking in persons' shall mean the recruitment, transportation, transfer, harboring or receipt of persons, by threat or use of force, by abduction, fraud, deception [inducement], coercion or the abuse of power, or by the giving or receiving of payments or benefits to achieve the consent of a person having control over another person, for the purpose of exploitation [irrespective of the consent of the person]; exploitation shall include, at a minimum, [the exploitation of prostitution or other forms of sexual exploitation], forced labour or services, slavery or practices similar to slavery [or servitude] (United Nations Office on Drugs and Crime [UNODC], 2014). The protocol pronounced the legal terminology that would allow for the prosecution of traffickers. In its 2000 iteration, the protocol emphasized differences between "exploitation of prostitution" and "prostitution" (referring to "voluntary" prostitution or "sex work"). This allowed many countries to sign the protocol even if prostitution was legalized either partially or completely. However, what this also did was create two perspectives: either an accused-oriented/law-and-order perspective or a victim-oriented one. In the United States, all 50 states have defined trafficking as a crime, but this still does not ensure complete understanding of the issue or a uniform way to address it. If we are going to tackle this issue in a dynamic and multidisciplinary way, we must expand those perspectives and definitions. The Palermo Protocol will be discussed in more depth in chapter 9.

The term "modern-day slavery" is used broadly to encapsulate human trafficking and to establish the difference between historical aspects of slavery and current trends. It is a term that is meant to invoke comparisons to chattel slavery, which was prevalent in the 18th and 19th centuries. Remember, this form of slavery is where one person owns another as property they have purchased. The definition of modern-day slavery has been expanded to include debt bondage, indentured servitude, and other forms of control. "Modern-day slavery" began to be used because the term "human trafficking" assumes that transport must take place across borders. In truth, the phenomenon can and does occur in victim's own neighborhoods.

There are many facets to defining slavery based on the "type" of slavery and trafficking and individual experiences as well as a number of typologies to consider. These typologies are based on movement (domestic versus international), type of labor (sexual versus nonsexual), age (minor versus adult), and consent versus coercion (Nawyn & Birdal, 2014). "Free the Slaves," a nonprofit advocacy, antiabolitionist organization that was founded in 2000 and believes in a community based strategies, identifies distinct occurrences of slavery ("Free the Slaves," n.d.). These are as follows:

- Contract slavery: workers who are deceived into slavery through false employment contracts. The contracts serve as lures because of the promise of genuine employment. For instance, in Saudi Arabia and Qatar, many construction projects lure migrant workers with the promise of lucrative contracts. When they arrive at the site, their passports are taken and in some cases they are physically restrained until their work on the project is completed. During this time, they are compensated little, if at all, and often their families and lives are threatened if they attempt to run.

- Debt bondage: this type of slavery is based on high usury loans where an individual accepts from moneylender and the borrower is then indebted due to the high interest rates until they are forced to "work off" the loan. The debt continues to grow, despite the work, as more and more items may be added to the principal, which in turn raises the already outrageous interest. In both sex and labor slavery, this type of debt bondage is prevalent. Acute examples of this type of debt bondage is exemplified in almost all countries where domestic workers are located. They are usually hired through an employment agency, which starts with exorbitant fees they are expected to pay, and which only increases with the addition of other "debts."

- Forced or servile marriage: where a girl or woman has been forced into marriage against her will. This is a form of "selling" a woman or girl, usually to pay for family debts or to restore the girl's honor (even if there is sexual assault involved). In China, there are a number of stories of women and girls who are kidnapped and then forced into marriages, particularly in the provinces (countrysides or rural areas), where life is difficult and there are very few women to wed.

- Domestic servitude: where household workers (such as maids) are not permitted to leave their employers' residences and typically receive little/no pay and are vulnerable to any number of abuses including rape. In Hong Kong, there is a "live-in" rule for domestic workers. Domestic workers who are found "living out" of their employers' homes can be arrested and deported.

- Sex trafficking: prostitution or commercial sex acts engaged in as a result of force, fraud, threat, or coercion. "Consent" is not relevant if threat or force, whether physical or psychological. Child sex trafficking can never be considered consensual.

- Child soldiers: children who are forced to become soldiers and engage in combat and/or forced into armed forces. For example, in the conflicts occurring in the Democratic Republic of the Congo, tens of thousands of children have been either forced or illegally recruited into military forces.

- Organ trafficking: the illegal sale or procurement of organs for transplant. This is particularly rampant in the sale of kidneys, followed by livers. According the United Nations, the trafficking of organs and the trafficking of persons for organ removal are two different crimes. The latter is generally straightforward and covered in the protocols against trafficking. However, there has yet to be an agreed-upon definition for the trafficking of organs. This could be due to the ambiguous nature of what countries define as "consent." A vast majority of those who are trafficked are males. This phenomenon began as "transplant tourism" with those who could afford it traveling to areas where donor rules had been relaxed. Soon, however, it turned into a clandestine trafficking trade that flourishes far and wide from India, South Africa, and Kosovo (UNODC, 2015).

- Cyber trafficking: refers to the use of the Internet and cyberspaces for the recruitment of victims, advertisement and engagement of victim services, and attracting clients. To date, there is no legal definition. Only a 2001 Council of Europe Convention on Cybercrime (CETS No 185) made reference to cyber trafficking in terms of child pornography (Sykiotou, 2013).

Depending on the country of focus, there are nuances to each of these definitions that may only be relevant for that country, further adding to the variance in defining trafficking and modern day slavery. These nuances may be due to legal definitions of trafficking, cultural considerations, political contexts, economic factors, and more.

Since this book provides a global scope, international definitions are most useful and will take precedence over regional. Keeping this in mind, this book will utilize the definitions provided by the United Nations (UN), as they have been the most widely adopted internationally. Any other definitions will be clarified when necessary if they differ from the United Nations. Further, it should be clear that this definition is a strict definition of trafficking and cuts through many of the discussions and debates around typology and taxonomy, but that we are in no way trying to simplify what is complicated. For example, the lack of an agreed-upon definition is a tremendous problem because it causes fluctuation in numbers (of incidence and scope) and makes identification fluid and difficult. The UN definition, taken strictly, is a necessary stance we take to uphold a more universal interpretation of what we should consider trafficking: any exploitation and commodification in the trade of human beings.

The largest definitional categories used to define and describe trafficking and modern-day slavery is the deceptively dichotomous use of the terms "sex trafficking" and "labor trafficking." On the surface, it might seem that these are two different categories, but there are many fine lines that make it difficult to discern between the two. For example, women who are trafficked for domestic services are vulnerable to rape and other types of sexual assault, which could be construed as sex trafficking. In fact, though sex trafficking actually constitutes a smaller percentage of those who are trafficked, there is much more attention paid to it. There are various reasons for this, including the outrage that the public feels when they hear about instances of sex trafficking, especially as it relates to children. Further, reasons such as the fact that many nations do not acknowledge forced labor as human trafficking are also why sex trafficking may be more prominent in the literature and social consciousness (Hepburn & Simon, 2013). This is also reflected in the policies and sentencing between the different forms of trafficking (we will talk more about this in section 3 of the text).

SEX TRAFFICKING

Sex trafficking has its own distinct characteristics. As we have mentioned, it is the smaller of the two areas of trafficking, but the one that people most readily identify because of the way it has been handled by the media, governments, and the public in general. It is an area of trafficking that is dominated by women and children but almost always perpetrated by men (Pearce, Hynes, & Bovarnick, 2009). This is the case even when it seems as if women are procurers, traffickers, or pimps. Often, these women are working on the behalf of a "bigger boss"—usually a man. It is impossible and would be wrong to minimize or even equalize the victimization of women and girls over that of men and boys. However, it is important to note that boys and men are also victims of sex trafficking, especially in international settings or instances of what is referred to as "survivor sex" that many runaway and homeless youth are forced to engage in. Although it is a rare statistic, one study found that 90% of children who were sexually exploited were boys (Todres, 1999). Sex trafficking of boys also feeds into the high demand for child pornography, which is related to trafficking, with almost half the exploited being boys (UNICEF, 2001). LGBT persons are also vulnerable to sex trafficking. Particularly notorious are the "ladyboys" of Thailand, Burma, and Cambodia, but there are also documented cases from of LGBT victims trafficked from the Caribbean and Latin America into Western Europe and African victims trafficked in the Arab Gulf States. In the United States, homeless LGBT youth are much more likely to be vulnerable to trafficking than are heterosexual homeless minors (Martinez & Kelle, 2013).

The full extent of sexual exploitation and slavery is unknown, though often the United States will cite an estimate of 800,000 persons a year trafficked across borders (UNICEF, 2005). The numbers may be somewhat unclear because some countries vary in their definitions of sex trafficking, often not including prostitution or other aspects such as mail-order brides, surrogacy, and "legal" prostitution. Sex slaves are usually found in red-light districts, usually in some type of brothel or in clubs. However, they are also found in more private settings such as homes, apartments, and hotels. With the emergence of cybersex trafficking, there are any number of areas where sex trafficking may be occurring. Most slaves are never allowed to leave or are forced to live together. Brothels can house anywhere from a handful to hundreds of sex slaves, often in deplorable conditions whether in rich or poor countries.

Understanding Sex Work

One of the most controversial discussions is the debate within sex trafficking over the question of prostitution. This is prevalent in much of the sex trafficking literature, which is riddled with discussion over the difference between "forced prostitution" and "sex workers" as well as the overarching question as to whether or not prostitution is a choice and matter of women's agency (Bishop, Morgan, & Erickson, 2013). Some researchers and practitioners believe that if the persons themselves do not classify their experiences as being "victims," then they should not be considered "trafficked" (Bishop, Morgan, & Erickson, 2013). The assertion of "sex work" as empowered behavior, or at the very least chosen, is cited as the reason for legalizing prostitution, thereby, somehow being able to alleviate the differences between "sex worker" and "trafficked victim." To understand this debate better, one has to understand the differences in terminology, the legality and policy discussions regarding prostitution, and the ideologies surrounding the various perspectives.

(Continued)

(Continued)

Terminology

There are several terms that are used in this debate, especially in the choice of words and terminology are preferable and/or should be used. Here is a nonexhaustive list of the main terminology used (Panchal, 2013):

- *Prostituted Women:* referring to women who are coerced into sex work
- *Sex Worker:* income-generating activity seen as a form of employment; negotiation and performance of sexual services for remuneration; meant to be nonjudgmental; a move away from the term "prostitute"
- *Prostitute:* generally a derogatory term meant to refer to women who sell sexual services, but also used to describe promiscuous women
- *Commercially Sexually Exploited:* trafficked victims who have been forced and coerced
- *Commercially Sexually Exploited Survivor:* trafficked victim who is rescued and reintegrated after their experiences

It is very difficult to get around the differences and the assumptions present in the terminology because by selecting one term over another, one declares also their political or ideological position(s). For instance, people can easily be lured into a morality debate based on what terminology they select, even if that was not their intention. Equally dangerous is the fact that people feel they can use the terms interchangeably, not aware that there may be repercussions, or at the very least assumptions made on all sides. For instance, if one is working with a client, it is important to let that client define their identity, regardless of your own personal belief system.

Legality

Internationally, the laws around prostitution generally fall into one of three areas: criminalization, legalization, or decriminalization.

- *Criminalization:* makes prostitution illegal. Everyone involved in prostitution are penalized. The idea is that if you criminalized, you would reduce or eliminate prostitution. This is mainly supported by moral, conservative, and religious groups as well as some feminist groups. Countries that have done this are: most states in the United States, England, Canada, and Sweden. In the case of Sweden, they have only criminalized the buyers.
- *Legalization:* legalizes prostitution under specified conditions, which include registration, licensing, and mandatory health checks. The countries that have legalized prostitution include the Netherlands, Germany, Iceland, Austria, Turkey, and many Australian states.

- *Decriminalization:* Decriminalization has no legal binding conditions against prostitution, meaning there is an absence of anything that criminalizes prostitution. The regulation of prostitution then becomes subsumed under other laws or policies. It is a way of avoiding the discussion—making prostitution neither a crime nor eligible to be legal. The only examples of decriminalization are New South Wales (an Australian state) and New Zealand.

Regardless of one's stance in this debate, there have been no studies that demonstrate legalization makes prostitution better (safer, less exploitative) for those involved or that it lowers the incidences of illegal trafficking. Rather, studies have revealed that in areas where legalization has occurred, the situation has actually gotten worse (Mishra, 2013).

Ideologies

Ideology, or theoretical perspective, guides the actions of different feminist groups. Thus, depending on their ideologies, they hold various opinions about what is best out of these options. For instance, radical feminists believe in sexual liberation and so they believe in either legalization or decriminalization (Patkar, 2013). Materialist feminists believe that any objectification, commodification, and commercialization of women's bodies introduced or existing in the market is equal to sexual slavery (Kotiswaran, 2011).

Currently there are a number of issues that are layered on this debate. For instance, there are the conceptual and ideological notions of work; sociological definitions of work as a space of self-actualization; economic aspects of work as a site for wage, production, and profit; structuralist interpretations that every society has roles to fill, which take the form of jobs, whether formal or informal. This is but a quick span of the value that individuals and society in general may attribute to work. The dictionary defines work as being "activity in which one exerts strength or faculties to do or perform something: *a.* sustained physical or mental effort to overcome obstacles and achieve an objective or result. *b.* the labor, task, or duty that is one's accustomed means of livelihood. *c.* a specific task, duty, function or assignment often being a part or phase of some larger activity." (Merriam-Webster, n.d.). Comparatively, while "sex worker" may speak to aspects of work such as the ability to negotiate or operate through choices, it does not address deeper structural and sociological issues related to work such as mastery, self-esteem, or level of stigma (Overs, 2009). Finally, while it is true that many girls and women claim that they "choose" to engage in what they term as "work," it is also acknowledged that there are different degrees of coercion, abuse, and violence in all parts of the process (i.e., all women in this "system" are violated and sexually exploited in what is an inherently unsafe and dangerous environment) (Panchal, 2013). For instance, in Thailand, prostitution has become a type of cottage industry because of the amount of profits that pimps and traffickers make off women's bodies. However, it has also thrived because women do not see any other ways to make the same kind of money (Brown, 2000). The problem is that if a person is being coerced or exploited,

(Continued)

(Continued)

they are very likely also being threatened into these "admissions of choice." Equally problematic is the shallow treatment that some of this literature gives the topic, not allowing for deeper reasoning and explanations that cause the masking or defensive posturing of the victims who may not be able to admit their experiences.

One can understand the complexity of this debate just by looking at how pervasive prostitution and "pimp culture" has been inculcated into society. For instance, the past few years have seen an emergence in the popular lexicon of "pimp culture," which essentially has elevated and misappropriated the prostitution and commodification of women into situations that are depicted as glamourous or even powerful. In fact, this type of pimp culture has added to the increase in sexual assaults and domestic/dating violence. At the very least it has created an environment of hypersexuality that begins at a young age. For example, television commentators used terms such as "prosti-tot" and "pimp-fant" to describe girls' fashions, indicating this is the new, "hip" way to dress children (Oppliger, 2008). Melissa Farley (2003) writes, "Prostitution today is a toxic cultural product, which is to say that all women are socialized to objectify themselves to be desirable, to act like prostitutes, to act out the sexuality of prostitution." The contradictions that exist in these dynamics of this supposed sexual "power" are glaring. For instance, many women are in situations involving pornography and prostitution may define their experience as being in control or actively making a living, but they are also women who have documented pasts of severe sexual trauma and abuse. Other aspects associated with the notion of "work" such as self-esteem, confidence, self-actualization, and self-efficacy are absent from these women's narratives. These examples indicate that sex is indeed a commercial act where it is exchanged for money or other things (Levy, 2005). Even more of a detriment, it has normalized for young women that the commercialization of sex, assault, and female subjugation are signs of status—or worse, genuine affection.

To further complicate matters, the debate has been exacerbated by the agenda of the far right and the religious community who built arguments against sex trafficking that are based on moral indictments of those involved. In 2003, U.S. president George W. Bush stated that the sex trafficking was a "special evil," and created an immediacy tantamount to moral crusades that was effective in bringing the public attention to this important issue, but that also created a framework where the discussion of sex slavery began and ended in circumstances of prostitution. This impacted a number of things, but most notable was that other aspects of sex trafficking were eclipsed and as an excuse to police women's sexuality in the guise of abolishing prostitution.

Palermo Protocol

However, if one were to strictly adhere to the definition provided by the Palermo Protocol, this divide and debate would be rendered redundant and in some cases (except for the aspect of agency) would cease to matter. According to the Palermo Protocol, *all* sexual exploitation, *irrespective* of the consent of the person, and including prostitution and other forms of sexual exploitation, shall be considered trafficking. Strictly speaking then, the debate around "choice" or "coercion" should not exist, because all sexual exploitation is and should be considered a form of trafficking. In other words, in an attempt to understand trafficking definitions, lexical shifts cannot gloss over or ignore concrete circumstances of exploitation even when agents themselves may describe situations of perceived control as empowered. As we have witnessed, regardless of what semantics you wrap around these power differentials, slavery is still slavery.

LABOR TRAFFICKING

Labor trafficking includes forms of indentured servitude, contract slavery, and domestic servitude. There is more of a gender equity seen in those who are trafficked for labor (56% women and girls; 44% men and boys) (Hepburn & Simon, 2013). As noted, it is within labor trafficking, which may be harder to discern than sex trafficking, that almost half of victim composition is men and boys. These numbers are extremely sensitive to industry-specific details. For instance, if you are talking about domestic helpers, usually maids, most who are trafficked or enslaved are women and girls. This is contrasted to the agricultural industry, where men and boys compose the labor force. For example, in the United States, which has the greatest demand for farm labor globally, 79–90% of the work force is composed of men (Carroll, Samardick, Bernard, Gabbard, & Hernandez, 2005).

While labor trafficking can happen in virtually any industry, it is most prolific in agriculture, fisheries/fishing, construction, factory work, and domestic service. Other than coercion, most labor trafficking occurs through the lure of false economic opportunities such as jobs abroad, followed with huge fees charged for recruitment, visas, housing, travel, and other needs. These "fees" accrue so that someone can never truly get out of debt. In many cases, some trafficking situations do not even bother with debt bondage and instead will literally enslave their workers. In these cases, documents and papers are taken away and slaves are isolated or locked away. For example, in Brazil, traffickers hire their own armed guards to make sure slaves are put into isolated locations where they cannot possibly get access to help (Hepburn & Simon, 2013).

CONCEPTUAL APPROACHES TO HUMAN TRAFFICKING

Lee (2011) proposes that the definition of human trafficking and modern-day slavery should be determined by the type of theory or lens that one utilizes in their "approach" to the topic. Depending on your profession or your perspective, one approach may be more dominant or fitting. Similarly, because of this, the growing multidisciplinary lens used to understand trafficking and modern day slavery, may also be combined and used. This might mean that different interventions as well as how trafficked persons are treated will be developed according to the specific conceptual frameworks one ascribes to. Lee hypothesizes there are six main areas or approaches that are most salient in the discussion thus far:

1. Modern Form of Slavery. Perhaps one of the most-oft references to trafficking is that it is a modern form of slavery. "Old" forms of slavery (kidnapping, auction blocks, chattel slaves, etc.) have given rise to a more modern practice. Modern-day slavery is not about legal ownership (as it was with older forms of slavery) but is part of an illicit, unregulated economic world (Bales, 1999). This conceptual approach relies on the framework of absolute control, economic exploitation, and violence (Bales, 2000).

2. Exemplar of Globalization of Crime. Although there are discussions of the impact of globalization on economics and how this has contributed to trafficking, this conceptual approach takes a different perspective. This approach asserts that the conditions created by globalization have resulted in new contexts for crimes to occur (Findlay, 2008). This approach also proposes that because globalization created larger rifts between rich and poor, with more and more cuts to the basic social welfare programs, large portions of the population realize that unless they are willing to engage in illegal actions, they will never be able to attain their goals or gain the lifestyle they want (Passas, 2000). Another aspect this approach states is globalizations' use of technology and connectedness has worked in the favor of organized, global crime syndicates and gangs, who have followed the same patterns and opportunities of migration flow and flow of money and goods (Shelley, Picarelli, & Corpora, 2003).

3. Problem of Transnational Organized Crime. Unlike the previous conceptual approach, this one proposes that trafficking occurs through transnational organized criminal groups that are sophisticated and complex enough to shift from economic pursuits previously engaged in (for instance, the drug trade) into something more profitable and sustainable (human trafficking). This occurs, according to this approach, even without the direct impact/effects of globalization's economic policies. This approach naturally leads to the resolution of trafficking from a law enforcement perspective, which would include counter trafficking interventions but also possibly a stricter implementation of protocols used by law enforcement to address/deal with the issue.

4. Synonymous with Prostitution. The most common approach is to consider that prostitution and trafficking are often discussed as if they were one and the same. Based on the experiences and propaganda of the "White Slave Trade" and the xenophobia of the 19th century, which was built on the idea that foreigners would kidnap and force women into prostitution (Enloe, 2000), this conceptual approach

highlights an area where the most heated debates have occurred, usually based on moral codes and ideological lines (Outshoorn, 2012). Debates that have split sex trafficking have been based around notions of "sex workers" versus "sex slaves" as well as "voluntary" prostitution versus "forced" trafficking, raising the issue of women's agency. What this has meant is that this approach has dominated the discussion of sexual exploitation, even though prostitution is only a small portion of it.

5. Migration Problem. Simply stated, this approach assumes that trafficking is only a subset of illegal migration. Thus, the approach examines breaches and gaps in immigration and migration policies and interventions such as border controls, interception, document verification repatriation agreements, migrant detention, and other exclusionary methods (Grewcock, 2007). On the other hand, this approach has been instrumental in the perspective that examines the conditions that cause transnational migration to begin with. This perspective also assumes that trafficking is the consequence of restrictive migration policies that make it difficult to have a trajectory of either asylum or immigration displaced persons (Lee, 2011).

6. Human Rights. The final conceptual framework relies on the definitions of several UN Protocols beginning with the UN Declaration of Human Rights in 1948, which clearly state the right to be free from slavery (Assembly, 1948). Subsequent conventions such as the UN Convention on the Elimination of All Forms of Discrimination against Women (UNEGEEW, 1979), the UN Convention on the Rights of the Child (1989), and the International Covenant on Civil and Political Rights (1966). The Office of the UN High Commissioner for Refugees (UNHCR) can also provide support and protection of those trafficked if their own countries are unable to do this. The human rights approach reframes the discussion of trafficking from more than just moral and economic perspectives to the belief that all people have intrinsic liberties. These rights include the right to safe passage and opportunities for migration. Intervention wise, this conceptual approach has relied on practices of empowerment, righting social wrongs, and mobilization of populations to fight against trafficking. While this conceptual approach contains the most global, grassroots' response, that has been very little in practice that reflect true empowerment (Munro, 2008).

These conceptual approaches have been included as they exemplify the most comprehensive break down of varied and sometimes competing theoretical understandings of the nature, causes, and interventions toward trafficking. We have included them here to make sure that the intersectional and multilayered nature of how trafficking is understood and discussed in the literature is well represented. For the purposes of the book, we will be focusing on Concepts 1 (Modern-Day Slavery), 2 (Globalization), 4 (Migration), and 6 (Human Rights). These main concepts have been selected as they fit closely to the book's theoretical premises.

SCOPE OF THE ISSUE

The U.S. State Department estimates anywhere from 4 to 27 million people are trafficked and/or existing in modern-day slavery around the world. The International Labor Organization (ILO) estimates this number to be at 21 million—3 out of every 1,000 people in the world. As of 2016, the Global Slavery Index estimated that there were 45.8 million people in the world who were enslaved or trafficked (ILO, n.d.). The Asia-Pacific region has the largest numbers of trafficked persons at around 12 million, or 56% of the total, followed by Africa at 3.7 million (18%) and Latin America at 1.8 million (9%) (ILO, n.d.). There are an estimated 900,000 persons who are trafficked across borders annually. Over one million children are in the global sex trade. Eighty percent of transnational victims are women and girls. Over 150 countries (identified as either sending or receiving, or both) have been identified as being affected by trafficking. The extreme variance in the numbers speaks to the nature of this issue, mainly, the difficulties with victim identification. U.S. Ambassador-at-Large to Monitor and Combat Trafficking Luis deBaca (Schott & Weiss, 2016) stated, "We are only seeing a mere fraction of those who are exploited in modern slavery." The need to address this growing epidemic has led to the need to understand the global scope as well as to exchange information and learn from the actions of countries around the world where trafficking is most concentrated. However, the taxonomy of how

Figure 1.2 Global Slavery Index, 2016

Source: The Walk Free Foundation: globalslaveryindex.org/media

trafficking and modern-day slavery are understood is extremely important in uncovering the variety of the estimates or in some cases even "guesstimates" of the true number of those exploited (Amahazion, 2015). Therefore, how trafficking and modern-day slavery is defined (and how these definitions are interpreted) will directly impact the scope of the issue and indirectly the scale of possible interventions.

TRAFFICKING IN PERSONS (TIP) REPORT

The U.S. State Department began to generate the Trafficking in Persons (TIP) report, which monitors efforts to combat modern day slavery in 2000 (Gozdziak & Collett, 2005). The TIP Report details (1) country-level efforts in the area of the three P's (prevention, prosecution, and protection); (2) categorization of countries as origin, transit, or destination (or a combination thereof); and (3) tier rankings of countries (Horning, Thomas, Henninger, & Marcus., 2014). While this report has become a type of "gold standard" for measuring efforts against trafficking, it is important to note that it is composed of government self-reports and information that is sent to a centralized e-mail (providing means for nongovernmental organizations, institutions, and individuals to share their input). U.S. Embassies were also utilized to collect information. This information is gathered and used to organize countries into one of three tiers (tier 1 is the highest ranking, tier 3 the lowest). Placement on the tiers is dependent of government efforts with the rational that governments bear the primary responsibility for responding to trafficking. The need to address this growing epidemic has led to the need to understand the global scope as well as to exchange information and learn from the actions of countries around the world where trafficking is most concentrated. Because of the transnational nature of trafficking, prevention and intervention practices must also be created with an internationalist perspective. As of October 1, 2013, countries that are given the "tier 3" label countries will be subject to a number of sanctions, including withholding of U.S. government nonhumanitarian, nontrade related foreign assistance. The report is composed annually with the hope that countries will improve and build on their efforts to combat trafficking (Wyler, 2010).

There are number of controversies around the TIP report because the evaluation of countries is facilitated exclusively by the U.S. government. Further, the TIP report is dependent on self-disclosed actions and numbers from the reporting bodies. This creates a system of estimating that is somewhat based on guesses (Amahazion, 2015). While this might be true—countries taking a guess at their numbers—the result is extremely real. Nations who do not demonstrate that they are improving on their response to trafficking can be economically and/or politically sanctioned by the United States (TIP Report 2015). There is a lack of specificity between each tier (Horning et. al., 2014). This has led to criticisms of favoritism and bias in support of certain countries because of reasons other than their efforts around trafficking (Gallagher, 2001). It remains unclear exactly how data is compiled for the report, especially how tier markers are assessed (Gallagher, 2012; Woodtich, 2011; Woodtich et. al., 2009). Some critics have stated that the report is not culturally sensitive, resulting in an inability to understand interventions that may not fit into U.S. paradigms of intervention but may be effective in country contexts (Sharma, 2003). For instance, the United States has been accused of the TIP report rankings being "ideologically and politically motivated" (Kempadoo, 2004).

For tier 3 countries, the United States can also oppose support from the international financial institutions (U.S. Department of State, 2013). According to the TIP report, countries in Southeast Asia range from tier 2, 2WL (watch list), to 3 because of the prevalence of trafficking in those countries and the noncompliance of their governments to eliminate trafficking. Some critics believe that the reason has less to do with noncompliance to eliminate trafficking and more about noncompliance to agree to other political agendas of the United States. Regardless of these issues, the TIP report is the most utilized mechanism for obtaining country by country data. It is widely referenced and used to further intervention and policy.

ALTERNATIVES TO THE TIP REPORT

Although the TIP report is the most often used report because of the sheer breadth of it, this does not mean that there are no other alternatives. Before the TIP report, the nonprofit and nongovernmental (NGO) world was already providing anecdotal and qualitative data on trafficking and modern-day slavery. These were not the terms they used per se but they were definitely building the case for what would constitute this phenomenon. As the issue persisted, data collected from these organizations also became more sophisticated. The data from this NGO and nonprofit perspective are still garnered from a number of areas, including communities that the organizations work with, services that are provided, and estimates based on campaigns and awareness raising drives that continue to be the backbone of anti-trafficking and abolitionist efforts. Further, this sector has been able to identify situations that are not recognized by governments. For instance, in some countries, the definition of trafficking is so strict and hinges on prosecution, that there are scores of victims who are not counted and whose numbers are not reflected in the TIP report. Because of this, in some ways, critics of the TIP report believe these alternative methods are more true to what is actually happening in countries. This is especially true in countries that also may have high incidences of corruption and/or may have vested interest in gaining the favor of the United States. For instance, whereas it was recognized that the Indian government's efforts to fight trafficking could be classified as uneven at best, Indian NGOs are known internationally to lead in their anti-trafficking activities (UNODC, 2009).

CALL TO ACTION: A MULTITUDE OF LENSES

We are used to hearing about trafficking from politicians, law enforcement, and nonprofit or nongovernmental organizations. It is not surprising to hear feminist groups and other grassroots organizations lay out their viewpoint. And of course, there are people like us—professionals, scientists, and academics—who are attempting to make sense of what is happening at the micro-mezzo-macro levels and within the areas of clinical intervention, policy implementation, and ongoing advocacy. While there are efforts to bring all our ideas together, for the most part we have existed in a silo during one part of our journey or another. This may be one reason that our impact has not moved us very far toward a pathway to freedom. But this can change. True collaboration, examining the issue from different perspectives, and supported rather than reinvented efforts will set the course we need to be on.

The statistics speak for themselves: millions of trafficking victims that form the basis for billions of dollars in profit. And yet, as many victims that we are able to actually count, there are more that we never know about or who remain invisible. However, these numbers do not mean anything until you begin to meet and hear the stories of those who have survived trafficking and modern-day slavery. Therefore, in each chapter, you will "meet" some of the remarkable men, women, children, and organizations that were interviewed to provide you/us with a unique standpoints life, experience, and inspiration for this book.

DISCUSSION QUESTIONS

1. What is the unique or specialized perspective your helping profession defines and approaches human trafficking and modern-day slavery? Which conceptual approach is the closest to this perspective?

2. What are three events or policies that impact trafficking and modern-day slavery in your country or a country of your interest?

3. Select a country of interest (or use the country you reside in) and look up its most current TIP report submission or section in the TIP report. What are the notable points? What might be missing or underreported based on what you know about that country's relationship to the United States?

4. Many researchers, policymakers, and activists have said that the disagreement around trafficking taxonomy makes it difficult to arrive at genuine points of unity for a basis of working together. Identify at least three areas where taxonomies have been difficult to define.

5. Given the controversies around the TIP report, what are some viable alternatives and why?

CHALLENGE

Log onto the Podcast: Ending Human Trafficking from Vanguard University's Global Center for Women and Justice. Click on the first podcast, "What is Human Trafficking," and check out at least one other program. If you could design your own episode for this podcast, what would it include? Would you have special guests or an organization you highlight? What is the power of podcasting? Once you have an idea of what you would do, carry out your plan. Record a podcast and share it with your networks, or with existing podcasts. Get the word out about trafficking using this type of social media.

CHAPTER 2

The Law of Supply and Demand:
The Business of Trafficking

Chapter Objectives

1. Readers will comprehend an economic perspective of human trafficking and modern-day slavery.

2. Readers will be able to compare the market demands between sex and labor trafficking.

3. Readers will deconstruct the factors for price elasticity and its impact on trafficking and modern-day slavery.

4. Readers will integrate the driving factors of the market into their analysis of trafficking and modern-day slavery.

5. Readers will attribute the role of globalization and other trends in trade as a factor of consideration for the origins of trafficking and modern-day slavery.

My footsteps are rushed as I pass over one picturesque bridge after another. The students are way ahead of us, but I'm still trying to keep up with my friend and guide–with her pace and with her commentary. She is in the middle of telling me how the sex industry has changed once they made the Red Light District in Amsterdam legal. "They regretted it almost as soon as they did it," she says in a matter-of-fact manner that left no room for disagreement.

Still, I ask, "How come?"

"Well, you know," she slows down a bit, "I suppose it's because trafficking has exploded. It's like this, they made it legal to literally put women in store fronts. It's like a magic trick."

"A magic trick?" I ask, taking advantage of the slower pace to finally catch up with her.

(Continued)

(Continued)

She stops completely then, and says, "Yeah, a magic trick. Everyone is so busy paying attention to what is in front of their faces that no one asks what is going on behind the doors or inside the building or under it. It's ridiculous how much it's opened up the market." We cross another bridge. The sun is bouncing off the waters of the canal and small houseboats bob with the slight waves caused by the wind. It's just beautiful, this country. I wave at a little girl who trundles ahead of us and take a moment to peer into a tourist shop, making a note to purchase some things before I returned home. I'm also looking ahead to see where our small group of students have gotten to. I see that they are just a few steps ahead. I'm about to say something to them so I almost miss it, the transition happens so quickly. I turn a corner and bam! There it is—right in front of me, a row of "storefronts." I am trying not to be shocked. I've seen the world and I'm prepared for anything, I think, except I wasn't—not for this.

The girls look bored. It's early in the evening, the sun isn't even down, but they sit on stools behind their glass windows. They wear flimsy lingerie, with their high heels swaying slightly. Some of them are intently looking at their cell phones. Others look almost sleepy as they stare out, empty eyed, into somewhere beyond you. There are a few whose doors are propped open or who are even leaning on them as they call out to the street, enticing the next customer. We all stand there for a minute, taking it in. A student's voice interrupted my thoughts and said to me in a whisper, "See, look how empowered they are." Or, maybe what I'm not prepared for were my students' responses.

It's the role of a teacher not to force students into your perspective but to provide them with all the information they need to make their own decisions. I smile at her uncomfortably, knowing that I think differently. To me, the storefronts, even the nice ones, look like gilded cages, but cages nonetheless. I nod, encouraging her to continue. She says, "They are filling a need and people are addressing their demand or at least what they want. It's like a business. All of them look free to do what they want to do." She tilts her head toward the row of doors.

I turn her attention to the opposite side of the street where groups of two or three men congregate, smoking cigarettes, just talking, but always watching. "What about them?" I point out.

"What about them," she shrugs.

"Them. The pimps, " I say.

"What?" Now she looks shocked. "Why do you think that?"

"Because they are." I emulate my friend's tone. I say it like a fact. Then, I realize that some things just have to be experienced. I take out a hundred Euro note from my wallet. "Here. Use this. See if one of these women will talk to you. Ask about her empowerment." She looks at me with wide eyes. I nod again to her, "Come on, it's not a trick. I can't answer you. You have to find out for yourself. Think of this as field work." She agrees, very serious, and takes the money. I watch as she engages a friend and the two of them approach a young woman from Eastern Europe. Another woman joins them. I see the slight exchange of money. My attention is turned away and I attend to the other eight students

who are with us. Thirty minutes later, I feel a tug on my sleeve and see that my student and her friend have returned. There are tears in her eyes. I don't say I told you so. I don't even ask. I just hug her. She mumbles something. I lean closer to listen, "What was that?" I ask.

"I was wrong," she says. "I was really wrong."

I hold her a little tighter and sigh. "If it makes you feel better, I wanted you to be right." I say, "Really."

—Annalisa Enrile

It is the same story in countless countries—shifts in the economy, industries transitioning (and sometimes closing down), multinational firms driving down the costs and the wages, and other factors that result in mass poverty. Markets are pushed beyond capacity and communities have to reconfigure not just their financial basis but their very relationships. It sounds like the background for a behavioral economic case study; however, it is the foundation of almost any trafficking discussion. In an industry where net profits are estimated at 150 *billion dollars* annually, it is not any wonder that perhaps the best way to understand trafficking and modern-day slavery are through an economic lens—through the process of supply and demand. In fact, five of the six conceptual approaches toward trafficking that were introduced in chapter 1 are represented by a fiscal analysis. These are Concepts 1 (Modern Slavery); 2 (Exemplar of Globalization of Crime); 3 (Problem of Transnational Organized Crime); 4 (Synonymous with Prostitution); and 5 (Migration Problem).

In very simple terms "supply" and "demand" are the basic concepts of a free market economy with "demand" referring to how much buyers want a certain product and "supply" being that product and its availability. It is a symbiotic relationship in many respects, with demand somewhat determining the cost of goods and alternatively, the ready access to the products driving the demand. For example, if something is in high demand, then sellers may charge more for it, particularly if there is a small or limited supply. Conversely, if the market is flooded with the same or like goods, then there is the opportunity for buyers to leverage their demands and drive the price lower. This relationship is also apparent in the way that quality is maintained. This is where the notion of perceived benefit or value is influential. The perceived benefit or value is the opinion of the consumer/customer's on a product or service's worth, regardless of its market price, with more of an emphasis on the product or service's ability to satisfy. For instance, in the tourism industry, establishments that are of higher caliber or more luxurious can charge more because of the extra perceived benefits or value.

While there are many situations that can be explained by an economic analysis, there are few as fitting as the issue of human trafficking and modern-day slavery. Every aspect of trafficking and modern-day slavery is commodified, centered around the main product: human beings and the capacity to exploit them for sex or labor. Unfortunately, though the demand is high, the supply also seems endless. Kara (2009) states that when we examine modern-day slavery, we are witnessing a system where the "products" can be transported across or within transnational lines, can be bought and re-sold countless times (theoretically, until their death), and are exploited and re-exploited. This being the case, the "return on investment" (ROI), so to speak, is high. For the traffickers, their ROI is the most important thing to consider as they know they will always have both supply and demand. Therefore, the concern is how to generate the most profit from the least effort and expense. Although only a small percentage of slaves are trafficked as sex slaves specifically, they generate almost half of all slaveholders' profits, creating a net profit of almost 70% (Kara, 2009). This is in comparison to Google's average net profit margin of 22.88% over the between 2010–2015 (Alphabet Profit Margin, 2016). By further comparison, the average business would consider they were strong if they had a 10% profit margin. Kara (2009) estimates that slaves can generate 300 to 500% of what they are purchased for. Moral imperatives, when they may exist, are quickly overridden by the sheer amount of profit to be had. In other words, there is a high incentive for traffickers to continue to exploit their slaves. The goal of the trafficker is to be able to make the most profit from their slaves. Meanwhile, the consumers demand the greatest "deal" or least expense possible. What we have here is both the "supply" and "demand" side driving down the cost of human lives.

DEMAND DYNAMICS

Profits

Understanding demand of human trafficking and modern-day slavery is like any industry that is susceptible to market forces and disruption. Economist John Mill (2004) states that the demand side of slavery can be isolated to three specific market forces: profit, male sexual demand, and elasticity of demand. We have already seen the tremendous profit margin that trafficking can command. In most industries, labor is the primary expense, so it is not surprising that forms of slave labor are utilized. By using slavery and trafficking, perpetrators are not only saving money from this type of labor provision, but they are also making immense profits (Crane, 2013). Labor trafficking can generate profits ranging from $2,300 (domestic work) to $4,800 (labor exploitation excluding domestic work) *per* slave according to the ILO (2012a). Profits to be made from sex trafficking is even higher. For instance, a brothel owner can purchase a slave anywhere between $200 and $8,000 depending on where in the world they are; but they make a return of over 1000% per slave (Bales, 2000). It is also interesting to examine what other drivers of profit exist. For example, in many countries, people believe in what is called the "virgin cure." This is the belief that having sexual intercourse with a virgin can cure medical diseases, including HIV/AIDS as well as other STDs. This cure not only drove up the demand and cost for virgins but it also created other markets as well. In Southeast Asia, a common practice was developed where the blood of doves was used to line the vaginal walls of trafficked girls and women so that those having sex with them would think that they were virgins. This allowed the traffickers to charge more (Bulawan, personal communication, 2013).

Figure 2.1 The Business of Modern-Day Slavery

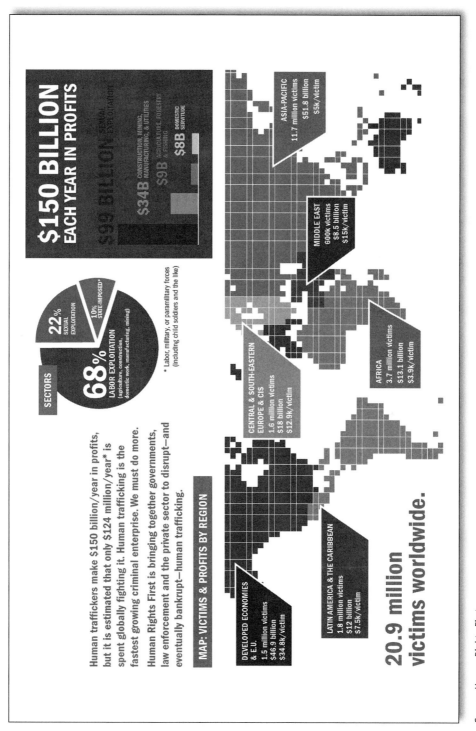

Male Sexual Demands

While the basic premise is the same, there are unique demands within sex trafficking that have to be understood focused on male sexual demand. While there are males who are victims of trafficking, the demand has been primarily unilateral, from heterosexual male to female. There are growing instances of males and transgendered persons, but these numbers are slight. Thus, we understand demand from the perspective of the highest prevalence. Sex trafficking thrives on the type of "commodity" that women's bodies have been fashioned into by the demands of (mainly heterosexual) male sexuality. Patriarchy and gender stereotypes have shaped the perfect commodity through racism and sexism. Literature on prostitution, especially in areas of Southeast Asia during times of conflict (and afterward), demonstrate how local women are constructed as being "exotic," and "sexually fetishized," playing the role of the "other." In describing women with these words, the connotations and the assumptions have constructed the perfect "commodity"—a woman who is no longer a person but a being that deserves to be bought and sold because of her proclivities or the fact that she can divert men's animalistic needs away from white women (Sturdevant & Stoltzfus, 1992). Research on the Vietnam War and militarization state that men felt that they were even "saving" or "maintaining" the purity of American or Western women by using Vietnamese and other Southeast Asian prostitutes. The objectification of women and eventual commodification does not stay trapped within borders indefinitely. Like other "products," there is an explosion of types and brands. Metaphorically, the construction of this "type" of woman had the potential to be located in every country that one encountered and more. For example, in Amsterdam, there are locations within the famed red light district that cater to different ethnicities and tastes from appearances to activities (Maarsen, personal communication, 2014).

In sex trafficking, the price of inexpensive sex means that anyone can be exploited. It is no secret that male sexual demands have supported commercial sex in many facets from pornography to cybersex, as well strip clubs and prostitution. As hard as it is to identify victims of trafficking, it is also difficult to get a grip on the prevalence of perpetrators, especially in sex trafficking. Even in regions where "sex work" is regulated, those regulations do not include gathering data on the perpetrators, only on the women. Those that pay for sex, commonly called "johns," "male clients," or "customers," are hard to count because of stigma, legality, and the nature of self-disclosure overall. This has meant that the numbers that have been gathered have been low. Kara (2009) found that even if a majority of men did not purchase commercial sex (or any derivatives thereof), a little under 10% of all males in the world over the age of 18 purchased sex from a slave at some point each year. Few studies have examined the motivations of the men who purchase sex. Of those, a literature review found the following reasons men have given for "paying for sex" or "using a prostitute[1]": desire for specific sex acts (oral sex, anal sex, fetish sex—in this order); no commitment or limited nature of contact; clandestine or secret nature; "good sex"; and companionship or intimate contact. One of most comprehensive studies has

---

1. Methodologically, in most of the research conducted examining male demand, the question has been framed in these two ways: "Why do you purchase sex?" or "Why do you use the services of prostitutes?"

been conducted by the Chicago-based group, Chicago Alliance Against Sexual Exploitation (CAASE), which examined not only motivations but also demographics and characteristics of male demand. Of the 113 men surveyed, the study found that their average age was 39, but that they bought sex on average at the age of 21; 62 % of those who had bought sex have regular sex partners in their lives; and more than half (53 %) stated they bought sex as frequently as every month up to several times a week (Durchslag & Goswami, 2008). Internationally, an Australian study (Pitts, Smith, Grierson, O'Brien, & Misson, 2004) surveyed over a thousand individuals and 23.4 % of men reported that they had ever "bought sex." They found that men[2] were motivated to "buy sex" because of ease (more than half), arousal, and engagement. Their average age was a little younger at 33.7 years old, almost half (45.1 %) had a regular partner, and most "purchased sex" through a brothel (63.6 %).

One of the main arguments for demand has been one that many feminists categorize as patriarchal and sexist. This argument is one that posits that there is a male "biological need" for sex and therefore, they "cannot help" but exploit women for sex when it is unavailable any other way. Mainstream, Western men's magazines even contain articles that express males "need" to have sex and think about it every 7 seconds, so it follows that it should be understandable that sex be for sale. However, research shows that this is false and hyperbolized. Another reason that is given is that this biological need necessitates multiple partners (Raymond, 2004). This perspective has relied on anthropological, even evolutionary perspectives (Ryan & Jethá, 2012). The concept is that this is the way that biological diversity is created. For example, in Bangladesh and Cambodia, men are considered to have "insatiable" sexual appetites so much so that it would be impossible for one woman to satisfy a man. It is even ingrained in Cambodian proverbs, and men believe not only that they are entitled to have sex with many women but also that they should be able to purchase it (Brown, 2000).

Psychologically, there have been many misused and misunderstood ways that perpetrators have provided as rationales for sexual exploitation and sexual demand. In some cases, the argument has been that the point of exploitation is not to have sex but to find some sort of connection. As research has indicted, this is not usually the reason that is given by perpetrators, but it is a small segment of the population (Pitts et al., 2004). In these situations, perpetrators may genuinely be looking either to replicate a former attachment or create a new one based on their own internal working representations. Founded on object relations and constructivist theories, one's earlier experiences with relationships may have shaped situations where it is plausible to believe that intimacy can be gained even through monetary or other types of material transactions. In these instances, internal working models of relationships have been constructed so that, at least from the perspective of the perpetrator, emotional connections are being created. However, the reality of the matter is that there is a constant power differential that is not taken into consideration. It is a one-way exchange that misses the reciprocity of intimacy, even if that is what the perpetrator is supposedly looking for (Davidson, 2003).

---

2. Of the 1,225 subjects surveyed, only 11 women and 1 transgendered individual say that they had ever purchased sex. Because of the low number, researchers decided to focus their research on male responses.

With the availability of women and children to exploit, trafficking drove the price for sex down, the more men participated. Couple this with advances in technology and the accessibility to multiple facets of commercial sex exploded exponentially. Pornography and even procuring sex moved into greater availability (and convenience); literally, men had the tools to purchase sex slaves on demand at the palm of their hands through their mobile devices. For example, a popular app in the United States called Tinder allows one to "like" someone else using the app by a simple swipe of their hand. Connections made within this app could result in a "hook up" (sex) or a date for those looking for a more traditional relationship. However, it has also become a venue for traffickers to sell their product, often providing price lists for commercial sex acts. Websites such as Craigslist, BackPage, and any number of sex tourism sites are also examples of the ease at which women can be exploited. This type of mobility is supported by pop culture, which has become more and more hypersexualized in a way that constructs women and girls as commodities within a "game" or an "industry" (Niemi, 2010). For instance, earlier we discussed the role of "pimp culture." This phenomenon is similar to the normalization of sexual fetishism into the mainstream so that such things as bondage, group sex, and anonymous sex are no longer taboo (Ryan & Jethá, 2012). In turn, the push into the mainstream has meant an increase in commercial sex markets who share the same values of the patriarchal, male, sexual demands (Skinner, 2008).

Price Elasticity

Price elasticity *of demand* refers to the sensitivity of pricing. When there is a change in the demand, there is also a change in price. Price elasticity refers to the any small changes in price resulting in a change in the demand. There are some things that are immune to changes in price, such as gas (because people view this as a necessity). This makes gas inelastic because no matter how much the price changes, people still need it and will purchase it (changes in price did not result in a change in the demand). For example, in labor trafficking, this is the case; the necessity for workers is nonnegotiable as is the necessity to make a profit. Therefore, to a certain extent, labor trafficking is somewhat inelastic. Or, at least, this is an argument that businesses make—that the need to pay the lowest wages is a necessity to protect their profit. This mind-set leaves businesses vulnerable to modern-day slavery in multiple forms (i.e., debt bondage, indentured slavery, coercive practices). It has been argued that as long as there is modern-day slavery, there can be no other way of doing "business" without cutting labor costs. Further, without the cost of labor, the actual price of the product or service can be lowered and it will still be competitive. While this may be a "convenient" argument for exploiters and perpetrators, we must also ask the question: What would motivate slave-free businesses?

In terms of sex trafficking, we have seen that changes in the price of slaves result directly in a change in demand. We have already identified that both cultural acceptance and availability of cheap sex have resulted in the increased use of sex slaves. Further, Keynesian economics states that people increase their consumption as their income increases. Thus, the elasticity of sex trafficking coupled with increases (or decreases) in income will determine the prices and demand for sex. Replicating Kara's (2009) elasticity curves through interviews of brothel customers, we found that when the price increased even just 50 pesos (about $1.10 U.S. dollars) in the Philippines, there was a reduction in purchased sex. If one takes into account the average minimum wage in the Philippines, which is 481 pesos in the National Capital Region ($10.45 U.S. dollars), then even a slight increase will price out those earning at or below minimum wage.

Sociocultural conditions also have the ability to drive price elasticity. For instance, within labor trafficking, especially where migrant labor is exploited, there are aspects of both racism and classism or caste. Racism and discrimination may be operating either consciously or unconsciously in the procurement and treatment of workers (on the spectrum of modern-day slavery). For instance, in migrant situations, the workers are almost always a different race and culture than the "boss" or the traffickers. This provides the ability to "other" workers who are exploited, relying on stereotypes to justify treatment. Similarly, cultural conditioning and tradition may create situations where one class is expected to do a type of work. For instance, workers of a lower class who are uneducated may be treated a certain way and those in charge may justify it as such. Caste, or economic station, plays a similar role. All these aspects have to do with power and status expressed through the exploitation of one human being over another. In this sense, there is not only the necessity for workers that become a driver for cost but also the referent value that it bestows. For instance, in developing countries, where the price of labor is cheap, nannies, maids, and other forms of domestic help become status symbols of rich households (Crane, 2013). It is not coincidental that these spaces in the "private sphere" are also where unique and widespread abuse takes place, so much so, that the International Labor Organizations categorizes domestic help in its own category (ILO, n.d.).

Factors for elasticity also include whether there are any close substitutes and if what is being purchased is considered a necessity or a luxury. In terms of commercial sex, there are a number of options that may be considered close substitutes such as strip clubs, pornography, or even drugs and alcohol. Further, the use of sex slaves is not considered a "necessity" by most. In India, the restructuring of the economy to rely on global consumerist technology is directly related to the growth of sexual slavery (Prabhakaran, 2013). This makes it even more elastic and sensitive to market forces. Theoretically, if one were to follow this logic, then cutting into the profitability of sex trafficking would be one way to help significantly end it. However, since the slave owners and the traffickers are not going to willingly cut into their own profits, then this continues to be a situation where the exploiters are gaining immense profits with quite minimal risks involved.

SUPPLY SIDE

The highest cost to the supply side is the cost of labor. Trafficking and modern-day slavery bypasses that cost, either by paying a pittance or nothing at all. Since this cost has been eliminated, suppliers like traffickers and slavers are able to drive the labor market down as a whole. With modern-day slaves readily available, in jobs such as domestic servitude, construction, agriculture, garments, and just about any other industry that slave labor dominates, "legitimate" jobs in the area are often underpaid, contractualized, and deregulated.

Once poverty is figured into the equation, we have an overabundance of laborers that are willing to work, sadly, under any circumstance. They are also willing to take risks that are high to be able to find work that will allow them to support themselves and their families. Using this framework, with more "supply" and no seeming end to it, there is virtually no way to leverage the position to the advantage of the impoverished.

Where are slaves procured? The supply of slaves may come from a number of different sources. Many slaves are tricked into debt bondage or may be lured into slavery through a false contract (Hepburn & Simon, 2013). In sex trafficking, slaves are sometimes seduced or romanced by their traffickers or even recruited by former (or current) slaves. One of the most difficult incidences to understand is when children are sold by their own parents. Often when the sellers are hawking their own children, there is the image society puts forth of gold-digging parents who would rather sell their child and get the money than to keep their child and care for them. However, the truth is that most parents are pushed to this option either by current or past financial necessities or feudal practices where they must provide slave labor for the "master." Surprisingly there are also thousands of parents who don't get a penny for "selling" their child (Skinner, 2008; Plan International, 2005). These are parents who have hope for their children and their future, so they are often tricked by traffickers who promise to educate and care for their children. In fact, these parents may never know what happened to their children. The high cost of education exacerbates these practices. Parents, believing that education is the only sure way to success, will see this as an opportunity to provide for their children and unwittingly send them off with traffickers.

Price elasticity, which we discussed in the previous section, is also relevant here. The seemingly unending supply of slaves creates a situation where demand can determine prices. Also, the reason that people are vulnerable to being slaves in the first place underscores the income disparities in many countries (especially sending ones). We saw that when one's income fluctuates, the prices will as well, determining elasticity. The price of human lives is shockingly low. For instance, in the 1980s, a slave was $90; by the late 1990s, the cost of a slave was down to $15 (Skinner, 2008). Slave wages hovered around $1.25 an hour all the way down to a few pennies, if anything at all (Skinner, 2008). Second, the actual industries using slave labor drive down the costs of their own products. For instance, in a globalized world, one can buy anything, anywhere and so this makes the supply of cheaper, less specialized products extremely low. Slaves can also be manipulated to "produce" more. Slaves who are labor trafficked often report working 18–20 hours a day by psychological force (such as threats made against their families) or physical threats. Pimps report using meth to make their "girls" perform longer such as through consecutive days where they are in high demand (Friday, Saturday, Sunday) (De Los Reyes, personal communication, 2015). Finally, the unique nature of this "product" is that it is renewable. In other words, slaves get bought and sold countless times. Unlike guns or drugs (the other two most trafficked products in the world), human beings can be sold and profited from again and again.

As with demand, supplies are affected by external social/economic and political realities. "Slaves" and those who are trafficked are produced by events such as genocide, civil war, and even environmental disaster. Almost 10 million slaves and persons who are trafficked come from or reside in refugee camps (Healy, 2015). In Europe, we see in 2014 that between 3,500 and 5,500 women and girls were kidnapped and trafficked by militants in Syria and Iraq for sexual slavery (Agence France-Prese, 2015). Between 2011–2014, most of those trafficked in the area of Lebanon, Iraq, and Syria were for sexual exploitation and these persons were directly connected either to the conflict or to the migration following the conflict (Healy, 2015). Further, the structure of these camps help collude to provide a supply of labor. For instance, in the mountains of Chiang Mai, Thailand, Burmese refugees are considered "nonpersonages." Because of this, when refugees go missing, the Thai government does not necessarily have to look for them. There are currently thousands of Burmese refugees living in camps in the Chiang Mai area, with the largest camp numbering over 40,000—a large pool of slave labor ready to be transported across and within the Thai borders.

BEYOND SUPPLY AND DEMAND

Once the relationships between supply and demand are understood, the more complex aspects of trafficking should also be considered to provide a more comprehensive picture from an economic lens. There are a number of different economic models that have been suggested as the impetus for how trafficking and modern-day slavery remains a profitable and desirable business. Traffickers have been referred to as entrepreneurs, taking advantage of circumstances that allow them to make the highest level of profits from the commodification of human lives (Wheaton, Schauer, & Galli, 2010). Structuralist and rational economic models have been applied to trafficking but are no means the only ones that can be used to analyze the issue vis a vis an economic lens. However, in the literature, they do offer interesting perspectives that have been replicated or adopted by others in an effort to understand the economic impetus for trafficking especially in relation to profit.

Structuralist Economic Model

More than an understanding of supply and demand, other economic models can be used as a lens to understand trafficking. If this is the case, for instance, a structuralist model allows economists to make the argument that poverty and prostitution should be considered utilitarian. This approach would perceive that adults have sexual needs, which are usually met within relationship structures (traditionally: within heterosexual marriage), and if these needs are not met or the structure not available, then prostitution takes its place (Patkar, 2013). Further, traffickers argue that poor women are more compliant and that poverty keeps them from being demanding (Skinner, 2008). Indeed, there are links between poverty and human trafficking. ITEMP (n.d.) found they could observe differences between sender (source country) and destination countries is based on as little as $1,000 fluctuations in GDP. For every increase of $1,000 to the GDP there was 10% more of a chance of being a destination country. For every decrease of $1,000 GDP there was a 12% increased chance of the country being a source country. Even countries who experience economic upswings may be vulnerable as these periods of growth occur at such a rapid space that for them to be successful, there will be a creation of the demand of cheap labor, especially to keep up with supposed development.

Rational Choice Theory

Rational choice theory states that individuals take all the information they are able to have and use that economic information to help create a cost-benefit analysis on which to base their decisions (Wheaton, Schauer, & Galli, 2010). This is particularly fitting for labor trafficking as many people who are vulnerable first make the decision to migrate for the purposes of working abroad. The hope is that they will earn more working abroad than they could possibly earn staying in their own country. Components that are considered in this cost-benefit analysis include not only the possibility of higher wages and opportunities but the workers' own skill-set—the lower the level of skills, the more vulnerable they may be to trafficking, but ironically, it is these populations that are targeted and encouraged to migrate (Borjas, 2008). The cost of relocation is often a mitigating factor, but when recruiters or traffickers promise to cover those costs, workers may believe that migration is a viable option. Obviously, they do not know that they will end up incurring more and more fees as debts, which will limit their agency and restrict their freedom at being able to leave the situation (Borjas, 2008). This cost-benefit analysis also examines noneconomic aspects, such as the needs of the family, the psychological benefits (feeling as if one is doing something active to help the family), and physical well-being. It may seem to migrating workers that they are making a rational decision. However, in most of these cases, even with knowledge about the possibilities of trafficking, individuals may still feel that the foreseen benefits outweigh any other threats. They may decide, despite the danger, to continue with the migration process. While this economic model provides a framework to understand how trafficking may occur beyond the dichotomous relationship of supply and demand, it begins with a fallacy as it does not take into account that it is very rare for workers to be given *all* the information regarding their situations and operates on the assumption that even if they were to be provided with all relevant information, that they would be able to process it correctly.

Push and Pull Factors

While similar to the concept of supply and demand, equally important to understand are the push/pull factors that dominate the discourse on trafficking. There remains a lot economic basis but this model also looks at broader aspects. As with supply and demand, push and pull factors are not difficult to understand. Push factors tend to be those things literally pushing people out of either rural areas (and into urban centers) or out of poorer countries into richer ones, looking for a better life through opportunities or promises of work. Push factors tend to be environmental, political, social, cultural, and, as we have already discussed, economic. For instance, political unrest or political machinations can be responsible for the movement and migration of people. Pull factors include industrialization, urbanization, communication and the mode of transportation becoming more simplified (and cheaper), and technical advancements (Mishra, 2013). Roe-Sepowitz, Hickle, Dahlstedt, and Gallagher (2014) also look at the incidence of domestic violence as a push factor, especially into sex trafficking. Further push factors, include aspects such as caste (for instance in India, this plays a major role), class structure, discrimination, race, and ethnicity (primarily if they are part of an indigenous population) (Mishra, 2013).

It is not a clear-cut analysis when trying to understand the business of trafficking and modern-day slavery. For instance, the countries do not fall easily into either sending or receiving categories. As we can see from the sensitivity of the GDP, patterns and routes of trafficking are not static (Sanghera, 2005). While this can be due to economic circumstances, the sociopolitical and cultural dynamics between countries of origin, transit, and destination (as well as the dynamics between these interactions) are important and will be discussed further in chapter 3. The measures that are available are also extrapolations and assumptions using approximations because, although traffickers operate similarly to multinational corporations (steady growth and immense cash flows), they are still illegal, criminal entities. Therefore, to understand the pervasiveness of trafficking and its profits, one needs to understand that they are produced through not just the selling of cheap labor and even cheaper sex but because of the effects of globalization. In fact, in many ways, trafficking (especially sex trafficking) is "one of the ugliest contemporary actualizations of global capitalism" (Kara, 2009, p.66). The understanding of globalization is essential. Sophisticated market assessments based on where victims come from and where they go are only important if one also understands the relationship of the countries involved as well as other sociopolitical, economic, and cultural contexts. Globalization policies, rural poverty, increased economic disenfranchisement, migration, supply chains, and the feminization of all these aspects must be understood to get a comprehensive/full picture of forces affecting slavery.

Globalization

Globalization is often referred to as one of the catalysts for widespread trafficking and modern-day slavery. A commonly used definition is based on the economic foundation of globalization, which is the integration of the world into one economic space through the mechanisms of international trade agreements, internationalization of products and financial markets, creation of a commodity driven culture, and international telecommunications that have revolutionized communication (Gibson-Graham, 2006). Economically, globalization favors free trade, private enterprise, contractualization, and liberalization, opting to treat nations as markets, supposedly erasing borders (Stromquist & Monkman, 2014). Supporters of globalization have said that it has the potential to leverage opportunities and support the poor. Critics of globalization have referred to it as neoimperialism, opening up the developing, poor world to the richer, developed countries so that they may further exploit labor, infrastructure, and political relationships (Bhanji, 2008).

Globalization's economic polices began after World War II and with renewed interest in the 1990s and was supposed to lead to the promise of development, industrialization, and wealth, especially for countries in what was commonly referred to as the "Global South" through the increase and expansion of international trade and foreign investment occurring through a series of economic agreements such as NAFTA (North American Free Trade Agreement) and APEC (Asian Pacific Economic Cooperation) (Sachs, 2006). One of the reasons that globalization was so popular was that it rapidly became associated with modernization, but as with industrialization, its promise could only occur with great structural inequities (Mishra, p. 78). A key feature of globalization policies is the role that the International Monetary Fund (IMF) played in offering and mandating support in exchange for market economy formulas that regardless of context were mandated (Kara, 2009). Most detrimental to this process were as follows:

- the IMF mandated austerity measures, which cut government expenditures in health care, education, and social services (the very areas that were needed in most developing countries);

- products, services, and commodities should be dictated by market forces, which resulted in massive inflations that eroded local currencies;

- push for rapid market liberalization, which opened up markets to foreign investors and interests. These same investors would pull out their money quickly, leaving countries in financial ruin.

- market privatization, which resulted in the selling off of government-run industries to the private sector and rise in prices of basic goods (like electricity) that the population could not keep up with.

Globalization was also the catalyst that started migrations from the rural to urban areas and then into transnational migration (Kabeer, 2008). Essentially, this created a global division of labor, driving the gap between the rich and poor even greater. The main beneficiaries of globalization were Western countries that were able to take advantage of cheap labor, raw goods, and new markets in which to sell their goods.

Poverty and Increased Economic Disenfranchisement

Poverty levels actually soared with globalization. Daily wages and minimum wages in countries hovered around less than $5 U.S. dollars. In Eastern Europe in 2001, ninety-three million people lived on under $2 per day (UNDP, 2005). In Thailand during this same time period, all currency reserves were used up trying to keep stable, which effected the confidence of investors in Malaysia, South Korea, Indonesia, and the Philippines, resulting in recessions and currency crashes (UNDP, 2005). Although the IMF stepped in with bailout money, they were loans whose high interest rates and policies further sunk economies into recessions. It would be the worst economic crisis in the history of these countries (Kara, 2009). On a micro level, this meant increased unemployment rates, higher costs of basic staples, and the largest income disparities in history. In fact, it is the level of income disenfranchisement had never been seen in many of these countries. In addition to the practical reactions to income disparity, socioemotional and even cultural reactions are important to note. If people do not think that they can earn decent livings or provide for their families, they are more vulnerable to being trafficked and exploited.

It is also important to consider that even when it seems like countries are doing well. For instance, in times of great economic growth, people can be even more vulnerable to trafficking. As countries experience this "boom" in growth, there are a couple of things that happen: (1) The country becomes a destination for migrant workers from poorer nations, and (2) there is an internal migration that occurs from rural or poorer areas into urban, wealthier areas. Growth wise, by 2020, Russia, Brazil, China, and India will be among the world's six largest economies (Hepburn & Simon, 2013, p. 393). While this may seem like a positive, it does have other repercussions such as in Russia, where progress has been slow and those who have flocked to the cities for work often have to resort to begging, may become homeless, and are in danger of being trafficked. In Brazil, the economic boom is a result of the global response to the biofuel movement, which is ethanol created from sugarcane. Unfortunately, most of the labor in sugarcane plantations continues to be supplied by labor trafficked individuals; at least half of those trafficked in Brazil are slaves in the sugar cane industry (Hepburn & Simon, 2013).

Migration

One of the biggest reflections of external realities that impact supply and demand is the global migration of workers. Countries who do not provide legal avenues of migration or whose migrations costs are too high experience the most susceptibility to trafficking. Lee (2011) notes that global neocapitalism is responsible for prompting circuits of undocumented and irregular migrants. Both types are more vulnerable to experiencing trafficking. To understand the dynamics of countries (both between and within) that are origin points, transits, or destinations, one should trace the migration patterns of their workers. Migration is caused by a number of things but can first be witnessed in countries that are still largely agricultural in nature. The lopsided development between rural and urban areas, in addition to the loss of agricultural lands for various reasons, results in large numbers of the rural population migrating to their urban areas (Leung & Xu, 2015).

Supply Chain

Supply chains are simply the network of businesses and steps required to produce and distribute a commodity. The importance of trafficking in relation to supply chains is that slave labor is usually found in the "supplier of workers," such as subcontractors, contract employment agencies, or even gangmasters, which are not included in "official supply chains" (Barrientos, 2008; Plant, 2008). The practice of subcontracting makes understanding supply chains and who is responsible much more difficult. Workers who are subcontracted may not be covered under basic corporate rights. Because there is a technical shift of commercial/corporate responsibility, it creates places in the production line that are all but invisible. This, in turn, makes it very arduous to identify what is occurring. Similarly, labor standards especially around inspections or enforcements become almost impossible to carry out (Anderson, 2007). With the rise of transnational and multinational companies, this becomes even more difficult, because it is hard to track what local laws are being enforced, if at all. Though there are a number of international trade agreements, most of them actually add to the ambiguity than clarify consistent standards of practice that should be followed. The industries most vulnerable to modern-day slavery affecting their supply chains include garments, chocolates, seafood, sugar, flowers, and so forth. This list is not exhaustive, but what they have in common are they are commodities that are dependent on products that are raw resources or products that are exports from poor countries (Satyarthi, 2013).

Feminization of Poverty and Migration

The two largest aspects that we have looked at in terms of impact have been poverty and migration. Both are said to be mainly composed of women, so much so that the term "feminization of poverty and migration" is often found in the literature (Chant, 2006). The poverty that women experience tends to be multidimensional and multisectoral (Cain & Howe, 2008). Structural conditions of globally stratified order have always placed women's work and labor under that of men, and children under adults. This hierarchy has created a positioning of women in all areas of society that is secondary, or under their male counterparts (Lee, 2011). As a result, women are the larger portion of 1.3 billion persons who are living in absolute poverty. The lack of economic opportunities and this patriarchal framework that makes women secondary creates a social climate that not only condones violence against women but also encourages it.

During times of industrialization, particularly current trends of globalization, we see that women have been given supposed economic opportunities. However, as Prabhakaran (2013), points out, women's labor in these instances are just an extension of their already traditional gender roles. The "work" that women dominate are in areas that they are already expected to be responsible for in more informal sectors. Thus, these are the sectors that are built on emotional and reproductive capabilities, which women's traditional gender roles tend to focus on. For instance, Kabeer (2008) discusses how retail jobs, domestic service, assembly line work, meal services (kitchen help and servers), some forms of manual labor, nursing, and teaching are all areas of women's roles within households that have been extended into the formal workforce. More insidiously, in the areas of trafficking and modern-day slavery, this commodification takes the form of surrogate mothers—the actual "renting" of wombs; mail-order brides or bride markets; sexual services; and slave labor through domestic servitude primarily as nannies and in elderly care. In fact, domestic servitude is one of the worst forms of trafficking according to the Organization for Security and Cooperation in Europe (OSCE) (2010). This is due to the excessive working hours, especially if the slave is living with the trafficker because there is literal access 24 hours a day; low or nonexistent salaries; lack of private life; and the physical and sexual abuse they are vulnerable to. Largoza-Maza (1995) states that most of these domestic slaves have to deal with situations that are difficult, dirty, and dangerous. Mishra (2013) found that 60% of girls and women who are trafficked for sex are also trafficked for forced labor. This further emphasizes how lucrative it is for traffickers to focus on women and girls—they are able to get double their "product."

The Political Economy of Sex

While labor trafficking and modern-day slavery outnumbers sex trafficking nine to one (roughly nine incidences of labor trafficking for every one case of sex trafficking), the economic discussion of sex trafficking remains unique. In part, this is due to the fact that one cannot separate the discussion of sex trafficking from prostitution. Therefore, the distinction of all prostitution as a form of trafficking as stated in the Palermo Protocol is an important one, although it is not being enforced by any country. In fact, the debates and controversies that exist around prostitution overshadow the fact that the Palermo Protocol, which many countries have signed and agreed to, has in fact redefined the parameters of trafficking. Because it has not halted the debate, it also has not stopped the growth of economic "markets in women" (Lee, 2011). These markets are almost all in domains of sex tourism and are also in places where legalization of prostitution have occurred. Even in these areas where legalization has occurred, research has found that migrant women who are prostitutes bear the burden of so-called legalization policies because they earn the least but are also exploited by a larger number of perpetrators and are even sought out by them in what Lee refers to as the "commodification of desire" (Long, 2002). In chapter 3, we shall see how these markets developed from current and former "rest and relaxation" zones (usually former military, but not exclusively so).

Central to this discussion is the question of prostitution as a legitimate form of "work." Proponents of that argument do not believe that all sex trafficking is a form of sexual slavery. In fact, supporters for legalization believe that women are exercising the use of their own agency by making the decision to become a sex worker. However, feminists contend that countries that are patriarchal in nature (some would say all of them) make it impossible for women to have real consent in the decision to sell their bodies (Outshoorn, 2012). If one takes this argument and brings it to a global scale, then each country should be taken into account to measure not only patriarchy but also the concrete conditions of poverty, violence, and migration that might push a woman into selling her body. For these women, it may be argued, that the selling of their bodies may be nothing more than a survival strategy instead of a practice on empowerment. There is also a question of whether national infrastructures are able to fully support legalization of prostitution. As with the case of Amsterdam, the brunt of the protectionist laws fall on migrant women as opposed to Dutch women, who can charge more and in some instances operate independently (Outshoorn, 2001). Until these issues can be addressed, there is no real policy that can be taken seriously because the circumstances that landed women and children in this situation will continue to exist.

CALL TO ACTION: CHANGING THE BUSINESS MODEL

Understanding the business of trafficking and modern-day slavery is one way to begin to comprehend the immensity of the issue. The incredible profit that is literally being made from the slave labor of people is to understand how much is at stake for both sides. Kara (2009) believes that by being able to discern what is driving these types of profits, we can formulate ways in which we could end trafficking for good. There are several ways to operationalize this type of tactic. For example, as we mentioned earlier, you could attack commercial sexual exploitation by just raising the cost of sex. While this is highly unlikely, we cannot ignore or fail to address the economic aspects of sex trafficking which are driving its growth. The need to attack both the supply and demand include taking responsibility for the growth and commercialization of sex, including the aspects we believe are innocent and not tied to the issue such as dating, relationships, and pop culture (Levy, 2006). This would include areas where sex trafficking thrives: brothels, clubs, massage parlors, apartments, hotels and motels, and of course, what happens on the streets.

Similarly, another attack on profitability is to create a radical shift in the conduct of how economic globalization and multinational businesses work (Kara, 2009). While this might seem like a task that does not have a solution, many companies are in favor of working to end trafficking. This is a key aspect as the problem exists within the auspices of multinational company supply chains and must be targeted as part of how business is run. To this extent, the partnership between industry and the nonprofit or service sector and law enforcement agencies may be one way to combat trafficking and modern-day slavery. For example, consumers could play a part in swaying businesses to be more responsible, which we will discuss later. Companies, as well, have taken control of the situation once they understand their part within the larger ecosystems or production and supply chain. For example, Cadbury (now owned by Kraft) is the largest producer of chocolate in the world. They are unique in that they have sourced their chocolate for over a hundred years from Ghana. At the turn of the 21st century, the cocoa sourcing market saw a slowdown in growth because of a number of things, one of them being the lack of new farmers entering the space; young people were simply not farming but rather migrating internationally or at least to urban cities to find work. Cadbury commissioned a study that identified a number of poor socioeconomic challenges the farmers faced. Because of this study, Cadbury did two things. First, they convened a collective impact group, the Cocoa Partnership, that included the farmers to get their ideas on how to reduce the challenges. Then, they did such things as supporting farming sustainability through direct partnerships with farms that sourced the chocolate. In some situations, Cadbury created their own farms or financially supported those of small farmers (Barrientos, 2011). This type of collective impact and ecosystem thinking (see Table 2.1 and Figure 2.2), is what can help solve the problem and is preferable to simplistic answers such as "close the borders," which have been proposed by conservative politicians. The idea of even being able to have the capacity to police borders, much less close them, is economically impossible. Admittedly, while it would shut down the supply chain in one area, the low cost of transportation would just mean that there would be another way that traffickers would find to circumvent the barrier. Conversely, if one takes the collective impact approach, there is a creation of solutions that target the actual root causes of the problem.

A final factor to note is that it is not only the traffickers that have vested interest in keeping their "businesses" profitable. There are deep barriers in the form of government and other possibly unseen beneficiaries to trafficking. For instance, many governments do not even classify labor trafficking as such; they only recognize sex trafficking. Even in these cases, countries may not want to create legislation or policies with real "teeth" or avenues for concrete enforcement because they may stand to lose substantial income that adds to

Table 2.1   The U.S. Government's Anti-Human Trafficking Initiatives

Agency/Office/Organization	Services/Advocacy/Research
Health and Human Services (HHS)	• Reports/publications: Comprehensive study of HHS AHT programming agency-wide • Victim services: "Services Available to Victims of Human Trafficking" booklet outlines available services for victims and service providers • Victim services: Anti-trafficking in Persons (ATIP) program provides services to victims of human trafficking
U.S. Agency for International Development (USAID)	• Funding: ~$16.3M of annual funding for Counter-Trafficking in Persons (C-TIP) programming • Policy: C-TIP policy integrated into development programs • PPP*: C-TIP Campus Challenge for youth-led solutions to human trafficking
Department of Homeland Security (DHS)	• Outreach: Single Department voice to end trafficking through the Blue Campaign • Prosecution: Illicit Pathways Attack Strategy (IPAS) identifies illicit pathways and dismantles human smuggling networks • Prosecution: National Victim Identification Program integrates technology to rescue child victims of sexual exploitation
Department of Defense (DOD)	• Interagency collaboration: DOD Combatting Trafficking in Persons (CTIP) engaged in interagency task forces and policy groups • Reports/publications: DOD CTIP Strategic Plan outlines DOD efforts and vision to end human trafficking • Training: Required human trafficking awareness training for DOD personnel
Department of Transportation (DOT)	• PPP*: Transportation Leaders Against Human Trafficking partnership • Training: Required human trafficking awareness training for DOT personnel • Training: Training for Amtrak personnel to better identify trafficking indicators
U.S. Equal Employment Opportunity Commission (EEOC)	• Interagency collaboration: Increased participation in inter-agency efforts through "New Frontier Against Human Trafficking" • Prosecution: Enforcement of laws prohibiting employment discrimination • Victim services: Certifying agency for U visas

(Continued)

Table 2.1 (Continued)

Department of Labor (DOL)	• Prosecution: Investigations into violations of labor law standards • Reports/publications: Annual reports on goods produced by child and forced labor • Victim services: Trafficking in Persons guide for NGOs with relevant laws and victim services
Department of Justice (DOJ)	• Data collection: Human Trafficking Reporting System collects key data from DOJ AHT task forces for analysis • Meeting/forum: Agency-wide quarterly meetings to coordinate activities across components • Prosecution: Human Trafficking Prosecution Unit engaged in ongoing trafficking investigations
U.S. Department of Agriculture (USDA)	• Training: Training available to all USDA employees worldwide • Victim services: Special and supplemental nutrition assistance program
Interagency	• Outreach: National Slavery and Human Trafficking Prevention Month initiatives • Reports/publications: Federal Strategic Action Plan on Services for Victims of Human Trafficking in the United State • Training: Blue Lightning campaign training airline personnel on trafficking indicators
Department of Education (ED)	• Reports/publications: Fact sheet on trafficking for distribution to schools and educations • Training: Survey of school emergency management personnel on trafficking prevalence
White House	• Interagency collaboration: President's Interagency Task Force to Monitor • Policy: Executive Order (E.O. 13627) Against Trafficking in Persons in Federal Contracting • PPP*: Partnership for Freedom Innovation Awards for creative solutions to human trafficking
Department of State (DOS)	• PPP*: Partnership with Made in a Free World to increase demand for responsible sourced goods • Reports/publications: Annual Trafficking in Persons Report serves as a guide for governmental AHT efforts • Victim services: Refugee assistance and admittance programs

Note: PPP = Public/private partnership.

Source: Copyright © 2015 Deloitte Development LLC. All rights reserved. Member of Deloitte Touche Tohmatsu Limited.

Figure 2.2 Mapping the U.S. Government's Anti-Human Trafficking Initiatives

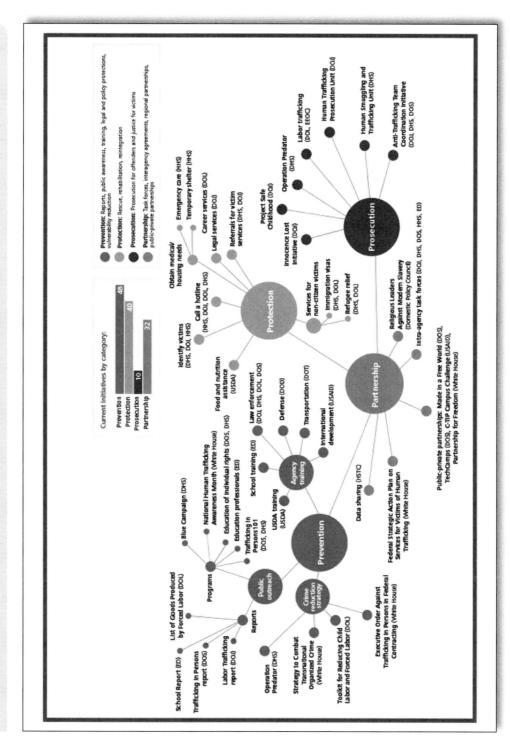

their GDP. For instance, in an ILO report, it was stated that the trade in sex contributes up to 14% to Thailand's annual GDP (Prabhakaran, 2013). To contrast, in the United States, professional and business services contribution to the GDP is 12%.

Being able to apply an economic analysis is just one piece of the puzzle. Even if one were to fully understand all the economic implications, the politics, polemics, and root causes around trafficking would still be impediments to ending trafficking and modern day slavery. Otherwise, it might be as simple as to raise the prices (especially given the elastic nature) or to target the right portion of the supply chain. But, we know it is not this simple. It is difficult for those engaged in human rights work to bifurcate their social justice world view from the economic realities. Thus, the next chapter will examine these root causes, how these causes have historical bearing and policy implications, and their current manifestations. Now that you understand the role that economics, profits, and business practices have on trafficking, you can see where the rest, especially root causes and origins, fit.

DISCUSSION QUESTIONS

1. Identify at least one driver of profit for the demand of trafficking and modern-day slavery. What does this entail? What are the implications to your practice?

2. How have women been fetishized into the perfect "commodity"? Try to be as concrete and specific as possible. Provide at least three real-life examples.

3. How does "pop culture" support sex trafficking and the commodification of women and/or children? How would your field address this?

4. Research the type of work visas available in your country or in a country of your interest. What are they? How do they protect or increase vulnerability to labor trafficking?

5. What is the role or power of consumers as supply chains become more transparent?

CHALLENGE

Understanding supply chains is important to understanding human trafficking and modern day slavery. Your challenge is to select a company. This could be a company that you are familiar with, for instance, one whose product or service you use. Once you have selected one, see how far you can re-create the supply chain. Then, identify where in the supply chain there are vulnerabilities to trafficking.

Social Determinants of Human Trafficking and Modern-Day Slavery

Chapter Objectives

1. Readers will be able to summarize the key social determinants involved in human trafficking and modern slavery.

2. Readers will identify and explain the root causes and social determinants of human trafficking and modern slavery.

3. Readers will evaluate different institutions and the role they play in human trafficking and modern-day slavery.

4. Readers will assess the impact of corruption on human trafficking and modern-day slavery.

5. Readers will consider the global feminist response to human trafficking and modern-day slavery.

I shift slightly to my left, trying to shake the tingling feeling away by balancing on my toes; I've been there so long that I think my foot is falling asleep. My hands slip and for a second the banner I am holding slips down as well. Lucky for me, I am flanked on the right and left by two other women who smile in sympathy. We have been standing outside for quite some time, watching the police assemble across from us. It is 1996 and we are at the World Trade Organization, International Monetary Fund World Bank meetings protesting the increased collaboration between global corporations and militarism in poor countries. To me, it is another protest—a massive one—but still a political rally. Later, it would come to be known as the "Battle in Seattle."

(Continued)

(Continued)

As the police presence grows and the sun begins to set, fire trucks drives up and there are large hoses being unrolled. A guy, wearing a shirt with a big peace sign spray painted across it, comes up to me, a tube of toothpaste in his hands, gesturing for me to take it. The woman on my left, who is from Puerto Rico, takes it, squeezes the tube, and puts some under her eyes and nose, and smears it on a bandana that she has tied around her neck. She nods at me and says, "For the tear gas. They are going to gas us or hose us. I don't know which." I've never had this experience before but I follow her example. When I'm finished, she nods again and says, "Now we are ready. Sometimes that's all you can be." I shrug and look out at the sea of growing police in front of us.

"There are so many of them," I say.

"Oh, mi hija," she says, "This is nothing. In Puerto Rico we have the police and we have the soldiers. My beautiful island is filled with military and more military. That is why we are here right? We are tired of living in a military state. We are tired of the cowering before the powerful."

"Is that what you are fighting for? freedom from the United States?" I ask because I know that Puerto Rico has been a territory of the United States since the turn of the twentieth century.

She shakes her head and her laughter is musical. Then she sighs, "Do we want freedom? We don't just have the military, we have corporate greed, we have racism and colonization, and we have a machismo[1] that just will not stop. Freedom? I would settle for my island not turning into one big red light district."

—*Annalisa Enrile*

---

1. Machismo is a concept of maleness and standard of behavior, usually tied to the Spanish or Latino cultures. This standard of behavior is a hyper masculinity that is composed of sexism, chauvinism, and the belief that men are violent, aggressive, and sexual. Further, traditional notions of machismo are also connected to the domination or submission of women (Arciniega, Anderson, Tovar-Blank, & Tracey, 2008).

We have to delve deeper than just statistics and indices to understand trafficking and modern-day slavery. While it is important to understand how to define trafficking, where it occurs, and what leaves populations vulnerable, it is imperative that we also understand its deep root causes. In doing so, we can see how trafficking and modern-day slavery evolved into what it is today. Also, by understanding wicked problems such as trafficking and modern-day slavery from its roots, we will be able to come up with prevention plans and interventions that will eradicate and not just temporarily alleviate the situation. This chapter will examine the social determinants of trafficking and modern-day slavery. It is important to consider that we are not talking about individuals here. Rather, we are talking about institutions and ideologies.

SOCIAL DETERMINANTS

According to the World Health Organization (WHO), these determinants are "conditions in which people are born, grow, work, live, and age, and the wider set of forces and systems shaping the conditions of daily life." Social determinats include socioeconomic contexts, social norms, policies and development agendas, and political systems. Perry and McEwing (2013) conducted one of the only comprehensive research reviews examining 1,148 articles within a ten-year period (2001–2011) and deeply analyzing 61 articles to identify what social determinants impact trafficking in the Southeast Asia region. Southeast Asia was selected because of the high concentration of trafficking that occurs in that region, accounting for one-third of all trafficking in the world, including accounting for 60% of trafficking into the United States (Congressional Research Services, 2000; Richard, 1999). Similar studies have not been conducted in other parts of the world. The review found that key social determinates that create vulnerability to trafficking include poverty, female gender, lack of policy and enforcement, age[2], migration, displacement and conflict, ethnicity, culture, ignorance of trafficking methods, and caste status. For the purposes of this chapter, we will examine the main social determinants of poverty, militarization (i.e., conflict), female gender, ethnicity, culture, and caste[3].

POVERTY

As you have learned in previous chapters, poverty is the biggest reason people cite as to why a supply of slaves in the world exists. Additionally, it is the ever-growing divide between the rich and the poor, which also drives slave labor. According to the World Bank, poverty affected the world in 2012 in these ways:

- 12.7% of the world's population lived at or below $1.90 a day.
- Over 2.1 billion people in the developing world lived on less than U.S. $3.10 a day.
- 77.8% of the extremely poor lived in South Asia and Sub-Saharan Africa.

Further, according to DoSomething.Org, a social change challenge website, the impact of poverty in the world is far reaching:

- 2.1 billion children worldwide are living in poverty. According to UNICEF, 22,000 children die each day because of poverty.
- 805 million people worldwide do not have enough food to eat.

---

2. Age will not be discussed in this chapter because, for the most part, it refers to the connection with the "virgin cure." In sex trafficking, this is the higher value and price that is put on virgins, thus making young(er) girls more vulnerable.

3. Poverty, migration, displacement, and ignorance of trafficking methods are discussed in other areas within the text.

- More than 750 million people lack adequate access to clean drinking water. Inadequate drinking water causes diarrhea that kills an estimated 842,000 people every year globally.

- 25% of all humans live without electricity.

- Oxfam estimates that it would take U.S. $60 billion annually to end extreme global poverty (that is less than 1/4 the income of the top 100 richest billionaires).

- Hunger is the number one cause of death in the world, killing more than HIV/AIDS, malaria, and tuberculosis combined.

In the United States, we define poverty based on a standard of living that we assume is minimal (Di Nitto, 2011]). According to the U.S. Census, the official poverty rate in 2014 was 14.8%, or 46.7 million people in poverty (DeNavas-Walt & Proctor, 2015). More women (16.1%) than men (13.4%) were in poverty, with the most notable differences being in those aged 65 and older (12.1% for women and 7.4% for men). The longer someone is in poverty, the harder it is to get out of over time and can increase throughout the life cycle (Rank, 2004).

The largest mitigating factor of fighting poverty, after fair wages and access to resources, is the equalizing factor that free education has. The popular campaign, *The Girl Effect*, succinctly demonstrates the benefits to girls who are able to access and receive an education. In 30 seconds, the campaign's effective multimedia presentation provides the following facts:

- An extra year of primary school education boosts a girl's eventual wages by 10–20%; an extra year of secondary school adds 15–25%.

- When a girl in the developed world receives 7 years of education, she marries 4 years later and has 2.2 fewer children (thus reducing her vulnerability to poverty).

- Girls who stay in school during adolescence will have a later sexual debut, are less likely to be subjected to forced sex, and if sexually active, more likely to use contraception than their age peers who are out of school.

- Girls can't succeed when they are living in fear; ending violence is the first step to end poverty of girls.

- When girls are educated, they end up reinvesting in the country and building onto the country's overall GDP.

Parents are willing to do almost anything to educate their children. Skinner (2008) found that some parents accused of "selling" their children actually only traded them for the promise that their children would be educated. This is a common occurrence, with many families hoping that by letting their children work as domestic helpers or in other industries (fisheries, mining, and other industries), they will be able to gain an education.

Poverty leaves families vulnerable not just for the reasons that we have seen but also for overall physical and mental health. Even when families are able to get ahead and move slightly above the poverty line, the level of debt they find themselves in, as well as low wages, may still keep them only one or two paychecks away from being homeless.

For many poor families, work is a collaboration between all able-bodied members of a household, which makes child labor a necessity. It is estimated by the International Labor Organization (ILO) that about 168 million children are involved in child labor, with more than half (85 million) working in hazardous conditions. Asia and the Pacific still has the largest numbers, but Africa has the highest incidence (about 59 million; 21 %). Most labor occurs in agriculture, fisheries, and the service industry, which are informal, where it can be hidden.

The growing gap between the rich and the poor, lack of health care, and decreased access to free education create the "perfect storm" of desperation that characterizes the daily life of those mired in poverty. In fact, traffickers prefer to procure from the poor, not just because of desperation to earn money but because they feel that the impoverished will value any amount they are given (or think they are being given) and will be less likely to complain. However, it is not enough to say that poverty is the only reason for the proliferation of trafficking and modern-day slavery. It is a catalyst, particularly in terms of vulnerability, positionality, and sustainability of slavery, but there are other systemic factors and contexts to consider.

MILITARIZATION

Some of the basic conditions that led to trafficking were facilitated through a military presence. Though these are the institutions that were designed to keep people "safe" and "secure," they became the breeding grounds for the construction of what we would come to think of as the "sex industry" and later know as trafficking. Though this may be difficult to accept, it does not hide the facts that one can trace most, if not all, red light districts to the presence of either military bases or areas of conflict. Leading researcher on militarism, Enloe (2000) states that this is not new, that we can see from the early twentieth century how the military and government policed women's bodies and sexuality vis a vis the needs of the soldiers during World War II and earlier. For instance, the Japanese military instituted sexual slavery as a method for "servicing" their soldiers. The sex slaves, now known as "comfort women," came out in the 1990s to reveal the wartime atrocities done toward them. An estimated 200,000 Asian women were kidnapped to serve as military sex slaves for the Japanese military. Their existence was proof of the collusion between the Japanese government and military[4].

During the colonial era, European military powers recognized the role that commercialized sex would play in their militaries. Indeed, the construction of militarized masculinity included the idea that *real men* had sexual appetites that needed to be met, preferably by women, and that the appeasement of these appetites would actually aid in their role as soldiers. Ancient Roman garrisons (on the British frontier) left evidence of hundreds of women's sandals, providing some truth that women were used by soldiers even then. In 1589, a Spanish officer discussed how prostitutes were necessary to well-run militaries (Chapkis, 1981). The presence of women with the military has never been contested, but it was not until modern warfare and the super military industrial complex that we saw major changes resulting in sex trafficking and modern-day slavery.

---

4. Council on Foreign Relations. N.d. "Global Conflict Tracker." *CFR.org*. Retrieved from https://www.cfr.org/global/global-conflict-tracker/p32137#!/

World War II Sex Slaves ("Comfort Women")

During World War II, the Japanese ruled the Pacific Theater, taking over many countries in the Asia-Pacific region. "Comfort women" was the euphemism used to label prostitutes and later sex slaves that were used by the Japanese military. The rationale for this practice was to deter rape and sexual assault that the Japanese military might enact (Hayashi, 2008). What the Japanese called "comfort stations" actually began before the war in the 1930s where volunteer prostitutes were recruited. After the start of the war, Japanese women who volunteered for war effort to work as nurses or in factories found themselves pressed into sexual slavery in these comfort stations. As the war progressed, comfort stations were set up on the front lines and in occupied territories where local women and girls were kidnapped and forced into becoming sex slaves. Girls as young as 11 and 12 were taken. Girls and women were kidnapped from Korea, China, the Philippines, and Indonesia (mainly) and then other outposts later. They were also taken from Thailand, Vietnam, Malaysia, and other Japanese territories, as well as a small group of women from Australia and the Netherlands (Kumagai, 2014).

It was not until the early '90s that these women even began to come out in public and tell their stories because of the deep sense of shame that it cost them. At times, the women were told to service from 20–30 men a day; 75–100 if it was during the weekend. From the first testimonies of the Korean Comfort Women who came forward, others followed, emboldened by the fact that women were now speaking out. In 1993, "Kono Statement," after these statements the Japanese government confirmed to coercion being involved in getting women to the comfort stations, but in 2007, they stated that there was "no evidence that the Japanese military was involved." In 2014, a joint commission between South Korea and Japan upheld the Kono Statement. Although this was the case, there was no public apology issued by the government.

In 1991, three Korean women filed a suit against Japan demanding compensation and an official apology. A few thousand dollars was awarded, but the government refused to apologize. Even by 2015, though the Japanese government agreed to pay $8.3 million dollars in damages to all surviving comfort women, they did so contingent on the removal of statues commemorating comfort women and also refraining from any further public demonstrations in front of Japanese embassies. However, the Korean, Philippine, and Taiwanese women were not satisfied with this because they were motivated less by money and more by making sure their experience would be part of the historical record. As a result, many turned the money away. Despite the numerous denials of the Japanese government, there have been several memorials, in Palisades Park, New Jersey. Several homes have also been set up for the surviving comfort women in the Philippines, Taiwan, South Korea, and China. The homes were set up because many of the comfort women were turned away by their families either because of shame or because they were not believed. This is why it was so important to the survivors to obtain an apology and to be recognized in the annals of history. As comfort women Rosa Henson, who wrote a book describing her experiences, the plight of survivors was to make sure that these atrocities against women did not happen ever again.

With the Vietnam War in the 1970s, the formal establishment of what was euphemistically referred to as the "rest and recreation" industry, which according to Enloe (2000) was the "prostitution system militarized, capitalized, and masculinized" (page 70). Four criteria had to be met for the organized, widespread prostitution that occurred. These were as follows:

1. Large numbers of local women are treated by the government and businesses as second-class citizens or cheap labor, even though there are women who are part of or joining the middle class;

2. Prostitution is seen as a "necessary evil" by foreign militaries basing in local countries;

3. Tourism is imagined by local and economic planners as the fast track to development;

4. Local governments hosting these foreign troops believe that there are certain human rights violations (including rape) that are necessary for national security.

Eventually, these were the actions that constituted the rationale of sex as an industry (Barry, 1995). Before this, prostitution in the form of streetwalkers or even camp followers was a matter of personal choices and proclivities, and did not have this level of organization, or more importantly, exploiters in the form of pimps and (later) traffickers.

It was not only sex that the military acknowledged. From the earliest wars, "camp followers" also included women who would provide the comforts of home such as laundry and meals. Generally, the role of these women was to ease the soldiers' needs (Meyer, 1996). They were not known first or only as prostitutes, although sex was something that was also provided in their "services." For some of the men, this was described as a necessity, a reminder of something or someone "back home." The expectation of fulfilled gender roles combined with sexual urges were integrated the perception of what these women were supposed to be or at the very least, symbolize. What is more salient to modern times is that red light districts that have transitioned from military to tourist areas have the need not just for sex slaves but for labor trafficking as well. From the construction of these areas to other services (construction, hospitality, and other domestic chores), labor traffickers have taken advantage of the situation. For instance, while the brothel may be the central focus for trafficking (dancers, strippers, prostitutes, and hostesses), it also supports a number of persons vulnerable to labor trafficking: those that build the brothel; provide security; medical help; even small convenience stores are all examples of how trafficking may have any number of influences into the community. In fact, whole communities were supported by trafficking. This does not change despite the transition from military rest and relaxation sites to tourist hubs (Enloe, 2000).

Enloe (2000) writes that "in both military and civilian corridors of power, women figure in this debate as allegedly passive creatures whose sexuality is merely designed to service individual men and male-defined institutions" (p. 63). Everything we have stated about the role of the military, politicians, and law enforcement has been from mostly male institutional perspectives. The central idea has been an attempt on how to maintain and control women's sexuality both in the sense that their sex (and bodies) are for sale and also that it must be regulated. For instance, from the beginning, the military did not try to regulate the actions of their soldiers but the women. Health services were always directed to the control of women's bodies for the protection of the soldiers. For the most part, the need for protection, beginning in the 1990s was protection against HIV/AIDS where most of the international models still placed the onus on prostituted women or sex slaves. It was up to them to enforce the use of condoms. Even though it was U.S. military policy to provide condoms and encourage their use, most commanders admitted that they did not think that the soldiers would use them. It was decided that the women would have to be mandated to use them so it was the women who could be fined (although this happened infrequently). Women were told they were to blame if the disease were to begin and/or spread. For example, South Korean women who were prostituted in GI towns called "Americatowns" were in danger of being picked up by U.S. military officials and being sent to VD (venereal disease) clinics in an outside provide for two weeks (Enloe, 2000). Nothing was done to soldiers, who were not monitored for having unprotected sex.

Gender role norms and sexual abuse were also ways to control women's bodies and their "sexual proclivities." German Nazis felt that women forced into prostitution that were lesbians could be "cured" of what was seen as incorrect sexual desires. Similarly, they also felt that if prostitutes were readily available, they would be able to "correct" the homosexuality of German men who needed "reforming." This type of control over women's bodies was not just for the prostituted women or sex slaves but also for the women "left behind." For example, American women were told that they should excuse the behavior of their husbands who exploited Vietnamese prostitutes because they were doing so to "save their wives" from unnatural asexual appetites caused by war (Lawson, 1989).

Rest and relaxation zones were located not only in areas where conflict took place, such as Vietnam and Cambodia, but also in areas where military bases were located such as in Thailand, the Philippines, and Okinawa (Japan)[5]. These zones would become booming red light districts, especially in the 1980s when they were fully established. If there was any question as to whether there was military collusion in the setup of these districts, one only had to take a look at the policies developed to know that the military directed much of the activity. For instance, in Subic Bay, Philippines, the United States based its largest Pacific Fleet, and had a complex policy of health regulations related to their soldiers and the prostitutes beyond the gates of the base. Within the base, bulletin boards were located where women's "pink health" cards would be posted so that men would know who was "safe" and "clean." Although prostitution was illegal in the Philippines, any woman who was employed by the "entertainment" industry (hostesses, waitresses, dancers, etc.) would be required to have monthly health screenings and be given copies of these cards to prove they were clean of STDs. Men did not have to prove a similar level of health. In Thailand, also at U.S. military bases, military commanders kept track of the women by labeling them as "special job workers" (Enloe, 2000).

---

5. Okinawa is an island in the southern part of Japan, with a total area of roughly 455 square miles. Strategically, the island has been the location of U.S. bases with almost 20% of the island being covered by U.S. military bases (74% of all bases in Japan).

Militarized prostitution shaped the stereotypes of whole populations of women, and created mental maps of femininity that would continue to exist and fuel rationale around trafficking. The archetype of the "whore" is depicted not only in the literature but also in the pop references related to these periods of conflict. For instance, well into the 1980s and 1990s, Hollywood portrayals of the Vietnam War include the obligatory prostitution scenes such as in *Full Metal Jacket* where women offer "sucky sucky" (Lawson, 1989). While this may seem to be innocent and just another film, it reflects the common ways in which women and girls were being constructed. The famous pictorial essay by Sturdivant and Sturdivant highlighted the way that women were seen during this period in time (and presumably until today). The acronym LBFM is perhaps the most illustrative of the way that most women were seen— *Little Brown Fucking Machines* (powered by rice). This acronym decorated t-shirts, baseball caps, graffiti, and was even the name of some of the clubs all throughout Southeast Asia.

Once the military bases left and the world began to demilitarize or shift their basing options, women and children were left more vulnerable than ever. It was already too late because the sociological and economic damage was done. Most bases that were left behind stood as wastelands until it was decided what would be done with them. The only portion of the community that thrived were the clubs and bars, which had transitioned from servicing the military to servicing local police, politicians, and business people. This period would lead to a boom in the tourism market. Because of the excellent infrastructure of the bases, they were areas that were ripe for tourism development. While some in the community was offered job training to help them with the transition, this was not an option to prostitutes. Even within this system, there were accessibility issues that continued to exist based on class and even race. In addition to the fact that prostituted women and girls still had no other (or limited) recourse, there was the added consequence of military bases and rest and relaxation areas—the Amerasian children that were left behind

Table 3.1   Global U.S. Military Presence, 2015

Country	U.S. Presence
Russia	143 active duty personnel in place
South Korea	28,400 troops and 15 bases
Japan	16,000 troops, 40,000 troops inland, and 6 active bases
Philippines	500 recreational troops, has existing Mutual Defense Treaty
Guam (U.S. Territory)	Has existing 4,500 troops, Anderson Base
Saipan (U.S. Territory)	Direct U.S. airfield, old base during WWII
Australia	2,521 troops and access to the Royal Air Bases in Dowell and Perth

Source: Adapted form Asia Pacific Research Network.

Figure 3.1 Global U.S. Military Presence, 2015

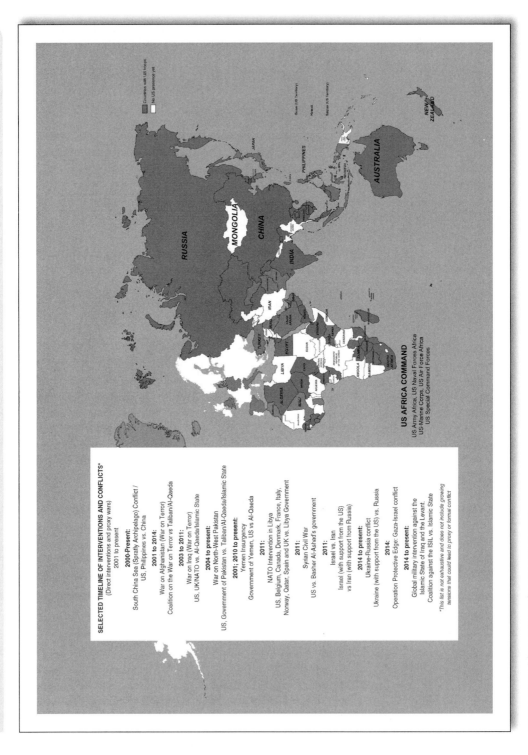

Source: Adapted form Asia Pacific Research Network.

Case Vignette: Chien

Chien is a middle-age woman who was formerly sex trafficked in Vietnam. An Amerasian woman whose mother was prostituted during the Vietnam War and who suspects her father was an American soldier, Chien always knew that she was different from her pale brown hair and her green eyes. Chien was one of thousands of Amerasian children left behind in Vietnam. After the war, only 3,000 orphans were evacuated. Another 21,000 Amerasian children were able to repatriate to the United States after the 1987 Amerasian Homecoming Act, but Chien did not have enough money to take advantage of the policy. She grew up with her grandparents until the time she was 10 years old and her grandfather, a farmer, passed away. Her grandmother, unable to care for her, sent her to live with her mother in the city. At first, her mother, then working in a nightclub, did what she could to keep Chien in school. But, it was difficult and the children often made fun of her obvious mixed background. Chien said until then, she had never worried or even thought about her father. She only knew this his name was James and was forbidden to talk about him. Her mother was afraid they would be sent to a "reeducation camp." Chien stated, "Every time I looked into the mirror, a foreigner looked back. I grew up to think that the enemy looked like me so they must be me." She had no friends in school and no family other than her mother. Her mother became sick when she was 14 and Chien was forced to leave school and earn money. She was trafficked by a local bar who took advantage of the fact that she was a virgin. Chien was forced to sexually service many men a night until she became ill when she was 24. "I felt like an old woman," she says, "but I was lucky because it got me out of the club. I didn't know how long I would last." By then, her mother had passed away and there was no one for her to turn to. After Chien was thrown out of the club, she was homeless and found help with a local NGO. As she healed, she started to work with them as an outreach worker, providing education and contraceptives to women who were trafficked as she was. She keeps her hair short and wears brown contact lenses because she reports still being discriminated against because of how she looks. "I am still the enemy," she sighs, "I cannot erase it from my face completely." Recently, Chien found out important information from an organization called Operation Reunite, which matches DNA of children to their soldier fathers. Chien had done the test as a whim when one of her friends suggested it. She never imagined she would find a match. Chien has now "met" her father and his family via Skype and is planning a visit in a few months to the United States.

Of special note is the role that child sex slavery and pornography has played especially in the 1980s and beyond. During this time, civil servants in the U.S. Pentagon began to raise the issue of militarized prostitution to no avail. They decided to change tactics and talk about *child* prostitution and abuse, pointing out the vulnerability of Amerasian children (usually left behind by soldiers who had been with prostitutes during the Vietnam War and shortly after). This was a growing issue in Thailand and the Philippines where hundreds of young children were entering the sex tourism industry. To illustrate, although the U.S. military left Thailand after Vietnam in the mid-1970s, leaving in its wake, over 1,400 brothels and hundreds of bars, massage parlors, and other locations of the "sex industry," by the early 1990s, there were some estimates of anywhere from 100,000 (Thai police estimates) to 800,000 (Centre for Children's Rights estimates) of child "prostitution" (sexual exploitation), demonstrating the foundation of sex tourism that endures (Jones, n.d.). The Okinawan rape of a 12-year-old girl by three U.S. military personnel in 1995 pushed the issue into the forefront. Department of Defense officials had no choice but to address the issue after over 85,000 people in Japan and thousands more around the world protested the sexual abuse, especially because it involved a child. Since then, there have been continuing levels of violence (though not all directed toward children) with 26 cases of murder and 129 cases of rape that involve members of the military industrial complex (soldiers, contractors, and dependents) according to Okinawan law enforcement (RT, 2016). In 1996, a conference sponsored by UNICEF and ECPAT approved work for antichild prostitution efforts that continue to be ongoing. This in turn helped build current antichild pornography, sex tourism, and commercial sexual exploitation that we have today.

Global feminists from many different areas attempt to raise the issue of militarization and its detrimental effects on women and children, as well as whole communities where military bases are located. From the late '80s onward, feminists have been building the case of trafficking and modern-day slavery. While there was a certain amount receptivity to the growing issue of trafficking, there was strong opposition to highlighting the role of the military, particularly the U.S. military and its complicity in the creation of the problem. In the United Nations Fourth World Conference on Women in Beijing (1995), women delegates from the United States led by then first lady, Hillary Clinton, discussed sex trafficking and child labor but removed any reference to the function or presence of military prostitution. This omission effectively removed militarization from the discussion of trafficking and into the realm of moral discussions (Enloe, 2000). However, as we can see, no matter how much politicians and the military want to ignore the connections, there is a clear relationship between homegrown and international militarism, foreign bases, tourism, politics, and industry as it relates to trafficking and modern-day slavery.

CORRUPTION

For the militarization to thrive and for the "sex industry" to grow, there has to be local cooperation. This is mainly provided in the form of international peacekeepers (such as the United Nations) or local police forces. With so much of the anti-trafficking initiatives based on law enforcement efforts, the ability of police to be allies in the fight and not exacerbate the issue is paramount. Unfortunately, one of the areas that cannot be ignored is the corruption and abuse of power by law enforcement. The United Nations has about 125,000 troops, police, and peacekeepers all over the world (Moran, 2015). In 1994, the United Nations Transitional Authority in Cambodia (UNTAC) was sent to restore peace after Vietnamese troops withdrew from Cambodia. The main purpose other than the restoration of peace was to remove land mines in the area. What happened in addition to these things was an upward surge in prostitution; the UNTAC peacekeepers themselves became customers and there was a growth of over 150% (Cambodian Women's Association, 1996). Many of the women who were prostituted were ethnic Vietnamese or from migrant communities of Vietnamese living there before the war and because of this, the Cambodian government was slow to respond. There were similar cases in Sarajevo, where UN peacekeepers had reputations for keeping sex slaves (Skinner, 2008). In the Congo and Eritrea, UN "peacekeeping" became synonymous with "rape." (Skinner, 2008). In 1996, human rights' and women's organizations called for UN troops to be mandated to have training on respecting local women (Crossette, 1996). Another study by Beber, Gilligan, Guardado, & Karim (2015) found that UN peacekeepers engaged in sexual exploitation (transactional sex) with as many as 58,000 women and girls in Liberia from 2003 to 2012.

Defense contractors and other ancillary people related to the military machinery must also be considered. In many cases, they get paid large sums of money, are given the same access and courtesies as military officials, but do not have any of the responsibility nor do they have to report to a commanding officer. This is not to say that their actions go unnoticed. For instance, U.S. Pentagon contractors were being investigated for keeping Eastern European sex slaves in their residences (Skinner, 2008).

Local police continue to be one of the most pervasive areas of corruption especially as it affects sex slaves. Local police carry a lot of power, especially in their ability to protect the women in the community. Rather than seeing them as a source of help, sex slaves have found that police will often require bribes or even sexual favors in exchange for their protection. One woman from the Philippines explained that she was picked up for walking the street when she was taken to the police station. There, she was forced to perform sexual acts for the police until she was released (BUKLOD, personal communication, 2013). In South Africa, most of the women and children have been trafficked for domestic servitude, usually domestically, from rural areas to cities (Swart, 2012). The issue of police corruption in South Africa has been identified as a major barrier to combating trafficking; because criminal syndicates traffick people within and across borders, some rely directly on the police to help smuggle people through supposed checkpoints (Swart, 2011).

The police also became key players in the transition between militarized prostitution and the tourist industry. For example, the Thai military and police, along with American support and businessmen (both Thai and American) were key figures in the setup of many of Thailand's red light districts. Their connections to businessmen as well as their ability to "control" border regions were essential in setting up districts where they would not just promote sexual slavery but also participate in it. Local police were often "regular customers." This collusion with businessmen and entrepreneurs (both local and foreign) would also be repeated in other countries. Most often, there would not be enough interest in the powers that be to prosecute these men. However, in the mid-1990s Thai feminists formed a women's rights movement calling for it to be illegal to have sex with children. A law making it a crime did not pass until 1997 (Enloe, 2000). Similarly, in the United States, there were policies against sex tourism that were also passed. Along with these institution structures is the ideologies that supported the proliferation of trafficking and modern-day slavery.

FEMALE GENDER

Being a female in the world is a detrimental factor in and of itself. We discussed in chapter 1, while the numbers are lower in sex trafficking, the largest public response has been directed toward this area. In chapter 2, we talked about how women have been packaged as a viable commodity—cheap and easily replaced—whose very bodies can be sold over and over. While the role of male sexual demand has been a direct factor in the business of trafficking, the proliferation of the idea that women are nothing more than objects to be used for sex drives the rationalization of the necessity of a sex "industry." Likewise, how this has shaped ideas around sexuality and control of women's bodies has been key to the continued commodification of women and girls.

These root causes that we have discussed are all tied into one commonality that resides in all nations is the ways in which women are regarded and raised based on traditional gender roles. There is an invisibility at best of women and a blatant abuse at worst. The ways in which trafficking and modern-day slavery have been able to take hold is based on patriarchal, feudal, and other cultural beliefs about the disposability of women. Selective abortions wherein women choose to abort female fetuses is one example of how society favors men over women. To be fair, many of these women have had awful lives and do not want the same for their children. One woman we interviewed said, "There is nothing in my country that a girl can benefit from. I don't want to bring a child into the world so that she can just be used." It is estimated that over 160 million girls are "missing" from the world because of such abortions and infanticides (Hvistendahi, 2011).

Girls and women around the world are more vulnerable to any number of violences throughout their life span. The defining factor of how girls are raised in the context of patriarchy is that girls are taught to be subservient, secondary to men and boys. Gilligan (1982) proposed that girls are raised to be relational. In the Western world (and arguably in the whole of the world), relationships are not as valued as hierarchy and power. Therefore, girls are raised to understand the nuance and context of situations so that they do not engage in direct confrontation or competition especially with men; they are being set up to be unable to engage in areas that would be considered "successful." They learn, in effect, to know when to "stand down." By the time girls are in their pre-teen years, they experience the lowest levels of self-esteem and mastery (Gilligan, 1982). It is not a surprise then, that this is also the age when it is easiest to lure girls into being commercially, sexually exploited.

The social construction of what it means to be a woman or a girl in the world is enforced by strict gender roles. For example, in Mexico, a highly patriarchal country, women and girls are expected to be subservient to males. This has resulted not only in unequal treatment but extremes of gender violence. In one of the most horrendous examples of femicide in the world, the killings of women workers who migrate to the border town of Cuidad Juarez to work in one of the many export processing zone factories, hundreds of women have been found killed, raped, and tortured with the authorities doing very little to look for the perpetrators (Women's Media Center, n.d.). This sends the message that women's lives are not valuable. Following this rationale, perhaps it is not surprising that this is also a country with rampant rape statistics, where a woman in raped every four minutes (roughly 120,000 women annually). Literally women and girls have become vessels to use. The drug cartel and the infamous drug wars in Mexico (between warring cartels and between law enforcement/government officials) have used the abuse and traffic of women and girls in multiple ways. First and foremost, women and girls are trafficked both for labor and sex; they are used as drug mules and then are sexually exploited (Cave, 2011). Further, female bodies are used as symbols for power of the cartels and to send messages to each other—that of destruction (rape, murder, prostitution) and even celebration (rape, murder, prostitution). This does not end when Mexican women leave Mexico. Amnesty International estimates that 6 out of 10 Mexican women who migrate for work into the United States (mainly) are victims of rape. The cheapness of female lives is never more apparent than when it is used in these multiple ways.

In the same vein, girls are not taught to fight back. Instead, they are taught to understand how they might have caused the problem, yet another layer of victim blaming. Girls are taught to be silent, subservient, agreeable, nice, and not question authority. Traffickers find that girls are more compliant than boys (Kara, 2009). When intersected with further oppressions such as race, class, or even specific cultural challenges, the ability to take advantage of girls becomes exponential.

RACE AND ETHNICITY

Race and ethnicity are important social determinants that facilitate trafficking and modern-day slavery because it is predicated in the ability to "other" whole populations, including indigenous and native groups. Especially with sex trafficking but also with labor, the need to create a "other" operates on the emphasis and overexaggeration of differences. The dehumanization of women to mere objects especially coupled by being of another race was the ultimate in "othering." This was the case with African slavery in the United States where rape was used as a way to "subdue" slaves who were treated like chattel. Black men and women were treated and depicted as animals in an effort to keep races from mixing where black men and women weren't sexually fetishized to keep white women away from slaves. Then, we see this same type of rationale both in Eastern Europe and Southeast Asia with the growth of the exploitation of both men and women. The psychological ability to distance oneself to the subject of exploitation and cruelty allows for traffickers to treat humans as their "product."

Globally, the history of colonialism in most poorer countries have set up natural color lines, with "white" being the most sought-after hue. This is because the lighter one's skin, the more benefits they received in society. For example, in Mexico and other Latin American cultures, *meztizas* were characterized by (usually) their white father and their indigenous mother. Their lighter skin helped them "pass" as the ruling class. This was the same with Creoles in the southern United States. All this was very different from Eastern European women who easily translate into the American mainstream because of their white skin. They do not carry the same stigmas that Asian, Latina, or African women do. One reason may be because it is easier then to imagine these types of sexual fetishes with women you cannot relate to. The lack of identity of women of color in the American mainstream continues to be based in stereotypes and racist representations. One only has to look at present racial caricatures to understand the extent that race plays in the labor and sexual exploitation of women of color. This extends across borders and affects women as they migrate and globalization pushes more and more workers across the world. For instance, in Vietnam, the term "gook" was often used to describe the Vietnamese as being "lower" than Americans. The same can be said about all racial epithets (Lawson, 1989). The use of language to construct "other" is one of the easiest methods.

In the United States, women of color experience more violence in their lives and are vulnerable to more violence than white women. This may be due to the fact that women of color tend to have poorer structural challenges, discrimination, and living conditions, which make them more susceptible to violence (Kelly, 2010; Williams, Oliver, & Pope, 2008). This is not surprising, especially if we tie it into the past colonial legacies as well as militarization and conflict. American Indian women are twice as likely to be victimized than any other women (Modi, Palmer, & Armstrong, 2014). In Mark Baker's *Nam* (1981), he says, "Let's face it. Nature is nature. There are women available. Those women are of another culture, another color, another society. You don't want a prostitute. You've got an M–16. What do you need to pay a lady for? You go down to the village and take what you want" (pg. 206). It is not difficult to imagine going from this type of thinking to the belief that all women that are of "another culture, another color, and another society" are there for the raping.

Instances of labor trafficking mainly occur in receiving countries with large populations of migrant labor. This creates an inherent and built-in othering. In some cases, this may be founded on preexisting colonial relationships such as between Africa (sending country) and countries within the European Union (receiving countries), and in others, it is a type of neo-colonization that is being established. Either way, the creation and treatment of the "other" is apparent. For example, Singapore's booming construction industry is run through the use of thousands of the migrant labor force coming from Pakistan, India, and Bangladesh. Most migrants to Singapore are either males in the construction business (over 326,000 of them) or as domestic helpers (232,000) who are vulnerable to abuses, trafficking, and modern-day slavery because of policies such as recruiter fees (regulated in Singapore but not in many of the sending countries) and laws that tie workers to their employers (either literally as in the case of domestic helpers who must live with their employers or construction workers whose visas are connected to specific employers). Despite these restrictive policies, migrant labor constitutes 38% of Singapore's labor force (Piper, n.d.). In 2013, the first race riot in 40 years occurred after an accident happened in the Little India district of Singapore where an Indian migrant was allegedly pushed out of a public bus by a Singaporean citizen. The riot included hundreds of migrant workers and the response of the government were heightened patrolling of migrant areas and deportations, blaming the rioting on ethnic tensions between migrant workers and Singaporean citizens (Nghiem, 2013).

CULTURE

In addition to societal constructs of patriarchy, one has to also examine contexts of culture that are unique to countries and their populations. "Culture" can be construed as broadly as possible to include social mores, shared rituals, common values, and even religious practices. This is especially true in countries where there may be little separation between church and state or when one religion dominates within a country. In India, a primarily Hindu country, the practice of "sacred prostitution" exists and exacerbates the trafficking of girls and young women (Dkhar, 2015). *Devadasi*, a concept that is well practiced and literally means "female slaves of the deity," is a cult that dedicates girls to goddesses and temples (Jena & Pandey, 2012). Girls, particularly of lower caste, are sold to the highest bidder in elaborate ceremonies of "deflowering" in the name of devadasi. From this point on, she is then "promised" to priests or other temple men, living now in sexual slavery (Giri, 1999). Annually, anywhere from 1,000–5,000 young girls are enslaved.

Although culture plays a role when we look at trafficking and modern-day slavery, practitioners often will put an exaggerated emphasis on the impact of culture, almost blaming culture exclusively for situations (Agustin, 2005). This "pathologizing" culture creates environments where the blame is put squarely onto the victim and may inhibit slaves from reaching out for help (Berg, 2013). There is intersection between the issue of culture and that of racism. If practitioners are not careful, they will not only be overlooking or oversimplifying what is happening with those who are trafficked but also expressing these sentiments in the language of racism even if that is not the intention. Abolitionist Kevin Bales (2007), cofounder of Free the Slaves, was even guilty of stating that the problem was not poverty and violence, but the "toxicity of some cultures." Even in nations where there are solid cultural mores that support or even encourage trafficking and modern-day slavery, this does not mean that they cannot be challenged. Indeed, the protections that have been gained by movements to end trafficking and slavery of children have had to assert universal child rights, despite current cultural standards. This is not to say that it is easily done but to emphasize that practitioners and others who work in this field need to be aware of cultural biases so that they don't become broader ethnocultural discriminations (Samuels & Ross-Sheriff, 2008). This means more than cultural competence; it extends into relying on real understanding of contexts and also honoring different perspectives of how to define, view, and intervene in the problem.

CASTE AND CLASS

The role of class brings us full circle with our discussion in this chapter, which started with examining poverty. As we saw earlier, women are more likely to suffer from poverty. What is an important detail here is to examine how poor women are regarded in society and again, their disposability and invisibility. In some cases, such as India, poorer women are literally considered "untouchable." In other areas such as Colombia, poor women, especially from rural areas, are seen as not being sophisticated or knowledgeable, thus, it is easy to expose them to a traffic situation. In addition to the hierarchal nature of class and the deep divides between the rich and the poor are the stereotypes built around the poor. For instance, it is not rare to hear the insinuation that the poor stay poor because they "want to." Even more detrimental are the arguments that poor families sell their children or their women because they are "gold digging" and looking to make a quick profit. The truth is, as we saw earlier, most parents who sell their children are told that by doing so they will be able to get their children education, a job, or something to help them break out of cycles of poverty. The allegation that people perpetuate their poverty does not take into account other structural and contextual issues that may make someone vulnerable to trafficking simply because of their income (or lack thereof).

Caste is most notable in India and other Hindu societies that are divisions of the population which are mutually exclusive, hereditary, occupation specific, and determinate of social class and privileges (Thorat & Neuman, 2012). According to Hindu tradition, there are five different castes (in this order from highest to lowest): Brahmins (priests, teachers); Kshatriyas (warriors, royalty); Vaisyas (moneylenders, traders); Sudras (menial jobs); and the Ati Sudras (the untouchables, lowest menial jobs) (Deshpande, 2000). India is an interesting country example because it encompasses the entire continuum of trafficking in large numbers from organ to sex to labor. However, forced labor (20–65 million people) is the largest area, mostly through bonded labor in industries such as brick kilns, factories, and carpet weaving. Because the nature of the caste system is hereditary, some of these victims are literally "inherited" as bonded laborers. Similarly, those that are sexually exploited are usually a member of the scheduled caste (50%) or other backward classes (30%). Those in the lowest socioeconomic classes and lowest castes are also subject to organ harvesting, supporting the growing "transplant tourism" business.

CALL TO ACTION: ENDING TRAFFICKING BY TARGETING SOCIAL DETERMINANTS

The emphasis on social determinants comes from the health field. It is an approach that asserts the importance of nonbiological or behavioral models that may affect vulnerable risks such as trafficking. The importance of this approach is that it provides specific insights to the context and ecosystems that affect populations and groups. It also allows the acknowledgment of the major influences that some determinants may play over others (depending of course on the group), provides practitioners with a midpoint or average to consider, and emphasizes determinant specific traumas or vulnerabilities (Raphael, 2006). Research in this area also shows clear connections between specific determinants and health and wellness outcomes. For example, Perry & McEwing's (2013) literature review shows that social determinants can also serve as protective factors. Formal education, maternal education, higher castes, birth order, and citizenship have all been found to be determinants that reduce vulnerability to trafficking.

By understanding social determinants, we move further away from pathologizing individuals (i.e., victim blaming) or generalizing circumstances (i.e., all poor parents are willing to sell their children) so that we can understand nuance and significance of certain circumstances. This type of insight can help direct the formation and improvement of interventions. It can also inform policy objectives and advocacy. However, perhaps the greatest benefit is that understanding social determinants broadens the spectrum of possible solutions because it identifies a variety of influences, which may reframe the way we understand the situation or the issue overall. Finally, social epidemiologists have begun to build structural methodologies to show the role of these environmental aspects and their relationships and intersections, which provide insight into all the aspects that may mediate the situation. This, in turn, will give providers more sensitivity to these important determinants but also, depending on the case, what areas should be considered most important and/or focused on. For instance, should the purpose of your work be focused on horizontal structures (gender, race, ethnicity), which are more individualized and clinical, or on vertical structures (political, economic, and social forces), which are aimed at macro forces such as community capacity building, economic reforms, and employment training. By expanding our knowledge base to include the necessity of social determinants, practitioners level the playing field to help explain the gap between what we know and what is actually being practiced in the field. By including everyone involved in the situation, there is the further advantage of expanding the impact of other areas such as clarifying power (in providers' services as well as within the trafficking situation) and influencing existing ideologies (Labonte, Polanyi, Muhajarine, Mcintosh, &Williams, 2005). The traditional ways of thinking that we currently default to is not creating enough of a dent to end or even destabilize trafficking and modern-day slavery, so, by adding the framework and perspective of social determinants, we can expand our perspectives and hopefully amplify the reach of effective solutions.

DISCUSSION QUESTIONS

1. What are the largest impacts of poverty in a country of your interest or your country of residence? How does this increase vulnerability to trafficking and modern-day slavery? (Remember to be specific to the country you are focusing on.)

2. Identify one innovative antipoverty program or service in your field. How does it help in the fight against trafficking and modern-day slavery, if at all? If it doesn't, why not?

3. What is the utility of militarized masculinity and femininity in warfare or conflict? Give at least three examples to illustrate your points.

4. From the perspective of your field or profession, what are three detrimental aspects of police corruption? Provide examples.

5. What is the effect of race, class, and gender on the social determinants discussed in this chapter?

CHALLENGE

Identify a campaign or project that originates from the local, regional, and/or global women's movement which addresses trafficking and modern-day slavery and describe it. How would this campaign fit into your field? What would your field contribute to the effort? Take the challenge to the next level and contact the organization, campaign, or project to spend a day or attend one of their events. How did their actual work meet (or not meet) your expectations?

Clinical Interventions

Trafficking and modern-day slavery is not an emerging field, in fact, as we have discussed in the last section, there has never been a complete abolition of slavery. New and emerging clinical interventions are being developed to provide help and healing to those who have been trafficked. Many of these interventions have been developed in the last ten years and are just now being evaluated. Some of them are applied from interventions that have been developed for other situations such as anxiety and depression. It would be a fair assessment to say that there is not a lot we have in terms of clinical tools, much less having full evidence based interventions that could be applied universally. This is a period of building and testing.

What is becoming more available to us are guiding strategies and evolving best practices that have shown promise and potential in the field. These strategies include those interventions that are based on an empowerment model—driven by stages of change—and take into account the unique aspects of each part of the cycle of trafficking (recruitment, exploitation, rescue, recovery, and reintegration). For the purposes of this section, we concentrate mainly on the areas of recovery and reintegration, which is where most of the interventions are directed toward. When there is paucity of literature or even a gap, we support that literature with informed practice evidence.

These models have one thing in common and that is they all stem from or are grounded in empowerment theory. Empowerment theory does not espouse one particular type of treatment or therapy per say but rather it guides treatments so that they are strengths based and action oriented. Unlike theories prior to its development, empowerment theory is not wholly concerned with psychological or sociological dysfunctions that underlie how therapy would be conducted. Since this is the case, the basic concepts of empowerment theory should be understood as a foundation for the interventions rooted in it. These concepts include critical consciousness, social justice, and a strengths-based perspective. The intervention models are also all based in a trauma informed perspective (discussed further in chapter 4), even the more psychodynamic or cognitive behavioral theories. Both trauma-informed care and empowerment theory call for practitioners not only to partner with their clients but also to take action as an advocate.

Most of the practices that are included in this next section are driven by some type of theory of change. Before we discuss different theories, we will discuss overall stages of change so you can see how a general understanding of change is necessary to these interventions. Stages of change is a transtheoretical model that hypothesizes change goes through five stages:

- Precontemplation—no intention to change because either an individual is unaware they have a problem or they are underaware. However, others around them know that there is a problem.

- Contemplation—an individual knows a problem exists and may be thinking about changing, but they have no commitment to action.

- Preparation—individuals intend to take action and are making "baby steps" to do so, but they have yet to take action.

- Action—individuals begin to modify their behavior to overcome their problems. The most obvious behavioral changes occur during this stage.

- Maintenance—individuals in this stage work to prevent relapses.

There is no set time that an individual stays in each of the stages, and each stage focuses on different processes, including relational stances. The stages represent when people are ready to change and what type of changes they would open to making (Norcross, Krebs, & Prochaska, 2011). Stages of change is important to understand regardless of what theory of change is being utilized for the intervention because most theories of change are sensitive to the process of change as outlined here. Being able to determine where someone who is trafficked falls in the stages can help practitioners decide on what course of action or portion of a curriculum or intervention may be most relevant and timely.

The cycle of trafficking begins with the recruitment into the trafficking situation, either knowingly, getting tricked, or being coerced. Again, for our purposes, we are not splitting differences in the degree of "coercion" because we assume that there is some level of coercion or force inherent in all forms of trafficking (even if it is through trickery or "relationship"). Because of this wide definition, the first difficulty that practitioners encounter is the difficulty in identifying trafficking victims. Moreover, the ways in which identification of those who are trafficked and for what reason will differ based not only on trauma specific experiences but also on demographics of gender, age, income, and other factors. For instance, Grace, Starck, Potenza, Kenney, and Sheetz (2012), describe that the best way to determine whether an adolescent may be being trafficked is to ask them directly. This might work as a rule, but it would definitely be different if you were working in another country where direct communication is unheard of or even taboo.

This is a common challenge in all types of trafficking but it is also detrimental to most interventions since the recognition of an individual as a "victim" or as someone exploited by trafficking is important to determine before services are offered. Research shows that this issue of identification is a large and difficult task due to two things: (1) the complexity of the issues, which includes, safety, language barriers, and fear (Macy & Graham, 2012), and (2) often, the victims themselves will not label their experiences as trafficking even when where is irrefutable evidence to the latter. Most of the time, the process and need to build rapport and trust must begin even before the individual has been fully identified. There are several inventories that exist as well as trainings that provide information on how to identify risk factors such as the Polaris Project's indicators (2015b). The social stigma involved especially with sex trafficking and the invisibility of labor trafficking make it hard to identify victims. Education and public awareness continue to be the best ways to begin to identify victims as does the sharing of information between systems. For example, the Blue Campaign is a collaboration led by the U.S. Department of Homeland Security (DHS) that includes law enforcement, government, nongovernmental organizations, and private organizations to create what they call "victim-centered investigations" to maximize identification and recovery efforts (U.S. Department of Homeland Security, n.d.).

Section 2 of this text examines strategies that are demonstrating the most favorable outcomes in regard to recovery and reintegration for individuals who have been trafficked. In keeping with the conceptual foundations of this text, we make sure to provide a lens that looks at shifting perceptions and behaviors as methods for creating transformational change. We begin in chapter 4 with setting the overall tone with the most important strategy to consider: a trauma-informed care framework. This framework is the basis for all the other strategies and interventions that we have included. Almost all individuals who are trafficked experience some level of trauma and can benefit from a perspective that directly considers complex trauma and the effects of PTSD and other trauma-related symptoms.

In chapter 5, we analyze the pivotal role of case managers in the provision of intensive case management. Every individual who has been trafficked and is going through recovery and reintegration is in need of coordination services. This is a global phenomenon, and in some countries, it is the only "service" that is offered. While intensive case management is sometimes considered a logistical necessity, we argue that it is a central tool and/or partnership for intervention strategies and that the role of the case manager is much more than a logistical administrator but someone who ends up becoming a confident, advocate, and stakeholder for the client.

We recognize that trauma-informed care is about shifts in self-worth and self-esteem but that it is also about changes that are behavioral. Chapter 6 describes the most studied intervention in this area (as well as being efficacious in other areas)—trauma focused cognitive behavioral therapy (TFCBT). This evidence-based intervention follows a number of principles and steps that we go through in-depth, providing examples of how it might manifest with trafficked individuals. Practical assessment tools, worksheets, and suggested methods are in this chapter to help practitioners utilize this best practice.

Chapter 7 highlights the survivor advocate model, which is firmly rooted in empowerment theory. Survivor advocate models go beyond paradigms of peer supports and group work. Although all these paradigms incorporate sharing with those who would understand their experiences as well as to be able to provide empathy and non-judgmental support, survivor models are specifically designed for victims to move into roles where they are spokespeople and advocates to end trafficking. Models such as this may begin as ways to incorporate survivors into organizational programming but have evolved into survivors taking leadership and creating direction of movement (Clawson, Grace, & Salomon, 2008).

Chapter 8 focuses on a special population of trafficked individuals: children. The phenomenon of commercial sexual exploitation of children (CSEC) has been referred to as a "public health epidemic" and is the strongest example of domestic slavery in the United States. In the past few years, funds have dramatically shifted from the international scope to the domestic, with the mandate of child welfare, juvenile justice, probation, and educational systems to provide services and solutions. Hundreds of protocols have been developed but there has been little evaluation research to let us know what is *really* working. Despite this, we have reviewed four interventions that are used across the board in different settings and in regions in the country. They include the following: My Life, My Choice; Ending the Game; Empowering Young Men; and shelter/transitional housing services.

This section also includes the complex case of Cynthia. As you will note, each chapter has a version of Cynthia's case. The slight differences in her outcome emphasize the sensitive nature of human trafficking and modern-day slavery to events that occur within a person's ecosystem. Any slight disequilibrium may shift one's trajectory. In a perfect world, Cynthia's case may look like this (see following case), but as you will experience in these chapters, the vulnerabilities that many who are trafficked or enslaved face will result in traumatic circumstances. This section provides us with beginning tools to address such circumstances and a place on which to build.

THE CASE OF CYNTHIA O.

Cynthia O. grew up in Tacloban, Leyte, a provincial city in the Philippines. Tacloban is somewhat industrial, housing the factories for Coca Cola and many garment factories as part of its Philippine Economic Zone. However, much of it remains rooted in agricultural production. Since it is outside of the National Capital Region of the country, it is considered a "province" and therefore does not have all the resources available that one would find in an urban center. While it is rapidly developing, it is an economically stable region that is precarious because of its geographic location in the middle of what geologists and meteorologists call the "Typhoon Corridor." Being on this pathway means that it is just a matter of time until they will experience severe natural disaster. The region has some notable colleges and vocational opportunities for education. It has a population of about 240,000 persons.

Cynthia is the oldest of five siblings. Although she is only 10 months older than her brother, she has always had a bulk of the responsibilities to help with the family, but it has always been like this so she doesn't mind or complain. Cynthia is 16 years old and in her last year of mandatory education (public high school). Her siblings are 15 (male), 13 (male), 10 (male), and 5 (female). Her parents own a small bakery and they make a modest income, although her mother often must take in laundry to make ends meet. Since there is a lot of work in the bakery, Cynthia often must wake up at 3 or 4 in the morning to help with the baking. Sometimes she is asked to help with the laundry, but rarely. Many times, she must also help watch the other children. This makes Cynthia late for school or sometimes she misses school completely. Her parents try to make sure she doesn't because they want her to finish school, but it cannot always be helped.

Cynthia is of average height and is very slim. She is attractive and often mistaken for younger than her age. She is very outgoing and has a positive attitude. Their neighbors always comment on how lucky her parents are for having such a good *manang* (oldest sister). Cynthia has no history of health problems and has reached all her developmental milestones. Because of her family responsibilities, she is not able to participate in many after-school activities but whenever she can, she likes to play volleyball. For the same reason, she also does not hang out with classmates or have very many friends. Cynthia has never had a boyfriend nor does she have any close male friends. Teachers and peers describe Cynthia as being well liked, helpful, and friendly.

Despite the fact that Cynthia has a lot of responsibilities at home, she continues to persevere in school and is able to graduate with a high school diploma. With the help of a well-meaning teacher, she is able to apply to a local college and also get a scholarship. She majors in physical education and she has dreams of becoming a teacher so that she could help youth like her teacher helped her. Her parents are very proud of her. She continues to help them at home in the bakery and with her siblings.

Cynthia finishes college with an undergraduate degree in education and specialization in kinesiology. She has just finished taking her licensure exam and finds a job as a physical education teacher for a private primary school. Although the pay is not that large, it is enough to help supplement her family's income and help pay for her brother's college tuition. To earn more, Cynthia also helps tutor children when she can. She is well liked by her students and their families. They often invite her to their homes for dinner. Cynthia has gone out on a few dates and has had people interested in her but she does not pursue a relationship. She is focused on her work.

On November 8, 2013, Super Typhoon Yolanda (also known as Typhoon Haiyan), the strongest storm to ever hit land, strikes the Philippines. The first place it hits is Eastern Samar, and then Leyte, where Cynthia and her family live. The family is home when the typhoon begins and they evacuated to a local public school. They think they are safe, but the school quickly floods and the family is forced with everyone else to climb up to the roof of the building. Cynthia helps keep her younger sister safe when the water starts rising and she describes her panic as the water is rising. They stand on the roof for four hours while the storm and the winds rage around them. The family isn't able to return home until a week later because of all the debris. The roads are closed, phone lines are down, and there is no electricity. Aid can barely reach the for almost two weeks. They are grateful that they do not lose any family members, especially since so many of their neighbors are not as lucky. They have nothing left of their home or any of their things.

Current Situation: As a teacher, Cynthia helps with the international UNICEF volunteers who set up temporary day-care facilities at the Astrodome—the largest area where hundreds of people are sheltered. She also is helping her family set up their bakery again and has the idea to help provide bread to the many volunteers who are arriving into the city to help. Cynthia volunteers with UNICEF three days a week where she works with the children. While there, she meets a volunteer from Manila. He is an engineer who is helping with getting the electrical grid back up. They spend a lot of time together and eventually start dating. Cynthia and he are very happy.

GLOSSARY OF TERMS

ABC—Antecedent behavior consequence is a behavioral analysis measuring tool commonly found in the CBT therapy model. ABC measures the events that happen before a behavior and the consequences that follow in an effort to identify behavioral patterns.

Best Practice—commercial or professional procedures that are accepted or prescribed as being correct or most effective.

Biopsychosocial Assessment—systematically considers biological, psychological, and social factors and their complex interactions in understanding health, illness, and health-care delivery.

Case Management—collaborative process of assessment, planning, facilitation, care coordination, evaluation, and advocacy for options and services to meet an individual's and family's comprehensive health needs through communication and available resources to promote quality, cost-effective outcomes.

CBT—Cognitive behavioral therapy is a psychosocial intervention that is the most widely used evidence-based practice for treating various mental disorders.

Collective Impact—framework to tackle deeply entrenched and complex social problems. It is an innovative and structured approach to making collaboration work across government, business, philanthropy, nonprofit organizations, and citizens to achieve significant and lasting social change.

Compassion Fatigue—The emotional residue or strain of exposure to working with those suffering from the consequences of traumatic events. Often referred to as secondary trauma.

CSEC—Commercial sexual exploitation of children is defined as criminal practices that demean, degrade, and threaten the physical and psychosocial integrity of children. There are three primary forms of commercial sexual exploitation of children: prostitution, pornography, and trafficking for sexual purposes.

Cultural Competency—awareness, understanding, and reacting to a variety of cultural variances. It is important in a client/patient relationship.

Cultural Humility—encourages an individual to recognize their biases when working with those from other cultures and backgrounds. It acknowledges that balance of power between individuals to more effectively interact and engage with other cultures and communities.

Cultural Sensitivity—awareness that cultural differences and similarities between people exist without assigning them a value—positive or negative, better or worse, right or wrong.

DST—Domestic sex trafficking (sometimes referred to as CSEC—commercial sexual exploitation of children)

EMDR—Eye movement desensitization and reprocessing is an evidence-based therapy commonly utilized for PTSD. The therapy utilizes various sensory inputs, such as side-to-side eye movements or rapidly flashing lights.

Empowerment Model—theory of human behavior based on the ideology that people have inherent strengths and should build on those strengths. The empowerment model is concerned with awareness raising, building individual and community capacity, and the ability to increase self-efficacy and mastery to create change.

Evidence-Based Practices—integration of the best available research with clinical expertise in the context of patient characteristics, culture, and preferences.

Maslow's Hierarchy of Needs—This five-stage model can be divided into basic and psychological needs, which ensure survival (e.g., physiological, safety, love, and esteem) and growth needs (self-actualization). This model has been utilized by traffickers to best manipulate their victims.

Mindfulness—maintaining a moment-by-moment awareness of our thoughts, feelings, bodily sensations, and surrounding environment.

PTSD—Post-traumatic stress disorder is a disorder that develops in some people who have experienced a shocking, scary, or dangerous event. The disorder can manifest via disrupting thoughts, vivid dreams, feelings, or physical reactions. These symptoms will last for more than a month after the traumatic event.

SAMHSA—Substance Abuse and Mental Health Services Administration is a branch of the U.S. Department of Health and Human Services.

Self-Care—activities that an individual engages in to relax or attain emotional well-being, such as exercise, meditating, or other enjoyable activities. This is especially important within the context of trauma or secondary trauma.

Strengths Based/Strengths Perspective—social work practice theory that emphasizes people's self-determination and strengths. It is a philosophy and a way of viewing clients as resourceful and resilient in the face of adversity.

Survivor—a person who continues to function or prosper, in spite of opposition, danger, trauma, hardship, or setbacks.

TF–CBT— Trauma Focused-Cognitive Behavioral Therapy is evidence-based treatment for children and adolescents impacted by trauma and their parents or caregivers. Research shows that TF–CBT successfully resolves a broad array of emotional and behavioral difficulties associated with single, multiple, and complex trauma experiences.

Victim—a person harmed, injured, or killed as a result of a crime, accident, or other event or action.

Trauma-Informed Care

Annalisa Enrile and Wilhelmina De Castro

Chapter Objectives

1. Readers will develop an awareness of trauma-informed care.

2. Readers will be able to contrast trauma, complex trauma, and specific trauma.

3. Readers will implement basic principles of trauma-informed care.

4. Readers will integrate the trauma-informed model as an overall lens to understand treatment of individuals who have been trafficked and/or enslaved.

5. Readers will adapt trauma informed care in both traditional and nontraditional settings.

The survivors we work with hold complex traumas. We have to take time to acknowledge the depth and breadth of their experiences because they will inform how we ask questions, what working environments look like, what we suggest, and how we ultimately carry out our service. In my experience working with survivors of violence, abuse, and/or trafficking I have found it particularly important to validate their experiences and create opportunity for them to make their own choice and hold control. In so many circumstances agency has been taken away and they have been disempowered, and as a service provider I find it to be such a valuable experience to help survivors reclaim their lives.

A huge shift that helped me become more trauma informed was to first take an inventory of myself, my views, and my preconceived notions. I constantly work on unlearning bias and being open to creative approaches to ensure that clients are not retraumatized or triggered by my approaches. Before becoming a social worker, I always heard these questions or comments:

- *Why doesn't she just leave?*

- *Why doesn't she stick up for herself?*

(Continued)

(Continued)

- *That's her choice if she wants to sell her body.*

- *She could just say no.*

If I were completely honest with myself, I had similar thoughts when I was younger, but quickly learned the questions and comments are complicated and loaded with lots of assumptions. There is nothing better to test your assumptions than when they are sitting there staring at you in the form of a family of four. Theresa and her three kids, Audrey (14 years old), Mary (13 years old), and Darren (1 year old), were screened into the domestic violence shelter I managed. Based on how she looked and her lack of interaction with her kids, I had assumed that Theresa was one of those mothers who was so concerned about herself that she could not care for her children. I braced myself to struggle with her. I couldn't have had it more wrong.

Right away Theresa told me that she wanted desperately to connect with her children but that she didn't know how. They were a handful—truant, rebellious, doing things like smoking in the shelter. She was tearful when she told us her own story—runaway at age 13, her own mother addicted to meth, and chronically homeless. Theresa said she felt helpless because she knew that her decisions had been bad and she had lost her kids for a while when they were placed in foster care. Both her daughters had been identified as CSEC victims and Audrey had been mandated to a residential facility, which she went AWOL from to return to her pimp. She was picked up by authorities again during a felony auto theft her pimp made her participate in. Theresa felt that there was no way to reach the girls and feared that if she couldn't they would be sexually exploited again. She knew how hard life on the streets was.

As I worked with them and learned their story of intergenerational trauma, I saw how resilient the family was. It would have been easy to just blame Theresa for not caring for her children, but the truth was she loved them and was trying to learn how to be a good mother. Theresa and her daughters taught me such a powerful lesson. They taught me to zoom in on personal experiences and zoom out to consider underlying and overarching themes within the family. It could have been so easy to blame, stigmatize, or place judgment them. I had to remember that survivors were trying to protect their family from being hurt because their perpetrators threatened to hurt them. I had to acknowledge how poverty acts as a strong push factor and a reason traffickers prey on people. I had to consider past traumas can lead to use substances as coping mechanisms. I had to learn there may be a long string of generational events that act as precipitating events to exploitation and the ever-present vulnerability girls face at being objectified and hypersexualized.

To refrain from making assumptions and unlearn bias, I now create time to actively reframe my mindset and truly take time to understand what influences the client. It's common for lots of people to want to care and help people, but truly caring for people means you must keep their life experiences, trauma(s), and context in mind. I have found trauma-informed care to be a crux of our practice. The clients, families, and communities we work with have history and accounts that get overlooked and ignored, but knowing them, truly knowing them, is a catalyst to healing. In fact, I believe this is the first step in helping someone—understanding and being open to their experience without a biased or tainted stance to inform what their healing or recovery process may look like.

—Melanie Ferrer-Vaughn

INTRODUCTION

Human trafficking and modern-day slavery is predicated on varying levels of formal and informal coercion resulting in situations against one's will where threat is always assumed. The nature of trafficking and modern-day slavery naturally increases a person's susceptibility to experiencing trauma, and in most cases, complex trauma. Because of this, the understanding of trauma is central to providing services for people who have been trafficked. The California Child Welfare Council (2015) provided a list of six promising strategies and services for trafficking victims, including the "trauma informed programming." In actuality, all six of these strategies can fall under the general heading of "trauma-informed care." These include safety planning, collaboration, trust and relationship building, cultural competence, and survivor involvement in treatment (California Child Welfare Council, 2013). Under the framework of trauma-informed care, we can begin to provide services that are responsive and sensitive to the needs of those who have been trafficked.

Trauma is harmful and impacts all populations regardless of gender, age, socioeconomic status, ethnicity, or location (Perry, Pollard, Blakley, Baker, & Vigilante, 1995). Having a history of trauma is considered a significant determinant that increases the risk for trafficking (Mezzacappa, Kindlon, & Earls, 2001). The frequency of abuse has been found to be directly correlated to increased vulnerability to experiencing more trauma (Deshpande & Nour, 2013). West Coast Children's Clinic, a leading children's clinic, assessed that approximately 75% of foster youth have been abused or neglected prior to being trafficked. Moreover, most of women who have been trafficked, particularly those for sex, report having similar common traumatic events or risk factors before being trafficked such as physical or sexual abuse. Sadly, for many, their first sexual encounter is usually rape; and it is usually rape by a family member or friend of the family (Hom & Woods, 2013). In other forms of trafficking, the Department of Health and Human Services reports that victims of labor trafficking often experience a trauma bonding, which is when the victim develops attachment and bonds with their captor. This is considered a human survival instinct in which the victim develops cognitive distortions of reciprocity to cope with their captivity (Trauma-Informed Care, n.d.). Furthermore, in the case of child soldiers who are forcefully recruited to commit violent acts against others are assessed to have a higher likelihood of experiencing PTSD symptoms.

This chapter will examine how trauma informed care is a necessary approach for those who have been trafficked and even those who are vulnerable to being trafficked and experiencing traumatic stress reactions. We will define trauma and complex trauma, understand the impact of trauma on neurobiological development as well as relationships and connectedness, and walk through the principles of what trauma-informed practice might look like. When used correctly and appropriately, trauma-informed care is an approach that has the opportunity for providing the most holistic form of treatment for those who have been trafficked.

DEFINING TRAUMA

Trauma is defined as a direct personal experience of an event that involves actual or threatened death or serious injury, or other threat to ones' physical integrity. Similarly, if one witnesses or even hears about violent death, serious harm, or the threat of death or injury experienced by someone close to them, they may also be vulnerable to traumatization (Cohen, Mannarino, & Deblinger, 2006). The response to trauma is expressed through intense fear, helplessness, or horror. Context exposure to these types of harmful experiences can lead to chronic and complex traumatization, which we will discuss in the next section.

Trauma has been shown to not only affect psychological and mental health situations but also shape physical health outcomes and brain development. The Adverse Childhood Experiences Study (ACES) is ongoing collaborative research between the Centers for Disease Control and Prevention in Atlanta, Georgia, and Kaiser Permanente in San Diego, California (Felitti & Anda, 1997). With over 17,000 participants in routine health screenings, the data from this study reveals some of the key findings in how trauma affects physical health. For instance, ACES has found that childhood abuse and neglect increases a person's risk for serious health problems and higher mortality rates. Moreover, in the cohort of youth studied, their reports of significant psychological stress (which may include trauma) created potential pathways to depression and post-traumatic stress disorder, which could then lead to substance abuse, sleep disorders, and anxiety, which could then lead to further vulnerability for future exploitation and abuse. The experience of trauma and its lasting effects are also mitigated by genetics, personality characteristics, capacity to cope, emotional and physical resources, and familial and community support.

COMPLEX TRAUMA

Complex trauma exposure refers to the "simultaneous or sequential occurrences of maltreatment" (National Child Traumatic Stress Network, 2003). This could include a number of different experiences as mentioned above (emotional abuse, neglect, sexual assault, physical threat, etc.) but they are chronic (happening over and over) and usually begin in childhood or early adulthood. Complex trauma has several distinctions from simple trauma. It is more persistent, diffuse, and complex than PTSD. It is also characterized by personality shifts most apparent in distortions of attachment and identity. As we have mentioned, complex trauma heightens vulnerability to revictimization either through self-harm or through further abuse from others (Muraya & Fry, 2015). In one of the only cohort studies of trafficked women, Abas et al. (2013) found that 40% of the women who were trafficked in their study developed PTSD six months or later after being rescued. The development of PTSD was found to be directly correlated to the trauma itself, mainly if the trauma was chronic based on type and severity of violence, exploitation, and restriction of freedom. Also, it was found that multiple traumas made it more difficult to process because of the multilayered nature of the trauma but also because of its longer duration. It was also found that sexual trauma or any traumas that centered around interpersonal violence were the most detrimental (Courtois, 2004). When considering Cynthia's complex case, it is important to understand the potential to experience chronic trauma in the form of extreme poverty in the context of a natural disaster. The constant deprivation of resources in her environment increases her vulnerability to experiencing additional forms adversity, thus increasing her susceptibility to experiencing trauma. At the time of assessment, it would be essential to explore these dimensions of complex trauma to obtain a thorough understanding of her presenting situation.

NEUROBIOLOGY AND TRAUMA

Psychological trauma is considered neurophysiological and can often stem from an injury to someone's neurobiology. A holistic understanding of the relationship between the psyche, the brain, and the body is essential in providing trauma treatment. The impact of trauma on the developing brain has a significant determinant of the brain's structure and function. With the astoundingly complex nature of the brain, it has the capacity to store a remarkable amount of experiences from early childhood and onward through development. Optimal development is accomplished when individual's experiences are consistent, predictable, stimulating, and nurturing. All children will face new and challenging experiences and most will entail predictable stress and moderate activation of the stress response. Development is disrupted when a child experiences cognitively or relationally impoverished environments, unpredictable stress, and persistent fear and threats (Perry, 2007).

Basham (2011) writes that children who experience trauma at a young age have more negative consequences because of the fact that their brains are still developing. Early trauma and complex trauma impacts the right hemisphere of the brain, and infants who experience trauma are shown to have developmental differences with their right hemispheres (Basham, 2011). This impacts emotional and affect regulation, attachment, and self-soothing techniques that are used when in stress. It could be implied that the prolonged and chronic trauma children experience has a longer lasting impact on their neural circuitry. Also, there are more delays in development because it was a persistent and recurring trauma. When a child experiences repetitive activation of the stress response, their baseline state of arousal functioning is distorted. This results in a heightened fight physiological response that can cause significant impairment to daily functioning. Untreated, this state of physiological and psychological arousal can increase synaptic activation in areas of the brain that deal with survival while pruning areas of the brain that are in charge of developmentally appropriate tasks such as bonding, judgment, learning, and memory (www.childtrauma.org; Muraya & Fry, 2015).

IMPACT OF TRAUMA-INFORMED CARE

Trauma-informed care is a powerful and growing movement in health and human services that exhibits potential to help people recover from adverse life experiences. Trauma-informed care is basically an approach to services where the delivery of services is driven by an understanding of the impact of interpersonal violence and victimization on an individual's life and development. However, to provide trauma-informed care, it is not only practitioners who must be trained but also the entire staff or anyone that victims may come into contact with. This ensures a clear message as well a continuum of care that is consistent. The use of trauma-informed care has integrated a more visible level of empowerment that can often be lost in other forms of practice. An example of this is when a practitioner is asking questions during an initial assessment, they are framed in a safe, open-ended way that the victim can speak as specifically or as generally as they wish and are also encouraged to shape their own care. From the very beginning of treatment, the victim has the choice of how their systems of care support them. It is through approaches such as this that it is clear the victim has the power to influence their environment and the way they receive support. At the very minimum, those in the organization must understand how violence impacts the lives of the people you are serving so that every interaction is consistent with the recovery process and reduces the possibility of retraumatization. We do not suggest that a trauma-informed care approach will solve all challenges with this population, so it is essential that the approach is utilized within a larger, systemic and contextual framework. SAMHSA's key assumptions in trauma informed care are that services

- realize the widespread impact of trauma.
- recognize the symptoms of trauma.
- respond by fully integrating knowledge about trauma into policies, procedures, and practices, and thats service actively resist retraumatization.
- provide basic knowledge about how trauma can affect multiple systems such as individuals, families, groups, and communities.

Screening tools and assessments should be based on this approach and will help in creating processes that contain the recognition of trauma from all points of engagement. Coupled with proper training, all parts of the system can now respond in a trauma-informed manner whether providing direct or indirect services.

TRAUMA-INFORMED CARE AND TRAFFICKING

Trauma-informed practice is the implementation of the framework and has shown to be effective with persons who have been trafficked because it recognizes the impact of violence and victimization on an individual's development and their capacity to develop coping strategies. Multiple systems of care are involved when one leaves a trafficking situation, including child welfare, juvenile justice, social services, law enforcement, and criminal and/or civil court (Harris & Fallot, 2001). Many victims of trafficking have experienced developmental trauma that has led to further trauma through trafficking, while others have had traumatic experiences due to episodes of trafficking. The many variations of a trafficked person's experience can result in a highly complex trauma response, which involves an intersection of professional and social systems that could promote or impede the healing process. Much of the symptoms of those who are trafficked—health, psychological, social—are directly related to the trauma of their experiences and must be treated as such (Clawson et al., 2008). The use of trauma-informed care helps guide the navigation through these systems in a way that decreases vulnerability to retraumatization and promotes overall recovery.

PRINCIPLES TO GUIDE PRACTICE

Over the past decade there has been a steady movement toward implementing evidence-based trauma practices. The variety of evidence-based practices have been proven as effective

Figure 4.1   Trauma-Informed Primary Care

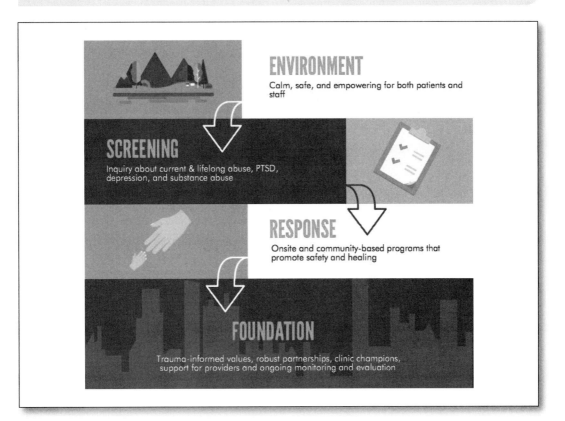

Source: Honey Imbo.

ways of mitigating the effects of trauma across the life span (www.nctsn.org). Because of the complexity of trauma involved in human trafficking, the need for collaboration across settings has increased, thus making it critically necessary to implement trauma-informed practice. Placing a trauma-informed lens on the current practices will enhance the effectiveness of the interventions and will ensure that the following trauma-informed principles are integrated into all aspects of "service." Evidence-informed and evidence-based practices have been geared toward providing for victims of trauma, but which intervention is selected for use should be decided by the practitioner on a case-by-case basis. The following is a set of trauma-informed principles to help a practitioner decide what is the proper direction/care for persons who have been trafficked.

Safety and Acceptance

Providing services to those who have been trafficked must provide a safe and welcoming environment where there is a culture of acceptance and respect. The physical environment of the organization must be one that promotes safety and privacy. It must also be one that protects against exposure to violent and sexual material that might be emotionally triggering. For instance, the waiting room of an organization should not be playing television shows or music that may have provocative or triggering content. For example, in the lobby of an organization should not be playing shows or music that promote pimp culture and violence against women. Furthermore, organizational policies should be stringent because it relates to confidentiality. These policies should be clear, well-defined, and predictable to those who are receiving treatment/services/care. Clear roles and boundaries help provide a feeling of safety both emotionally and physically. For instance, once someone begins treatment, they would be informed of all the policies and then introduced to *all* individuals that may be directly or indirectly involved. Roles, in addition to their names, would be provided for everyone ranging from that of the front desk administration to case managers and therapists. Descriptions and expectations would be discussed and clarified. These actions serve to decrease any chance of confusion and would minimize any worry about having unfamiliar people around. Both are important at providing a sense of ease, acceptance, and safety.

Adaptation Over Disease

In providing trauma-informed care, it is important to highlight adaptation and coping over disease and pathology. Frequently, organizations operate with a diseased-based medical model, often labeling someone who has been trafficked with a diagnosis to qualify for services. This model indicates that the person is damaged and deficient. Conversely, trauma-informed care recognizes that symptoms of trauma are rooted social determinants and experiences. Moreover, trauma-informed care also recognizes an individual's capacity to adapt to a traumatic event. This makes it important to recognize and develop an individual's coping skills and level of adaptation rather than to treat them as diseased individuals. In fact, trauma-informed care denies the claim that individuals may have some type of mental or personality disorders, which either make them susceptible or drive their experiences in trafficking. In a trauma-informed lens, the development of adaptive coping skills can mitigate the symptoms of trauma. For example, agencies/organizations are encouraged to use "strengths inventories" as part of the assessment process. While it may be difficult for people to identify strengths, the inventory starts the discussion and possibility of strengths-based language in the relationship (SAMHSA, 2014).

Collaboration and Peer Support

People who have been exploited by a trafficker has experienced isolation and many times betrayal. Often persons who are trafficked do not know who to trust or have been put in situations where they are alone and have no one but their exploiter, rapist, or trafficker in their lives. When they are coming out of trafficking, it is important to provide a range of supports during this recovery process, including provision of basic needs, such as shelter and food, to social emotional needs that can take place in crisis management and support groups. Peer support and self-help supports are essential for creating a space where there is hope and rebuilding trust. This also allows them to identify with others who have been trafficked and/or may have shared experiences, which can normalize what they are feeling as well as remove feelings of isolation and loneliness. When engaging in mutual aid there is an increased capacity to vicariously experience self-efficacy and mastery through like-minded people who have experienced similar adversities. Mutual aid paired with shared experiences is one of the strongest means of developing self-efficacy, which is a key component to the healing process.

In providing services to those who have experienced trauma, power dynamics between practitioners and their clients can often be imbalanced. The natural tendency for power to fall into the hands of practitioners is unhelpful in the healing process because it maintains a lack of power and control. The psychological foundations of practice have historically put the power of the treatment in the practitioners' hands and takes form as "the powerful healer healing the wounded." This framework is inherently antithetical to a true empowerment practice. To reduce the tendency to do this, the creation of collaboration and mutuality is essential. This can be done by partnering with all levels of organizational staff and even other organizations in service of the trafficked person, which would help level power differentials, while modeling and supporting healthy communication and relationships. In trauma-focused care, everyone has the responsibility and accountability to provide services that are not just sound but also supportive. In many countries, collaboration is not only promoted but also absolutely necessitated to obtain desired outcomes especially if cultures are more collaborative or if agency/organizational resources are limited. Because of the complex nature of trafficking, it is rare that one organization has the capacity to meet all the needs of persons who have been trafficked. This makes collaborative partnerships between systems an essential component for success.

Saving Innocence, an organization that works with child victims of sex trafficking in Los Angeles, is a strong example of peer support and collaboration. Savings Innocence's mission is "To rescue and restore child victims of sex trafficking through strategic partnerships with local law enforcement, social service providers, and schools, while mobilizing communities to prevent abuse and increase neighborhood safety" (http://www.savinginnocence .org/about/). Through their programming at Saving Innocence, they work to meet the girls at every step of their recovery process. The organization provides intensive case management and advocacy for the survivors to create a new support system for the victims. Saving Innocence also works to collaborate with various organizations, including probation, the Los Angeles Police Department, and children services to empower the victims to become as successful as possible. Saving Innocence also utilizes advocates for their victims to help them navigate their transition. These advocates act as anchors for the victims who are traversing a difficult and sometimes isolating recovery. The organization also works on mentoring the victims to help them understand they are not the only ones going through this and that they can learn from those who also share similar experiences. This organization works to combine both peer support and collaboration to ensure the success of all the victims they work with. This example of peer support is a powerful vehicle in creating reparative relationships and healthy bonds that are fundamental in recovering from trafficking trauma.

Empowerment Model Supporting Choice: Victim Versus Survivor

An organization that provides services for trauma must also make a concerted effort to build on the strength of each person. This means that the organization's culture must be embedded in a strengths-based framework and promote the growth of not just those they service, but also that of the staff and practitioners. A strengths-based framework focuses on the inherent strengths, talents, and assets of an individual and capitalizes of those strengths to propel them into a more successful outcome (Rashid, 2015). In every aspect of treatment, the client's voice and choice is the driving force for services. This same type of model of advocacy and empowerment is also repeated, and therefore modeled, throughout the organization. For instance, staff in the organization who are empowered and practice advocacy can then act as facilitators for recovery as opposed to being responsible for "healing." It is critical here that the goal is empowerment. In most cases this means moving someone from the role of victim to survivor. The use of the term "survivor" is used to indicate an individual's capacity to take control over their lives and not to solely be identified by the trauma they experienced. The use of either "victim" or "survivor" can be appropriate depending on where the individual is in their recovery process. An individual can enter into the empowerment process in multiple places of their recovery, but they can also vacillate from victim to survivor. This is dependent on their environment and where they are emotionally, physically, and mentally. They may land in a certain place in the process, which may indicate their positionality as a victim or survivor.

Context and Cultural Sensitivity

The aspect of culture is central to most practices, but it is essential to a trauma-informed care approach. At the minimum, culture may be used to leverage familiarity of positive customs and rituals as well as incorporate diversity responsive protocols. Practitioners should have the knowledge and skills to work with each individual's culture and understand how one's own cultural perspectives may influence the client (Fong & Furuto, 2001). "Culture" includes not only race and ethnicity but also gender, sexual orientation, and religion or spiritual beliefs. Understanding these aspects will deepen relationships between practitioners and their clients to facilitate a more effective recovery (Whaley & Davis, 2007). This is

Figure 4.2 Challenging Unequal Power Relationships

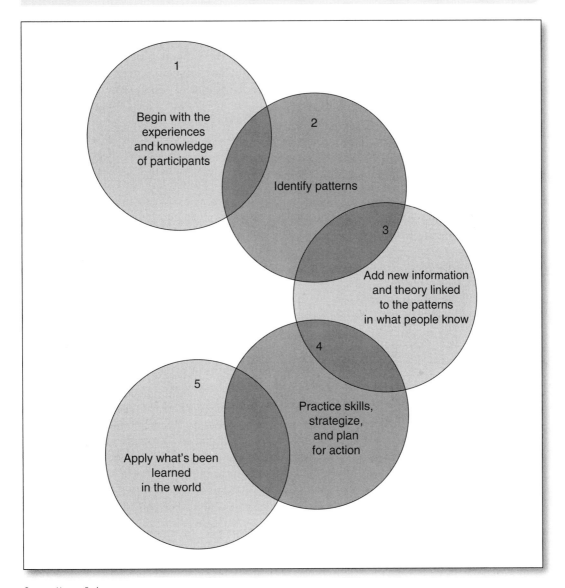

Source: Honey Imbo.

due to the reality that culture is a large influencing factor in an individual's perspective and decision-making. Understanding culture provides practitioners with an understanding of meaning that an individual may attribute to the trafficking situation, trauma, and recovery process. Also, when culture has been used against the individual and actually assisted in the trafficking exploitation, it is important to know that as well. For example, someone who has strong religious and spiritual beliefs may be inclined to thinking that their misfortune, even traumatic events, is an outcome of fate, destiny, or karma. If someone has this perspective, it is important for the practitioner to take into full account their reports around their beliefs and understand where those beliefs are rooted.

In Cynthia's case, it is important to understand the context of culture and religion in which her situation takes place. As noted in the complex case, Cynthia and her family were victims of a natural disaster, which has placed her in a situation where she must leave her family to find work. It would be important to explore her thoughts and beliefs on how she makes sense of her current situation. Dependent on her culture and religion and her relationship to the two, the natural disaster could be perceived as "punishment," "fate," or "a sacrifice." Each of these perceptions is tied to a mental and emotional process, which are essential components of her assessment and treatment.

Belief systems can also be used in the recovery process. For instance, in this same example with the religious beliefs, practitioners can help clients deconstruct their perspectives and/or realign them with other religious values and help them reframe their experiences within the context of important cultural values and norms. A thorough assessment of an individual's cultural belief systems can assist the practitioner in how the individual is actualizing their experiences and provide deeper considerations for the course of treatment.

In many situations where the victims have had a history of adverse childhood experiences, that individual's perception of a healthy relationship and healthy attachment is often distorted and unhealthy. Frequently "Romeo Pimps" or "Loverboys" target young women with this vulnerability and often win their trust by entering into a romantic relationship with them and gradually making the women dependent on them. Once the women are dependent on them, they use this level of power to threaten or intimidate the women to do exploitative work such as prostitution and drug dealing. This leads the individual to perpetually seek out similar unhealthy relationships, which tend to reflect unregulated expressions of attachment. The interpersonal violence often experienced in trafficking can be more traumatic than other traumas such as natural disasters because it is more disruptive to our fundamental sense of trust and attachment and is typically experienced as intentional rather than a natural force of nature (International Society for the Study of Trauma and Dissociation, 2009). Therefore, building a trusting and reparative relationship with an individual who has experienced trafficking an essential component in recovering from trauma-related symptoms.

IMPLEMENTING TRAUMA-INFORMED CARE

It is one thing to understand the principles of trauma-informed care, but a larger challenge to take this perspective and operationalize it into trauma-informed *practice*. One of the biggest challenges is to have a strong understanding of how trauma at different life stages may lead to developmental arrest, deficiency, or disruption. For example, a practitioner treating someone who has experienced early childhood trauma must be knowledgeable about the developing brain and internal working models. Children regulate and modify their behavior according the response of their primary caregivers. These internal working models, as defined by Bowlby, are the internalization of the affective and cognitive characteristics of their primary caregiver (Orlans & Levy, 2014). Because many of these early childhood experiences, including traumatic experience, occur in the context of a developing brain, it is essential that knowledge of neural and social development is used to understand the significant impact of these experiences on the overall development of a person's brain as it relates to their current functioning. Thus, to operationalize into trauma-informed practice, the practitioner needs to have knowledge of trauma-specific concerns as well as developmental stages. This will help craft an appropriate practice response that can address the actual symptoms of those that have been trafficked (Harris & Fallot, 2001). Those who are trafficked present a variety of symptoms that in total or even individually are unique and should be addressed as such (Pearlman & Courtois, 2005).

There are a range of approaches that are utilized to treat trauma such as psychological first aid, cognitive behavioral therapies, exposure therapy, eye movement desensitization reprocessing, and integrated CBT. An ongoing discussion in the field is the identification and use of these trauma-specific interventions. Depending on the nature of the trauma, researchers and practitioners are currently discussing if one approach is more suitable to a client than another and if so, why. SAMHSA (2014) states that individuals who are recovering from a more recent trauma would benefit more from a present-based approach that teaches coping skills and challenges cognitive distortions, while individuals who have experienced more complex and chronic trauma may benefit from a more narrative approach to address more repressed traumas (SAMHSA, 2014; Trauma Informed Care in Behavioral Health Services. Treatment Improved Protocol No. 57). People who have been trafficked can experience a range of trauma dating back from early childhood or may have experienced recent trafficking trauma with no history of prior trauma. Considering the broad range of possibilities, it is important that, when adapting a trauma-informed lens to practice, trauma-specific considerations are also reviewed. It has been clear in other violence-related traumas (such as domestic violence or sexual assault) that specialized services which are more specific are also more effective (Campbell, Patterson, & Lichty, 2005; Fry, 2007). Although there are unifying factors of victimization that intersect and are universal, there are special needs and issues that exist for those who have been trafficked. For example, issues of shame, oppression, and relatedness (or lack thereof) are unique to those who have been trafficked in overt and also nuanced ways.

Just as with creating space of collaboration, one of the most crucial aspects in operationalizing trauma-informed care approach is constant monitoring of the power dynamics that exist in the relationship. Some of the most salient aspects to the relationship and power should always be monitored because of the dynamic of uneven distributions power. For instance, in most situations you have a practitioner who is a highly educated, paid professional. Their background may be, and often is, very different from their clients. In some cases, the trafficked person may not have a choice in whether or not they receive services. While in the United States trafficked persons are no longer required to comply with services or in cases against their traffickers, in many other countries that is not the case. Trafficked persons must participate in getting services and in the prosecution of their traffickers. This may cause a further power dynamic with practitioners because the option of choice is again removed from the clients.

In some experiences, trafficked victims had no choice whatsoever and were in positions where all power had been stripped from them. However, practitioners can use these situations as a way to create healing experiences. One of the most impactful areas that women who have been trafficked gain their sense of control and self-worth is through economic empowerment. Many times, practitioners are strongly encouraged to link them up to government resources and work opportunities. Although the practitioner can identify options for the client, it is imperative that the practitioner promotes the client's freedom of choice and level of participation and supports the client through that decision. This can challenge a client's previous perception of power dynamics and create mental and emotional room for reparative experiences. Throughout this process, practitioners should always be aware, however, of actions that may trigger or retraumatize (Clawson et al., 2008).

Most evidence-based practices also contain guidelines for the timing to conduct various elements of treatment. Although fidelity to treatment models and curricula are critical, the movement of treatment should be guided by the practitioner's assessment of client readiness for change and client drive in terms of empowerment goals to determine movement forward.

Because of the emotionally acute nature of trauma work and the relationships that are formed when conducting such work, practitioners and clients may find themselves in positions where they experience significant transference and countertransference. Transference is when the client projects thoughts, wants, needs, feelings, and fantasies on the practitioner. Countertransference is the opposite; it is the practitioner who projects those elements on the client. When this work has a significant relational component (which this does), transference and countertransference, need not be an impediment and instead could be helpful to the process. It is, of course, unhelpful when unhealthy relationship and communication patterns are re-created or triggered. In these cases, the practitioner must temper and even call to attention what is occurring so as not to repeat or play out these patterns. However, if a practitioner recognizes what is occurring and has a good understanding of the relationship with the client, this awareness can be brought into the therapeutic process by using these thoughts and feelings to facilitate change and transformation in the therapeutic work.

Working with people who have been trafficked calls for abundant compassion, dedication, and sometimes a high level of emotional investment. The consistent usage of these emotions can have an adverse impact on the emotional well-being of the individual providing care. This emotional residue and strain is called compassion fatigue, or secondary trauma, and is a consequence of working with people who have suffered from the consequences of traumatic events (Figley, 2013). In the state of Colorado alone, 48.9% of emergency response personnel have committed suicide after exposure to distressing events (Jamison, Herndon, Bui, & Bol, 2014). Compassion fatigue builds up over time and could be a result to exposure to multiple cases of trauma or could be a result of exposure to one case. Compassion fatigue can be a physical and emotional response where individuals experience a strong reaction that can overpower their usual coping mechanisms. Some symptoms of compassion fatigue can include feelings of exhaustion, nervous system arousal, depression, loss of emotional modulation, physical aches and pains, decreased interactions with others, depersonalization, and reduced sense of meaning in work. To ensure the care of the practitioner, the implementation of self-care techniques that include both emotional and physical tools can promote practitioner well-being. The implementation of self-care by the practitioner can alleviate symptoms of compassion fatigue and will help them more effectively deal with the trauma involved with people who have been trafficked.

Practitioner Note

Jaime was one of the first clients who I served when I started my career as a social worker. Jaime was a transgender client who was transitioning from male to female. She was cursing, yelling, and shaking as she entered my office. Jaime was completely dysregulated. After ten to fifteen minutes, Jaime was able to catch her breath and speak to me. When I attempted to ask her what was happening, she wasn't able to articulate exactly what was happening in her mind and body. At the moment, I wasn't sure what to do with her, so I began my regular assessment. Jaime was able to share information clearly around her family and some areas of her childhood. When it came to discussing her adolescence and her history of exploitation, Jaime began to show some of the same symptoms of dysregulation and agitation. Noticing her affect, I paused the assessment to check in. Again, Jaime had a difficult time identifying what was happening in her mind and her body. It was evident that she was triggered. I worked with her in regulating her emotions and feelings and we ended the session. Jaime agreed to come back next week.

The following week Jaime returned to my office and entered my room in similar fashion: agitated, shaking, and dysregulated. I worked with her with grounding techniques and attempted to identify why she was presenting in this way. Again, she didn't know why she was feeling these emotions and appeared confused and upset. We went through session as usual and scheduled for another session the following week.

The next week, twenty minutes before Jaime's scheduled session, I decided to wait near the front desk. When Jaime walked into the clinic, the front desk clerk instructed Jaime to, "Please sign here, Sir, and have a seat." I observed that Jaime rolled her eyes and took a seat. Then I noticed that in the waiting room there was a television that was playing old episodes of *Maury* and *Jerry Springer*, which entailed loud and aggressive yelling and insulting violent language. I observed Jaime becoming more agitated, and I called her name and brought her into my office. It was evident that the lack of sensitivity of the front desk clerk and the aggressive content in the waiting room were triggers to Jaime's trauma. It was clear that the organization I was working with lacked practices in trauma-informed care. Jaime's experience was a clear example on how it is necessary for every dimension of an organization, from the front staff to the administration, to be sensitive to the trauma of all people who enter the clinic. Jaime's experiences prompted this organization to revisit its approach on providing care to ensure that clients and staff are not retraumatized by their experience at the clinic.

—Wilhelmina De Castro

TRAUMA-INFORMED PRACTICE EXAMPLE: SEEKING SAFETY

Seeking Safety is an empirically validated present-focused intervention that helps individuals attain safety from trauma and/or substance abuse (Najavits, 2002). It is utilized to decrease the risk factors involved with individuals who suffer from co-occurring disorders of PTSD and addiction, both of which are also prevalent in trafficked persons. Traffickers often use substances to create compliance. The use of these substances may eventually result in addiction. Similarly, many adults find themselves vulnerable to being trafficked because of their substance abuse and addictions (Lloyd, 2011). *Seeking Safety* focuses on developing coping skills and support systems for the identified client through the implementation of the following principles: safety as a priority of treatment; integrated treatment of PTSD and substance abuse; focus on ideals; and four content areas, including: cognitive, behaviors, interpersonal, and case management (http://www.seekingsafety.org). The format is a group therapy structure in each of these content areas. There are 25 module topics in *Seeking Safety* that cover areas such as building healthy support systems, identifying triggers, and understanding PTSD and substance abuse. *Seeking Safety* was created by Lisa M. Najavits, PhD (1993) and has been translated into eight languages. Facilitation of *Seeking Safety* is best done by a clinician, but has been manualized and marketed in such a way that "even those without training" could facilitate the model.

Seeking Safety is particularly concerned with not triggering the client's substance abuse or PTSD. A large amount of time is spent on discussing the potential for retraumatization. In every group session, there is a check-in and check-out where practitioners make sure they assess whether individuals are feeling safe enough to share vulnerable information. If practitioners assess that all group members feel safe and are also capable of providing a safe containing environment for others, then they continue with the planned module. If they assess otherwise, they might direct the group to adjust the group content that feels safer. This level of flexibility on the part of the practitioners can determine the success of a group because it helps group members feel as if they have a certain amount of control in their treatment and that their emotional safety is a priority.

Another aspect of *Seeking Safety* is that each client creates a safety plan. Parts of the plan may be shared with supervisors and administrative staff so that they may know how to responsively and appropriately respond to any behaviors clients may exhibit in between sessions, but while they are at the organization. Sharing significant components of the safety plan with organization staff and administration can help the client feel heard, safe, and understood. Finally, *Seeking Safety* also incorporates techniques such as progressive relaxation and meditation, moving toward holistic approaches.

Cognitive behavioral therapies have been the most studied interventions but they are not the only avenues for treatment to reduce PTSD symptoms or other trauma-based symptoms (Ugarte, Zarate and Farley, 2004). Indeed several treatment strategies have been used effectively, which are deemed to be "nontraditional." While some of these strategies are "outside of the box," many veer away from individually Western-focused conceptualizations (Herman, 2003). These strategies still focus on empowerment and building self-esteem, reconnection to self and others, and expression. Strategies include art therapy, music therapy, journaling, poetry, drama, yoga, body work, and meditation. For example, progressive relaxation is a strategy that increases body awareness and assists in grounding during periods of cognitive dissonance (Cohen, Mannarino, Deblinger, 2006). Through grounding, an individual can stop unhelpful cognitive processes that often lead to unhealthy and even high-risk behaviors. Challenges for those who experience trauma revolve around recognizing and differentiating current emotional experiences and physical cues. Additionally, another challenge is in learning how to regulate emotions and behaviors that allow the healthy and beneficial fulfillment of current life goals. Elements of many meditative practices such as calming visualization, positive self-talk, and mindful breathing.

MEDITATION AND MINDFULNESS

As the complexities of trauma are more widely understood, the integration and effectiveness of nontraditional interventions have been more widely accepted. The most commonly used nontraditional practices are meditation and mindfulness. Meditation and mindfulness hold their roots in Eastern religion and philosophy such as Buddhism, date back over 2,000 years are and beginning to have a more profound integration into modern health-care practices (Greenberg, Reiner, & Meiran, 2012). Meditation is a practice that induces a mode of consciousness to realize some benefit to self or for the mind to recognize and acknowledge a thought without an embodied attachment to the thought (Bach & Guse, 2015). Meditation has been specifically proven to decrease anxiety-driven symptoms that many trafficking and trauma victims suffer from. One significant source of anxiety can be rooted in what mental health specialists call cognitive rigidity. Cognitive rigidity is the inability and inflexibility of the mind to integrate different perspectives or thoughts into ones existing thought processes (Ottaviani et al., 2016). Research has shown that cognitive rigidity is a source that contributes significantly to symptoms of anxiety (Lee & Orsillo, 2014). Through the multitude of techniques used in meditation, such as mantras, deep breathing, repetitive positive self-talk, acknowledgment, and nonattachment to thoughts, an individual can enhance their cognitive flexibility, subsequently decreasing their anxiety (Lee & Orsillo, 2014).

In the movement toward integration of meditative and mindful practices, there is an inextricable relationship between the well-being of the mind and the body. When trauma is experienced, it crosses boundaries between the emotional, mental, physical, and metaphysical and causes significant imbalance to one's natural state. Some Eastern philosophies have long believed that when a person attains balance in the mind and body and ensures that energy is flowing consistently through oneself, then optimal well-being is achieved. This is exemplified in practices such as acupuncture, which aims to release tension in areas where there is a blockage of "chi" or "life force energy" (Errington-Evans, 2012). There was a study that found that acupuncture was promising for the treatment of trauma-related symptoms such as anxiety, sleep disturbances, depression, and chronic pain (Lee et.al., 2012). In Western culture, these physical indications are understood as the somatization of symptoms, which is the manifestation of mental emotional ailments in the physical body. Somatization of symptoms can range from tension headaches and back pain to sleeplessness and other forms of chronic pain. With the foundations of Eastern philosophies integrated into Western environs of treatment, there has been an expansion of capacity to provide healing, support, and recovery for those who experience trauma. In the complex case of Cynthia, the susceptibility of PTSD and the somatization of her emotional symptoms are high. At the time of the typhoon, Cynthia was not only worried about her and her sister's physical safety but was also emotionally traumatized when she was filled with panic as the storm and winds ranged around them. The layering of these types of traumatic experience increases vulnerability to reexperiencing trauma in the emotional, mental, and physical form.

Complex Case

Overview (for all scenarios)

Cynthia O. grew up in Tacloban, Leyte, a provincial city in the Philippines. Tacloban is somewhat industrial, housing the factories for Coca Cola and many garment factories as part of its Philippine Economic Zone. However, much of it remains rooted in agricultural production. Since it is outside of the National Capital Region of the country, it is considered a "province" and therefore does not have all the resources available that one would find in an urban center. While it is rapidly developing, it is an economically stable region that is precarious because of its geographic location in the middle of what geologists and meteorologists call the "Typhoon Corridor." Being on this pathway means that it is just a matter of time until they will experience severe natural disaster. The region has some notable colleges and vocational opportunities for education. It has a population of about 240,000 persons.

Cynthia is the oldest of five siblings. Although she is only 10 months older than her brother, she has always had a bulk of the responsibilities to help with the family, but it has always been like this so she doesn't mind or complain. Cynthia is 16 years old and in her last year of mandatory education (public high school). Her siblings are 15 (male), 13 (male), 10 (male), and 5 (female). Her parents own a small bakery and they make a modest income, although her mother often must take in laundry to make ends meet. Since there is a lot of work in the bakery, Cynthia often must wake up at 3 or 4 in the morning to help with the baking. Sometimes she is asked to help with the laundry, but rarely. Many times, she must also help watch the other children. This makes Cynthia late for school or sometimes she misses school completely. Her parents try to make sure she doesn't because they want her to finish school, but it cannot always be helped.

Cynthia is of average height and is very slim. She is attractive and often mistaken for younger/older than her age. She is very outgoing and has a positive attitude. Their neighbors always comment on how lucky her parents are for having such a good *manang* (oldest sister). Cynthia has no history of health problems and has reached all her developmental milestones. Because of her family responsibilities, she is not able to participate in many after-school activities, but whenever she can, she likes to play volleyball. For the same reason, she also does not hang out with classmates or have very many friends. Cynthia has never had a boyfriend nor does she have any close male friends. Teachers and peers describe Cynthia as being well liked, helpful, and friendly.

Case Twist: On November 8, 2013, Super Typhoon Yolanda (also known as Typhoon Haiyan), the strongest storm to ever hit land, struck the Philippines. The first place it hit was Eastern Samar, and then Leyte, where Cynthia and her family lived. The family was home when the typhoon began and they evacuated to a local public school. They thought they were safe, but the school quickly flooded and the family was forced with everyone else to climb up to the roof of the building. Cynthia helped keep her younger sister safe when the water started rising, and she describes her panic as the water was rising. They stood on the roof for four hours while the storm and the winds raged around them. The family wasn't able to return home until a week later because of all the debris. The roads were closed, phone lines were down, and there was no electricity. Aid could barely reach them for almost two weeks. They were grateful that they did not lose any family members, especially since so many of their neighbors were not as lucky. They had nothing left of their home or any of their things. Because there was nothing left, her parents asked her to go to Manila to some distant relatives to find work. Cynthia did not want to leave her family alone but she knew that she had to do whatever she could to help.

CALL TO ACTION: STRENGTHS-BASED AND TRAUMA-INFORMED

Of all the approaches that have shown to be effective in helping individuals who have been trafficked, a trauma-centered approach is the most promising. This is a framework and the advantage of that is that it can be used to guide most, if not all, interventions and strategies that are being utilized in the field. Also, because of this, it can be used in multiple settings and by multiple disciplines so that those we are providing services for can experience a consistent continuum of care. We now know how central experiences of trauma are to almost all aspects of human development and behavior. This knowledge base can be a start and also help direct how we develop and create evidence-based practices for the trafficked population, not just for recovery and healing but hopefully for prevention as well.

DISCUSSION QUESTIONS

1. How can you ensure that every person in your agency is trained in practicing from a trauma-informed care approach?

2. What can you do in your agency to assess the level of understanding of each employee for trauma-informed care?

3. What can clinicians do to increase awareness on countertransference?

4. What can agencies do to address the risk retraumatization with their clients?

CHALLENGE

Try the meditation application Headspace (headspace.com) for 10 days. During that time, pay attention to what mindfulness and meditation practice does for you. What difference does it make? How might you imagine these differences help those who have experienced trauma? Would you suggest meditation as a supplementary practice?

CHAPTER 5

Case Management

Annalisa Enrile and Wilhelmina De Castro

Chapter Objectives

1. Readers will be able to connect case management to a trauma-informed lens.

2. Readers will be able to recognize the benefits of case management in helping individuals who have been trafficked and/or enslaved.

3. Readers will establish an awareness of effective approaches in implementing case management.

4. Readers will determine the pivotal role that case management has as an intervention for human trafficking and modern-day slavery.

5. Readers will apply the principles of case management to larger mezzo and macro efforts to end human trafficking and modern-day slavery.

I first met Dania when I was working as a clinical social worker at a transitional housing unit in Compton, California. I worked with a case manager and found out firsthand how important intensive case management could be. I had gotten the call from someone looking for housing and when Dania showed up she banged on the door. When my staff and I opened the door, there was Dania, looking as if she had not showered in a week, with bruises on her body and looking agitated and scared. With her, she only had an expired ID and a TAP card (used for public transportation). After doing an initial safety assessment with Dania, I began my clinical assessment. It was hard for her to fully explain her situation. Parts of her story did not align and details seemed hazy and inconsistent. The only parts that were clear were that she was a former foster child in need of housing and that she was currently breaking up with someone whom she called her "boyfriend." During my assessment, Dania made mentioned that she did not want anyone to know where she was and when I asked her if she was in immediate danger, she remained quiet and had a difficult time making eye contact.

(Continued)

(Continued)

After her first day there, I attempted to assess Dania's financial situation. Again, she gave me stories and excuses about why she never went to the Department of Public Services. She said that all her official documents were lost between homes. Her stories seemed fragmented and she would immediately change the subject when I attempted to obtain more details. It was like peeling layers off an onion. She was doling out information so sparingly and it was all we could do to be patient and wait for her to be ready. But, every time she told us something new, it meant more resources we had to find, more services we had to help coordinate, and definitely more healing she would have to do. After a few days with us in transitional housing Dania gave us permission to run her information through the county data base, which would let us know if she had a criminal record and would also give us access to her social workers. After some of our staff looked through our records, it was clear that there was a warrant out for Dania's arrest, including charges of prostitution. It also stated that she has also been in the foster care system since she was 6 years old.

I met with Dania to clarify why there was a warrant out for her arrest. She was very defensive and stormed out of the room stating, "This is why I don't tell you guys anything! Everyone is always judging me!" I tried to talk with her but to no avail. After giving her some time to cool down, Robin, her case manager and I returned to Dania's door and asked to come in. Robin sat with Dania and helped her make dinner and set up her apartment. While she was with her she encouraged Dania to share a little of her story. During that time, Robin was able to understand Dania's circumstances and that her warrant for "prostitution" was actually a consequence of her being trafficked. The "boyfriend" that Dania was also speaking about was found out to be her pimp. Dania came to us fleeing her trafficker and also fleeing the law. Between myself as her clinician and Robin as her case manager, it was evident that we needed to work with law enforcement and Department of Child Protective Services to ensure that Dania was protected from her trafficker, and protected from retraumatization and exploitation from the system. With Dania's permission, Robin was able to contact her previous social workers, the courts, and probation officer to meet to discuss the nature of Dania's situation. I've been doing this long enough to know that it takes a village to help our clients, but Dania's case was a reminder that in trafficking cases, the village had to include a case manager; they were the only ones who had a perspective of every moving piece and when the cases are as complex as these, that skill is invaluable.

—Wilhelmina De Castro

INTRODUCTION

The complex challenges faced by individuals who have been trafficked require the use of intensive case management. The main goal of intensive case management is to provide comprehensive community-based treatment to rehabilitate and support those who suffer from mental health issues. The nature of trafficking is that an individual faces multiple traumas and layers of exploitation. Further, the transnational nature of trafficking poses a challenge for victims in obtaining government-funded resources. A signature part of this treatment model is the use of an integrative approach that harnesses a multitude of resources to support the range of life domains, including physical, psychological, and emotional health, life skills, finances, and education and employment, that are inextricably impacted by trauma and mental health issues often rooted or exacerbated by trafficking and other forms of exploitation (Enrile & De Castro, 2015). At a domestic and global level, there is a significant importance of case management in working with victims of human trafficking from the point of identification until a victim reaches self-sufficiency. In some countries, intensive case management is the extent of their services, making it all the more critical. Case management is an effective practice not only for victims but also for law enforcement, service providers, and all key people involved in serving this population and eradicating this problem. This chapter will describe case management as a service modality, provide implementation suggestions, and look forward at the potential of case management within the overall movement against trafficking and modern-day slavery.

DEFINING CASE MANAGEMENT

Case management is service that provides comprehensive community-based treatment to rehabilitate and support those who suffer from mental health issues. The purpose of case management services is to establish the physical and psychological safety of the client (Clawson, Grace, & Salomon, 2008). Case management services provide a multifaceted approach to ensure that all the needs of the client are met. The main components of almost all intensive case management models include multidisciplinary teams, community-based services, highly individualized services, long-term planning, vocational planning, and attention to health-care needs (Allness & Knoedler, 2003).

Role of the Case Managers and the Use of Trauma-Informed Care

Case managers are the conveners at the center of the collaborative process in serving victims of trafficking. The collaboration of multiple stakeholders and service providers is intended to lead to the most effective outcome that supports the physical, psychological, emotional, intellectual, and spiritual healing and well-being of the participant. Although it is common for social service organizations to offer case management to their participants, it is critical that case management is an integral part in servicing the trafficking population and not thought of or treated as an ancillary or merely logistical service. There are a multitude of systems involved, including mental health professionals, housing providers, shelters, law enforcement, prosecutors, attorneys, and employers. Each of these systems includes a different set of policies, protocols, or stakeholders. Unfortunately, there does not exist any true coordination of care. In a study reviewing the unmet need for coordination of care for children and families, they found that approximately 40% of children and families with mental health issues reported that their need for coordination of care was left unmet (Brown, Green, Desai, Weitzman, & Rosenthal, 2014). Managing and navigating through all these systems can be overwhelming and can easily propel someone who has been trafficked into feeling lost and alone and to create higher vulnerability for retraumatization. Despite the lack of coordination, at the minimum, it is important for the systems involved to all operate from a trauma-informed care approach. This way, those who are trafficked will be treated in a consistent manner and begin building trust with an ecosystem of providers and practitioners. In the example of the complex case, a coordination of services is extremely important due to the financial needs of Cynthia and her family, which is further exacerbated by the challenges brought on by geographic distance between Singapore and the Philippines. To address these challenges, effective practice of case management utilizes a trauma-informed lens to ensure that all systems involved are actively practicing the highest level of care and sensitivity to the individual being served.

Significant rehabilitation for this population involves participation of multiple systems. These systems are often difficult to understand and require advocacy skills to ensure that one's voice and best interests are heard and addressed, language abilities to guarantee transparency and clarity of communication between systems, and capacity to synthesize and utilize information to guarantee action and accountability (Summers, 2015). Individuals who are in the initial phases of garnering support may not have immediate accessibility to these interpersonal skills, thus making the role of the case manager that much more significant. Having the case manager as a single point of contact is a fundamental component in providing victims with essential resources. As the single point of contact the case manager will ensure not only that information is communicated effectively and sensitively but also that the information is synthesized and utilized effectively, organized in one place to reference.

In many organizations, case management is often used as an ancillary supportive service, but when it comes to the realm of trafficking, they become one of the single most important people in supporting the rehabilitation of the trafficking victim. Case managers serve many roles in addition to being the convener of services. For example, in managing a case of a trafficking victim, the case manager will be the central point of contact to coordinate the clients access to doctors' appointments, financial supports, housing, and legal services. As a central component of services, case managers conduct needs assessments, identify and coordinate services, spearhead communication across settings, and serve as an advocate for the participant and a liaison between systems. In many trafficking cases perpetrators induce significant levels of trauma by destroying a victim's self-worth, sense of self, and relation to others. The amount of physical and emotional entrapment that victims experience often leave them feeling helpless, hopeless, and shut down (Heffernan & Blythe, 2014). Although it may not be overtly stated in their role definitions, case managers play a crucial role in the emotional and psychological rehabilitation of victims. When case management is executed effectively, it offers a valuable currency to often resistant clients who have difficulty trusting others. When actions that are beneficial to the client are successfully completed there is a strengthened bond of attachment between the case manager and client. As long as the case manager is professional and does not use the task completion to pressure the client toward an expedited recovery, the bond can be helpful and healing. Often this level of dedication and rapport building results in significant participant cooperation and an unparalleled therapeutic relationship the drives meaningful change. In Cynthia's case, a relationship of trust and clear expectations must be communicated. Because of her perpetrators use of "debt" to manipulate her forced labor, it would be likely that Cynthia could perceive any form of support as another form of "debt" accumulation. A healthy relationship between her and her case manager could be pivotal in her recovery.

One of the main ways that case managers build rapport and keep clients safe is through trauma-informed care. For example, they ensure that clients feel emotionally and physically safe is by taking them on a tour of the agency so that they are aware of the physical space and are also aware of everyone's role and purpose. This helps clarify expectations and mitigate possibilities that a client will feel confused or overwhelmed. From the very beginning of their work with the client, case managers also create safety plans. These safety plans are frequently revisited to ensure they continue to speak to the client's needs (Asquith & Turner, 2008). In the beginning of every meeting, case managers conduct a check-in with the victim by asking them if they are feel safe talking and that the safety plan they initially developed was still active and applicable. A study done by Heffernan and Blythe (2014) assessed that the repetitive nature of these check-ins is important in working within a trauma-informed lens because it helps the victim feel a sense of consistency and continuity of safety.

Another tool that is utilized to deepen emotional rapport and safety with victims is "The Participant Bill of Rights" (Heffernan & Blythe, 2014). This it is provided to each participant once they agree to receive service and is meant to remind them of their power and capacity to practice their power. The Participant Bill of Rights reads as follows:

You have the right to put yourself first.

You have the right to be you.

You have the right to be safe.

You have the right to love and be loved.

You have the right to be treated with respect.

You have the right to be human—NOT PERFECT.

You have the right to be angry and protest if you are treated unfairly or abusively by anyone.

You have the right to your own privacy.

You have the right to earn and control your own money.

You have the right to ask questions about anything that affects your life.

You have the right to make decisions that affect you.

You have the right to your own opinions, to express them, and to be taken seriously.

You have the right to grow and change (and that includes changing your mind).

You have the right to say NO.

You have the right to make mistakes.

You have the right NOT to be responsible for other adults' problems.

You have the right not to be liked by everyone.

YOU HAVE THE RIGHT TO CONTROL YOUR OWN LIFE AND TO CHANGE IT IF YOU ARE NOT HAPPY WITH IT AS IT IS.

With the use of these practices with additional trauma-informed interventions, case managers undoubtedly have the capability in providing services that are highly beneficial for victims of trafficking.

IMPLEMENTING CASE MANAGEMENT

Case management has proven beneficial not only to victims but to stakeholders as well. Since case managers are at the center of treatment, they are highly utilized by other systems such as law enforcement and legal entities. Law enforcement's main goals are to obtain information and to complete the investigation. Because of the severity of their trauma and conditioning, victims often become closed off and apprehensive toward officers and refuse to share information (Connell, Jennings, Barbieri, Reingle Gonzalez, 2015). Many victims of trafficking are aware that the activities that they often unwilling participate in are criminalized. For example, many trafficked individuals get arrested for prostitution, but they do not know that there are also laws that categorize their experience as victimization and could actually be protected from such experience. This lack of knowledge makes victims that much more reluctant to engage with law enforcement. Foreign victims of human trafficking have the added complication of a lack (or perceived lack) of lawful immigration status. These victims may have voluntarily come to the United States, perhaps under the bondages of the smuggler, only to become a trafficking victim. Though, the looming threat of deportation makes these victims particularly hesitant to engage with law enforcement (Helton, 2016).

The litany of challenges that come in stabilizing a victim of trafficking are often beyond the means of law enforcement, thus making the case mangers role critical for stabilization, resulting in time and space for the officer to conduct their investigation. A victim's stabilization may lead them to share pertinent information, which can aid in the investigation and potentially lead to the apprehension of the trafficker. Prosecutors also find case managers to be very helpful in creating movement in a case. Since case managers provide a consistent support system, this lends to a greater sense of stability for a client. The prosecution assesses that a greater sense of stability frequently results in a more consistent and credible witness (Moser, 2012). Since many cases of trafficking heavily rely on the victim's testimony, there is significant benefit to having a case manager involved.

To implement intensive case management, first a comprehensive intake of the trafficked individual must occur. Usually organizations that work with this population do not need to re-create what they are already using as long as it is exhaustive and focused on resources. One way to think about this is as one would think of a larger needs assessment inventory. Macy and Johns (2010) emphasize the importance of understanding a victim's history as well as the circumstances surrounding their exploitation. This follows a trauma-specific lens, which we discussed last chapter. When possible, the needs assessment should be in simple, vernacular, and if applicable, in the trafficked individual's native language to increase accuracy of response. In true coordinated fashion, if the trafficked individual has to move or change services, ideally, this assessment would follow them (ILO, 2006).

In Australia, under the Support for Victims of People Trafficking Program, trafficked people are eligible for supportive services and resources such as food, living allowances, counseling, and shelter. One form of eligibility for this program is if the person trafficked makes a contribution to the investigation. Case managers would be an essential liaison to support this this possible route of eligibility. Often trafficked persons are unable to put together or fully understand the totality of what they need, much less what they can access. In these situations, the role of the case manager is essential. Though Australia might have laws in place, there are challenges within those laws. For instance, the anti-trafficking law is located in two different divisions: movement (Division 271) and exploitation (Division 270). Prosecutors, incorrectly believing that the key to determining trafficking is movement, rely on Division 271 even though it is a more difficult burden of proof (Hepburn & Simon, 2013). Afterward, those who are trafficked can apply for a visa that also comes with a number of benefits. The case manager's involvement in this area would not only support a client's access to resources but would additionally support the systems movement toward obtaining justice and eradicating trafficking (Interdepartmental Committee on Human Trafficking and Slavery, 2015).

Resources for Case Managers

Government Resources:

Food and Nutrition Assistance
  fns.usda.gov

Job Corps
  jobcorps.gov

Medicaid
  medicaid.gov

Office of Family Assistance/ TANF
  acf.hhs.gov/ofa

Substance Abuse and Mental Health Services Administration
  samhsa.gov

Suicide Prevention Lifeline
  suicidepreventionlifeline.org

U.S. Committee for Refugees and Immigrants
  refugees.org

(Continued)

(Continued)

U.S. Department of Education

www.ed.gov

U.S. Department of Housing and Urban Development

hud.gov

U.S. Department of Labor

dol.gov

U.S. Department of Health and Human Services, Mental Health

mentalhealth.gov

Office for Victims of Crime

ovc.gov

Special Supplemental Nutrition Program for Women, Infants, and Children (WIC)

fns.usda.gov/wic

Trafficking Resource Organizations

Asian American Advancing Justice

advancingjustice-la.org

Catholic Charities

catholiccharitiesusa.org

Career One Stop

careeronestop.org

Children of the Night

childrenofthenight.org

Coalition for Humane Immigrant Rights Los Angeles

chirla.org

Coalition to Abolish Slavery and Trafficking

castla.org

Dream Center

dreamcenter.org/about-us/

Dress for Success (Career Development and Clothing Resources)

dressforsuccess.org/client-services/

Catholic Legal Immigration Network

cliniclegal.org

GEMS

gems-girls.org

Goodwill Job Assistance

goodwill.org/find-jobs-and-services/

Hope for Justice

hopeforjustice.org

International Justice Mission

ijm.org

Childhelp National Child Abuse Hotline

Phone: 1-800-422-4453

National Human Trafficking Hotline

humantraffickinghotline.org

Not for Sale

notforsalecampaign.org

Polaris Project

polarisproject.org

The Salvation Army

salvationarmyusa.org

Saving Innocence

savinginnocence.org

Alliance of Career Development Nonprofits

acdnonline.org

United Way

unitedway.org

(Continued)

(Continued)

Unlikely Heroes

   unlikelyheroes.com

211

   211.org

   Phone: 2-1-1

EFFECTIVE APPROACHES

There are many approaches that agencies use in working with trafficking victims, including housing, economic empowerment, life skills training, or mental health. The most promising approaches to effective case management with trafficked people include culturally appropriate provision of services, individualized/client specific services, collaboration across settings, and support for the case management practitioner (Frederick, 2005). At times, a case manager can see themselves as a coordinator of others or even a convener of services that may be needed. If the needs of the individual are great and complex, it is suggested that a case management team be put together and meet regularly (Frederick, 2005; ILO, 2006).

To adequately serve the vast diversity of individuals impacted by trafficking, culturally appropriate services must be implemented. Case managers should be inquisitive and seek out education about the beliefs and norms of each person's culture. A case manager that is aware and proactive in learning about a client's culture and religious beliefs can ensure that services are appropriate and that all experiences, starting at the initial meeting, are positive and sensitive to the client's needs. Furthermore, this level of awareness can help the case manager adapt their interventions appropriately. For example, if a case manager is attempting to obtain information surrounding a potentially taboo subject, they will be more equipped to identify ways to obtain the information in a sensitive and noninvasive manner. This can prevent the client from being offended or from shutting down. Cultural sensitivity and knowledge could also support the case manager in identifying services that would best meet the needs of the client and services that the client would actually be open to receiving. The more a plan of service is adapted to the culture of the client, the higher the likelihood is for success (Blue Blindfold, 2012).

The inability to speak out on behalf of one's own needs is an example of the patriarchal (or feudal) family systems in many Latino cultures. This expectation has become integrated into the cultural fabric of Latino society as a whole, even though it applies more specifically to the treatment of women and children. Essentially, when a woman speaks out or advocates for her needs, she is often seen as disrespectful and nontraditional and is often shamed for doing so. On the contrary, in providing services for trafficked victims in the United States, service providers often teach the skills of self-advocacy as an avenue toward self-reliance. It is important that when providing services to Latino individuals who identify with these customs, that an adaptation toward self-reliance is considered. The practitioner must be mindful of the delicate balance between cultural conservatism and advocating for women's empowerment. A substantial imbalance between the two could be detrimental at many levels (Ugarte, Zarate, & Farley, 2004).

In the situation of trafficking, cultural competence also extends to an understanding of trafficking and modern-day slavery. As we have demonstrated, there is a complex taxonomy around terminology and definitions as well as practices and processes. Being sensitive to these things allows case managers not only to create rapport and build trust but also to not engage in missteps that will retraumatize at most, or not be effective in the least. For instance, many shelters and transitional housing utilize token economies. While it is an effective method, it is not useful for victims who may have been trafficked and who are used to having to "earn" privileges or "work off" debts. In fact, it may trigger negative feelings of being back in an exploitative relationship (Morgan, personal communication, 2016).

Another widespread approach in providing case management is the individualization of services. This entails the case manager approaching the client and meeting them where they are in their healing process toward self-sufficiency. Often clients enter into services at different stages of readiness. It is important for the case manager to assess which stage their client is in and begin there. In the beginning of services, the case manager should take a more flexible approach. This flexibility will allow the client to feel in control of their trajectory and will help the case manager learn about the client's strengths and abilities. In addition to meeting the client where they are, the case manager can also take on the role of teaching a client skills toward self-sufficiency. Teaching and developing the skill sets of a client versus providing or doing tasks for a client results in a more empowered survivor. Once clients have learned skills and have effectively practiced these skills, they will be more self-sufficient, which leads to a more meaningful, lasting recovery. It is important that the case manager is keen to assessing whether the client is in need of a more hand-holding approach or if they are ready to practice their skills on their own. A consistent check-in will help the client feel safe and supported while promoting opportunity for growth and change. For example, many women who have been trafficked are often fearful of riding public transportation due to anxiety of encountering their trafficker or distress of being identified by people who were involved in their trafficking. Case managers often provide an interactive approach in situations such as this by working with the client to identify safe transportation routes, coaching them through the process as they join them on transportation, and providing praise and emotional support before, during, and after the task.

In the realm of social services, there are an array of services housed in different systems and organizations that could meet the needs of trafficking victims. Largely because of the financial capacities of many organizations, there are no organizations that house all the appropriate legal, financial, emotional, medical, psychological, and housing resources necessary to meet this population's needs. Therefore, it is vital that effective collaboration takes place to ensure that all the client's needs are met. One way of doing this is by developing collaborative partnerships. The ways that partnerships are cultivated and practiced are through formal memoranda of understanding, coalitions, committees, and focused task forces.

In San Bernardino, California, a multi-disciplinary team (MDT) is in place to serve people who have been trafficked. MDTs are a diverse group of professionals ranging from social workers, attorneys, nurses, and law enforcement, which collaborate in service of an individual or family. This MDT is coordinated by the Children's Network and includes a probation officer, a Department of Behavioral Health social worker, Children and Family Services social worker, and a public defender. This allows a team to work specifically on CSEC cases with a higher coordination of focus on at-risk youth. As more MDTs are formed, more forms of collaboration and methods of collaboration will occur. For instance, in Orange County, California, they have followed the example of San Bernardino and added to the model by physically housing these different entities in the same building complex. This makes it even easier to coordinate services allowing for continuous communication (Global Center for Women and Justice, 2013). The next level of the MDT is to utilize technology. Currently this group is working with application developers to streamline their communication and coordination (Morgan, personal communication, 2016).

Last, an important theme that is echoed across service providers in multiple settings is the need to support case managers. Providing services to the trafficked population often entails a significant commitment of time and emotion. Because of the nature of many trafficking cases, case managers are at risk for experiencing vicarious trauma (Newell & MacNeil, 2010). Although supportive systems are not always built into the case managers' work environment, it is important that spaces are created for case managers to process their stress, frustration, and other feelings around the individuals they serve. While case managers are not categorized under mental health practitioners, they still experience the psychological processes of transference and countertransference. The emotional intensity of many trafficking cases ignites these two processes in which case managers must holding difficult emotions for their clients (transference) and while also navigating their response to their client's experience (countertransference). In addition to executing their tasks as case manager, managing these processes can become overwhelming for the case manager (Korićanac, 2013). If there is a lack of support for the case manager in this area, it is highly likely that the case manager will become exhausted and burned out. Although in many settings case managers are not considered mental health practitioners, they often are the first providers to hear the firsthand, primary accounts of trafficking victims' traumatic experiences. This speaks to the need for formalized support and supervision for case managers so that they can manage their emotions in a healthy manner and decrease vulnerability to compassion fatigue and secondary trauma.

CHALLENGES

Though it is evident that case managers play a crucial role in serving people who have been trafficked, in many settings they are still perceived as ancillary and or secondary to mental health practitioners. Mental health practitioners are often perceived (socially and legally) as the centralized practitioner that holds responsibility for the care of the client. Although this is effective in some environments, it may impede on the case manager's ability to centralize and coordinate services. Because of the education and degree that is required from case managers, they often lack the necessity leverage to manage and sustain long-lasting change.

Complex Case

Overview (for all scenarios)

Cynthia O. grew up in Tacloban, Leyte, a provincial city in the Philippines. Tacloban is somewhat industrial, housing the factories for Coca Cola and many garment factories as part of its Philippine Economic Zone. However, much of it remains rooted in agricultural production. Since it is outside of the National Capital Region of the country, it is considered a "province" and therefore does not have all the resources available that one would find in an urban center. While it is rapidly developing, it is an economically stable region that is precarious because of its geographic location in the middle of what geologists and meteorologists call the "Typhoon Corridor." Being on this pathway means that it is just a matter of time until they will experience severe natural disaster. The region has some notable colleges and vocational opportunities for education. It has a population of about 240,000 persons.

Cynthia is the oldest of five siblings. Although she is only 10 months older than her brother, she has always had a bulk of the responsibilities to help with the family, but it has always been like this so she doesn't mind or complain. Cynthia is 16 years old and in her last year of mandatory education (public high school). Her siblings are 15 (male), 13 (male), 10 (male), and 5 (female). Her parents own a small bakery and they make a modest income, although her mother often must take in laundry to make ends meet. Since there is a lot of work in the bakery, Cynthia often must wake up at 3 or 4 in the morning to help with the baking. Sometimes she is asked to help with the laundry, but rarely. Many times, she must also help watch the other children. This makes Cynthia late for school or sometimes she misses school completely. Her parents try to make sure she doesn't because they want her to finish school, but it cannot always be helped.

Cynthia is of average height and is very slim. She is attractive and often mistaken for younger/older than her age. She is very outgoing and has a positive attitude. Their neighbors always comment on how lucky her parents are for having such a good *manang* (oldest sister). Cynthia has no history of health problems and has reached all her developmental milestones. Because of her family responsibilities, she is not able to participate in many after-school activities but whenever she can, she likes to play volleyball. For the same reason, she also does not hang out with classmates or have very many friends. Cynthia has never had a boyfriend nor does she have any close male friends. Teachers and peers describe Cynthia as being well liked, helpful, and friendly.

Cynthia's father gets injured helping his brother on their small farm during harvest. Because of his injury, he cannot lift heavy objects and this limits his work in the bakery. To help the family, Cynthia drops out of school. She takes over her father's baking duties and the running of the bakery almost completely because her mother's time is now split between taking care of her father and taking in laundry. For about six months, the family is able to survive. However, her younger sister is afflicted by dengue and her hospital bills push the family to the edge. Luckily, the Cruz family, one

(Continued)

(Continued)

of the families that her mother does laundry for is looking for another maid and her mother suggests that Cynthia can take the job. Cynthia does not want to do so, but the hospital will not release her sister until the bills are paid. The Cruz family agrees to pay the hospital bills as an advance on Cynthia's pay and within the week Cynthia moves in with them. She must work long hours and because she lives in the home, it is not uncommon for the wife of the household to wake her up to do things. For the first year of her employment, Cynthia does not see any money because in addition to "working off" her sister's hospital bill, she is also working off her daily expenses, which her employers keep a detailed list of, such as soap and food. Cynthia has no choice in the matter as the family purchases these items and Cynthia is responsible for "paying" for her share of them.

The Cruz family business is growing and they decide to move to Manila. They have lots of family in the national capital and are planning to live with Mr. Palma's parents. They will not be bringing Cynthia with them. They give her the equivalent of $100 U.S. dollars for her work and Cynthia returns home. Although her parents are very disappointed that she must now look for work, they are happy she has stopped working for the Cruz family because they were not paying her well and she could not contribute a lot to the family. Her father has never been able to work full time since his injury and they are relying on her help. Cynthia is able to find a job waitressing in a local tourist restaurant.

Current Situation:

Cynthia continues to look for work in her community but it is very difficult. She returns to Manila twice, trying to find work with people she met when she was there the first time, but there is very little available. On her third trip to Manila, she is approached by another woman who says that a club is recruiting girls to dance in Japan, but that they must first "train" in a bar in downtown Manila. Cynthia does not want to do this, but it is the only job that she can find. She feels a lot of responsibility to help her family and pressure to provide financial support.

CALL TO ACTION: COORDINATION, COMMUNICATION, CASE MANAGEMENT

The importance of intensive case management cannot be overemphasized. As this chapter has demonstrated, the role of the case manager is crucial to the healing and recovery process. Moreover, it is key in terms of successful reintegration, and when applicable, successful repatriation should trafficked persons choose to return to their countries of origin. On a micro scale, intensive case management is coordinating the ecosystems of trafficked persons. If we were to magnify this work to mezzo or even macro levels, we could see intensive case management as microcosm of larger movements for collective impact groups. Consultant groups such as Deloitte (2015) and academic institutions such as the Stanford Center for Social Innovation suggest that the next step in the fight against trafficking and modern-day slavery be to bring together groups for "collective impact." Collective impact brings together likely and unlikely stakeholders to the issue from a variety of perspectives for the express purpose of solving social problems. Based on an ecological systems model, it is easy to imagine all these systems as those that case managers are already balancing in their work with individuals who are trafficked. Taken to the next level, case managers are the experts who can already identify and coordinate needs on an intimate level and who will be able to lead such initiatives in regional and global arenas.

DISCUSSION QUESTIONS

1. What is the role of the case managers in your organization? What are their main duties? How would this be different if they were working with individuals who have been trafficked?

2. What kind of training do you suggest case managers need?

3. What are the challenges of intensive case management?

4. How would you suggest intensive case managers deal with large caseloads?

5. How would you suggest beginning or joining a collective impact project in the city you are in? Does one exist already?

CHALLENGE

Contact a local trafficking organization in your city. Ask them for a list of needs that their case managers have identified are important for the clients that they serve. Have an event, contact friends, or use social media to do a "drive" of those items that are needed by the agency. Make your donation!

CHAPTER 6

Trauma-Focused Cognitive Behavioral Therapy

Annalisa Enrile, Gabrielle Aquino, and Charisma De Los Reyes

Chapter Objectives

1. Readers will be able to construct cognitive behavioral-therapy through a trauma-informed lens.

2. Readers will be able to recognize the benefits of trauma-focused cognitive behavioral-therapy in helping individuals who have been trafficked and/or enslaved.

3. Readers will establish an awareness of effective approaches in implementing cognitive behavioral therapy.

4. Readers will apply methods to assess a client, create a treatment plan, and track progress.

5. Reader will recommend solutions to challenges raised by trauma-focused cognitive behavior.

I wasn't always a subject matter expert for CSEC victims. I started as a social worker at an emergency center for the county. It was there that I met and handled my first cases like Jennifer. She was 15 years old and in our group home. Jennifer was of mixed ethnicity—Mexican and African American. She grew up in Sacramento where her father was not present and her mother was homeless and drug addicted. Once she had Jennifer, they were in and out of many homes. The first time Jennifer was molested was when she was 9 years old. By the time she was 11 years old, she was being commercially sexually exploited by one of her mother's boyfriends. Jennifer was brought in by law enforcement, who had caught her in a hotel room being sexually assaulted while her supposed "boyfriend" (i.e., pimp) waited in a parked car.

(Continued)

(Continued)

Jennifer was upset about being caught and being here, but she was also hopeless. She said things to me like, "This is all I know how to do. I've been supporting myself since I was 11. No one cares about me. I'm just a ho. I'm damaged goods." I couldn't blame her for being upset. I also felt anger toward her parents and her family who were supposed to keep her protected and safe but didn't.

I thought, "How was I supposed to change her mind?" She sat in front of me, obstinate, stubbornly repeating everything that had ever been told to her. Despite this, she was a survivor. But, how could I help her see that?

It took everything to hold myself back and not just tell her she was strong, that she was bigger than this. . . . This needed to come from her. She needed to see that despite and in spite of all the ugliness, she is still standing, standing and not defeated. I had to force myself from just telling her to take back her power and her truth—that no one could own this but her. It was so hard for me to watch her go through her pain, but I also knew this was the only way; she had to be the one to reclaim her strength. I could not do it for her.

First, I really needed to listen to all the trauma that lay underneath the words of anger and self-hate. Then, I had to gently challenge her dysfunctional thoughts and beliefs about herself. We were at an emergency shelter so I wasn't going to have a lot of time to work with her, but I had to make sure we started to reset her frame of mind. This is the good thing about trauma-focused cognitive behavioral therapy: It can work fast. I didn't have to go too deep with her, I just had to start the foundation toward stabilization into her next placement, helping her to feel psychologically and emotionally safe enough not to run.

As she spoke, I heard recurring themes of disempowerment. I helped point out that she was exploited, that people took advantage of her vulnerabilities particularly as a child. As she continued to speak, I asked her to really think about the "choices" she was forced to make and the quality of those choices. Were they really good choices, or were they more like the lesser of two evils or even things she felt she had to do? Often, the girls I encounter don't even recognize the exploitation, let alone the victimization, because of the stigma attached to commercial sex. But, it is trauma, and she had to see that to start to gain control.

We went around and around. She vacillated between a range of emotions and sentiments. She kept saying, "Look no one cares about me. I ain't got no one." Nothing I said could convince her otherwise. Finally, I took a deep breath and then put a piece of paper on the table between us. "Here," I said, "let's make a list. I want you to write down everyone you feel safe with." She chewed on the edge of the pen and made no move to write. "Do you feel safe with Olivia?" I asked, naming her case worker. She nodded reluctantly. "Then write her name down." She slowly wrote O-L-I-V-I-A. Then she followed it with another name. And another. And another.

After a few minutes, she looked up at me and for the first time, she made eye contact. "I have people," she said with surprise.

I saw the aha moment had arrived. "Yes," I told her, "you have people."

—Charisma De Los Reyes

Trauma-focused cognitive behavioral therapy (TFCBT) is one of the most oft-cited evidence-based models of practice that has shown to be efficacious in a number of different mental health areas and the most promising for individuals who have been trafficked (Clawson, Grace, & Salomon, 2008). The complexity of working with this population includes the persistent and often complex trauma experiences endured by those who have been trafficked. This trauma has the capacity to impact the way they think, the way they connect to others, the way they think about themselves, and ultimately their well-being. Trauma-focused cognitive behavioral therapy (TFCBT), when applied appropriately, can be a strong tool in the recovery process of trafficking victims. The therapeutic aspects of the counseling relationship coupled with the goals of cognitive restructuring is extremely helpful in the healing process. This chapter will clarify what TFCBT is, how to implement it, and how to address possible challenges when using it with this population.

DEFINING TRAUMA-FOCUSED COGNITIVE BEHAVIORAL THERAPY

Cognitive behavioral therapy is a form of psychotherapy that examines the relationship between an individual's thoughts, feelings, and actions or behaviors. It is based on the premise that one thing is powerful enough to influence their feelings and in turn, their behaviors. Often, a trafficking situation not only contains physical abuse but also emotional and psychological—preying on the way that people think. Paranoia, feelings of helplessness, thoughts of being threatened—all these ideas may last long after someone has been freed. Practitioners assist clients with identifying irrational thoughts that lead to destructive behavior. One of the main components of cognitive behavioral therapy is the assumption that clients have irrational beliefs that influence how they behave. The practitioner's goal is to help the client identify the negative beliefs and modify them so they could produce healthier behaviors.

Practitioners may view victims of trafficking and victims of domestic violence in a similar manner. This is also similar to how practitioners would treat a victim of sexual assault since many of the experiences parallel that of trafficking. For instance, the same cycles of violence and power that exist with domestic violence are also present in trafficking relationships. It is not unheard of for traffickers to use romance, praise, or appeasement to keep victims in place and then revert to abuse. Even the neurobiological effects of domestic violence are similar for those who experience trafficking because both are forms of trauma. Research shows that trauma impacts the development of the amygdala in the brain (Anda et al., 2006; Chemtob & Carlson, 2004; Creeden et al., 2008). The amygdala is a brain structure that is responsible for the autonomic response individuals have when in situations of fear (Cozolino, 2010). Trauma also alters the prefrontal cortex of individuals, which is responsible for the executive control and decision-making in individuals. After a traumatic experience, both the amygdala and the prefrontal cortex experience a rupture in development. The underdevelopment of these brain structures impacts the mental well-being in the same way for both victims of domestic violence and of trafficking. This is expressed by impulsive decision-making, impaired emotional regulation, and limited ability to self-soothe. Based on what we know about domestic violence, a trauma-informed framework is necessary and can be applied to individuals who have been trafficked. However, one caveat is that victims of trafficking should also be treated as if they were victims of sexual assault because of the feelings of powerlessness and worthlessness that they may also experience, which may differ from domestic violence. These types of comparisons (to domestic violence and sexual assault victims) are helpful because they can provide practitioners with a starting point for how to approach and help those who are trafficked. Further, in lieu of evidence-based practices, it is helpful to know what interventions have worked with similar populations or similar traumas.

As mentioned in chapter 4, having a trauma-informed care approach is essential to working with individuals who have experienced trafficking. First and foremost, the practitioner must understand that implementing a trauma-informed care approach modifies the trauma-focused cognitive behavioral therapy curriculum. It changes the language because this framework allows the client to tell his or her story. This change is necessary to meet the client where he or she is. For example, standard cognitive behavioral therapy typically prompts practitioners to ask clients, "What's *wrong* with you?" On the other hand, with a trauma-informed care lens, practitioners are advised to ask, "What *happened* to you?" focusing on the empowerment of the client. There is an active attempt to not pathologizing or starting from a point of dysfunction.

Research shows that CBT is the most effective treatment for individuals who have PTSD (Cahill & Rauch, 2003; Cardoso & Fong, 2010). CBT is also very effective with individuals who have anxiety and depression (Gearing, Hoagwood, Lee, & Schwalbe, 2013). This intervention helps decrease symptoms of depression. CBT helps identify distorted thoughts that affect behavior. It not only targets the behavior but it also examines the thought process of the individual who has PTSD, depression, or anxiety. CBT provides interventions that identify distorted thoughts that provoke symptoms of PTSD, depression, or anxiety. CBT intends to distinguish maladaptive thoughts and modify them to thoughts that empower the individual. Again, the belief is that the changing of thoughts of individuals will influence behavioral change. For example, a woman who was attacked at a park tends to avoid the location because she has PTSD and negative thoughts that she would get attacked again. The woman could also be fearful to leave her home because of the trauma from the attack. CBT would target her fear of being attacked again and help her change the automatic thoughts. The use of CBT in this scenario will empower the woman to overcome her situation so she could live a life without fear again. There is also research in neuroscience that suggests cognitive restructuring helps modify the neural pathways of the individual (Cozolino, 2010). Furthermore, this specific intervention takes into consideration the cultural background of the client. Hodge (2014) states that cognitive behavioral therapy is more effective with clients because some cultures are not congruent with the modalities of Western talk therapy. For example, one individual from Thailand utilized Buddhist practices like chants and mindfulness to help her overcome the trauma she has experienced. These chants gave her a sense of spirituality that allowed her to move forward from the horrific experiences she endured. When she would have flashbacks of men raping her, she would use chants or prayers to help soothe her anxiety. This was more helpful to her than explaining or discussing what happened with her or having a therapist work with her to understand subconscious motivations or defense mechanisms, as might occur within traditional modalities of talk therapy. Also, there are many cultures where it is difficult to talk about adversity or where they may feel things such as self-blame or even shame at dishonoring their family or community by further talking about it. For those with cultural taboos against "therapy," cognitive behavioral methods work well because it is highly structured and may not feel as invasive. This is not to say that this type of intervention will not get individuals to open up or have insights. On the contrary, some of the concrete exercises will do just that, especially since most will happen on the client's timeline and with them being able to have enough room for reflection.

IMPLEMENTING TRAUMA-FOCUSED COGNITIVE BEHAVIORAL THERAPY

Assessment for Diagnosis

Assessment and intake is important to CBT. The initial intake interview provides the background information of the client that will set the foundation for the rest of the intervention. Remember, CBT is very context specific so the more information the better. Practitioners must be open to actively listen because this will help guide the questions during the session. This portion is also an opportunity to begin building rapport with the client. It is important to build trust and connect with the client because this will help guide the practitioner with his or her primary evaluation and will provide insight on any treatment history. Knowing an individual's cognitive level is necessary before treatment because a minimum threshold must be met. There is a minimum cognitive threshold that clients must meet for cognitive behavioral therapy to be the best fit for them. In other words, they have to have enough cognitive ability to participate. Clients with significant cognitive impairment may not benefit from this type of treatment. For this reason, young children or those who have extenuating circumstances such as traumatic brain injury (TBI) are not capable of participating in TFCBT. The practitioner should also assess the home environment because the intervention requires homework and other at-home exercises for the individual. If their home environment is not optimal, the practitioner should know so that they can take this into account when assigning homework. Home environments that may be problematic are not detrimental to CBT, but they must be considered by the practitioner to make the necessary allowances. Intake interviews also help decide which practitioners available are a best fit for the client's individualized needs. Specifically, clients and practitioners need to be optimally matched for treatment compatibility based on things such as temperament, scope of practice, and knowledge base. Most essential to the relationship is that both the practitioner and the client feel comfortable with one another. This is crucial for individuals who have been trafficked because the relationship should not trigger any feelings of threat or power differentials that might mimic the situation they were just removed from or escaped. Additionally, assessments are important because they establish the baseline of cognitive ability for the clients as well as a starting point for the work to begin.

The steps of TFCBT typically proceed in this sequence: assessment for cognitive ability, biopsychosocial assessment, assessment tools for diagnosis, creation of treatment plan, psychoeducation about trauma (previously explained in chapter 4), cognitive restructuring, exposure therapy, review of automatic thoughts, and positive affirmations. The purpose of a diagnosis is to help guide the treatment plan for the individual (Hepworth, Rooney, Rooney, & Strom-Gottfried, 2012). It is recommended to create the treatment plan with the client to ensure that she or he has ownership for her or his progress. After establishing the treatment plan, the practitioner proceeds with the intervention. It is imperative to be aware of cultural factors when working with the individual.

The practitioner must administer a thorough biopsychosocial-spiritual assessment before proceeding with any treatment and must remember to let the client tell his or her story. The practitioner's main role here is to listen to the story of the client because what the client shares will guide questions that could help with the assessment. While having a checklist of questions may be intrusive for clients, it is also important to have a reminder of what to learn and what areas to explore about. This assessment will help evaluate important factors, such as language barriers, cultural beliefs, perceptions on therapy, and social support, that may help support treatment. Hutchinson (2013b) suggests that the following information should be included in the biopsychosocial-spiritual assessment: general description of individual, presenting problem, family composition and background, educational background, medical and developmental history, psychological functioning and background, social activities, faith background, current and past physical and economic environment, access to basic life necessities, other psychosocial factors, individual's strengths, and access to resources. Below are examples of areas to cover for each dimension of the assessment.

A thorough biopsychosocial-spiritual assessment should also take into account the circumstances that may have led to the individual being vulnerable to or being trafficked. Many times, a victim may not want to talk about the details of their actual experience once they were enslaved or exploited, but they will usually emphasize the events leading up to their being trafficked. They will also spend time discussing how they were able to escape their situation or how they were rescued or freed. The latter is extremely important to the empower process of this intervention because it may help determine how much control the individual feels they may or may not have in their

Table 6.1 CBT Dimensions

Dimension	Example
Biological	Last medical checkup
	History of health issues
	Accidents
	Sleep patterns
Psychological	History of trauma
	History of mental illness
	Stressors in life
	Deaths in life
Social	Social support
	Ethnic background
	Socioeconomic status
	Access to services
Spiritual	Faith background
	Values
	People you look up to
	Core beliefs

current situation. The biopsychosocial-spiritual assessment can also provide the practitioner with insight on how the individual copes with adverse situations as well as their role in societal networks (including family, community, and other groups). Further, this type of assessment is the best way to gain an understanding on any particular values or cultural perspectives the individual who was trafficked may have. The assessment is crucial so it is advised that practitioners make sure their questions are thorough and open-ended enough to provide a wide interpretation and room for a variety of answers. Whenever the practitioner may suspect or perhaps not even know if the client is correctly interpreting the question, or if the practitioner suspects that there is more to an answer, they should gently but firmly press the issue or ask the question from another angle to obtain the most complete response possible.

Following the biopsychosocial-spiritual assessment, assessment for diagnosis should be facilitated. We will provide the tool for diagnosing PTSD because it is one of the common diagnoses for victims of trafficking. There are tools that could be utilized to assess both youth and adults for trauma and PTSD (Cohen, Kliethermes, Mannarino, & Murray, 2012). One example of a tool for assessment is the UCLA PTSD Index. The UCLA PTSD Index is one of the most widely used tools for assessing symptoms of trauma (Cloitre et al., 2009). The UCLA PTSD Index is a 48-item interview that evaluates the individual's exposure to different traumatic events (Briggs et al., 2013). Categories of trauma in this index include loss or separations, circumscribed, and chronic or repeated trauma (Briggs et al., 2013). There are also different assessments depending on the age of the individual. For instance, the PTSD Index for children asks specific questions about their experiences using the language of this age group such as

- "Did you feel what you saw was disgusting and gross?"
- "Did you run around or act like you were very upset?"
- "I feel grouchy, angry, or mad."

To view the full assessment tool for children, adolescents, and adults, please see: tdg.ucla .edu/sites/default/files/UCLA_PTSD_Reaction_Index_Flyer.pdf or ptsd.va.gov/professional/ assessment/child/ucla_child_reaction_dsm-5.asp.

Treatment Plan and Intervention

After assessing for diagnosis, the practitioner uses that data to help guide the treatment plan for the individual. The treatment plan includes the intervention used to help the individual reach his or her goals. CBT is an intervention that targets the dysfunctional beliefs and thoughts of individuals in hopes to alter his or her behavior and emotional state. It focuses on the relationship between thoughts and behaviors (National Alliance on Mental Illness [NAMI], 2012). The goal of CBT is to modify maladaptive behaviors into healthy behaviors. It is a task-orientated type of therapy that requires time and collaboration between the practitioner and client (NAMI, 2012). One type of CBT is trauma-focused CBT. Research suggests that trauma-focused CBT is one of the interventions practitioners typically utilize with individuals who have experienced complex trauma, which includes individuals who have endured trafficking (Cohen, Kliethermes, Mannarino, & Murray, 2012; Cardoso & Fong, 2010; Johnson, 2012).

CBT is a combination of two components: cognitive restructuring and behavioral modification. There are several factors of cognitive restructuring: negative automatic thoughts, irrational beliefs, hot cognitions, core beliefs, and Socratic questioning. Negative automatic thoughts are organic cognitions that are related to negative emotions and questionable behaviors. According to NAMI (2012), there are different types of negative thoughts, which are shown on the table below.

Table 6.2   Different types of negative automatic thoughts

Type of Negative Automatic Thoughts	Example
Personalizing	He really loves me.
Overgeneralizing	He knows everyone and has connections everywhere. I can't escape. I have no choice.
Emotional Reasoning	He is watching me wherever I go, I feel it.
"Should" Statements	I should have known better than to talk back to my trafficker.
All-or-nothing Thinking	I have to make $500 to make him or her happy. He will leave me if I don't do this.
Fortune Telling	The police will take me back to the trafficker, I know it.
Mind-reading	He is going to hurt my family if I don't agree. My family is going to hate me for being like this.
Catastrophising	This is the worst thing that has ever happened to me.

Identifying negative automatic thoughts are a challenge because individuals are so accustomed to their style of thinking and are committed to their perceptions. For instance, a victim of trafficking who was in a juvenile camp in California for prostitution and another nonviolent crime shared she feels safe being in camp rather than in the "outs" because her trafficker has access to her entire life. This is a type of negative thought that overgeneralizes the power of the trafficker. Another example of automatic negative thoughts is what held Maria from Mexico captive as a sex slave for several years. Her captor said that he would hurt her family if she ever tried to escape from his home. When her captor would leave his house, she was left behind. She had thoughts of trying to escape but then she would remember that he would hurt her family if she ever left. She stopped trying to escape after several attempts because of her negative thoughts through mind-reading. She did not want him to hurt her family.

Below are examples of Socratic questions that practitioners could use when in session with their clients and a worksheet that practitioners commonly use to help their clients identify these negative automatic thoughts. This worksheet could be used in two ways: in session (client with practitioner) or as homework (practitioner sends it home with client, instructs client to complete it during the week, and they discuss it at next session).

Table 6.3   Examples of Socratic Questioning

	Questions
1	Could you give me an example?
2	Is there any evidence that this is not true?
3	Let me see if I understand you correctly. Are you saying that . . . ?
4	Could you explain that further?
5	What leads you to think this is true?
6	How could we find out whether that is true?
7	What's the worst that could happen?
8	What is an alternative way of seeing this?
9	Have you always felt this way?
10	Who made up this rule? Where did it come from?

Table 6.4   Worksheet to help identify negative automatic thoughts

Automatic Thought Record			
Situation	**Automatic Thoughts**	**Feelings**	**Behavior**

In addition, irrational beliefs are rules or assumptions that influence our behavior. The rules could be unreasonable and unrealistic. For example, in sex trafficking, victims tend to feel more connected to their trafficker because that is the only relationship in their life. This relationship then influences the irrational beliefs and meanings the victim has in his or her life. Similarly, in labor trafficking, the victims feel indebted to their trafficker. They might see their trafficker as the same person who gave them an opportunity out of poverty or believe that the trafficker in some way protects them from worse harm. Neither of these examples assume there is a type of "Stockholm syndrome" occurring. Indeed, this would be an extreme response. Rather, we suggest that there may be some identification with the trafficker or cultural aspects that encourage feeling indebted to the traffickers (thereby making them stay in the situation or at the very least, not fight back). Practitioners must be aware of this connection between the victim and their trafficker because, most definitely, this dynamic influences the irrational beliefs of the client. One example of irrational beliefs that a victim of trafficking has is that they may believe their family will not accept her or him because they were sexually exploited. This was evident in Cynthia's situation from the complex case study. Cynthia was fearful of reuniting back with her family because of her experiences in the clubs. She was filled with shame and did not want to face her family because of the shame and guilt around her traumatic experiences. Another example is the individual who was trafficked may believe that she or he deserves this mistreatment and is a worthless human being due to intense manipulation. The individual goes through a process where his or her identity is stripped. The trafficker typically grooms the individual, making them feel powerless and hopeless. The trafficker uses power and control to strip the individual of his or her dignity and respect. Verbal, physical, emotional, and psychological abuse are persistently thrown at the trafficked individual and over time, this individual begins to slowly believe what the trafficker tells them. In Cynthia's case, the men who raped her in the bar and her pimps told her messages that she is worthless and deserves to be mistreated. Cynthia began to internalize these messages. Eventually, the trafficked individual's cognitions are restructured to believing the lies the traffickers throws at them. Of note are what is known as "hot thoughts" in cognitive therapy. These "hot thoughts" are persistent, negative thoughts that shape our behaviors and decisions. Because they are persistent, it is difficult for practitioners to reframe the experience, or even attribute negativity or blame where it should be directed toward. This makes TFCBT extremely challenging, especially if the individual refuses to let go of such hot thoughts.

After the client is educated about cognitive restructuring and the different aspects of it, the practitioner and the intervention moves forward to the next step: exposure therapy. Exposure therapy asks the client to remember details of the trauma he or she experienced to help decrease heightened feelings of anxiety around the trauma. This portion of treatment depends on what the client experienced. For example, if the client was physically punished in a certain room with no windows, the practitioner would then help the client imagine that. It is imperative that the practitioner does not retraumatize the client. The practitioner must assess if it is the proper time for exposure therapy. In Cynthia's situation, the practitioner must be aware and mindful of when she is ready to have exposure therapy around her experiences in the bar. The practitioner could ask questions such as, "Are you ready to try the exposure therapy out around the bar experiences?" or "Please let me know how comfortable you are talking about the details of your experiences in the bar." These questions will help assess Cynthia's comfort level and readiness to try this aspect of the intervention. It is also up to the client if they are ready to face his or her trauma. For clients who were trafficked, this could be imagining the trafficker selling or coercing the client. It could also be the perpetrators violating the client. The practitioner should periodically check in and assess the client during exposure therapy to evaluate if the client is able to handle the trauma. The practitioner and client can make up a sign or code word if the client feels uncomfortable and wants to stop the imaginative process.

When the practitioner checks in with the client during exposure therapy, the practitioner should ask the client directly what negative thoughts automatically arise. This will help the client identify the negative cognitions. The practitioner could then ask the client how to modify his or her thoughts. Reviewing the automatic negative thoughts during the session is important. The practitioner's goal is to help the client modify the negative beliefs, restructure the thoughts, and empower the client to take control of his or her thoughts. Reviewing the automatic negative thoughts helps remind and challenge the client to modify his or her negative cognitions.

The last key portion of CBT is positive affirmations. This tool should be used throughout treatment to help build confidence and rapport with the client. Typically, most victims of trafficking (especially those with depressive symptoms) display hopelessness. Positive affirmations help boost the self-esteem of the client. Positive affirmations can come in different modalities. The use of encouraging cards that could be distributed as often as one desires could help remind survivors of their progress. Verbal praises and gratitude activities could also be used to express positive affirmations to survivors. Acts of kindness such as giving a gift to survivors is another way to positively affirm survivors and their progress. There is also jewelry with positive phrases that could help spread positivity among survivors. Some necklaces say "fearless," "brave," "courage," and other empowering words that remind survivors of their strength and resilience. In a larger scale, positive affirmations could include a celebration night that honors survivors for their journeys. This could be a night at a sports event that honors or acknowledges women, a benefit concert, or an art show that portrays the journey and courage of survivors. For Cynthia's situation from the complex case, the use of positive affirmations through weekly reminders in one-on-one counseling sessions will help her build her identity as a survivor of trafficking instead of an individual who is filled with shame and defined by the trauma she's experienced. The use of encouraging cards also provides a great visual reminder of Cynthia's identity.

PTSD: COMMON DIAGNOSIS WITH VICTIMS OF TRAFFICKING

Research shows that the common diagnosis for individuals who have survived sex trafficking is post-traumatic stress disorder (PTSD). The American Psychiatric Association describes several diagnostic criteria for PTSD. The individual must either have a direct experience with a traumatic event, witness the traumatic event in person, hear about a traumatic event that occurred to someone close to him or her, or have extreme exposure to aversive details of a traumatic event such as war or rape (American Psychiatric Association, 2013). The individual who has PTSD experiences significant levels of distress. To be clinically diagnosed with PTSD, four behavioral categories must be met. These categories include reexperiencing, avoidance, negative cognitions and mood, and arousal (American Psychological Association, 2013).

CURRENT ISSUES WITH COGNITIVE BEHAVIORAL THERAPY

One limitation with cognitive behavioral therapy is that there has to be a minimum threshold of ability for the practitioner to use it with her or his client. The client should be able to articulate his or her thoughts. There should also be an understanding of language because it requires a lot of dialogue between the client and the practitioner. Language barriers are another limitation. If the practitioner does not speak the main language of the client, there will be a gap in services since this intervention requires verbal communication between the practitioner and client.

There is also a limited track record of the utilization of CBT with victims of trafficking even though it has shown the most promise. This speaks to the lack of research evaluation for interventions used for survivors of trafficking. This intervention seems like the best match because of the similar symptoms displayed by survivors of trafficking and individuals with PTSD, anxiety, or depression. This intervention is most used with individuals with PTSD, anxiety, or depression as a result of sexual abuse and not specifically trafficking trauma. However, similar symptoms between both populations suggests that trauma-focused cognitive behavioral therapy is promising for trafficking survivors. Moreover, cognitive behavioral therapy relies heavily on homework and worksheets. This may not be culturally relevant for those whose primary language is not English, unless the worksheets are translated into the native language of the trafficking survivor. Translating the intervention to the primary language of the client may be needed to yield the best results. However, there is a lack of translating services able to convert homework and worksheets for practitioners.

Complex Case

Overview (for all scenarios)

Cynthia O. grew up in Tacloban, Leyte, a provincial city in the Philippines. Tacloban is somewhat industrial, housing the factories for Coca Cola and many garment factories as part of its Philippine Economic Zone. However, much of it remains rooted in agricultural production. Since it is outside of the National Capital Region of the country, it is considered a "province" and therefore does not have all the resources available that one would find in an urban center. While it is rapidly developing, it is an economically stable region that is precarious because of its geographic location in the middle of what geologists and meteorologists call the "Typhoon Corridor." Being on this pathway means that it is just a matter of time until they will experience severe natural disaster. The region has some notable colleges and vocational opportunities for education. It has a population of about 240,000 persons.

Cynthia is the oldest of five siblings. Although she is only 10 months older than her brother, she has always had a bulk of the responsibilities to help with the family, but it has always been like this so she doesn't mind or complain. Cynthia is 16 years old and in her last year of mandatory education (public high school). Her siblings are 15 (male), 13 (male), 10 (male), and 5 (female). Her parents own a small bakery and they make a modest income, although her mother often must take in laundry to make ends meet. Since there is a lot of work in the bakery, Cynthia often must wake up at 3 or 4 in the morning to help with the baking. Sometimes she is asked to help with the laundry, but rarely. Many times, she must also help watch the other children. This makes Cynthia late for school or sometimes she misses school completely. Her parents try to make sure she doesn't because they want her to finish school, but it cannot always be helped.

Cynthia is of average height and is very slim. She is attractive and often mistaken for younger/older than her age. She is very outgoing and has a positive attitude. Their neighbors always comment on how lucky her parents are for having such a good *manang* (oldest sister). Cynthia has no history of health problems and has reached all her developmental milestones. Because of her family responsibilities, she is not able to participate in many after-school activities, but whenever she can, she likes to play volleyball. For the same reason, she also does not hang out with classmates or have very many friends. Cynthia has never had a boyfriend nor does she have any close male friends. Teachers and peers describe Cynthia as being well liked, helpful, and friendly.

Despite the fact that Cynthia has a lot of responsibilities at home, she continues to persevere in school and is able to graduate with a high school diploma. With the help of a well-meaning teacher, she is able to apply to a local college and also get a scholarship. She majors in physical education and she has dreams of becoming a teacher so that she could help youth like her teacher helped her. Her parents are very proud of her. She continues to help them at home in the bakery and with her siblings.

Cynthia finishes college with an undergraduate degree in education and specialization in kinesiology. She has just finished taking her licensure exam. Before she is able to get her scores, her parents are killed in a car accident. Her younger brothers are in college and her little sister is still in school. Cynthia does not know what to do but returns home to take care of everything. They don't have enough money to pay for the funeral expenses so Cynthia borrows money from a money lender. The loan has a high interest rate but they are able to at least pay for the funeral and keep the bakery open. For a while, Cynthia and one of her brothers keep the bakery open, but it is difficult to keep up with day-to-day expenses as well as the loan payments. Someone suggests to that Cynthia might want to migrate to another country to work. She decides to migrate to Singapore and work as a maid. The cost of the migration (about $3,500 U.S. dollars) is high but the family decides to take out

(Continued)

(Continued)

another loan so that they can afford it. Cynthia goes through an employment agency and is placed with a family as a maid and nanny.

Cynthia begins working for a Singaporan family in their home. They have two children and Cynthia is asked to sleep on the floor of their room. For a year, things are fine and Cynthia is able to send enough money home to keep the bills paid. Often, her boss hits on her, often groping her "accidentally" or walking in on her as she is in the shower or changing. She is uncomfortable but does not want to jeopardize her job. One night, her boss tries to kiss her and she pushes him away. Outraged, he tells his wife that Cynthia tried to seduce him and his wife throws her out. She gives Cynthia the opportunity to get her things, but without her employers' sponsorship, Cynthia is now considered "undocumented." She is worried about her family and how to support them, but she is determined to find a way to make it work. While looking for a way to make money, Cynthia lives on the street, avoiding authorities.

Cynthia generally hangs out at Lucky Plaza. This is a hub for the Filipino community in Singapore. At the very least, she is able to usually find someone who will share food with her. On her eighth night on the streets, she is approached and befriended by another Filipina. Her name is JoVee, and she invites her to stay with her and her roommates. JoVee is a dancer at a club that is hiring. She suggests that Cynthia apply. She lets Cynthia borrow clothing from her because JoVee tells her that she must look "sexy" to get the job. Cynthia does not want to tell her parents what happened and she also does not know how to get home. She applies for the job, though she is uncomfortable with the situation. The manager, Patrick, explains to her that she would be "sexy" dancing to music on stage. Patrick showed her what they had to wear, which was skimpy lingerie. He also told her that she would get paid the equivalent of $300 U.S. dollars a week as well as 25% of the cost of alcohol if she can get the customers to buy drinks for her. Cynthia gets the job and is told that she has to live with JoVee and the other women. The "manager" of the club pays the rent but charges the women for utilities and "incidentals." She is also asked to turn her passport over so that he could get her papers in order.

On her first night, she is told that after midnight she must strip. Cynthia is not comfortable with this, but JoVee tells her she really has not choice. She suggests that Cynthia try to have some drinks with men so that she can "relax." Cynthia is also uncomfortable with this, but she thinks about the money she can make. When a customer buys them a drink, they are charged triple the price, and even though she is not used to drinking alcohol, she is willing to try. Cynthia decides to make the best of the situation and quickly gets someone to buy her a drink. He is from Australia and in Singapore for business. He buys her three shots of tequila and she must drink all three. By the time she leaves the table to get ready to dance, she is drunk and having difficulty getting the man to keep his hands to himself. Cynthia gets on stage and dances with about 12–15 other girls in the small area. JoVee dances next to her. There is not a lot of room for a real routine, they are just kind of swaying to the music. Some of the girls are more suggestive than the others.

After their first set, Patrick grabs Cynthia off the stage and tells her she is requested to have more drinks with the Australian. She says she does not want to because she does not want to drink anymore. Patrick roughly tells her she has no choice and sits her down at the table. He stands close to the table, watching her, and she takes four more shots. By this time, the man with her is constantly trying to touch her. She pushes him away and tries to move away from him. When the man leaves to use the bathroom, Cynthia notices Patrick sends JoVee to the table, and when JoVee gets there, she tells Cynthia in Filipino that she should stop pushing the man away and that they both will "get in trouble" if the customer complains. The customer returns, talks to Patrick, and then grabs Cynthia by the arm and says, "Let's go cherry girl. I just paid a pretty price for you and I'm going to see if you are worth it." Cynthia does not know what is happening and she struggles to get free. Before she leaves, JoVee says to her, "Don't struggle, it will be easier."

Cynthia is taken to a room next to the club. The room has a single bed, a chair, and a nightstand. The man takes off his clothes and dimly, Cynthia knows what is going to happen but she knows there is no way out of the room. She fights him and tries to get away, even though the door is locked. Cynthia cries and tells him to stop, but he rapes her anyway. When he is finished, he gets dressed and leaves her in the room, bleeding and crying. Five minutes later, Patrick comes in and throws a damp towel at her. He tells her to clean herself up because he has another man who is "interested" in her. He tells her to "act like a virgin still." That night, Cynthia is raped by four men.

Patrick never gives Cynthia her papers. He threatens to call authorities to deport her if she tries to run away. She continues to live with six or seven other girls in the small apartment. Later, she finds out that JoVee is a recruiter for Patrick, and she regularly goes to the mall to find girls like Cynthia who are in trouble. Cynthia dances and serves drinks at the bar for about 10 hours a day, and she is also forced to sexually service five–eight men a night. It's been over a year and she hasn't been able to call her family in the Philippines. She has gotten pregnant twice and been forced to have abortions. Cynthia uses drugs and drinks daily to cope "dull her pain." She doesn't get any pay because it all goes to her "debt" that she "owes" Patrick. Her goal is to be able to pay off her debt so that she can get paid even though she knows now that the dancers "pay" the bar a third of what they get as a "house fee" for letting them dance there. One night, she is raped by someone who is extremely violent; he beats her and she is taken to the hospital. At the hospital, she is approached by a Filipina social nurse, Grace, who asks her if she needs help.

Current Situation:

Currently, Cynthia is waiting to leave for the Philippines. When she was in the hospital, it was discovered that she had no papers; Patrick had never filed them. Because of this, Cynthia was given one

(Continued)

(Continued)

week before being deported back to the Philippines. Cynthia was not allowed to stay in the apartment and Patrick barred her from returning to the club. She checked into a cheap hotel with the last of her savings. Grace, whom she met in the hospital, has stayed in touch with her and has helped her get things ready to go home, even buying some things for her to bring with her for her family back home. Cynthia is nervous about going back to the Philippines and does not know what to tell her family. She is very tearful and despondent. Cynthia has a hard time sleeping and feels anxiety, especially when she is in large crowds or out in public.

CALL TO ACTION: REFRAME AND RETHINK

TF–CBT is a Western intervention that requires a certain level of critical thinking and communication skills. This intervention could be transferred into other cultures but little research has been done to assess its effectiveness. One way to modify TF–CBT so it is culturally competent for Eastern cultures is by having trainings on the cultural values for different cultures. For example, many Eastern cultures value the family unit over independence and independent success. Understanding this concept can help the practitioner understand the framework of a survivor who is from that culture. This allows the treatment process between the practitioner and survivor to look different from the typical TF–CBT session because the thought process and motives of behavior for the survivor is different. Learning different modalities to help understand different cultures and how their values and traditions affect one's behaviors is needed to ensure that TF–CBT is an effective tool for working with survivors of trafficking.

It is important to target people before they enter into the cycle of maladaptive thoughts that keep them chained to fear, worry, and doubt. Spreading awareness of what trafficking is, what it looks like in its different forms, and the power of advocacy equips communities to become advocates for themselves. Thoughts have power to influence one's behavior, which is why it is important to focus on education awareness around trafficking, trauma, stress, and healthy ways to cope with these adversities. Taking the time to engage in conversations before the cycle of distorted thoughts emerge is pivotal for empowering all communities, intergenerationally.

DISCUSSION QUESTIONS

1. What are ways to help promote cultural competency through the use of TF–CBT with victims of trafficking?

2. What settings is TF–CBT best utilized in?

3. What are some modifications that could be used to best meet the needs of victims of trafficking?

4. How can the practitioner build rapport with a victim of trafficking?

5. Do you think that trafficking victims have to be addressed through trauma-specific perspectives or are there universal responses to trauma, no matter what type is experienced?

CHALLENGE

Californians for Safety and Justice is a nonprofit project of the Tides Center that works with crime survivors, policy makers, community leaders, law enforcement, professionals, educators, and crime prevention experts. They launched Crime Survivors for Safety and Justice to help crime survivors join together and advocate for new safety priorities. They view the trauma experienced by survivors as universal and particular to what they experienced. One of their largest activities is to bring awareness to communities about the Victims of Crime Act (VOCA). Download their toolkit to learn more about VOCA: http://www.safeandjust.org/resources/2016-05-victims-of-crime-act -and-the-need-for-advocacy.

- To take the challenge to another level: Read the toolkit and practice at least one of their recommended advocacy action.

CHAPTER 7

Survivor Advocate Model

Annalisa Enrile and Gabrielle Aquino

(Continued)

about your family; you keep them together no matter what. Her parents did not believe her because they could not face the damage it would do to their family. They left her unprotected. Instead, when she was 15, they sent her to work in Pattaya, a city in Thailand known for sex tourism. They didn't send her to be sexually exploited, but they wanted her to earn money and help the family. Joy went because it was the only time her parents praised her and she wanted to please them and make them proud since they had always made her feel she was a "disobedient" daughter. This was her chance to make it up to them. Joy found herself on Walking Street, a congested alleyway filled with smoky bars and victims of sex trafficking. At first, Joy didn't know what Walking Street was, but she soon found out when a woman who promised to help her find work turned out to be a lady-pimp. Joy was lured to a bar and raped and beaten by its owners until they started to charge customers to do the same to her. She was slapped, hit, peed on, and mocked by the men who sexually abused her.

As Joy told us her story, I marveled at the way she smiled for us through her tears. I didn't know what to say and it seemed little to reach out to her and grip her hand. It was as if I could put all my outrage in our clasp of hands. She told us this story as she led our small group to Walking Street. I turned to her and said, "Joy, let someone else take us, you don't have to go back there." I could see the street now, and it filled me with equal parts despair and outrage on Joy's behalf.

I could feel her straighten her spine and sigh. She looked at me with equal parts bravery and sadness and said, "I never left."

"You did leave," I insisted. "Why return again and again? Isn't it too hard?"

She replied, "It's painful, yes, but I need to go and you need to come with me because we have to tell these women that there is a better life for them. I survived it and they can, too."

I pulled back for a moment and insisted, "There has to be other ways."

Joy smiled broader, her tears only a trace on her face now. "Come on, you all came here to make change. Let's break some chains. Even for one, it's worth it."

—Gabrielle Aquino

INTRODUCTION

The road from victim to survivor is one that is wrought with challenges and can often feel like one step forward and a hundred steps back. Despite this, those able to travel that road embody resilience and strength. Trafficking survivors are unique because of the multiple intersections that impact their well-being all under the context of literally being treated as an object, or a thing, by another human being or entity. We have already discussed the systems they must navigate in the recovery process such as law enforcement, the legal system, welfare and social services, and health care to name a few. Now, imagine each of these systems as layers they must go through to get out of their situation and claim survivorship. The intersecting layers include almost all these domains—psychological, emotional, social, spiritual, political, and physical—that are constant barriers to recovery. Of all the models that we include in this text, the survivor advocate model is founded concretely in empowerment theory and draws directly from the feminist principles of "the personal is political," solidarity, and sisterhood (Mohanty, 2004).

As practitioners, we must acknowledge that our clients cannot become advocates for themselves until their basic needs are met. Practitioners must take into consideration Maslow's hierarchy of needs, a concept used to describe the needs of individuals for survival. The priority needs are physiological needs, which include meeting basic needs for human survival (Poston, 2009). These needs include food, water, warmth, and rest. Practitioners must stabilize the victims of trafficking first before they can become advocates. For instance, one survivor told us, "I want to help my sisters who are still being sold, but I still have to worry about how to put food on the table for me and my family. Some days, I just survive" (Alvarez, personal communication, 2016). After their physiological needs are met, their safety needs should be met. This means that victims must feel safe and secure in their environment. For many people who experience trafficking, this is a tall order since it is usually what was most compromised for them. Even when they were not physically threatened or coerced into trafficking, their families or loved ones may have been. In either instance, their sense of safety and what it means to be safe would have been severely eroded. The practitioner may feel that they have to constantly assure the individual of their safety or help them relax their hypervigilance. Another way that might be effective is to remind them of how far they have come and to help them learn lessons from their adversity. For instance, someone who was subject to the whims of their abuser has probably learned to read microexpressions to anticipate a bad mood or explosion (Sciortino, personal communication, 2016). The third level of Maslow's hierarchy of needs is the necessity of belonging and love. This means that victims should feel a sense of belonging on a social level. This could occur when victims are able to build relationships with others. It may also be gained when they are able to express themselves emotionally or allow themselves to be vulnerable with others. This may present differently for victims of trauma who typically exhibit fear and feelings of distrust because of their experiences. The fourth level is esteem needs. Victims must feel a sense of self-respect before proceeding to the final level of self-actualization. Victims of trafficking must feel confident in themselves. The final level of Maslow's hierarchy of needs is self-actualization. This is the level where victims become advocates for themselves. Victims of trafficking will not enter the self-actualization level until all levels of needs are met: physiological, safety, belongingness and love, and esteem needs. Until then, they cannot realize the power in their voice and their potential to change society with their voice. Unlike some stages in psychological models, it is important to realize that Maslow's hierarchy of needs is not stable. Indeed, it is something that people experience in different ways depending on their context. For this reason, it is important to remind those who have been trafficked that their journey to survivor status is not a constant forward motion so that they do not become disheartened or discouraged when they have difficult times.

Pimp Appropriation

"To really be successful pimping you have to understand Maslow's Hierarchy of Human Needs; players call it the "Pyramid." These are the opening words of R.J. Martin (2009), who provides the lesson of "How to be a pimp: Using Maslow's hierarchy of needs to make the most money." This missive details how the prospective "pimp" or the "pimp" who is just starting out can benefit from understanding the basic psychology that Maslow's hierarchy presents and using that to take advantage of girls' vulnerabilities. Martin goes through each of the levels of Maslow's pyramid and points out where there is a possible entry point for the "pimp" to either procure or keep a girl that he wants to sexually exploit (or what he refers to as "turning out" or "turning tricks").

Martin begins with explaining that the bottom of the pyramid is composed of physiological needs such as food and water and that there is very little that a "'pimp" can provide that is not already being provided, unless you are talking about countries that are not the United States (though, thankfully, he doesn't extrapolate to the global). The next level of the pyramid are the needs for safety and security. He states that this might be where "pimps" may find their first opportunity to assert their influence on a vulnerable girl by promising that they can "protect her," though he cautions that this is more effective when combined with addressing needs from the next two levels of the pyramid: love and belonging (level 3), or self-esteem (level 4). For example, he encourages "pimps" to fall in love with the girl and explain that part of that love is the ability to "protect" her. Martin talks about the high probability that the girl has been abused or traumatized and so this would make falling in "love" even more of a possibility if someone is offering it to her. He does create a loophole for those who might not feel that they can fall in love by pointing out that one doesn't have to *really* fall in love; they do have the option to just pretend . . . if they are a good enough actor. The ability to create the illusion of love is what Martin titles the "Elevated Pimp" and what he feels they should aspire to.

Martin points out that once you get a girl to believe that you love them, she will do almost anything for you, but that if you really want her to be motivated to make money, you should also make her feel like she is respected. He suggests "showing her some sympathy" and that she will feel good about that. Another suggestion is to understand how she might have been treated or abused in childhood and to use that to help provide more self-esteem; again, it does not have to be genuine, just believable.

Finally, he ends at the top of the pyramid, which is the level of self-actualization. As Martin explains, it is a difficult level to master, but it is possible if you are able to convince the girl that there is a way "out of the life." For instance, the "pimp" might tell her that he knows she is better than what she is doing but that she is only doing it temporarily; you will eventually have enough to support her. He suggests that one may supplement any of the levels with sweet talk and endearments to bind her to him. Once he has found a way to meet their needs, especially in levels 3 and 4, he can then count on her to do anything for him (or "them"), including recruiting other women and girls. In fact, he says that if one does it correctly, she may even feel like a "business partner."

Martin's application of Maslow's hierarchy of need is an example of the complex and even educated nature of perpetrator and traffickers' ability to manipulate their victims. It is not a simple "street game" or Hollywood depiction (Sterry, 2009). Traffickers make a lot of money through the sexual exploitation of women and children and therefore, they treat it seriously—like a business in a rational, even scientific framework. Much of the research in this area demonstrates that "successful" traffickers (often referred to as "pimps") are those who understand the "wants" and "needs" of women and then try to meet them or use the vulnerability of them to threaten or coerce them (Williamson & Cluse-Tolar, 2002). For example, they may use the needs of their victims against them. One woman we interviewed stated, "I wanted to go back to my family, but my pimp said that they didn't love me; they were lying. No one loved me like he did. No one understood what I went through like he did. He respected me and I loved him. I couldn't just leave him" (Oliveros, personal communication, 2015). Therefore, those that are doing anti-trafficking work should not underestimate the cunning of traffickers or their ability to take our own tools for their advantage. This type of misappropriation is detrimental to providing strategic and timely services, and should be accounted for to better address the concrete circumstances our client's face.

SURVIVOR ADVOCATE MODEL

The survivor advocate model functions from the empowerment perspective. Empowerment is defined as the process by which individuals and groups gain power, access to resources, and control their own lives to reach their personal and collective aspirations (Hutchinson, 2013a). The way this is accomplished is through critical consciousness and effective action. Empowerment theory utilizes a strengths perspective and suggests that individuals have the power and self-determination to achieve any dream they set their mind to if given the opportunity. Hur (2006) suggests that critical consciousness rising involves three cognitive components: identification with similar others, reducing self-blame for past events, and a sense of personal freedom. The key is to understand the role of the environment in how they were exploited and to be able to identify those systems of exploitation either on a personal level or on a political one. Ideally, an individual would see the interplay of both.

The survivor advocate model views the survivor of trafficking as the expert in his or her life experience. This means that while they are able to access help, they themselves are the ones who know what they need to heal and to thrive. This is key especially in trafficking situations where individuals had so many decisions and control over their own lives taken away from them. For instance, in many trafficking situations, victims are not allowed to leave work or stop even when they are physically unable to continue. Their very natural cues are overridden by their trafficker. Similarly, they are unable to make decisions that most people take for granted, such as what to eat and or who they are allowed to talk to. For this reason, one of the most empowering things for those who are trafficked are to be able to make the most basic decisions concerning their own life and the lives of their family if they are able to be with them. Since survivors are viewed from a strengths-based and empowerment viewpoint, real "healing" and "recovery" is derived from the ability to access resources and make decisions for themselves. Practitioners are taught to assess the strengths of the trafficking survivor and incorporate those assets into their treatment plan. Again, these strengths are those that are defined by the individual. Practitioners may see strengths and they may even point them out during the intervention, but until the individual themselves can internalize and name those aspects as strengths of their own accord, it will not be effective or the individual may not believe them. This is acceptable. In fact, it is consistent with low self-esteem, lack of a feeling of self-efficacy and mastery that most trafficked victims feel. Helping them reframe their feelings is a big part of this intervention. The goal of survivor advocate model is to move individuals from being victims of trafficking to survivors of trafficking. Survivors become the authors of their own narratives, instead of having their stories written for them by their traffickers or as interpreted through others, however well-meaning they may be.

Empowerment is the increase of the personal power of the oppressed and the ability to help overturn oppression for a community (Turner & Maschi, 2015). The survivor advocate model seeks to empower survivors of trafficking into becoming their own advocates. There are key factors of this model, which include: trauma-informed care, a change of their personal narrative, a social justice orientation, a strengths-based perspective, and culturally informed practice.

These factors are essential for this model because they help guide the treatment plan for the survivor. As shown in the previous chapters, it is essential to operate from a trauma-informed care perspective when working with survivors of trafficking. Having a

Figure 7.1   Factors of Survivor Advocate Model

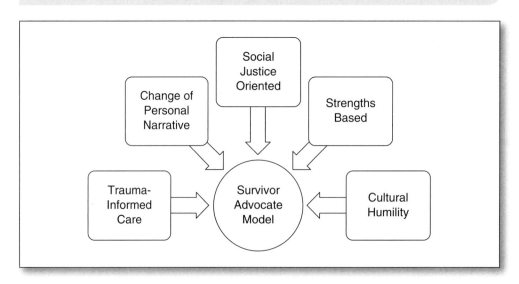

trauma-informed lens allows clinicians to prevent any retraumatization for the survivor of trafficking. Practitioners should be sensitive to the needs of the survivors to ensure that they do not unintentionally harm them. Practitioners should be warned, however, that they cannot control for every circumstance. For instance, as individuals come forward with their story, they may get a question from media or during a conference panel or even in a research interview that may be triggering. The best practitioners can do is to prepare them for coping with these types of situations.

Changing their personal narrative is a powerful tool that could be used for survivors because it helps them find their own personal voice. Changing the personal narrative of survivors helps them redefine their experiences. It also helps them become the masters of their own personal lives, instead of being enslaved to their traffickers' desires for them. Survivors of trafficking could also find that being the narrator of their own stories is very healing. A personal narrative is a story somebody shares that is true and from experience. Narrative therapy or narrative exposure therapy might also be useful where individuals are encouraged to tell the story from their perspectives and the practitioner can listen for any retelling or reframing. It is also an opportunity to understand how individuals have constructed or given meaning to their reality (Madigan, 2011). They may also discuss their trauma in several ways. Practitioners should encourage them to focus on the intersection of traumatic events. For instance, not just the abuse that was perpetrated on them, but also instances where they may have felt helpless or even forced to abuse others (Johnson, 2012). Individuals share their personal experiences through personal narratives, often narrating in the first person point of view. Personal narratives are a key component in survivor advocate model because their traffickers have always written the narratives of victims for them. Their traffickers dictate the trajectory of their lives. In survivorship, it is important for survivors of trafficking to become the authors of their personal life stories. This gives the power back to the survivor of trafficking and takes the power away from the trafficker. Using this intervention with Cynthia from the complex case study will empower her to become the author of her own story. Hopefully with this intervention, Cynthia realizes that she has advocated for herself to combat her feelings of shame toward her family. Even if it does not, it allows her the ability to name her own challenges as well as identify what she feels made her vulnerable to her situation. Furthermore, the practitioner will get a clearer idea of what Cynthia identifies as helping her get out of the situation.

Practitioners should have a social justice orientation when working together with survivors of trafficking. This perspective has two main premises: (1) the belief that all members of society should have equal rights, and (2) the belief that all members of society should have equal access to resources. Having a social justice orientation helps ensure that survivors of trafficking are provided with access to resources that will allow them to reintegrate back into society in a successful manner. The social justice lens helps practitioners recognize the dignity and worth of each survivor. Having equal rights is needed for survivors of trafficking. In addition, using the strengths of survivors of trafficking helps boost their self-esteem and confidence.

Strengths perspective allows survivors to view what they are capable of doing. Strengths perspective challenges social work's old ways of approaching clients from being problem focused to solution focused in terms of working as a collaborative team (Oko, 2006).

Operating from a strengths perspective empowers the client and professional to work together drawing from the client's strengths and not deficiencies (Oko, 2006). It is beneficial for practitioners to view survivors of trafficking from a strengths framework because it asserts that they believe in the worth and value of the survivor. Practitioners also believe that the survivors are resilient and capable of overcoming their adversities. The practitioner who is working with Cynthia should recognize that Cynthia's strengths include that she stood up for herself and her beliefs and she was did not succumb to the pressure of the club owner, despite being beaten by him.

Last, it is of utmost importance for clinicians to use a culturally informed practice lens because survivors of trafficking come from different backgrounds and may experience trauma in different ways. Culturally informed practice is the practice of not having assumptions about a certain culture. This encourages the practitioner to listen to the story and voice of the survivor, instead of assuming that they know their experiences and background. The practitioner recognizes that they do not know everything about the survivor of trafficking and empowers the survivor to educate the practitioner about his or her experiences. This also serves to redistribute the power within the relationship and emphasizes to the survivor that they are not only in charge of their own narrative but that they serve in a role of expertise within their experience that only they can articulate and share. The practitioner becomes more respectful toward the survivor of trafficking through this practice and the survivor themselves also become more trusting of their own expertise. For Cynthia's scenario from the complex case study, she shared that she was ashamed to go back to her family after the owner of the club punched her and left her in the alley. She was ashamed of what happened to her. These feelings of shame could be stemmed from cultural factors that include saving face for the family and having the responsibility to bring money back to the family. Cynthia had no money after she left the club because she refused to behave provocatively for the club.

EXAMPLES OF SURVIVOR ADVOCATE MODELS

Coalition to Abolish Slavery and Trafficking–Los Angeles (CAST–LA) Model

The Coalition to Abolish Slavery and Trafficking (CAST) in Los Angeles was one of the first organizations to operationalize a survivor advocate model as an intervention with their survivors of trafficking. CAST began in 1998 after a sweatshop case where 72 Thai garment workers were trafficked and kept in slavery for 8 years (CAST–LA, n.d.) Since then, CAST has provided comprehensive long-term services though three main components: social services, legal services, and outreach and training. Social services include meeting the basic needs of the client (food and shelter), job training, educational and vocational skills training, mental health services, and intensive case management. Ninety percent of CAST clients are able to establish basic needs security (CAST–LA, n.d.). In addition, it is apparent that safety and legal issues come up during the recovery of trafficking survivors. CAST's legal services work with numerous attorneys and organizations that ensure that survivors of trafficking are protected and advocated for. Legal services include preparation for criminal trials, help for filing T-visas, access to refugee benefits, obtaining child custody, and obtaining restraining orders against traffickers. All CAST's programming promotes the self-sufficiency and self-esteem of trafficking survivors (Shigekane, 2007).

In 2003, CAST launched a Survivor Advisory Caucus as part of its empowerment programing. This is a three-tier program that seeks to stabilize clients and empower them to become survivors. Each of the Tiers focuses on services and training. Tier one is direct case management. Tier two is the development stage, where survivors are not in crisis but they still need services. Last, tier three is the Survivor Advocacy Caucus. This caucus includes former clients who are trafficking survivors to mentor current clients. Mentors of the program assist clients to build their own capacity until they can become a part of the caucus as well but as leaders. Trafficking survivors are given leadership trainings on how to become effective advocates. Since its founding, the Survivor Advocacy Caucus works mainly on policy advocacy and public awareness campaigns. Each year, they identify key areas where they want to focus on to help abolish trafficking. Their track record is exemplary. They were instrumental in the passage of several key policies such as the Trafficking Victims Protection Reauthorization Act (TVPRA)(Polaris Project) in 2008 and the California Transparency in Supply Chains Act in 2010 (U.S. Department of State, 2010c). The activities of the Survivor Advocacy Caucus span the continuum of raising awareness of the issues by sharing their own stories, talking to media, and testifying to government officials as they support the passage of policies.

In 2011, CAST launched the National Survivor Network (NSN) to create connections between survivors of human trafficking. This is significant as it is the first network of its kind to bring together survivors internationally. As of 2016, there were 24 countries participating in the NSN with almost every state in the United States represented (NSN, 2017). The ability to bring survivors together is essential in the empowerment process. The dialogue they are able to engage provides much needed space not just to share their stories and their perspectives, but to heal and feel like they are an integral part in the fight against trafficking as well as in being able to gain measures of justice for what happened to them (CAST, personal communication, 2014).

Girls Educational and Mentoring Services (GEMS) Curriculum

Girls Educational and Mentoring Services (GEMS) is an organization based in New York State that was specifically designed in 1998 to work with girls who are survivors of commercial sexual exploitation and domestic trafficking between the ages of 12 and 24. Since then, GEMS has become the foremost nationally recognized organization and service provider for youth exploited in these ways. Their mission is to empower girls and young women who are survivors of trafficking through short-term and crisis care, court advocacy, transitional and supportive housing, and holistic case management. Their founder, Rachel Lloyd, a survivor herself, has worked to make sure that survivors are able to be heard in their own words. In fact, GEMS utilizes the perspective of survivors and brings them into agency leadership to run programs, set strategy, and be the face of the organization. GEMS utilizes the Victim Survivor Leader (VSL) curriculum to support girls and young women to create their own personal narrative change. Their curriculum is trauma-informed, gender-responsive, and developmentally grounded. This curriculum is also used in their Survivor Leadership Institute (SLI) and Resource Center. This is a platform of support for survivors of trafficking and CSEC victims. Survivors' leadership skills are developed and the resource center provides them with opportunities to excel in areas where their strengths lie. This resource center provides trainings, workshops, and materials to help survivors achieve their goals.

Also, their youth leadership provides a medium for peer support. GEMS believe that the only way to ensure a member's successful recovery from the commercial sex industry is to address the entire person and their mentoring and group component is the core of their youth leadership program. Each participant is matched with a staff member who they meet with once a week. Each staff member has been trained to provide peer counseling. The most rewarding outcome to this mentoring partnership is the relationship among the participants and an understanding and definition of the ways the commercial sex industry divides women. Through the mutual aid and support provided in this program, participants repair old wounds and learn specific skills to build genuine and rewarding relationships with other women.

One curriculum that GEMS created is called *The Survivor's Guide to Leaving* (White & Lloyd, 2014). This curriculum is for individuals who are in "the life" or "the game." This guide is for those who are commercially sexually exploited. Survivors of commercial sexual exploitation and trafficking who are members of GEMS created this book. Most of these survivors are now staff members at GEMS. Advocates at GEMS also contributed to the creation of this book. This guidebook has five sections: "Understanding What's Happened to You," "Taking Steps to Leave the Life," "Starting Over," "Adjusting to Something New," and "Continuing Your Journey." This guide's presentation is similar to that of a slam book, which appears like a journal that young kids write in, so those in "the life" can easily hide it.

This book is written for survivors by survivors. The authors recognized that everybody has a different journey and no two journeys are alike. There are commonalities, but each person experiences this journey differently. It is used to encourage those in the life, so they don't feel alone. The book is not divided into a specific timeline or series of steps. It is up to the reader to go at the pace he or she desires. This book also aims to validate the feelings of victims of trafficking. GEMS encourage those "in the life" to get support or to find a "support person" throughout their journey. They recognize that individuals can't get out alone. The message of the text is that everybody needs someone they can trust and connect with. We will now discuss each section of the guide.

Understanding What's Happened to You

This section defines what commercial sexual exploitation of children is. It defines the situation of children and youth who trade sex in exchange for something of value to them. It explains what trafficking is and demystifies the myth that trafficking only happens in developing countries, because trafficking also happens in the United States. Feelings of confusion about these traumatic experiences are then explored. The authors help identify with those feelings and confirm them. The end of the section contains 12 core beliefs that are used to reverse the negative messages that victims of trafficking constantly hear into positive ones filled with hope. The purpose of this section is to empower victims of trafficking by educating them about the cruel realities of trafficking. This awareness helps create bonds among victims of trafficking and encourages them by letting them know that they are not alone and that they can fight against negative messaging and thinking.

12 Beliefs

We Believe That

1. Commercial sexual exploitation and trafficking is something that happened *to me*; it is not *who I am*.

2. I'm not a criminal for being commercially sexually exploited and trafficked. I am a victim.

3. Acknowledging my victimization doesn't take away my strength and doesn't mean I will be a victim forever.

4. Although I may have made some choices based on my circumstances, I did not choose to be abused, violated, sold, or treated as less than human.

5. I *deserve* to be treated with respect and given services, love, and support.

6. The real criminals are pimps and johns who buy and sell us, and they need to be held accountable.

7. I deserve to live a life free of exploitation, danger, abuse, and pain.

8. I can heal and recover from my experiences and go on to live a happy and healthy life. I am not forever "damaged" or broken.

9. I am not defined by my experiences or my past. I am more than what has happened to me.

10. I am beautiful, strong, unique, and valuable. I have different talents and gifts inside of me, even if I don't see them yet.

11. I deserve to be loved, to have kindness, peace, and happiness in my life.

12. I am a survivor.

Source: White, Sheila and Rachel Lloyd. 2014. The Survivor's Guide to Leaving. New York: Girls Education and Mentoring Services. 30.

Taking Steps to Leave the Life

This portion of the book gives tangible steps on helping victims of trafficking leave the life. It first recognizes that leaving the life is a big and daunting task that often is repeated. In fact, it often takes seven–nine times before the leaving is permanent. This recognition affirms the feelings that the reader may be experiencing when contemplating if she or he should leave the life. This section also includes the National Trafficking Resources Center's hotline number and text number. This section dives into the different reasons why victims of trafficking don't get out of the life. It speaks about the intense fear toward traffickers that victims experience. This section also provides guidelines on creating a safety plan and tips to decrease risk of getting caught by their traffickers such as deleting text messages and having code names. Last, the authors share common reactions and emotions that arise right after victims of trafficking leave the life.

Breathing and Relaxing

This book also provides tools to help victims of trafficking cope with their emotions. This section teaches victims of trafficking on how to navigate the flood of emotions they are experiencing. These tools are supposed to help calm the nerves of trafficking, decrease the anxieties, and minimize the fears they experience, all of which are symptoms related to trauma exposure. Each page has a different tool that comes with a description and a prompt on how to apply it. There are two categories for tools: (1) breathing and relaxing, and (2) grounding. Each category includes different examples shown in the table below.

Figure 7.2   Coping Strategies

Category	Examples
Breathing and Relaxing	Take three deep breathes
	Breathe in positivity, breathe out worries
Grounding	Listen to music
	Stretch and/or clench your hands

Starting Over

The purpose of this section is to help victims of trafficking transition and reintegrate back into society. This section recognizes the difficulties victims of trafficking endure when starting their life again. It provides the reader with encouragement that there is help and hope for them. The book then breaks down the available resources to help victims of trafficking find a job, find a safe place to live, and enroll in programs necessary for basic needs. Last, this section recognizes the complex emotions victims of trafficking experience when leaving the life and recommends them to speak to somebody they trust or a counselor or therapist.

Adjusting to Something New

Transition and change is hard. This section identifies the possible challenges victims of trafficking experience after they have settled in their new homes. These challenges include experiencing symptoms of depression, feeling bored, wanting to go back to the life, and intense fear. This section also provides the reader with skills to help identify triggers that lead them to make choices such as running back to their trafficker. One tip this section gives is called "H.A.L.T.–STOP." This acronym means Hungry, Angry, Lonely, and Tired. The readers may experience times for "relapse" when they have a strong desire to go back into the life. The authors identify that the most common time readers have these thoughts is when they are H.A.L.T. However, the point of the acronym is the second half: STOP. This tip encourages readers to STOP their way of negative thinking when they are H.A.L.T. so they don't think about running back to the life. Other experiences from survivors of trafficking are shared in this section. These stories are used to build connection with the victims of trafficking who just got out of the life.

Continuing Your Journey

This last section positively affirms the reader through a collection of personal creations produced by survivors of trafficking. This intends to empower victims of trafficking who just got out of the life by creating solidarity in their experiences. The section includes poetry and essays with the following titles: survivor, fighter, faith, sisterhood, leader, and growth. There is also a final page full of quotes from survivors of trafficking that encourages the readers to persevere in their journey. Last, the end of this guide includes a list of survivor-led organizations and programs that the readers could reach out to for support.

CHALLENGES

There are several challenges with the survivor advocate model. The first challenge is voyeurism. When survivors of sex trafficking share their stories and explicitly state the details of their multiple rapes, individuals who are voyeurists tend to be turned on by the details. Also, there is a high chance that this model is triggering for survivors of trafficking because they have to face the truth and reality of their experiences. It can be traumatic. Last, there is a disparity between who should be administering this intervention. The disparity is if clinicians with expertise apply this intervention or on the other hand, clinicians with experience (who are survivors themselves) implement it. There are pros and cons for who should be administering the intervention. The clinician with expertise is trained in the intervention; however, he or she lacks experience with working with survivors of trafficking. On the other hand, the survivor who has experienced this trauma is not trained on how to implement the intervention.

Trafficking survivors also experience internal and external bases of chaos and terror. For survivors to become more than conquerors of their narrative, their internal trauma must be addressed. This process is ongoing. Survivors could experience flashbacks and nightmares—all symptoms of complex and persistent trauma. The mental health needs of trafficking survivors should be met through consistent one-on-one trauma informed sessions and support groups. Support groups should be consistent. These types of groups are similar to process groups, where survivors share their experiences and offer positive affirmations and encouragement to one another. A sense of trust and confidentiality is expected in support groups. Confidentiality is crucial in support groups because it is for the safety of the survivors. Pimps and traffickers have the ability to find the survivors to get them back into "the life." This is why confidentiality is necessary so survivors do not fear for their lives and are safe at their shelters.

Complex Case

Overview (for all scenarios)

Cynthia O. grew up in Tacloban, Leyte, a provincial city in the Philippines. Tacloban is somewhat industrial, housing the factories for Coca Cola and many garment factories as part of its Philippine Economic Zone. However, much of it remains rooted in agricultural production. Since it is outside of the National Capital Region of the country, it is considered a "province" and therefore does not have all the resources available that one would find in an urban center. While it is rapidly developing, it is an economically stable region that is precarious because of its geographic location in the middle of what geologists and meteorologists call the "Typhoon Corridor." Being on this pathway means that it is just a matter of time until they will experience severe natural disaster. The region has some notable colleges and vocational opportunities for education. It has a population of about 240,000 persons.

Cynthia is the oldest of five siblings. Although she is only 10 months older than her brother, she has always had a bulk of the responsibilities to help with the family, but it has always been like this so she doesn't mind or complain. Cynthia is 16 years old and in her last year of mandatory education (public high school). Her siblings are 15 (male), 13 (male), 10 (male), and 5 (female). Her parents own a small bakery and they make a modest income, although her mother often must take in laundry to make ends meet. Since there is a lot of work in the bakery, Cynthia often must wake up at 3 or 4 in the morning to help with the baking. Sometimes she is asked to help with the laundry, but rarely. Many times, she must also help watch the other children. This makes Cynthia late for school or sometimes she misses school completely. Her parents try to make sure she doesn't because they want her to finish school, but it cannot always be helped.

Cynthia is of average height and is very slim. She is attractive and often mistaken for younger/ older than her age. She is very outgoing and has a positive attitude. Their neighbors always comment on how lucky her parents are for having such a good *manang* (oldest sister). Cynthia has no history of health problems and has reached all her developmental milestones. Because of her family responsibilities, she is not able to participate in many after-school activities, but whenever she can, she likes to play volleyball. For the same reason, she also does not hang out with classmates or have very many friends. Cynthia has never had a boyfriend nor does she have any close male friends. Teachers and peers describe Cynthia as being well liked, helpful, and friendly.

On November 8, 2013, Super Typhoon Yolanda (also known as Typhoon Haiyan), the strongest storm to ever hit land, struck the Philippines. The first place it hit was Eastern Samar, and then Leyte, where Cynthia and her family lived. The family was home when the typhoon began and they evacuated to a local public school. They thought they were safe, but the school quickly flooded, and the family was forced with everyone else to climb up to the roof of the building. Cynthia helped keep her younger sister safe when the water started rising, and she describes her panic as the water was rising. They stood on the roof for four hours while the storm and the winds raged around them. The family wasn't able to return home until a week later because of all the debris. The roads were closed, phone lines were down, and there was no electricity. Aid could barely reach the for almost two weeks. They were grateful that they did not lose any family members, especially since so many of their neighbors were not as lucky. They had nothing left of their home or any of their things. Because there was nothing left, her parents ask her to go to Manila to some distant relatives to find work. Cynthia does not want to leave her family alone, but she knows that she has to do whatever she can to help.

Cynthia arrives in Manila and finds her relatives. She has never met them and she has only been to the city twice before. Her "aunt" says that it is hard for them to take on an extra person in the household but that she can sleep on the couch. Cynthia spends three weeks applying for jobs but cannot find anyone to hire someone who does not even have a high school diploma. She is able to find a job in a local karaoke club where she applies as a waitress. When she shows up to work, the owner of the club tells her that she will be dancing. She doesn't want to, but he says he will fire her if she doesn't. She is given an outfit to wear that is tight and short and is told to get up on stage. She gets through two songs, and the owner tells her she can come off stage because someone wants to buy her a drink. Cynthia says no because she does not drink but again, he insists. A man buys her a drink, and while they are at the table, he puts his hand on her knee and tells her he wants to have sex with her. She is shocked and says "no." Cynthia runs away from the table and out the door. She doesn't care if she loses her job and decides to say that to the owner when she sees him follow her outside. Before she can say anything, the owner punches her in the face and slams her against the wall. He beats her and leaves her in the alley next to the club. Cynthia wakes up in pain but does not go to the hospital. She cannot afford it. She is too ashamed to return to her aunt's house, so she asks one of the other girls in the club if she could stay with her. She is kind and lets Cynthia stay with her while she heals.

CALL TO ACTION: NO JUSTICE, NO PEACE

The survivor advocate model empowers survivors of trafficking to share their narratives and promotes them to become leading activists to abolish slavery and trafficking. The process of becoming a survivor is the process of obtaining justice for themselves and their cases. Ultimately, their role as survivor advocates is to gain justice as a whole. It is these individuals who are leading and informing anti-trafficking movements. Trauma-informed care, a change of their personal narrative, a social justice orientation, a strengths-based perspective, and cultural humility are the main components of this model, but it is not as directive as it may seem. In fact, the journey is dialectical and sensitive. Many victims never become survivor advocates. In some cases, this could be because they just want to forget or put the trafficking experiences behind them. In other cases, it may be that they do not want to be defined or feel residual shame about what they experienced. Others may not want to be narrowly defined as having been someone who was trafficked. For whatever reason, this process of advocacy is not linear and varies from individual to individual. It is important for survivors of trafficking to have their basic needs met first before they can become advocates. There are different curriculums based on the survivor advocate model. However, it is evident that there should be more research facilitated for implementing survivor advocate model programs to assist survivors of trafficking.

DISCUSSION QUESTIONS

1. Which curriculum could you use in your agency?

2. How can you create training and curriculum for your agency that centers on survivor advocacy?

3. In what ways is survivor advocacy advantageous? In what ways is it negative?

4. What are possible triggers to watch out for as someone speaks out or advocates for legislation using their own personal experiences?

5. How do we plan for and mitigate retraumatization, or being triggered?

6. How do survivors and nonsurvivors work together? What are possible tensions and how to process through them?

CHALLENGE

Read a survivor narrative in your area of interest through the lens of your field or profession. How would your field or profession relate the experience of the survivor to be used as an example or training for your colleagues? Share the narrative with them, highlighting the points that are learning opportunities to further understand trafficking and modern-day slavery.

Interventions for Commercially Sexually Exploited Children (CSEC)

Chapter Objectives

1. Readers will develop an understanding of the scope and breadth of CSEC in the United States, within an international context.

2. Readers will discover the differences between CSEC populations and other populations that have been trafficked and/or enslaved.

3. Readers will review the four most common interventions used with this population.

4. Readers will evaluate what intervention and/or curriculum is the most appropriate for varying settings and communities.

5. Readers will validate what key principles are important at developing further curriculum to address this population.

I was a 22-year-old graduate student sitting in the home of a child who was currently under house arrest, charged with being a CSEC victim. I thanked Faith for being willing to speak with me about her experience and what led her to this life. I was working on writing a short article about the those who get trafficked so readers could better understand how diverse of an issue it was. While I was grateful for the interviews, the social work student part of me could not imagine that her family would welcome me—a young, white woman with little to no journalism credentials—into their home. But there I was, in Compton to discuss their daughter's experience. While I was grateful, I was worried that

(Continued)

(Continued)

they were forcing her to do this, like some strange scared straight program or even worse, some other type of reality show opportunity.

It turned out that Faith was more than willing to meet with me and tell me all about her life. For Faith, this was what she felt was the siren song to her experience; she would tell me her story and then she would close the book on it. Except that her last pimp was not in jail. Except that she still talked about him with reverence. Except that she called her exploiters "daddy" and it was obvious how much she loves them. Except that when she talked about "the life," she tried her best to make to sound "glamorous."

Faith described being in the life like it was an E! Channel reality show. She talked about getting dressed up and wearing what she called "costumes." There was a gleam in her eye when speaking about how dressed up and well cared for she could be at times. She talked about the men who abused her with an almost affection. What Faith did not talk about was the risk she was in. She skated over her various beatings like when she was thrown out of her pimp's car on to her front lawn. She didn't talk about how hard it was to walk home from school because she would have to walk by and defend herself against her old pimps. And, maybe she didn't talk about it because she never learned how she should have been treated: She should have been cared for by her parents, but instead her father left the family and her mother's boyfriends abused her (just as they abused her mother). Her mother fought with her more than she tried to take care of her. In fact, it was after one of these fights when Faith ran away that she became trafficked.

I left the interview stunned. Neither Faith nor I found any healing out of the process. I was over-whelmed, feeling like I could never know enough. These victims suffered not only years of abuse but also generations. They were failed by the very organizations and institutions that were supposed to help them and support them. As someone who would go onto represent and work for some of these same institutions, I knew that I had a long way to go to best serve this community. I've been in the field for a few years now, and as I continue to work in it, I still am reminded of Faith every day. A week after our interview, she cut off her ankle bracelet that monitored her house arrest and was picked up by a new pimp. I rack my brain, trying to understand if there was something that I could have done different that would have helped her not be retraumatized or return to her abusers. Thinking of her reminds me that I am no expert. I can never assume that I will know every way or best practice to work with this population. I only know that I can do my best to meet each child with authenticity and partnership . . . and care.

—Megan Healy

INTRODUCTION

Globally, the trafficking of children is growing exponentially. Children as young as 7 years old have been trafficked for sex and labor from countries such as Mexico, Honduras, El Salvador, Guatemala, Southeast Asia, and Eastern Europe (Albanese, 2013). According to the

Inter-Parliamentary Union and United Nations Office of Drugs and Crime (IPU & UNODC, 2009), children make up over 20% of all victims globally, but this number can fluctuate when we look at specific countries. For instance, in some parts of Africa, children compose the majority of trafficking victims and modern-day slaves. Age is a factor of future exploitation. For example, in Ethiopia, 20% of girls are sexually exploited before the age of 11 and continue to be until adulthood (Rafferty, 2013). Commercial sexual exploitation of children (CSEC), or domestic minor sex trafficking (DMST) as it refers to children who live in the United States (domestic borders), refers to children who are sexually exploited by having to engage in sex for the exchange of money, goods, shelter, and other types of things that may be deemed valuable or necessary. For the purposes of simplicity, we will be referring to this topic as CSEC. In the past ten years, there has been a rise in the awareness of the CSEC. Prior to this, the lack of knowledge was based on two main things: (1) that trafficking only occurred when global borders were crossed, and (2) the stigma that exists around prostitution and the idea of "choice." There have been significant shifts in public perception around this notion of *choice* as more research and awareness campaigns have brought the issue to light. Currently, this is also the area that has experienced significant growth in terms of legislation and intervention, in part, because of the U.S. institutions designed to address the protection of youth such as child welfare and juvenile justice. As we are aware, each of these institutions come with its own set of complicated procedures and perspectives. To offer the most applicable best practices in this area, we will cover those used domestically, but include global examples when available.

OVERVIEW OF CSEC

CSEC has been called a "health crisis" and "an epidemic." It is estimated that roughly 300,000 children are at risk. As with other types of trafficking, it is difficult to get a real handle on the number. It is believed that even this number is underestimated. For instance, when different, local initiatives and surveys have been launched, there has been higher than average reporting or counting of actual victims. The average age of children who are exploited is between 12–15 years old (Grace, Starck, Potenza, Kenney, & Sheetz, 2012). In Asia, most "cherry girls" (virgins or near virgins) are between these ages. Traffickers make some of their highest profits from "cherry girls" especially in areas where the "virgin cure" (the idea that having intercourse with a virgin cures illnesses) abound (Brown, 2000). Most children are deceived, manipulated, or forced into this type of exploitation. These methods indicate that there are complex and multilayered psychological, social, and economic aspects that also become important in addressing children who are domestically trafficked (Goldblatt Grace, 2009). Therefore, the interventions developed for CSEC must be sensitive and specific to the needs of this population.

Theoretically, though all children are vulnerable to being trafficked, girls are proportionally at risk, especially girls who have histories of childhood sexual abuse and trauma (Raphael, 2004; Norton-Hawk, 2002). However, the extent of boys who are sexually exploited is not as clear because of the shame that they may feel, which hinders disclosure or reporting. In a 2013 study, ECPAT USA found that in some cities, boys and transgender youth may constitute almost 50% of victims, but it has been difficult to measure prevalence (Friedman, 2013). Other factors that increase risk include environmental ones such as chronic poverty. Family life makes a large impact. For instance, family disruption and loss, parents who have substance addictions, and where girls have witnessed their mothers in domestic violence situations are red flags to be aware of. This may be due to the fact that girls who go through these types of experiences will have lower levels of self-esteem, self-worth, and mastery of developmental tasks, especially at school (Clawson, Dutch, Solomon, & Grace, 2009). There are any number of determinants that increase risk, but the most consistent is the experience of sexual abuse and trauma, especially victims of incest rape (Raphael, 2004). The younger a girl is when she experiences this trauma and/or becomes sexually exploited commercially, the more likely the two are interconnected (Lloyd, 2011). LGBTQ youth also constitute a disproportionate number of youth who are homeless and susceptible to being trafficked and exploited (40%). Many have been turned away or rejected from their families and once on the street will often engage in survival sex (Durso & Gates, 2012).

The majority of girls are recruited and subsequently controlled by traffickers and also other girls whom the trafficker has designated. There is a process that is important for us to understand; in other words, this type of exploitation does not *just* happen. This means that by being able to understand the process, we have more opportunities to intervene and prevent. Traffickers will usually begin with recruitment, which does include force and coercion but can also take the form of offering friendship or even romance. This takes the form of "gorilla" and "romeo" pimps, referring to pimps who force, threaten, and coerce versus those who use romance and emotional exploitation (de Chesnay, 2013). Past traumas particularly make girls vulnerable to the phenomenon of the "romeo pimp," which is when traffickers use the lure of love and relationships as a way to exploit girls (Lloyd, 2011). Once the girls are recruited, there is a period of "grooming" or "seasoning" where the trafficker makes the girl dependent on him and isolates her from her old life and social connections. By the end of this period, psychologically and physically, the girl may be dependent on the trafficker for almost every aspect of her life. She will believe whatever he tells her. She will then be "turned out," which is when the trafficker will commercially sexually exploit her (de Chesnay, 2013).

Since most of these children continue to go to school or are involved in other systems such as child welfare or juvenile justice, it is imperative that practitioners be able to identify, intervene, and hopefully take a part in the prevention and protection of this population. In Canada, a study revealed that 64% of women they had surveyed who were commercially sexually exploited had been involved in the child welfare system. In the United States, nationally the average is 68%, with some states such as Connecticut reporting as high a number as 98% of women who are sexually exploited have been involved in the child welfare system (Center for Missing and Exploited Children, n.d.; Connecticut Department of Children and Families, 2012). In fact, traffickers often target these systems as their main areas of recruitment (Grace et al., 2012). It is not uncommon to see traffickers waiting across the street from known group homes or even locked facilities, waiting for girls to come out. There have even been instances where social workers have found that traffickers have sent in another girl so that she can recruit from inside (De Los Reyes, personal communication, 2015).

The Language of CSEC

Sociologically, the understanding of youth culture is one of subculture—in other words, a subset or margin of mainstream social norms or mores. This seems to be the case considering the youth have their own ways of fashion, trends, and especially language. The youth vernacular does tend to borrow from other aspects of mainstream and (other) subcultures, but for the most part, they take these strands and make it their own—with slight variations. This may explain the similar phrases and usage of language whether youth are from urban, working-class areas or more affluent suburbs. To a broader extent, it may also be why the phenomenon of youth subculture transcends even race and gender. Though there are specialized niches, there is also a shared knowledge and experience expressed through language. Exploiters, taking advantage of this subculture, have introduced a whole new "dialect" of trafficking. This includes the adoption of "pimp" language popularized in media. We must be aware of this vocabulary, as one of the ways in which children continue to remain exploited is through a complex practice of isolation and specialized language. Traffickers and slavers assume, in fact, count on the fact, that service providers, advocates, law enforcement, and the public in general have no idea what the language of child sex trafficking is. And, thus, with no translation, people will remain in the dark about what may be happening right in front of them. A challenge is that the language does tend to change all the time, but there are some basic terms that we can learn to identify, which should be red flags to look for and be aware of. Organizations, training curriculums, and even basic trafficking 101 presentations should include this terminology.

From: Shared Hope International, sharedhope.org/the-problem/trafficking-terms/

Automatic—A term denoting the victim's "automatic" routine when her pimp is out of town, in jail, or otherwise not in direct contact with those he is prostituting. Victims are expected to comply with the rules and often do so out of fear of punishment or because they have been psychologically manipulated into a sense of loyalty or love. All money generated on "automatic" is turned over to the pimp. This money may be used to support his concession/phone account or to pay his bond if he's in jail.

Bottom—A female appointed by the trafficker/pimp to supervise the others and report rule violations. Operating as his "right hand," the Bottom may help instruct victims, collect money, book hotel rooms, post ads, or inflict punishments on other girls.

Branding—A tattoo or carving on a victim that indicates ownership by a trafficker/pimp/gang.

Brothel (AKA Cathouse or Whorehouse)—These establishments may be apartments, houses, trailers, or any facility where sex is sold on the premises. It could be in a rural area or nice

(Continued)

(Continued)

neighborhood. Most brothels have security measures to prevent attacks by other criminals or provide a warning if law enforcement is nearby. The security is two sided—to keep the women and children in, as well as robbers out. The places often are guarded (and open) 24 hours a day, but some have closing times in which the victims are locked in from the outside. Victims may be kept in this location for extended periods of time, or rotated to other locations every few days.

Caught A Case—A term that refers to when a pimp or victim has been arrested and charged with a crime.

Choosing Up—The process by which a different pimp takes "ownership" of a victim. Victims are instructed to keep their eyes on the ground at all times. According to traditional pimping rules, when a victim makes eye contact with another pimp (accidentally or on purpose), she is choosing him to be her pimp. If the original pimp wants the victim back, he must pay a fee to the new pimp. When this occurs, he will force the victim to work harder to replace the money lost in transaction. (See *Reckless Eyeballing*)

Circuit—A series of cities among which prostituted people are moved. One example would be the West Coast circuit of San Diego, Las Vegas, Portland, and the cities between. The term can also refer to a chain of states such as the "Minnesota pipeline" by which victims are moved through a series of locations from Minnesota to markets in New York.

Daddy—The term a pimp will often require his victim to call him.

Date—The exchange when prostitution takes place, or the activity of prostitution. A victim is said to be "with a date" or "dating."

Escort Service—An organization, operating chiefly via cell phone and the internet, which sends a victim to a buyer's location (an "outcall") or arranges for the buyer to come to a house or apartment (an "in-call"); this may be the workplace of a single woman or a small brothel. Some escort services are networked with others and can assemble large numbers of women for parties and conventions.

Exit Fee—The money a pimp will demand from a victim who is thinking about trying to leave. It will be an exorbitant sum, to discourage her from leaving. Most pimps never let their victims leave freely.

Family/Folks—The term used to describe the other individuals under the control of the same pimp. He plays the role of father (or "Daddy") while the group fulfills the need for a "family."

Finesse Pimp/Romeo Pimp—One who prides himself on controlling others primarily through psychological manipulation. Although he may shower his victims with affection and gifts (especially during the recruitment phase), the threat of violence is always present.

The Game/The Life—The subculture of prostitution, complete with rules, a hierarchy of authority, and language. Referring to the act of pimping as "the game" gives the illusion that it can be a fun and easy way to make money, when the reality is much harsher. Women and girls will say they've been "in the life" if they've been involved in prostitution for a while.

Gorilla (or Guerilla) Pimp—A pimp who controls his victims almost entirely through physical violence and force.

"John" (AKA Buyer or "Trick")—An individual who pays for or trades something of value for sexual acts.

Kiddie Stroll—An area known for prostitution that features younger victims.

Lot Lizard—Derogatory term for a person who is being prostituted at truck stops.

Madam—An older woman who manages a brothel, escort service, or other prostitution establishment. She may work alone or in collaboration with other traffickers.

Out of Pocket—The phrase describing when a victim is not under control of a pimp but working on a pimp-controlled track, leaving her vulnerable to threats, harassment, and violence to make her "choose" a pimp. This may also refer to a victim who is disobeying the pimp's rules.

Pimp Circle—When several pimps encircle a victim to intimidate through verbal and physical threats to discipline the victim or force her to choose up.

Quota—A set amount of money that a trafficking victim must make each night before she can come "home." Quotas are often set between $300 and $2,000. If the victim returns without meeting the quota, she is typically beaten and sent back out on the street to earn the rest. Quotas vary according to geographic region or local events.

Reckless Eyeballing—A term which refers to the act of looking around instead of keeping your eyes on the ground. Eyeballing is against the rules and could lead an untrained victim to "choose up" by mistake.

Renegade—A person involved in prostitution without a pimp.

Seasoning—A combination of psychological manipulation, intimidation, gang rape, sodomy, beatings, deprivation of food or sleep, isolation from friends or family and other sources of support, and threatening or holding hostage of a victim's children. Seasoning is designed to break down a victim's resistance and ensure compliance.

Squaring Up—Attempting to escape or exit prostitution.

Stable—A group of victims who are under the control of a single pimp.

(Continued)

(Continued)

Track (AKA Stroll or Blade)—An area of town known for prostitution activity. This can be the area around a group of strip clubs and pornography stores, or a particular stretch of street.

Trade Up/Trade Down—To move a victim like merchandise between pimps. A pimp may trade one girl for another or trade with some exchange of money.

Trick—Committing an act of prostitution (*verb*), or the person buying it (*noun*). A victim is said to be "turning a trick" or "with a trick."

Turn Out—To be forced into prostitution (*verb*) or a person newly involved in prostitution (*noun*).

Wifeys/Wife-in-Law/Sister Wife—What women and girls under the control of the same pimp call each other. (See *Family/Folks* and *Stable*)

Source: Smith, Linda, & Martinusen, Cindy. *Renting Lacy: A Story of America's Prostituted Children*. Vancouver, WA: Shared Hope International, 2013.

SCREENING FOR CSEC

CSEC has been able to grow and proliferate because of lack of knowledge but also because of the stigma and stereotypes that the public, including service practitioners, have regarding this population. This is also what makes it difficult for the children involved to disclose their abuse. There is an intense sense of shame and also defensiveness at wanting to explain or justify their actions that make it important for us to be able to identify CSEC. The following is a list of possible indicators provided by child welfare services. Please note that this list is not exhaustive and it is extremely broad, but it is a starting point that has been identified by several researchers and practitioners.

Possible Indicators

- History of abuse
- Visible signs of abuse, especially those markings or bruises that cannot be explained or are in discreet areas
- Any behaviors consistent with PTSD (fear, triggers, anxiety, hypervigilance)
- Changes to physical appearance, especially any scarring or tattoos. Sometimes these are methods that traffickers use to literally "brand" the girls they are exploiting
- Multiple cell phones
- The language that is used
- Change in friends or social groups (could also be seen as isolating from previous networks, including family)

- Suicide ideation or cutting

- Unable to explain money or the exchange of money

- Current home situation includes poor supervision or neglect

- Behavior problems. For instance, is inappropriate in class or similar settings

- Sexually explicit behaviors especially in her online "life" or even in the topics that she talks about

- Excessive time on her phone or online, especially on social media

Once a provider has a suspicion of CSEC, then the challenge becomes actually being able to screen or positively identify those who have been exploited. This remains one of the biggest challenges. The West Coast Children's Clinic (WCCC, n.d.) compiled a summary of over 50 available screening tools used to identify CSEC. They attempted to look for and include tools that met the following criteria:

- *Validated.* The tool has some form of data collection and evaluation attached to it to ensure that the measurement contains reliability and validity. Only two tools fit this criterion: the Vera Institute of Justice Trafficking Victim Identification Tool and Covenant House Human Trafficking Interview and Assessment Measure.

- *Length.* The tool asks a number of questions aimed to get to the depth of the issues and be as comprehensive as possible. This is especially important when asking about past and present traumas.

- *Source of Information.* Does the tool rely only on victim or client disclosure? Does it ask for any other sources of information? This is especially important when screening younger children who may not self-identify as a victim. In an earlier WCCC study (2012), they found that 37% of children surveyed did not recognize their own exploitation. Only three tools they found did not rely solely on self-disclosure.

- *Domain/System specific:* Most of the tools can be used anywhere, but some were developed specifically for a setting such as juvenile justice.

- *Guide to Action:* Some tools have been developed to help practitioners decide what course of action to take. However, none of these tools have been evaluated for accuracy. Also, this falls more into the category of assessment. In particular, psychological assessments can be used to establish directions of treatment.

- *Format/Mode:* How is the tool administered? What type of questionnaire is it (i.e., structured, unstructured)?

- *Open or Closed Ended:* If the tool is composed mostly of open-ended questions, though they may yield a lot of information, they are not conducive, especially to large agencies or institutions that must take into account time and participation.

- *Appropriate for Minors:* Are the tools written for adults and then adjusted to minors? It is better to select tools that are made specifically for minors.

Figure 8.1 Matrix of Screening Tools to Identify Sexually Exploited Children

	Organization	Tool Name	Length	Source of Information	Domain/ System Specific	Guide to Action; Potential Use for Prevention	Format/Mode
1	WestCoast Children's Clinic	Commercial Sexual Exploitation-Identification Tool	10 key indicators plus 48 guiding questions	Any	Any	Yes	Checklist of indicators
2	Shared Hope International	Intervene	42 questions at intake plus 55 questions to explore or confirm possible trafficking	Self-disclosure by victim	Any	No	Structured interview
3	Vera Institute of Justice	Trafficking Victim Identification Tool (TVIT)	75 questions (long form) or 55 questions (short form), some questions are only asked as follow up if client answers "yes" to a previous item.	Self-disclosure by victim	Any	No	Structured interview

Open- or Closed-Ended	Intended Populations	Appropriate for Minors	Sexual Exploitation/ Trafficking	Labor Trafficking	Notes	References	URLs
Closed	Minors and young adults	Yes	Yes	No	Development of the CSE-IT addressed shortcomings of other tools; meets key criteria for multisystem prospective screening tool, including reasonable length, relies on all sources of information, does not rely on self disclosure, is not domain specific and can be used across systems, provides a guide to action, is closed-ended, avoids a structured interview, is appropriate for minors.	The CSE-IT is an open domain tool for use in service delivery systems that serve children and youth. The copyright is held by WestCoast Children's Clinic to ensure that it remains free to use. For permission to use or for information, please contact Danna Basson at dbasson@ westcoastcc.org.	
Open	Minors	Yes	Yes	No	Lengthy, assumes the victim identifies as such and is seeking help	None	Paper copy only; Shared Hope requires you are trained 4-8 hours; they provide training for a fee
Mixed	Adult and Minors	Only with significant modifications to questions and to language	Yes	Yes	Addresses transnational trafficking/ smuggling; authors note the tool is not as effective with minor victims of sex trafficking as it is with other populations; some items irrelevant and wording not appropriate for minors; identifies the situation as "work"	Weiner and Hala, Oct 2008, Measuring Human Trafficking: Lessons from NYC	ncjrs.gov/ pdffiles1/nij/ grants/224391 .pdf

(Continued)

Figure 8.1 (Continued)

	Organization	Tool Name	Length	Source of Information	Domain/ System Specific	Guide to Action; Potential Use for Prevention	Format/Mode
4	Loyola University Chicago Center for the Human Rights for Children & Intl Org for Adolescents (IOFA)	Rapid Screening Tool (RST) for Child Trafficking	12 questions	Self-disclosure by victim	Any	No	Structured interview
5	Loyola University Chicago Center for the Human Rights for Children & Intl Org for Adolescents (IOFA)	Comprehensive Screening and Safety Tool (CSST) for Child Trafficking	33 questions	Self-disclosure by victim	Any	No	Structured interview
6	Asian Health Services and Banteay Srei (also used by Native American Health Center)	CSEC Screening Procedure and Guideline	1 question	Self-disclosure by victim	Any	No	Verbal interview question
7	Polaris Project & National Human Trafficking Resource Center (NHTRC)	Comprehensive Human Trafficking Assessment	142 questions	Self-disclosure by victim	Any	No	Unstructured interview (suggested questions)
8	State of MD - Department of Juvenile Services (DJS) (Neil Mallon)	Deterntion Screening Interview: Tier One	17 questions	Self-disclosure by victim; observation	Juvenile Justice	Yes	Semi-structured interview

Open- or Closed-Ended	Intended Populations	Appropriate for Minors	Sexual Exploitation/ Trafficking	Labor Trafficking	Notes	References	URLs
Open	Minors	Yes	Yes	Yes	Tool is missing key indicators; no definitions or explanations offered for items; some wording is too general to be useful (e.g. child appears to be bought or sold)	Walts et al, 2011, Building the Child Welfare Response to Trafficking	luc.edu/media/ lucedu/chrc/pdfs/ BCWRHandbook 2011.pdf
Open	Minors	Yes	Yes	Yes	Requires knowledge or suspicion of exploitation, so not useful for identification; unrealistic indicators, e.g. victim refers to self as "slave"; assumes victim identifies as such and is seeking help.	Walts et al, 2011, Building the Child Welfare Response to Trafficking	luc.edu/media/ lucedu/chrc/pdfs/ BCWRHandbook 2011.pdf
Open	Minors	Yes	Yes	No	Direct, short, easy to implement in intake process, but not comprehensive and requires self-disclosure	None	ahsoakland .wpengine.com/ wp-content/ uploads/2016/12/ Confronting-Commercial-Sexual-Exploitation-and-Sex-Trafficking-of-Minors-in-The-US-1.pdf
Open	Not specified	Only with significant modifications to questions and to language	Yes	Yes	Needs to be tailored to the program where it is implemented; many items with inappropriate language (e.g. "commercial sex act"), many invasive questions are irrelevant for screening purposes; assumes victim is seeking help.	None	traffickingresource center.org/ resources/ comprehensive-human-trafficking-assessment-tool
Mixed	Minors	Yes	Yes	No	Tool is missing many key indicators. (Note: very similar to tool developed by Portland State Univ)	Neil Mallon, MSW, LCSW-C CANS Training Specialist, The Institute for Innovation and Implementation, Univ of MD School of Social Work	

(Continued)

Figure 8.1   (Continued)

	Organization	Tool Name	Length	Source of Information	Domain/ System Specific	Guide to Action; Potential Use for Prevention	Format/Mode
9	State of WA	Portland State University CSEC Screening Interview	25 questions	Self-disclosure by victim; observation	Juvenile Justice	Yes	Semi-structured interview
10	State of CT - Department of Children and Families (DCF)	None	---	In-depth case review and/or psychological assessment	Child welfare	No	In-depth case review and/or psychological assessment
11	Barnardo's	SERAF (sexual exploitation risk assessment framework)	42 items	Any	Any	Yes	Checklist of indicators, presence or absence
12	Covenant House, NY	Human Trafficking Interview and Assessment Measure (HTIAM-14)	37 questions	Youth self-disclosure	Any	No	Structured interview

Open- or Closed-Ended	Intended Populations	Appropriate for Minors	Sexual Exploitation/ Trafficking	Labor Trafficking	Notes	References	URLs
Mixed	Minors	Yes	Yes	No	Tool is missing many key indicators. (Note: very similar to tool used in MD-DJS)	Salisbury EJ, Dabney JD, Russell K. 2015. Diverting Victims of Commercial Sexual Exploitation From Juvenile Detention: Development of the InterCSECt Screening Protocol. Journal of Interpersonal Violence, 30(7):1247–76	ccyj.org/ Project%20 Respect%20 protocol.pdf
---	Dependents of the state	Yes	Yes	Not specified	In-depth, but not prospective since it uses case history files; not feasible for large caseload	Phone conversation with Tammy Sneed, Director of Girls Services, CT Department of Children and Families. 1/13/2014	
Closed	Minors and young adults	Yes	Yes	No	Incorporates many sources of information but missing several key indicators	Sam Clutton, Jan Coles. 2007. Sexual Exploitation Risk Assessment Framework. Barnardo's Cymru. Wales, United Kingdom.	barnardos.org .uk/barnardo_s_ cymru_sexual_ exploitation_risk_ assessment_ framework_ report_-_english_ version.pdf
Mixed	Minors and young adults	Some items	Yes	Yes	Unlike other interviews noted above, question wording is largely nonjudgmental; questions can be read verbatim with mature youth, especially youth seeking help. A few items and wording issues do not pertain to minors. Only 2 of the 37 items pertain to sexual exploitation, so missing some key indicators.	Jayne Bigelson. May 2013. Homelessness, Survival Sex and Human Trafficking: As Experienced by the Youth of Covenant House New York.	covenanthouse. org/ sites/default/files/ attachments/ Covenant-House- trafficking-study .pdf

(Continued)

Figure 8.1 (Continued)

	Organization	Tool Name	Length	Source of Information	Domain/ System Specific	Guide to Action; Potential Use for Prevention	Format/Mode
13	San Luis Obispo	CSEC Screening Tool	22 questions	Any	Any	Yes	Checklist of indicators
14	U.S. Department of Human Services (also Ohio Human Trafficking Task Force)	U.S. Department of Health and Human Services (HHS) Human Trafficking Screening Tool	14 questions	Self-disclosure	Health care but flexible for use elsewhere	No	Semi-structured interview
15	Florida Department of Juvenile Justice	Human Trafficking Screening Tool	60 questions	Self-disclosure	Any	No	Semi-structured interview

Open- or Closed-Ended	Intended Populations	Appropriate for Minors	Sexual Exploitation/ Trafficking	Labor Trafficking	Notes	References	URLs
Closed	Minors	Yes	Yes	No	A strength of the tool is that it allows for any sources of information, not reliant on self-disclosure; provides sample questions for arriving at the information. A challenge is that it is missing some key indicators that providers have noted are important for identifying CSEC.		cwda.org/downloads/tools/csec/SLO-CSEC-Screening-Tool.pdf
Open	Not specified	No	Yes	Yes	Wording is in many instances inappropriate. Very general, open-ended questions.		acf.hhs.gov/sites/default/files/orr/screening_questions_to_assess_whether_a_person_is_a_trafficking_victim_0.pdf
Mixed	Minors	Yes	Yes	Yes	A strength of this tool is that it groups items into domains, which facilitates information integration and identification of a potential problem. Challenges include: some items are irrelevant yet missing other key indicators; some items do not match the domain (e.g. the Unsafe Living Environment domain does contain questions that address unsafe living environment); relies on self-disclosure.		

Source: West Coast Children's Clinic.

There is no single tool for screening that they surveyed that was able to optimally fulfill all the criteria. This led to the creation of the Commercial Sexual Exploitation Identification Tool (CSE–IT) (Macy & Graham, 2012; McClain & Garrity, 2011). Even this, which was an improvement, was not a panacea for holistic or comprehensive screening that could be used universally. Therefore, the West Coast Children's Clinic compilation is still extremely valuable and commonly referred to as different situations will necessitate different approaches, including in assessment. The reality is that there may never be a tool that fits every ambiguity and uniqueness of situations given the distinct characteristics that distinguish CSEC cases. Knowledge about what assessments may be accessed and what they encompass is a rich resource for practitioners. Examples of assessments located on the West Coast Children's Clinic's Matrix include the following.

WIDELY USED CSEC INTERVENTIONS

There are over 50 identified anti-trafficking curricula, a majority of which are developed to target CSEC. However, none have completed comprehensive or longitudinal evaluations. This can be due to the fact that this is an emerging field of prevention and intervention. There has been a literal race to create tools and resources to stem this crisis. We have selected the most widely used curriculums based on what is being used in the major urban areas in the United States where CSEC is most prevalent. Usage was determined by contacting CSEC transitional housing (where available), child welfare agencies, juvenile justice facilities, and nonprofit organizations in San Diego, Orange County, Los Angeles, San Bernardino, Oakland, San Francisco, Las Vegas, Portland, Seattle, Chicago, and New York. The intervention was included if more than 10 entities reported they were using it. Many of these interventions are very similar or actually build on each other, though very few designers will admit that. For instance, My Life My Choice is the basis of the curriculum "Word on the Street," because they share the same theory of change as well as modality of delivery. Most curriculums will "sell" themselves as unique by necessity either stating that they are the "best, newest, miracle curriculum" or that they are addressing a niche market. While this is an advantage in marketing, it is detrimental to actual collaboration. We would hope that this would change, but for now, with the large amount of revenue that is garnered from viable curriculum, it will be a while before we see genuine collaboration and implementation.

My Life My Choice

fightingexploitation.org

My Life My Choice describes itself as a "national leader in the prevention of CSEC" and curriculum as "acclaimed." It certainly is one of the most widely used curriculums in the CSEC arena, partly due to the fact that it was one of the first written. Designed in 2003 by exploitation survivor Denise Williams and Lisa Goldblatt Grace, LICSW, MPH, My Life My Choice is a 10-session model that aims to prevent exploitation in girls ages 12 to 18. While this is a prevention curriculum, it is often used as an intervention as well, after girls have been exploited. The goals of this curriculum are based on a public health theory of change model of shifting behavior through attitudes, knowledge, and skills. Each session is led by a clinical provider with a background in trauma-informed care. For those agencies, organizations, or institutions that would like to use the curriculum, the developers offer training in facilitation. However, one does not need to be certified to use or implement. There is also an emphasis on survivor stories, so it is suggested that facilitation includes at least one survivor (but preferably two) on the team. Pre- and posttest surveys are used to evaluate the participants' progress over time during the sessions especially focused on the change in attitude. My Life My Choice also asks for access to journal entries as well as attendance levels for evaluative purposes. Currently, there has been no systematic review of My Life My Choice, but the fact that it is used in almost every setting and has been adopted by state systems such as Georgia, Massachusetts, California, and others (their website reports they are in over 20 states) indicate that there is a confidence level by practitioners who are in the field that this curriculum addresses their needs. Further, other curricula have used this one as a foundation either conceptually or literally in their creation.

The ten sessions of My Life My Choice are 75 minutes long and cover a variety of topics (see Table 8.1). Each of the sessions include clear learning objectives, icebreakers, content, interactive materials, and ends with relaxation exercises and journal writing. Whenever possible, real-life survivor stories are incorporated into the sessions. Each session is held in a type of support group/survivor mentoring facet. This allows for peer-to-peer exchange as well as an openness communication. As the curriculum has evolved, it has developed the survivor mentoring component. Originally, the sessions were designed as purely psychoeducational methodology.

Table 8.1   My Life My Choice

Session	Topic
1	Introduction and Welcome, including a baseline questionnaire
2	Game Recognizes Game: Understanding Predators and Recruitment
3	Do You Really Want to Hurt Me? Reducing Your Risk of Exploitation
4	Making the Link: Substance Abuse and Exploitation
5	I Come First: Developing Self-Esteem
6	Sexual Health: Part 1: Knowing What's Out There
7	Sexual Health: Part 2: My Body, My Choice
8	Making It Real: Stories from "The Life"
9	I'm Not Alone: Finding Help and Finding Safety
10	Celebration and Farewell

The largest strengths of My Life My Choice is that it is dependent on the use of a clinical and survivor facilitator that is trained in trauma-informed practices. Further, it is relational in focus. The importance of connectedness and attachment is central to trauma-informed care and in this curriculum, there is also an emphasis on its importance. Because of its group format, the curriculum encourages community building, especially if the groups are of girls who have been exploited. This process then also leads to survivor leadership as the modules progress. In many instances, the girls involved will continue to meet, work together, and support each other even after the whole of the curriculum has been delivered.

The challenges of this curriculum are in part due to its structure. For instance, because of the number of sessions, it cannot be used in emergency shelters or short crisis models because it takes too long to complete the program. Similarly, each session is 75 minutes in length, which makes it difficult to include in a high school or middle school class, which are usually only 50 minutes long. Finally, the curriculum is not geared toward males nor does it address demand from the perspective of males. Though the curriculum was designed as a prevention methodology, it is used interchangeably as an intervention for recovery. While it has been used for these purposes, it is important to remember that it this is not what the curriculum was designed for.

Ending the Game

endingthegame.com/etg/

Ending the Game (ETG) calls itself a curriculum of "coercion resiliency." ETG was created by four survivors Steven Hassan, M.Ed., LMHC, NCC (cult survivor); D'Lita Miller (a sex trafficking survivor and mother of a survivor); Carissa Phelps, JD/MBA (sex trafficking survivor); and Rachel Thomas M.Ed. (sex trafficking survivor). Steven Hassan has a background in mind control and cults since 1976. It is this perspective that he brings to the curriculum, which is why a large portion of ETG is based on psychological coercion. The curriculum is trauma-informed and psychoeducational. Areas where this curriculum purports to distinguish itself is that it is based on intervention (and not prevention), which is found in the support that it provides to survivors within the process of the program. Further, it states that it is "designed to educate and engage students intellectually as well as emotionally." This is operationalized through its goal of providing strategies of psychological coercion and how one would combat it. Finally, another unique aspect of this curriculum is that it is mainly delivered online, which means that there is constant web access and new material that can easily be added. ETG is said to be appropriate for questioning populations, transgendered individuals, and gay males. It is unknown if this curriculum would be effective with males who are heterosexual.

The ten lesson plans of ETG are meant to be given in either 2-hour or 1-hour group formats; although there is also a one-to-one version. The core lessons range from isolation to phobias to shame (see Table 8.2). Each of the sessions is composed of four parts: a lesson on psychological coercion, reflection, connection, and then rebuild their "true self." ETG operates on an empowerment model that seeks to raise awareness of the process of psychological coercion (this known as "The Game") and how survivors were exposed to the game as well as their own exploitation experiences.

Table 8.2   Ending the Game Core Lessons

Lesson	Topic
1	Introduction
2	False Promises: Students learn how unmet needs can cause vulnerability and how exploiters can cause victims to believe they provide solutions to these unmet needs. After reflecting on their unmet needs and previous beliefs about what The Game would provide, students learn a practical method to assess whether or not The Game has met their needs.
3	Isolation: Students learn how and why exploiters cause physical, mental, and emotional isolation. After reflecting on ways they have felt isolated, students are encouraged to do one or more suggested activities to foster reconnection.
4	Dissociation: Students learn basic psychology principles regarding human response processes. After practical examples and role play, students learn how exploiters can manipulate these natural response processes. On considering how their responses to sexual exploitation have changed over time, students then learn and practice a tool to identify changes in their responses to sexual exploitation.
5	Self-Defeating Thoughts: Students learn how thoughts can impact behavior and learn to differentiate degrading from healthy thoughts. Students also identify and examine personal thoughts that contribute to sexual exploitation. Lastly, students learn strategies to avoid degrading thoughts and enjoy the benefits of healthy thoughts.
6	Emotional Intensity: Students learn how exploiters cause emotional highs and lows as a method of coercion. After reflecting upon their emotional health in The Game, students learn strategies to embrace healthier emotional balance.
7	Self-Defeating Behavior: Students learn to identify coercive behavior modification techniques. After reflecting upon the impact of coercion in their behavior "choices," students learn how to create and choose healthier behavior options.
8	Identity Disturbance: Students learn basic mental health principles concerning identity and identity disturbance. After reflecting upon how their individual identity has been disturbed, students learn and practice strategies to spark recognition and appreciate of their true identity.
9	Phobias: Students learn the difference between a fear and a phobia and then reflect upon personal phobias that may contribute to their participation in commercial sexual exploitation. After reflecting on the impact of phobias, students will learn strategies to overcome phobias.
10	Shame: Students learn the negative impact of shame on personal growth and learn strategies to overcome shame, including self-care, self-compassion, and embracing survivorhood.

Source: Courtesy of Ending the Game (taken from: endingthegame.com/etg-lesson-descriptions!).

Anyone can purchase the ETG curriculum and receive lesson plans for each. There is also a membership fee where those who want to be a trainer or facilitator of ETG can purchase and this gives them access to the ETG website, which updates lesson plans, provides support trainings, and contains a library of resources. The lesson plans begin with session objectives and also directions in terms of facilitator materials and ancillary resources. Handouts and student materials are also included. There is also a suggested script for facilitators to follow. Anyone can sign up to be a facilitator and there is no general profile for them. However, because the curriculum also draws from trauma and dissociative disorders, there is a reliance on the DSM–5 diagnosis. Exercises associated to cognitive behavioral therapy (CBT) is also incorporated.

ETG is one of the only curriculums that offer a one-to-one model. This type of model would allow for optimum customization and flexibility. This goes along with the empowerment model, which is used in the framework. As with the other curriculums that have demonstrated effectiveness, ETG has the goal of moving victims through the process of becoming survivors. ETG is also web based, which allows for updated materials and an easy way to add materials as they become relevant or needed.

While being web based is a strength in terms of access, it is also a challenge to the curriculum. Being structured primarily online might be convenient, but the interface does make it difficult to build true connections between developers and facilitators. Issues such as transference, countertransference, and possible secondary trauma may arise and not be able to be handled sufficiently or appropriately addressed because of the online format. Another barrier is also that the facilitation of the curriculum does not require any specialty or clinical background. This is possibly an ethical issue because ETG does not require or even suggest a clinician even though there is a heavy reliance on diagnosis (via DSM–5) and labeling those who have been trafficked with some type of mental health issue, usually personality disorders. This latter aspect is also important because there is the tendency to victim blame once you have started to dispense these types of "disorders." It is antithetical to trauma-informed care, which espouses the principle of looking at adaptation versus disease models. Since ETG concentrates on psychological coercion, it also focuses on dysfunction and mental illness (via DSM diagnosis), and the "Game" becomes the primary case study, whether it fits common experiences or not.

Empowering Young Men

caase.org/prevention

The Chicago Alliance Against Sexual Exploitation (CAASE) is an organization whose mission it is to address "the culture, institutions, and individuals that perpetrate, profit from, or support sexual exploitation." Their signature gender-based psychoeducational prevention curriculum is "Empowering Young Men to End Sexual Exploitation," which is directed to high school boys. The curriculum is the first in the United States that is specifically designed for young men, ages 14 to 18. It was created in 2010 to address the "demand" side of prostitution and to move boys from being participants and abusers in the system to being allies in the fight to end commercial sexual exploitation. The curriculum is based on the theories of social norms, popular education, and media awareness.

The social norms theory is based on the idea that human behavior is influenced by our misperceptions of how our peers think and act; even though we may misinterpret them, we tend to then model our behavior after them. This theory coupled with media awareness challenges how these social norms are proliferated through the social media. The hope is that media can be used to correct misconceptions and instead promote more accurate norms. Another theory that drives this curriculum is that of popular education. Freire (2000) coined this term that refers to the education that is rooted in the analysis of class struggle, political context, and transformation. It is focused on the idea that the purpose of education is to be able to "liberate" or make give people true freedom to think and to act. The curriculum is interdisciplinary and covers a number of different perspectives on these topics. While this is geared toward young men, CAASE also partners with Rape Victim Advocates, who facilitate a similar program for young women. CAASE provides connections for schools who might be interested in that program as well.

The *Empowering Young Men* curriculum is composed of four sessions that are about 45 minute each and can fit into one high school class session. Mostly, schools have integrated this curriculum into health classes and where available, social justice courses as well. A large part of the curriculum is creating safe spaces for the discussion of these sensitive topics. The program also meets learning standards both set forth by Common Core guidelines such as English language arts, social science, and health as well as social emotional developmental needs in the areas of decision making and responsibility over behavior. The curriculum takes the stance that "prostitution exists because of men who purchase sex." Further, there is an emphasis on the roles that traffickers play in the procurement and continued exploitation of prostitution. The curriculum focuses on difficult issues especially around gender roles and perceptions of masculinity from the perspective of their peers, media, families, and their own views.

CAASE markets this curriculum as one that is able to fit into schools not only because it conforms to course time constraints, but also because it is integrated into the overall educational goals of the school. Currently, this program is offered in the Cook County area where CAASE is located. As of 2016, more than 1,600 young men in Chicago have completed the course. CAASE has its own facilitators that deliver the program but they also provide trainings for other states and areas that are interested. They respond to requests

Table 8.3   Empowering Young Men

Session	Topic
1	Introduction
	Creating Safety and Accountability
2	Commercial Sexual Exploitation
3	Commercial Sexual Exploitation within a Larger Context
4	Taking Action Against Sexual Harm

from schools, teachers, organizations, and so forth to deliver the curriculum and offer the program to schools at no cost. The only thing they require is that the school provide ample space and audiovisual equipment.

In addition to being one of the only curriculums and interventions that is geared to young men and the issue of demand, the curriculum is designed to fit seamlessly into the classroom space. Moreover, it's alignment with the Common Core guidelines makes it easier for schools to accept the curriculum. Any student can participate in the curriculum since it addresses universal prevention. There is also potential for more work to be done with girls because the overall themes are gender norms and gender-based violence. As schools become a main site for the identification and hopeful prevention of CSEC, curriculums such as this are well structured to help support these efforts.

This program has shown to have success in Chicago where it has been developed and piloted. The challenge will be how to bring this program to scale, especially since its current structure requires CAASE facilitators and educators to either administer the program directly or train those who are interested. Either way, this is time and resource consuming.

Shelter Interventions

Shelters are considered part of aftercare programs once children have been rescued. For aftercare, similar principles exist around best approaches such as trauma-informed care, rights-based care, and intensive case management. Human rights–based care refers to trafficked persons understanding their rights as would all service providers. This is predicated on the belief of a human rights platform being central to the service provision that occurs (Berthold, 2015). In addition to these principles, the following are areas that should be considered for shelter best practices:

- Safe and secure accommodations are a priority.

- Shelters should meet the country's minimum standard of care. At the very least, they should be clean and well lit. There should also be separate spaces for differing living functions. Most trafficked children have been in situations where they have been subjected to living in just one room for the duration of their trafficking if not something even more oppressive (it is not unheard of to find that children have been kept in cages or worse).

- The rights of the those who are trafficked as well as all those who may be residents or practitioners must be posted in a clear manner.

- As well as offering housing, there should be daily activities to participate in. If possible, the residents should help decide and give input as to what activities will be included. This not only creates buy-in but also will allow some measure of control.

- There should be some kind of complaint mechanism where residents feel like they are being heard and their complaints are being responded to.

- Shelter services should also be provided by people who are gender appropriate, child friendly, and well trained.

- Cultural competence—language, food, customs, religion—are just a few things. At the minimum, it is important for practitioners to listen to and be centered around the child.
- Provide access to medical care, legal care, and psychosocial care within the shelter where (hopefully) they have a level of comfort.

One difficult consideration during aftercare is whether children should have access to family (if the family is not abusive, neglectful, or part of the trafficking incident) as well as whether they should or could be minimally restrained, primarily in terms of movement. This is to minimize any resemblance to the trafficking situation. However, the challenge remains: How do you create that type of space and have a safe shelter, since most safe and secure shelters are anonymous and often hidden from the public? There is no simple answer to this, but what we do know is that the initial stages after recovery are so critical that the focus should be on stabilization and time to adjust. During this time, there is the susceptibility to miss their exploiter or be threatened or afraid of retaliation. Facilities and shelter staff need to be able to be flexible and adjust, knowing that CSEC victims will most probably run. As with domestic violence victims, researchers have found that it will take about five times for a victim to leave their trafficker. Other lessons from the domestic violence movement may provide some insight as to how to strengthen shelters and transitional housing (Kaufman & Crawford, 2011a; Rigby, Malloch, & Hamilton-Smith, 2012; Wirsing, 2012).

Although it might be tempting to place children in preexisting, general child (welfare) services or shelters, the argument for specialized services is that the needs of CSEC victims are extremely unique and their needs are not always easily predicted. Having them in the general population also means that they are vulnerable to a number of things such as "getting lost in the system" as well as being retrafficked or returning to their trafficking situation. It is not unheard of to have traffickers send in procurers or recruiters to get to the child. The latter is the most important reason that practitioners are specifically trained in trafficking, particularly in child trafficking (Taylor, personal communication, 2016).

There are only four specific CSEC shelters in the United States, run by GEMS, SAGE, Angela's Hall, and Children of the Night. Their best practices include having residential facilities that have a continuum of care (education-prevention-intervention), they partner with existing community-based programs, and they include long-term aftercare services such as support groups and mentoring programs. However, each of the four shelters recognize that not one program can provide everything so collaboration is a necessity (Clawson & Goldblatt Grace, 2007). Further, collaboration should practice open communication, common language, shared definitions, trust, and genuine motivations of partnership. Finally, supportive programs such as drop-in centers, mental health centers, and interventions that help rebuild attachment and trust skills show promise in the shelter care system (Taylor, personal communication, 2016).

GLOBAL CHILD TRAFFICKING

While we have been discussing CSEC from a domestic perspective (domestic being within the borders of the United States), it would be remiss of us not to discuss the child trafficking that occurs internationally. The practice of domestic trafficking is not unique to the United States.

Figure 8.2   Child Trafficking and the Child Welfare System

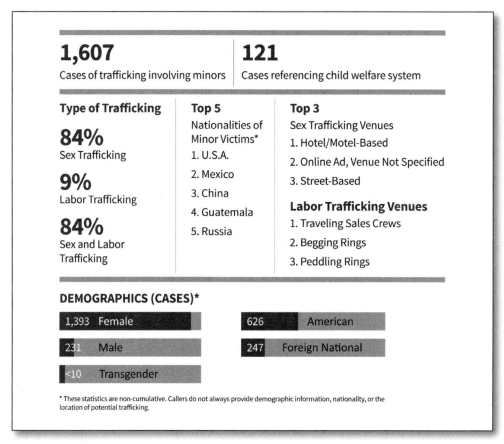

Source: Honey Imbo.

It is often the case that children are trafficked extensively within borders before they are trafficked across them. The Middle East and Africa have the largest percentages of children who are trafficked (UNODC, 2012). The International Labor Organization (ILO) estimates that 1.8 million children are globally trafficked every year, with two-thirds of the victims being girls (ILO, 2004; UNODC, 2012). Children are trafficked for labor, mainly in the fishing industries in Africa, but they are also trafficked for a host of other reasons. In countries where CSEC is criminalized, labor trafficking may still be tolerated. For instance, in Chile until 2011, experts estimate that there are over 200,000 children between the ages of 5 and 17 (with the average age being 12), who are slave labor (Hepburn & Simon, 2013). CSEC still encompasses about 58% of all children who are trafficked around the world. In the international definition, this also includes child pornography, prostitution of children (for cash and also in exchange of gifts), child marriage, and use of children in live sex shows. There is also a market for trafficked children for illegal adoptions as well as for organ removal (Ray, 2007; UNICEF, 2012; U.S. Department of State, 2012). The promising best practices that we are using in the United States have direct impacts around the world because we are currently leading the development of interventions. In a survey of 25 countries (both rich and poor), reported that there were no real protocols designed or used specifically for children. Most services operated on some of the principles that we discuss in this chapter, including intensive case management, shelter services, and trauma-informed care.

One of the things to consider with global child trafficking across borders is that aftercare includes the process of repatriation. Repatriation is part of the overall reintegration of the child and may include a return to the child's country of origin. This should only occur if the circumstances are safe and if it is the child's choice to return. There currently does not exist an assessment tool that allow practitioners across borders to share information that will help determine safety and security. If such a tool existed, it could help normalize the repatriation process. In some cases, when it is possible, practitioners may be able to do an ocular inspection of the intended repatriation site, but this takes a lot of time, effort, and money that often are not available (Muraya & Fry, 2015; Wirsing, 2012; Zimmerman et al., 2008).

Case Vignette: Amber

Amber is a 15-year-old African American female from Lancaster, California. Lancaster is about two hours outside of Los Angeles. For decades, Lancaster held the largest prison outside of LA, but in the late 1990s defense contractors and technical companies based themselves there. Even with this boom, Lancaster remains a largely working-class neighborhood. Both of Amber's parents worked at the prison until her father left because of a work-related accident and her mother was laid off due to cutbacks. With no work, it was difficult for her parents to provide for Amber and her three younger siblings, but the family moved in with her grandmother and made ends meet. Amber has had good relationships with her parents, though she is closer to her mother. Her father was barely home growing up and even now that he is home, he does not really interact with the children. She is not close to her siblings who are younger than her (5 and 6 years, respectively). Amber does not have a lot of close friends, but she is fairly well liked. She has average grades and enjoys playing volleyball.

In eighth grade Amber met Shaun, who used to hang around her school. Amber usually would walk home with her friends but one day she decided to ditch school and walked home early. Shaun saw that she was alone and offered to walk her home. On the walk, Shaun asked her if she had a boyfriend and told her how pretty she was. Amber knew that Shaun was older but thought it was nice having all this attention from Shaun. Over the next couple of weeks Shaun would send Amber text messages and would walk her home from school. One day Shaun asked Amber to be his girlfriend. Amber was very excited and said yes. Amber's parents had told her that they did not want her hanging around Shaun, but she felt they just did not want her to be happy.

(Continued)

(Continued)

Amber began to sneak out of the house to meet Shaun. Soon, they were together all the time. They would usually hang out with his friends, even though they would always look at Amber in a way that made her uncomfortable. One night, Amber and Shaun went to a party thrown by one of his friends. Shaun kept giving Amber drinks and even asked her to play a drinking game with him. Amber did not like drinking, but Shaun always told her it made her look older. Amber does not remember most of the night but woke up laying in a strange bed, with someone exiting the room. She could not tell who the guy was, but Shaun was yelling something about a payment and she did not have her clothes on. Amber was very scared and Shaun grabbed her and dragged her out of the home. Amber began to cry in the car and Shaun yelled that he was not going to take her to the hospital because she hurt all over. Shaun took Amber to his house, where she had never been before, even though she wanted to go home. He tells her that he doesn't want her to get into trouble because she is still drunk. She agrees and when she uses the bathroom, she notices there is blood on her panties and smeared on her thighs. Shaun gives Amber some medicine and tells her it will make her feel better. In the morning, when she wakes up, she still doesn't remember anything, and hopes that it was a nightmare.

She finds Shaun, who takes care of her by giving her breakfast. He is sweet and solicitous about how she feels. He asks her if she loves him and she says of course she does. Shaun tells her that he needs her to help make some money and that if he didn't need it, he would never ask her. Then, he asks her to sleep with one of his friends so that he can get some money to pay his bills. Amber does not want to and can't believe he is asking her to do this, but she loves him and he tells her it's just one time. Amber agrees and later that day, Shaun's friend, Ben, comes over and give Shaun $75. They go into his room. Amber has sex with Ben, but they have to stop halfway through because it hurt too much. He gets angry and begins to yell at her. She is afraid that Shaun will hear, so she lets Ben finish. He leaves and Amber showers then leaves the room to find Shaun in a hurry to leave. She thinks she has made him happy, but once they get into the car, Shaun turns to her and explains that Ben took some money back because she didn't do a good job. He says that she can make it up to him by doing it again for him. Amber says no. But, he says if she does it he will know that she is his "ride or die bae." She agrees to. Amber lies to her parents and tells them that she is staying at her best friend's house. She spends the rest of the weekend letting Shaun sell her to his friends. None of them use condoms.

When Amber returns to school on Monday, she feels like everyone is staring at her. By her third class, she knows that something is happening because people keep looking at their phones and pointing to her. A friend comes up to her during lunch and asks Amber, "How could you let them do this to you?" Amber does not know what she is talking about until her friend pulls up Instagram on her phone and types in "#shaunsvirgin" and "#notquitelegal." A series of photos comes up of her in bed with multiple boys—all friends of Shaun's that were at the party. Amber is shocked and can't even say anything. She runs out of school and calls Shaun, who picks her up a block away. When he asks her what is wrong, she tells him about the Instagram. He tells her that her friends are just jealous and then she gives her a gift—a new bag that he has bought her. He reminds her that he is the only one that really knows her and loves her.

Soon Amber is cutting school and doing whatever Shaun wants her to do.

When she catches him talking to another girl, he says it's only because he wants her to be able to "rest" and that she will always be his only girlfriend; the other girls are just for them to make some money. Amber begins to take drugs at the parties that Shaun takes her to to cope with everything. Sometimes Amber wants to tell her parents but she knows they will not understand because they often make comments about girls that they see on the streets. She knows that they will be ashamed of her and kick her out of the house.

One night Shaun asks Amber to go with him to Compton to hang out with some of his friends. When Amber and Shaun get there, he tells her that he wants her to walk Long Beach Blvd. so they can get some money. Amber is scared and does not know how to do this because Shaun would bring her men and boys and she had never done this. Amber agrees, but she is scared. She ends up soliciting an undercover officer who detains her after she is also found with meth on her person.

CALL TO ACTION: ONE CHILD IS ONE CHILD TOO MANY

We are only beginning to explore how to prevent the trafficking and slavery of children and how to provide empowering services for their rescue, recovery, and reintegration. We will see what is most effective and what does not quite reach the population. This area of practice is literally changing daily and it will be interesting to see what continues to evolve with the advancement of technology and more importantly, the growing awareness by society that trafficking and slavery is widespread and children one of the most exploited. The United States, in particular, is poised to take a lead in defending and treating child trafficking especially from a clinical stance. Almost all modalities of treatments that are being utilized, with exception to indigenous and cultural methods, originate from our service providers and practitioners. This should give us even more impetus to create interventions that work.

DISCUSSION QUESTIONS

1. Provide examples of global child trafficking in a country of your interest.

2. Select either the city you are attending school in or practicing or your hometown. Examine the status of children in that area. What are the risk factors that exist that make them vulnerable to CSEC? What are the protective factors?

3. What are some vulnerabilities that put children at risk for CSEC? Are they unique to children or could they fit even the adult population?

4. What are common stigmas or misconceptions about CSEC? How does this hurt public perception of the issue? Provide concrete examples.

5. How can we better coordinate services to identify and treat CSEC? What are the main barriers and how would you address them?

CHALLENGE

One of the biggest barriers to CSEC is the lack of understanding about the issue. Bring a group of your network of fellow professionals or even your personal tribe together for a viewing of GEMS' film, *Very Young Girls*. After you watch it, facilitate a discussion. You may want to download more information from the film's website to help structure the conversation: http://www.gems-girls.org

Policy Interventions

Before interventions were created at the clinical level and practitioners were struggling to define best practices, the world was struggling to gain agreement on definitions, how to prevent trafficking and modern-day slavery, how to end it, and of course, how to prosecute those who were found guilty of such crimes. The move from human rights–based paradigms and ways of thinking to criminal dichotomies of perpetrator and victim can be traced to developments in global policy interventions. Policy is rightfully perceived as a crosscutting direction to address issues in the broadest way possible with the potential to address international reach and local impact. Many practitioners do not find themselves engaging in policy or having difficulty imagining their role in what they might consider macro endeavors. However, it is precisely the arena of engagement that practitioners must take part in because they are on the front line of communities and working directly with individuals who have been trafficked or enslaved. It is the practitioner perspective that must inform policy interventions at all levels. This is when we see the most successful and relevant policy work. In the best-case scenarios, this type of policy-making can serve as a model for others.

The most significant policies in the area of trafficking and modern-day slavery have been in the area of what has been referred to as the "four P's": *Prevention, Protection, Prosecution,* and *Partnership.* The section begins with an international perspective in chapter 9, examining the work that the United Nations began with the Palermo Protocols. Questions and contentions around definitions of trafficking and slavery plagued the formation of the protocols and would spark various controversies especially around what should be considered "trafficking" and/or "slavery." For instance, should contract labor that turned into indentured servitude be considered slavery? Should commercial sexual exploitation be considered trafficking if those being exploited "agreed" to their situations? And, what should be the proper "punishment" for those who trafficked or enslaved people versus those who bought them? This section revisits the issue of the "demand side" of trafficking and modern-day slavery, particularly how understanding these things shifts the perspective and even focus of the legislation. Though laying down a foundation for future legislation internationally, the work of the United Nations was only the beginning and helped shape the legislative landscape for the next decade.

We highlight the legislative work that has been done in various countries, building on Palermo, or as in the case of the United States, built in parallel to the protocols. An analysis of the Trafficking Victims Protection Act and all its reauthorizations (2003, 2005, 2008, and 2013) are also included here. The TVPA is landmark legislation for the United States but also has global reach because part of its legislative power is the creation of the Trafficking in Persons (TIP) Report, which allows the United States to measure and then rank countries based on their anti-trafficking efforts. The TIP Report has real power in that it can invoke sanctions, except in the situation of natural disasters. Chapter 9 finishes with a survey of what other countries are doing and their versions of anti-trafficking legislation.

Chapter 10 takes a look at labor trafficking—specifically the work that is being done around supply chain transparency. Though labor trafficking is the more prevalent form of trafficking and modern-day slavery, there is relatively little attention paid to it in comparison to sex trafficking and this is true also in the legislative arena. However, migration patterns and labor trafficking must be understood because this is an area that leaves individuals vulnerable to sex trafficking as well. To understand the complexity of labor trafficking, we will look at how state, federal, and international policies have attempted to reveal the supply chain and other processes of labor. For example, we will look at the California Transparency in Supply Chains Act of 2010 and how this is changing the nature of how companies deal with trafficking and modern-day slavery. For example, even companies who want to engage in change have had difficulty positioning themselves as champions. One executive said that they believed that at the corporate level, the issues were so complex and varied that a systemic view had to be taken, including the formation, advocacy, and eventual implementation of policy. However, she also stated that many companies do not feel they can positively influence policy or whether that is even their role (GAP Inc., personal communication, 2015). Chapter 10 also examines federal moves to limit procurement of slave-labor produced goods and what this might mean for the future. As with the previous chapter, we round this chapter out with an international perspective on what is happening at a global scale.

This section will also look at key pieces of legislation such as safe harbor laws and the role of work visas. Furthermore, two case vignettes will be introduced and a number of different organizational highlights will be provided to give you a glimpse of what is happening in the field.

GLOSSARY OF TERMS

Act—formal decision, law, or the like, by a legislature, ruler, court, or other authority; decree or edict; statute; judgment, resolve, or award.

Audit—official inspection of an individual's or organization's accounts, typically by an independent body.

Bill—a draft of a law presented to a legislature for consideration.

Certification—the confirmation of certain characteristics of an object, person, or organization. This confirmation is often, but not always, provided by some form of external review, education, assessment, or audit.

H1B Visa—a non immigrant visa that allows U.S. companies to employ foreign workers in specialty occupations that require theoretical or technical expertise in specialized fields such as in architecture, engineering, mathematics, science, and medicine.

H2B Visa—is a temporary work visa for foreign workers with a job offer for seasonal, non-agricultural work in the United States.

Law—rule made by the government of a town, state, country, and so forth.

Multisystem Collaboration—group of organizations that are committed to meeting the same goal. Often collaborations are formed between law-enforcement, child welfare, and community-based organizations to better serve and meet the needs of the population.

Palermo Protocol—Three protocols that were adopted by the United Nations to supplement the 2000 Convention against Transnational Organized Crime (the Palermo Convention). They are as follows: the Protocol to Prevent, Suppress, and Punish Trafficking in Persons, especially Women and Children; the Protocol Against the Smuggling of Migrants by Land, Sea, and Air; and the Protocol Against the Illicit Manufacturing of and Trafficking in Firearms, their Parts and Components, and Ammunition. The convention marks great strides toward fighting transnational crime and identifies those member states in the United Nations who acknowledge the gravity of such crimes.

Policy—a course or principle of action adopted or proposed by a government, party, business, or individual.

Procurement—act of acquiring or buying goods, services, or works from an external source, often via a tendering or bid process.

Safe Harbor Laws—Safe harbor laws were developed by states to address inconsistencies with how children who are exploited for commercial sex are treated. Safe harbor laws are intended to address the inconsistent treatment of children and ensure that these victims are provided with services.

Sanction—a threatened penalty for disobeying a law or rule.

Supply Chain Transparency—The extent to which a company has the information on their suppliers and sourcing locations available and understandable to the public.

T Visa—visa for those who are or have been victims of human trafficking, which protects victims of human trafficking and allows victims to remain in the United States to assist in an investigation or prosecution of human trafficking.

TVPA—The TVPA, and its reauthorizations in 2003, 2005, and 2008, define a human trafficking victim as a person induced to perform labor or a commercial sex act through force, fraud, or coercion.

U Visa—a nonimmigrant visa, which is set aside for victims of crimes (and their immediate family members) who have suffered substantial mental or physical abuse and are willing to assist law enforcement and government officials in the investigation or prosecution of the criminal activity.

UNTOC—The United Nations Convention against Transnational Organized Crime is a United Nations–sponsored multilateral treaty against transnational organized crime. The Convention was adopted by a resolution of the United Nations General Assembly on 15 November 2000.

Verification—the establishment by empirical means of the validity of a proposition.

CHAPTER 9

Landmark Policies in Trafficking and Modern-Day Slavery

Annalisa Enrile and Melanie G. Ferrer-Vaughn

Chapter Objectives

1. Readers will gain a comprehensive understanding of the Palermo Protocols, the United Nation's response for transnational organized crime.

2. Readers will survey international anti-trafficking laws and policies.

3. Readers will compile ongoing and modifications to the United States' Trafficking Victims Protections Act of 2000 (and its subsequent modifications).

4. Readers will gain knowledge on laws and policies around the globe that affect trafficking.

5. Readers will consider how laws and policies can continue to be improved to become more effective at combatting human trafficking and modern day slavery.

I always thought this had been a big classroom, especially when the dividers were thrown open and we joined the two, but right now, I feel almost claustrophobic with the amount of people crowding the room. We are 3 lawyers, 7 social workers, 2 public health registered nurses, and several women rights' activists strong, but there are over 30 people in the room. They are from different countries, their languages musical as they meshed into a loud crescendo. Most of the people in the room are monolingual and so we have also a shortage in translators. They were roughly even in numbers, the men and women and representative of all ages.

(Continued)

(Continued)

Most of them come to us by way of Florida, having been trafficked there through the hospitality industry. Their story went like this: They were recruited to do work in hotels and country clubs ranging from being drivers to domestic workers to working in the kitchen. They signed up and paid exorbitant fees to the recruiters to help them with their papers, travel, and of course arrange their employment abroad. Before they even arrived in the United States, they owed the employment agency over $5,000. They were flown to Florida where their passports were taken away under the guise of having to make sure their "visas" were sufficient. They were then put in a house—about 35 to each 4-bedroom home. I did the slight math and realized that if there were 5 houses as they reported, we were only seeing less than one-fifth of them. Men and women were forced to share rooms and though none of the women reported sexual abuse or misconduct, they talk about making sure room doors were always left open. They were shuttled to work sites by two "security guards" hired by the company. The company turned out to be a subcontractor for several major hotel brands in the United States as well as private county club facilities. The workers did anything they were told and often had to work upward of 18 hours a day. They made no money the first year because they were told that the money they earned went to pay the recruiter. By the end of the year, their traffickers informed them that they owed almost $20,000 for their room, board, and food. They were transported all over the state and sometimes driven as far as New York. One woman was told to stop calling her son. She was told by one of the traffickers, "It doesn't matter if you call him. He is never going to see you again. You'll work for us until you are dead." They didn't know what to do because their traffickers constantly told them they would call the police and turn them in where they would go to jail because none of them had passports (they were never returned). Scared, this lasted for almost three years. One night, three of the workers were threatened by one of the traffickers. Knowing they had to do something soon, the 32 people in front of us bribed two of the "security guards" to drive them away, drop them off, and not report anything. From there, they bought a bus ticket to anywhere they could go. They made it as far as Chicago. Then, they made it to Los Angeles and to us.

Listening to this story told 32 times, we were stunned at the level of need—health care, mental health care, legal needs, reunification, and T-Visas all around. One of the major barriers that existed was that to get a T visa, you had to cooperate with prosecutors for the case. The problem here was the question of who to prosecute—the main employers? the subcontractors? the recruiters? Surely, they were all at fault but they each insisted they were innocent. As I observed the logistical mess, I felt an unreal sense of outrage and anger because while the prosecution and defendants tried to sort out whose fault it was, those who were wronged would continue to live in a strange type of purgatory where they had neither moral ground nor the proper documentation to go on with their lives. But I had to push that anger away, because in the middle of all this legal-ese, there were 32 people standing in front of us, and all they wanted was hope and a pathway to freedom.

—Wilhelmina De Castro

INTRODUCTION

In 2015, the United Kingdom ratified the Modern Slavery Act, which was designed to consolidate previous antislavery and anti-trafficking laws and to create new provisions. The comprehensive law addressed transparent supply chains, prostitution, tied visas, among other aspects of slavery and trafficking (Bayer et al., 2015). This law is one of the better examples of antislavery and anti-trafficking policies that have been added to the arsenal to mitigate and hopefully prevent any occurrence. However, as good as it is, the law has been criticized for not protecting victims enough, being too law-enforcement focused, and not providing options for civil litigation. These criticisms underscore the fact that there does not exist one comprehensive piece of legislation that fully addresses the complex issues of trafficking and modern-day slavery. Despite this, the need to keep perfecting and creating policies in this area is a priority. This is essential in countries whose only or main response is policy, with little else in the form of prevention or intervention practices. Further, there are some countries such as Uruguay, which have not enacted laws (and of the time of writing this book) are currently working to develop laws that will meet international standards on both sex and labor trafficking (U.S. Department of State, 2016).

THE UNITED NATIONS CONVENTION AGAINST TRANSNATIONAL ORGANIZED CRIME: THE PALERMO PROTOCOLS

In the late 1990s, it became clear that trafficking and modern-day slavery was not being abated by the anecdotal measures being taken country by country. Therefore, movements arose pushing the international community to create more organized and robust plans to tackle the issue (Gallagher, 2012). In Argentina, for instance, officials hoped to move away from a solely human rights perspective and instead represent some pragmatic plans rooted in transnational organized crime and law enforcement. At this same time, President Bush of the United States issued Executive Order 13387, an amendment to the military court martial, specified that any military personnel found "patronizing a prostitute" could be disciplined or court martialed (Executive Order 13387, n.d.). These two major events ignited awareness on the roles of governments and international bodies and their responsibility to create policies and legislations, at the very minimum that were able to really address what was happening.

The international community moved toward concerted efforts to create a global response to trafficking and modern-day slavery by framing it as a transnational crime. An intergovernmental ad hoc committee was formed in 1998, under the auspices of the United Nations to draft legislation that would directly address and combat transnational crime, of which trafficking and modern-day slavery was now considered part. The committee met for 11 sessions in Vienna with over 120 states involved, along with input from international nongovernmental organizations to gain various perspectives and insights on the topic. Over the next two years, the committee drafted what would become the

Convention Against Transnational Organized Crime. This Convention was supplemented by three protocols:

- The Protocol to Prevent, Suppress, and Punish Trafficking in Persons, Especially Women and Children;
- The Protocol Against the Smuggling of Migrants by Land, Sea, and Air; and
- The Protocol Against the Illicit Manufacturing of and Trafficking in Firearms, their Parts and Components, and Ammunition.

The three together became known at the "Palermo Protocols" since they were ratified and adopted in December, 2000 in Palermo, Italy. The convention marks great strides toward fighting transnational crime and identifies those member states in the United Nations who acknowledge the gravity of such crimes. Currently, there are 147 signatories of the Convention [https://www.unodc.org/unodc/en/treaties/CTOC/signatures.html], roughly only one-third of all member countries (Brusca, 2011).

The Convention aims to disrupt and eliminate any possibility of breeding or execution of criminal activities which are include any crimes that are committed in more than one country even in the planning of such crime and may have lasting effects on other nations. This extremely broad definition encompasses all types of criminal offenses. In terms of trafficking, this meant that nation-states should establish that there was a transnational offense and that the crime involved some organized group. For these aims to be addressed, there had to be more communication and cooperation among law enforcement authorities. The concern that was raised during the development of the Convention was that real collaboration could only occur through joint training, education, and simulation exercises, all which would come at a high financial price tag. This is a practical concern considering the limited resources of some member nations and the obvious need for considerable technical guidance and economic investment to adhere and implement the Convention and the Palermo Protocols. While this was raised during the development, it was addressed by the suggestion of a United Nations funding mechanism, though never resolved.

The main goal of the Convention and Protocols is to encourage collaboration between countries to fight transnational crime in a cooperative and comprehensive manner. To be able to do this, signatories must, at the minimum, be in agreement over how these crimes, including trafficking and slavery, are defined. Thus, one of the strengths that the Palermo Protocols accomplished was to get member states to agree on formally disparate definitions of trafficking and modern day slavery. According to the Palermo Protocols, the minimum definition of trafficking is:

(a) "Trafficking in persons" shall mean the recruitment, transportation, transfer, harbouring or receipt of persons, by means of the threat or use of force or other forms of coercion, of abduction, of fraud, of deception, of the abuse of power or of a position of vulnerability or of the giving or receiving of payments or benefits to achieve the consent of a person having control over another person, for the

purpose of exploitation. Exploitation shall include, at a minimum, the exploitation of the prostitution of others or other forms of sexual exploitation, forced labour or services, slavery or practices similar to slavery, servitude or the removal of organs;

(b) The consent of a victim of trafficking in persons to the intended exploitation set forth in subparagraph (a) of this article shall be irrelevant where any of the means set forth in subparagraph (a) have been used;

(c) The recruitment, transportation, transfer, harbouring or receipt of a child for the purpose of exploitation shall be considered "trafficking in persons" even if this does not involve any of the means set forth in subparagraph (a) of this article;

(d) "Child" shall mean any person under eighteen years of age.

(UNDOC, 2004)

Originally, the definition of trafficking and modern-day slavery that Palermo put forward attempted to parcel out different levels of "coercion." This sparked a continuing debate by the international community regarding how difficult to operationalize "coercion" was, especially taking into account various social, cultural, and political perspectives. For instance, many victims of labor trafficking became vulnerable to their exploitation by agreeing to subpar or slavery-like work contracts and were then tricked into working more or more. While there are some that might argue that this is an example of their agency and knowingly choosing to work in such conditions, others could also argue that they were *coerced* by poverty and oppression to make decisions that had dangerous consequences. Therefore, though Palermo had formalized international definitions of trafficking, it also left the door open in the interpretation of "coercion" and force.

Another defining area that is contentious is the treatment of sex trafficking and prostitution. There are a number of United Nations' member states where prostitution is legal. For them to sign onto the protocols, there would have to be some kind of exceptions in the protocols that allowed for them to maintain their current legal structure on prostitution. To avoid having to create any exceptions and in an attempt at unification, the protocol necessitated the vague language regarding consent. In some readings of this definition, there was enough ambiguity to justify the signing on by countries who have legalized forms of commercial sex but definitive enough to actually challenge the very notions of "consent." Under the protocols, "consent" becomes somewhat irrelevant, intimating that any victim of trafficking is incapable of consenting. Article 3 of the Protocol and Convention contains several notable points which we have included here (United Nations, 2010; Raymond, 2002). (See http://www.ohchr.org/EN/ProfessionalInterest/Pages/ProtocolTraffickingInPersons.aspx.)

- Trafficked persons are viewed as victims of the crime as opposed to the criminals;
- Victims do not need to cross countries to be protected, meaning women and children who are domestically trafficked within their own country are protected;

- State parties are to establish comprehensive policies, programs, and other measures to prevent and combat trafficking in persons and protect against victimization;

- State parties are to make efforts toward prevention by addressing factors such as poverty and lack of opportunity, which make women and children vulnerable to trafficking.

Successes

The Palermo Protocols were a catalyst in bringing together law enforcement around these issues, especially in defining trafficking and modern-day slavery as a crime. For the general public, this made trafficking and modern-day slavery more understandable than in the ways it was previously discussed, which was in terms of human rights and morality. Essentially, it became a dichotomous issue to defend and fight against, in the context of crime (i.e., innocence or guilt). This also helped construct an image of a victim as "deserving" law enforcements' assistance. Prior to the protocol, the discourse was rife with debates around consent and context of coercion, which could at times victim blame or even justify a trafficking or slavery situation. The credibility of the trafficked person may have been questioned and courts required proof of force to charge the trafficking in similar ways that sexual assaults and rape used to be proven. Because the definition of trafficking was not explicit and did not address consent, the fluidity of the court and its various perspectives could work against the victims or even acquit the traffickers. Palermo's more robust definition included the idea that almost anything could be construed as "coercion" and most importantly, that it did not need to be limited to physical force. This also demonstrated a growing understanding of the push and pull factors, and varying contexts that drove trafficking (Feingold, 2005).

Challenges

As we stated in the introduction, no legislation is complete or successful at addressing all aspects of the issue. Indeed, the Convention and Palermo Protocols were one of the first (if not *the first*) policies that attempted to address trafficking and modern-day slavery at a global scale. One of the largest challenges, not just to Palermo, but to the field in general, that was mentioned previously are the contentions around "coercion" and related to that—consent. Remember, Palermo serves as the foundation for other legislation. The presumption is that countries will use Palermo as a template to guide even more fitting definitions of trafficking and modern-day slavery as more is known about this issue.

One of the persistent challenges of Palermo is with the focus on "crime" the emphasis is on the perpetrators of that crime. Thus, the aim becomes naturally focused on them and not as much on the actual victims. Service or even working with victims is pushed to the backburner at the international scene, the prioritizing of victims being left to the discretion of individual countries. Again, while many countries may want to create genuine change or develop victim-centered programs, they may have limited material and political resources. In some of these areas, the Palermo Protocols could be the only legislation they have to address trafficking and modern-day slavery. For these countries, it is even more important that Palermo have "teeth" and the ability to be used for areas of enforcement and treatment, not just conceptually but practically. Unfortunately, what we have seen is that there has been little that Palermo could contribute in the latter. Its real advantage is to be able to further the conversation and help countries formulate both individual and transnational agreements against trafficking and modern-day slavery. For countries that are just beginning to formulate their anti-trafficking work, this is a good start.

Another challenge is that, in attempting to reframe the issue into one of transnational criminal activity, the Convention and the protocols swung far from a human rights model, losing those aspects completely. Critics state that the move toward a criminal activity prioritizes the needs and perspectives of law enforcement (Amahazion, 2015). Inarguably, the role of law enforcement is a large one, but it is not the only one. Often, those in the helping professions may be at odds with that of law enforcement, who are primarily interested in protection and prosecution. There has been an increasing move to bring law enforcement into multidisciplinary teams as well as provide more trauma informed trainings, but real integration of service providers and law enforcement still has a long way to go across the board.

10 Years of the Palermo Protocol

In 2010, the Palermo Protocol passed its ten-year mark. To date, it continues to mark a pivotal legislative decision for the international anti-trafficking movement. After ten years, the same struggles and challenges that hallmarked the protocols still exist. For instance, victim identification much less prevention has yet to be addressed or provided for. The lack of victim identification has been coupled with a growing absence of genuine victim services and a lack of alternatives to deportation for countries that insist on automatic repatriation (Heinrich, 2010).

Since Palermo, there has been an increase in convictions of traffickers. Thousands of traffickers have been identified and prosecuted successfully all around the world. The numbers of traffickers that have been convicted are a small percentage, and while that number may seem large, actually considering there are 147 nation-states that have signed the Convention and adopted the protocols, the aggregate is much lower than one would anticipate. This could be because some nation-states only report a handful of convictions (Heinrich, 2010), which could be based on how they continue to conceptualize trafficking. For instance, there are some countries such as Algeria where only sex trafficking is considered trafficking, and even then, very little is being acted on. Consequently, labor trafficking, which has larger numbers proportionately to sex trafficking, is not included. Even when sex trafficking is recognized, there are some countries where the age of "consent" is younger than 18 and therefore, differing understandings of "minors" or even of sexual assault make it difficult to make responses consistent. Regardless of the reasons, the small number of convictions may underscore the larger issue of inconsistent enforcement, or lack of enforcement altogether.

In the worst-case scenarios, victims are treated as if they are criminals; they are arrested, detained, or deported without clarifying their situation, a clear violation of the protocols. This is only one area where victim services are lacking. Palermo, Article 6, states that there should be implementation of physical, psychological, and social recovery for victims. This includes such things as housing, counseling (and other mental services), information about legal rights, medical assistance, employment, and educational opportunities. Article 7 plainly states that receiving states should consider victims of trafficking for temporary or permanent residence. Article 8 includes the requirement of voluntary repatriation with appropriate documentation. The problem is that often, they have no paperwork or have had their papers taken away. Even with these challenges, some nation-states have begun to create promising programs for victims. However, they are still woefully behind creating sustainable intervention and treatment modalities. The main function of Palermo is still to promote prosecution of traffickers rather than protection or prevention of victims (Raymond, 2002; UNODC, 2004).

With the growth of awareness, technology, and the world becoming a smaller and smaller place because of globalization and increased communication, Palermo is more important than ever. Its challenges notwithstanding, the Convention and the protocols still have the potential to influence a more effective global response to the issue (UNOHC, n.d.). However, this is really just the beginning of the direction that legislation needs to take. According to the special rapporteur in trafficking in persons in 2009, Joy Ngozi Ezelio, the protocols are not sufficient to bridge the gap between the international perspective and what is happening in individual countries (OHCHR, 2009). Therefore, it is imperative that domestic laws are also created, which address anti-trafficking legislation, even if the country has ratified the protocol.

UNITED STATES: TRAFFICKING VICTIMS PROTECTION ACT OF 2000

In response to the Convention and Palermo Protocols, President Clinton of the United States signed and enacted the Trafficking Victims Protection Act (TVPA) in 2000. The legislation set a high precedent for anti-trafficking policies and serves as a model to other countries. Prior to this act, there was minimal international legislation and nothing that contained cross border collaboration. In the United States, the only statutes that existed related to involuntary servitude and were enacted shortly after the Civil War such as the case *United States v. Kozminski* (Kim, 2007), which set the precedence that slavery was only defined as physical coercion, including force or restraint. Human trafficking crimes were also tried using the Mann Act of 1910, which is legislation that criminalized the wide range of offenses of what was known as "white slavery," or "commerce for the purpose of prostitution." Both this case precedence and the Mann Act were unable to address current human trafficking and modern-day slavery (Sheldon-Sherman, 2012).

The TVPA signaled that the U.S. government was finally acknowledging that human trafficking and modern-day slavery was a growing issue that required resources and policies to address its multilayered needs. Initially, the TVPA was created to address and establish the practice to prosecute traffickers, prevent trafficking from happening, and protect victims of trafficking within the United States. In other words, the TVPA mirrored the Palermo protocols' "3 P's": prosecution, protection, and prevention. Each will be discussed later in this chapter.

According to the TVPA, the president was required to establish an interagency task force to monitor and combat trafficking to be chaired by the secretary of state. This task force was then to do the following: (1) coordinate the implementation the TVPA 2000; (2) measure and evaluate the United States and other country's progress in preventing trafficking, providing assistance, and prosecution of traffickers; (3) facilitate and cooperate with countries of origin, transit, and destination; and (4) consult and advocate with governmental and non-governmental organizations to continually innovate and enhance the division. Out of this interagency task force and its mandates, the U.S. Office to Monitor and Combat Trafficking in Persons, housed in the U.S. State Department, was created to implement the division. An annual report, the Trafficking in Persons (TIP) Report, is generated from this office and is used to help facilitate relationships by determining rankings (categorized as tiers). Finally, this office had adopted a "4th P"—Partnerships—to address its final mandate: working to create innovative solutions to trafficking. One stellar example of partnership is the Partnership for Freedom (PFF) began in 2012 as a private-public partnership designed to be a catalyst for innovate solutions in trafficking. PFF is led by Humanity United (nonprofit), and the public offices of Department of Justice, Department of Health and Human Services, Department of Housing and Urban Development, Department of State, and the Department of Labor. There are also private entities who support the effort such as public donors, Steven Spielberg's Righteous Persons Foundation, Goldman Sachs' 10,000 Women Initiative, and the Ray and Dagmar Dolby Family Fund. PFF was assembled by President Obama to initiate three innovation challenges (2013 to 2017) for constructive solutions to end trafficking and support survivors (https://www.partnershipforfreedom.org/what-is-pff/#our-mission).

Prevention

Prevention includes raising public awareness, increasing coordination and communication efforts, and emphasizing effective policy implementation. The stated goal of TVPA has always been to prevent and service those who are vulnerable to trafficking. And, while there has been a lot of discussion and even planning in the area of prevention, there has been very little done in terms of implementation from the standpoint of this legislation. This is especially true if one were to view the TVPA contextually as a transnational piece of legislation since it clearly states that it will work to end trafficking from within the United States as well as targeting the sending countries of trafficking victims. In the latter, there has been very little done internationally except for the formation of the TIP report. While there have been efforts launched, such as mass media campaigns, it is not until recently with the formation of the national trafficking hotline that these campaigns were sponsored mainly by nonprofit organizations.

Protection

Protection includes all rescue, rehabilitation, and reintegration efforts. While this might seem to be one of the broadest areas of the legislation, in practice, most of its activities have focused on rescue (law enforcement) and reintegration (legal aspects such as being able to stay in the country). For victims of trafficking, this has taken the form of being cooperative in investigations against their traffickers, particularly in the stage of prosecution. Through different reauthorizations, the emphasis on cooperation has lessened but a lengthy and complicated certification process is still in place that may hinder the actual ability to access protection measures. The strongest instrument of protection in the United States for victims of trafficking and modern-day slavery is the T and U visas (U.S. Department of Homeland Security, 2009a). The U visa is considered a way for victims of certain crimes who meet eligibility to be able to stay in the United States so they can live and work for generally 4 years, while finding some other method to be able to stay. Eligible crimes include trafficking, but also other types of crimes such as torture, labor contracting, and other types of violent crime such as murder, kidnapping, or extortion. For this visa, an individual generally has to agree to cooperate with law enforcement, the investigation, and sometimes even the prosecution. The U visa also covers children under the age of 21, spouses, parents under the age of 21, and siblings under the age of 18 (if the U visa petitioner is under 21) (U.S. Department of Homeland Security, 2009b). There is a cap of 10,000 U visas given annually. The T visa is more specific to trafficking situations. It was created to encourage those who might otherwise not be willing to cooperate in prosecutions against their traffickers. The T visa allows people to remain and work in the United States, also for a four-year period. Just like the U visa, other family members are also covered by the T visa with the addition of the children of certain family members. There is a cap of 5,000 T visas given annually, though these numbers have never been reached and T visas are generally available to people who qualify. For both the U and the T visa, recipients may be eligible to extend or even make their stay permanent (via green card) depending again on "circumstances." The complicated process for either visa makes it necessary for individuals trying to apply for either to work with attorneys who are well versed with the process. Further, though there has been more and more built in flexibility to obtain the T and U visa, special certifications and exceptions still rely heavily on technical help.

Highlight: Kids in Need of Defense (KIND)

Kids in Need of Defense (KIND) helps children who arrive alone in the United States, typically fleeing abuse, human trafficking, and gang violence, to navigate the U.S. legal system. Without attorneys, children are almost five times less likely to win their cases. KIND and our pro-bono attorneys have helped thousands of children receive due process. KIND helps children who arrive in the United States alone by providing representation in immigration proceedings. When children are not eligible to remain in the United States, we facilitate safe reintegration. KIND recruits volunteer lawyers from top firms, corporations, and law schools, and provides them with training and resources to represent children. We currently work in Baltimore, Boston, Houston, Los Angeles, Newark, New York City, Seattle, and Washington, DC. Seventy percent of children arriving alone to the United States lack legal representation in immigration proceedings. Pro-bono representation, as provided by KIND, fills this need by

- Serving more kids: A private sector lawyer can take on 120 cases, while direct representation only serves 45 cases per attorney.

- Promoting cost-efficiency: Private sector brings increased in-house resources not available to NGOs that represent children directly; every $1 invested in KIND yields $5 is in pro-bono representation.

- Building a coalition of policy advocates: KIND has trained more than 8,500 lawyers to date. In addition to representing children, these lawyers advocate for improved policy and are driving increased public understanding of the issue.

Prosecution

Prosecution is concerned with the criminal trials of the traffickers, especially in terms of sentencing, accountability (for severity of involvement), and in some new trends, the use of restorative or transformative justice models (though very few are actually practicing this). The area of prosecution was not meant to be the priority of TVPA, but the ability to monitor and actually quantify impact through prosecutions moved focus to this area. Just as with the Palermo Protocols, the move from (human) rights-based definitions to crime-based ones naturally leaned toward a law enforcement paradigm. Also, when the legislation was written and through each reauthorization, there has been growing concern over the targeting, prosecuting, and punishing traffickers and slavers being the main focus of the legislation, with little real effort being made to prevent or treat populations who are vulnerable to trafficking. While this is the case, the criminal-victim paradigm that has been used in other instances is the same here, with little room for real understanding or target of the "demand" side, much less any movement toward more holistic restorative justice or transformative techniques, though both bear more consideration.

Partnership

The notion of "partnership" was introduced by U.S. secretary of state, Hillary Clinton, in 2009. The power of this paradigm addition was to be able to bring different and diverse populations to the decision-making table. Similarly, they would be able to leverage limited resources, which are often the largest barriers to practitioners to servicing victims of trafficking or even to launch activities such as training and capacity building. Other than the initial task forces that the TVPA mandated, this additional paradigm shift brought together international, national, and local NGOs and nonprofit organizations, public and private entities, and institutions for a number of different activities, including information sharing, service provision, advocacy, and recently, the creation of survivor networks. For instance, this is one way for transnational partnerships to be created. For instance, as Uruguay develops it's anti-trafficking laws, they partnered with the International Organization for Migration (IOM) in an interagency task committee to make sure that the laws created meet international standards (U.S. Department of State, 2016).

Reauthorizations to the TVPA

Since the inception of the TVPA in 2000, there have been four reauthorizations to the law, each with various amendments (protectionproject.org/wp-content/uploads/2013/06/TVPA-in-5-Colors_2013_FINAL.pdf). The reauthorizations have technically labeled the legislation to: Trafficking and Victims Protection Reauthorization Act, and will be referred to as TVPRA in the subsequent sections.

2003 TVPRA

The main changes in 2003 were focused on the improving T visa requirements to help the victims and their families remain in the United States. Congress increased the age for those who could receive the benefits of a T visa from 15 to 18 years old. Parents of victims, who were under 18 years old, could now qualify for T visas. Also, this reauthorization removed the requirement to cooperate with law enforcement for the prosecution of alleged traffickers. This made it easier for individuals who were trafficked to decide whether or not to apply. Although these changes were made, the actual number of T visas given each year was limited at 5,000. To date, there has never been more than 5,000 T visas rewarded.

Besides the T visa, victims also gained the ability to sue their traffickers civilly to reclaim lost wages and legal fees. The ability for victims to take their traffickers to court and reclaim their lost assets and wages is a game changer because it provides options that victims and survivors formerly did not have. Before this, the T visa and the required compliance to testify against their traffickers was their only option and one that was not often taken because of the many reasons associated with having to testify. Civil suits not only provide a way for those who were trafficked to gain material judgements but also provide a way to gain leverage. For instance, Southeast Asian domestic workers who had been enslaved by their East Asian traffickers took them to court after filing a civil suit. The traffickers opted for a settlement. The domestic workers decided not to pursue T visas or a criminal case because of their age, their level of PTSD, and the fact that they had been enslaved for over 20 years collectively and did not want to engage in lengthy criminal proceedings that they likely would not win (Garcia, personal communication, 2016).

One of the most pivotal changes was the ability to use the Racketeering Influenced Corrupt Organizations (RICO) statute in cases of trafficking. For instance, in San Diego, California, the use of the RICO statute was able to be employed to detain and convict sex traffickers who were operating and using gangs for their crimes. Twice, San Diego law enforcement worked with a federal task force to bring in over a hundred gang members who were charged with racketeering for the trafficking of underage girls and women, drug crimes, kidnapping, and murder (Kotiswaran, 2011). The gang members were from the West Coast Crips, a gang that had been in San Diego for over 30 years with over 300 members (Davis, 2016). Without the ability to use the RICO statutes the convictions would not have been as easy nor the consequences as severe.

2005 TVPRA

The largest shift in the 2005 TVPRA was the change in focus from international labor and sex trafficking to a more domestic lens—the trafficking within United States' borders. Since most of the emphasis was on domestic trafficking, the focus was on commercially sexually exploited youth. Congress recognized that children, especially runaway and homeless children, are at risk of being trafficked domestically. For the first time, the TVPRA made domestic trafficking an active part of the conversation. This salient turn in legislation was key because until this point, there was the misconception that trafficking *had* to occur across borders. The recognition of domestic trafficking opened up the potential for state by state legislation, federal and state funding, and mandated responsible institutions such as Child Welfare to engage in the situation. Because of this move, there begins to be an effort, under this reauthorization to create shelter services for minors that are trauma-specific to trafficking.

In 2005, there was also an effort to expand measurements to address sex tourism over-all, but especially with Americans who go overseas for the purpose of sex with minors. Sex tourism was a growing aspect of trafficking, especially in parts of Southeast Asia, Eastern Europe, and South Africa. The "sex tour" scheme was not a new one, with many travel agencies offering "sex tours," often with the marketing of unlimited sex with sub-servient women (in other words, very "different" from the women of the West). In several ways, these sex tours played on gender oppressive stereotypes in the United States and overseas.

2008 TVPRA

During this year's reauthorization, there was an initiative, beginning of what would become a trend in the anti-trafficking movement is the emphasis of data collection. TVPRA 2008 mandated more in-depth data collection. Further, this reauthorization helped jumpstart coordination efforts between different institutions or offices that were collecting trafficking data. Of course, there are still barriers around issues of confiden-tiality, limited resources, and technical know-how, but the prioritizing of data gathering is a positive movement toward understanding scope of the problem and scaling of the solutions.

2013 TVPRA

In 2013, the reauthorization of TVPRA made it an amendment to the Violence Against Women Act. Essentially, this strengthened the connections between trafficking and other forms of violence against women, especially in the areas of sexual assault. By doing this, shelters and services had to acknowledge the parallels and similarities between sexual assaults and trafficking. For instance, the connections between service provision of rape crisis centers and domestic violence shelters and trafficking opened up a greater area of cooperation and collaboration to the anti-trafficking and antiviolence efforts.

Also, this reauthorization refocused the issue on labor trafficking by including supply chain importance and also outlawing the purchase of goods made by trafficking victims. The issue of supply chain management and transparency will be discussed in chapter 10.

The issue of child marriage was also brought to forefront in this reauthorization. Child marriage is understood as marriage between minors under the age of 18 to those older than 18. The organization Girls not Brides estimates that if there is not a concerted effort to end child brides, 1.2 billion girls will be married by 2030. It is a practice that is preva-lent not only in countries such as India, Bangladesh, Nigeria, and Brazil but also in some areas of the United States (Girls not Brides, n.d.). Often, cultural practices are used to justify these types of marriages. In many cases, practitioners may not know how to deal with such obviously cultural aspects of child marriage but should be receive training on how to challenges such aspects that are truly detrimental to women and children.

Finally, 2013 addressed the increased vulnerability of populations experiencing natural disaster to trafficking. For example, after the Haitian 2010 earthquake, there were reports by UNICEF and other agencies that thousands of children were becoming *restaveks* (the literal meaning "to stay with" because culturally poorer children were put in the houses of more affluent families to exchange their labor for a place to live and food to eat). Currently, *restaveks* refers to "child slaves," mostly victims of sex trafficking in Haiti, but also in the United States, prevalent in Haitian-U.S. communities. Before the earthquake, the number of *restaveks* recognized by the Haitian government was more than 300,000 with the perhaps more abroad. Following the earthquake, there was a rush to the conflicted Caribbean island to claim children who were supposedly in the middle of being adopted by families. With the immense devastation, there was no way to verify who was telling the truth (Padgett & Ghosh, 2010). This experience and others led to recommendations to suspend any international adoption practices following a major natural disaster until more infrastructure and stability could be gained.

Additional Legislation

Approved in May of 2015, this law was passed. Highlights of the law include increased penalties for those who are convicted of trafficking and sexual exploitation of children as well as human smuggling. It also establishes the Domestic Trafficking Victims' Fund to award grants to states and localities to combat trafficking and provide protection and assistance for victims, especially to implement child abuse investigation and services for victims of child pornography. The law amends TVPA to allow U.S. citizens and permanent residents who are victims of trafficking to obtain benefits and services without official certification from the Department of Health and Human Services and requires that all Department of Justice anti-trafficking programs include technical trainings. The law also requires training for different provider areas, including nursing, Department of Homeland Security, as well as those within U.S. Immigration and Customs Enforcement (ICE). The law also establishes the U.S. Advisory Council on Human Trafficking to provide recommendations to the Senior Policy Operating Group (established under TVPA 2000) and the president's Interagency Task Force to Monitor and Combat Trafficking.

Preventing Sex Trafficking and Strengthening Families Act. Public Law No: 113-183

Approved September of 2014, this law includes specific compliance mandates for CSEC risks. It is mainly concerned with the identification and protection of youth who are vulnerable to trafficking within foster care and adoption assistance. The law requires the state to plan for identification, documentation, and determination of appropriate services to CSEC exposed victims. The law also improves supportive permanency and assistance to foster parents. At the same time, it allows for the youth ages 14 and above to participate in their own healing and case plans. This law also establishes a National Advisory Committee on the Sex Trafficking of Children and Youth in the United States who will advise the Secretary (U.S. Department of Health and Human Services, 2013) and the attorney general's office on practical and general policies.

International Laws:

Council of Europe Convention on Action Against Trafficking in Human Beings (2008)
coe.int/en/web/conventions/full-list/-/conventions/rms/090000168008371d

This is an open treaty that has been ratified by states (Denmark, Estonia, Finland, France, Germany, Latvia, Malta, Monaco, Poland, Portugal, Slovenia, Sweden, Switzerland, Former Yougoslav Republic of Macedonia, and the United Kingdom). The treaty is focused on all forms of trafficking, and its goal is increased protection and prevention. Further, they agree to take a human rights-based approach, use gender mainstreaming, and a child-sensitive approach in the creation and assessment of policies. This would be done through coordination between countries, including the creation of an independent monitoring system to guarantee that the provisions of this treaty are being followed.

Coordinated Mekong Ministerial Initiative against Trafficking (COMMIT) composed of China, Laos, Thailand, Cambodia, Myanmar, and Vietnam (2005)

no-trafficking.org/commit.

COMMIT was first conceptualized in 2004 and became official when the participating countries signed a Memorandum of Understanding at the Ministerial level in 2005. COMMIT is governed by six national taskforces, composed of government officials, police, social welfare, and women's affairs from each participating country. They make all the major decisions regarding the anti-trafficking programming and policy in their countries. Two representatives (also decided by each country) represents for COMMIT governance. Annually, a Sub Regional Plan of Action is created and then implemented in each country and between countries when needed through bilateral and multilateral agreements. COMMIT coordinates their efforts with local, regional, and international NGOs, United Nation agencies, and relevant government departments.

Justice for Victims of Trafficking Act, 2015. Public Law No: 114–22
congress.gov/bill/114th-congress/senate-bill/178

Challenges

The TVPA represents a federal initiative against trafficking and is undoubtedly a catalyst in the government's stance. Even though this is the case, this does not guarantee consistency between states or at local levels of government. Not all 50 states have created their own anti-trafficking legislation and only 9 states offer public benefits to individuals who have been deemed trafficking victims (U.S. Department of State, 2010b). Another area that needs to be improved on is that the T visa continues to be underutilized. This may be addressed by supporting victims of trafficking through lessening the pressure to cooperate in cases and making certification and eligibility more accessible and less cumbersome. Conversely, these things could be addressed if law enforcement, lawyers, and social services created stronger, more collaborative relationships.

Safe Harbor Laws

As CSEC has become a more widely discussed issue, the inequities of punishment to the abusers has become a major problem. A way to combat the lack of consistent punishment and legal action taken against those involved in CSEC has been the creation of safe harbor laws. "Safe harbor laws were developed by states to address inconsistencies with how children that are exploited for commercial sex are treated" (Polaris Project, 2015). Safe harbor laws are broken down into two parts: protection and services. The first was to work with children to protect them from prosecution from explicit offenses. The latter works to create programs for the children to be involved in as a path to exit the life. According to the National Congress on State Legislature (2014) the common goals enacted in the safe harbor laws are "that trafficked children be treated as victims and not prosecuted as prostitutes, that trafficked children be diverted from the justice system and placed in appropriate services, that states provide a protective response to prevent further victimization and that individuals who fund, profit from, or pay for sex with children are appropriately punished. At least 28 states have enacted legislation addressing safe harbor issues."

According to the Polaris Project, 2015, there are 34 states that have passed safe harbor laws. While the goal is similar, most of the states' laws vary greatly and have not been able to fully encompass appropriate protection for the victims. Some states protect children under the age of 18 while others will only protect children under the age of 15. According to the NCSL (2014) there are only 8 states who have created programs known as "john schools" to keep predators from reoffending. And there have been 13 states who have allotted funding for public officials to get training on CSEC and how to appropriately interact with victims. This is an important part of the education process to change the narrative with how these children are viewed and treated. These laws are also aiding in the creation of data collection for the states and public entities to better understand the true make up of CSEC, including the victims, abusers, and perpetrators. While these laws are not uniform nor are able to help combat the whole problem safe harbor laws are acting as a stepping stone to better legislation and understanding for CSEC victims.

ANTI-TRAFFICKING LAWS: A GLOBAL VIEW

A survey of different countries around the world and the status of their anti-trafficking legislation portrays just how uneven the state of policy remains from a global perspective. We have included a short survey of different countries and their laws to give you an idea of what is type of policy work is being done globally. The countries were selected to provide a perspective from different regions of the world. While the laws may vary, they all demonstrate that there is still much left to do overall, no matter what country we are talking about. For instance, there is still much to do if we are to get to point where there are sufficient protections and laws in every country much less begin to create multilateral agreements that would allow countries to work together. For instance, Japan is a both a transit and receiving country in that this is a destination for those who are trafficked, but it is also a "waiting area" while traffickers decide where to go next or await their next destination. It is also transitory in the sense that many exploiters on sex tours will use Japan as one of their many "stops" in the Asia Pacific region. Finally, Japan is unique in that there is also the criminal element of the Yakuza, or Japanese organized crime, who are extremely organized and drive trafficking. One branch of the Yakuza (the Yamaguchi-gumi) numbers roughly at 40,000 members and are required to study any anticrime laws so that they can stay ahead of the curve (McCurry, 2009). While Japan has had some preliminary statements about trafficking in 2004, they currently do not have any official anti-trafficking legislation. Japan also had extremes of both sex and labor trafficking, mainly from the Philippines, Thailand, Indonesia, Colombia, and China. Since Japan does not have any anti-trafficking legislation per se, it is difficult to create any progress between countries.

Colombia

Colombia has been engaged in decades of civil unrest, which has caused millions of internally displaced people, the involvement of children as combatants, and increasing numbers of children forced into labor (boys for labor and girls for sex). In 2005, Colombia passed anti-trafficking legislation (Law 985). This defined trafficking regardless of a victim's "consent," which meant that defense could no longer use consent to discredit victims and let traffickers go free. Law 985 also raised minimum sentences of imprisonment for traffickers. One of the strongest areas of the law was to assign an Intersituational Committee to Combat Trafficking in Persons to develop ongoing action plans and policies, including international coordination efforts with other South American counties such as Argentina, Bolivia, El Salvador, and Mexico (U.S. Department of State, 2010b, 2011). This join anti-trafficking cooperation effort focuses mainly on repatriation and investigations, but hopefully it can begin to focus on prevention and service coordination. Internally, all 32 departments in Colombian government have anti-trafficking committees, but it is unclear that they operate in any consistent or cooperative manner. While these are all certainly steps in the right direction, many analysts believe that nothing can truly change the situation until the civil unrest in the country is resolved (Vieira, 2010).

Iran

Iran is notorious for its uneven laws, sex/gender segregation, and sociosexual discrimination, causing deplorable conditions for women and leaving the vulnerable more vulnerable (Hepburn & Simon, 2015). Iran passed anti-trafficking legislation in 2004 that prohibits trafficking for prostitution, removal of organs, slavery, or forced marriage (Hosseini-Divkolaye, 2009). They also signed agreements with countries such as Afghanistan and Turkey as well as organizations such as the International Labor Organization (ILO) and the International Organization for Migration (IOM). The use of the anti-trafficking law is only available if the crimes do not fit under current Penal Codes and it is like all other laws in Iran, subsumed under shariah, or Islamic law. If this is the case, then women and girls will always be in an inherently unequal position. For example, under Islamic law, a women's testimony is worth half that of a man. This makes implementation difficult and inconsistent.

Thailand

In 2008, Thailand passed an anti-trafficking law. The law prohibits both sex and labor trafficking. This is an extremely important distinction because prior to this law, Thailand did not recognize male victims of trafficking, most of whom are labor trafficked. This law also created the provision of over 138 shelters in the country, with at least 1 in each region. One of the shelters also focuses on males, again, a positive move to recognize the thousands of men (foreign and Thai) who are trafficked especially through the fishing and shrimping industries (Skinner, 2008). The law also prescribes penalties for traffickers that range from 4 to 10 years' imprisonment. Interestingly, while most of the penalties that are actually given are in the 2-year range, there have also been death penalties that have been decided (U.S. Department of State, 2008b). Additionally, since one of the biggest challenges in Thailand are high levels of police and government corruption, under this law, any official found committing offenses is liable to twice the punishment (Royal Thai Government, 2008). Two large challenges to Thailand's effort is the growing issue of citizenship. Over a million of Thailand's people belong to Hill Tribes and over half of them are not recognized as citizens and their children are often not even given birth certificates, creating a cycle of nonrecognition. Added to this are Burmese refugees as well as other foreigners, some of whom may be in the country because of trafficking (Daughters' Rising, personal communication, 2015). There is also a lack of implementation or fragmented implementation that makes it difficult to enforce this law. To address these challenges, the Thai government has launched a number of policy initiatives and planning committees to help improve their efforts by addressing some of the intersecting issues and root causes of trafficking.

Organizational Highlight: Coalition to Abolish Slavery and Trafficking (CAST)

The Coalition to Abolish Slavery and Trafficking (CAST) began in 1998 in the wake of the famous El Monte sweatshop case. In this case, 72 Thai garment workers had been enslaved for 8 years. CAST's founder, Dr. Katheryn McMahon, was part of a group of concerned community members and service providers who felt that it was time to do something. Currently, CAST is a multiethnic, multilingual human rights organization that is recognized in Los Angeles, nationally, and internationally. They provide a three-pronged empowerment approach that includes social services, legal services, and outreach and training. CAST is constantly launching initiatives such as the Saban Free Clinic, a family clinic where they are now trained to address health and mental health needs of trafficking victims, the first national survivor network, and is a supporter and advocate of important local, state, national, and international legislation and policy. [adapted from: http://www.castla.org/about-us]

China

Because of its size, China is a microcosm of the world and as such, contains every form of human trafficking and modern-day slavery within its own borders (UNIAP, 2008). It is unclear what the trafficking statistics are in China, though we know that the country is a source, transit, and destination for trafficking. Some estimates have stated that trafficking of the Chinese alone (internal) is over 250 million people (Xin, 2012). The lack of solid statistics is partially based on the way that China has defined trafficking. Under Chinese definitions in Article 240 of their Criminal Code, trafficking is related only to "women or children" (UNIAP, 2008). The exclusion of men in this definition also excludes most forms of labor trafficking and thus, services to victims are also not available. The definition also excludes all forms of coercion except for abduction. Further, girls who are over the age of 14 are not considered trafficking victims (U.S. Department of State, 2011). The numbers may also be difficult to calculate because of the confluence of illegal adoptions, smuggling, and other criminal activities that are counted along with human trafficking and modern-day slavery. If these numbers cannot be delineated, it is difficult to gauge the true effects of any anti-trafficking legislation or efforts to stop trafficking all together.

France

In 2003, under their Internal Security Law, France added human trafficking (sex and labor) as a criminal offense. Imprisonment up to 10 years and fines up to 2.1 million are possible punishments (U.S. Department of State, 2009). Even though the law was enacted in 2003, it was not used until 2007 to actually convict traffickers of sex trafficking. Although the guidelines for the law, in theory, are stringent, they have been not only inconsistently implemented but trafficking as an issue has many times been overshot with other immigration issues such as unaccompanied minors and refugees. France has dealt with immigration issues by mass deportations and minimal protections such as housing minors in adult detention centers (with adults), and many obstacles toward asylum (HRW, 2009). This makes the biggest challenge the immigration policies and perspectives it has enacted, particularly toward the Roma populations and others. These policies have hindered efforts for clear anti-trafficking legislation.

Case Vignette: Cristela

Cristela was born in El Salvador where her parents were farmers. She was the eighth child and her mother was very ill after her birth. She was taken care of by her aunt, but she also had many children so Cristela was weaned early and since then had suffered from slight malnutrition and has always underweight. The family existed in abject poverty in a small village far from the capital of San Salvador, but Cristela traveled twice to go into the city because her mother's sister lived there and she was sent to help her keep her home. Both times, she traveled with another family. She did not

(Continued)

(Continued)

mind because her aunt only had two other children, who were already grown up so she grew very close to her. She was always a little sad to have to return home.

Cristela never went to school. She stayed at home and helped her family with the smaller children. Sometimes, she was sent to work in the coffee plantations with her parents during the harvest season. When she turned 9 years old, her parents started talking to someone who said that if they could send their children to the United States, the children could then send for their parents and they could get citizenship. Cristela had always heard about the United States but all she really knew about it was that it was very far away. It took her parents a long time to save, but by the time Cristela was 11 years old, they had enough to pay the Cayotajes (those who take smuggle people over the border into the United States) to take Cristela and her older sister, Delmy, who was 13 years old. Their 13-year-old cousin, Larissa, would also go with them. First, they traveled to the border of Mexico. This was not so hard, but Cristela missed home, especially her aunt whom she had grown close to. They were put on a train that everyone called La Bestia, which is a cargo train, so Cristela and her companions were placed on top of one of the cars. They stayed in the middle so that they would not fall off. Even though there were others around her, Cristela was very afraid. When the train finally stopped. Cristela, Delmy, and Larissa were met by a Cayotaje who was supposed to take them across the border into the United States. They were asked for money and when Delmy handed it to him, he told them they were $300 short. The three girls did not know what to do. They cried and begged him to take them. They were all worried they would get in trouble by their parents because they were not able to cross the border and they also had now given over all the money to the Cayotaje. He told them he would go to his boss and see what he could do and left them at the train station to wait.

The three girls waited overnight in the train station until he returned late in the night. He didn't say anything to them except to grab Larissa. Cristela and Delmy yelled at him and asked what he was doing with their cousin. Larissa struggled until he hit her in the face and picked her up. Cristela and Delmy were scared but they stayed where they were, hoping that he would return with Larissa. They did not ask any police for help because they were afraid they would get in trouble. Eventually, they fell asleep in a corner and were woken up when the Cayotaje returned, dragging Larissa with him. Larissa's clothes were torn and her lip was bloody as were her wrists. She did not look up when Cristela asked her what happened. The Cayotaje led them across the border through the dark and they walked for what felt like many hours to Cristela through the desert. Twice they had to hide from the border patrol. It became very cold and Cristela had several cuts on her feet. She was worried about her cousin, but Larissa still would not talk.

When they finally arrived across the border, the Cayotaje left them and told them to wait for the next person who would take them. As soon as he left, Larissa started crying and she told her cousins they had to get away. She told them that she had been raped and that they would be to if they did not run away from "these bad men." Cristela and Delmy had no idea where to go, but they believed

Larissa and they ran away, hiding behind a building. But, they were found by two men who separated them and took them to a building. The girls were put into rooms where they were raped and exploited daily. It was many days before Cristela was able to even get up, but she wanted to see her sister. She begged to be able to see her sister. She was told no. A month passed and Cristela, Delmy, and Larissa finally saw each other because they were put into a van to be taken somewhere else.

On the way to their destination, the three girls pretended they had to use the bathroom and made a run for it. The gas station attendant, who thought there was something wrong with three young girls who looked so bedraggled and fearful, found them hiding and helped them. He called the border patrol. They had been in the same neighborhood they first arrived at—never going farther into the United States. The girls were taken by Homeland Security and at first they were put on a bus to what they called a "resettlement area." Someone told Cristela they were going to go to a community near San Diego and for the first time, she had hope. But, when their bus entered the community, there were many people holding signs that said, "Go Home" and "We don't want you." Cristela could not read and definitely could not know what these foreign words said, but she could hear the same things being chanted. She was scared by all the yelling and scared that they would be returned to the men who hurt them, or at least found by them. The three of them huddled in their shared seat. Delmy started to pray.

The bus turned around and they were taken to another place that was a former detention area. It was already filled with children but they found a place to sleep and managed to stay together. Over the next month, they learned the rhythm of the refugee and resettlement area. They were finally approached by a lawyer who was there to help them. By then, they had also started to learn English. All three girls continued to have nightmares and disliked being touched. They rarely left one another and even in sleep, it was common to see them holding hands and holding onto one another. They are currently awaiting their court case. They have no family in the United States so they will be in the refugee and resettlement center until they are seen. Their only contact is the lawyer who has spoken to them.

CALL TO ACTION: CREATE AND ENFORCE ANTI-TRAFFICKING POLICY WORLDWIDE

Trafficking has gone from a specialized area where only a small number of activists, advocates, academics, and organizations were aware of it to a widespread social issue that almost everyone is aware of to some degree or another. With the advent of the legislation we have highlighted here, we can see the same challenges existing in many of countries. The need for legislation is paramount in being able to stop trafficking and modern-day slavery. As both Palermo and TVPA have passed their 15-year marks, we can see that there are many gaps and limitations to what type of impact the legislation really has, but this is still the first step of many and a decisive stance against the sale of human beings. While there continue to be huge challenges globally, they are not insurmountable and we can already see some positive changes and efforts occurring. For instance, in Congress just authorized a Human Trafficking Advisory Council that is composed of survivors to advise the president's Interagency Task Force on federal anti-trafficking policies. Also, as we looked at earlier, there are more and more multidisciplinary partnerships forming, bringing together many perspectives to address the issues. Moreover, while there are still improvements to be made in data gathering, there is now more information than ever, including our better understanding on how important our different perspectives may (or may not contribute to the work). More trauma-centric endeavors, genuine collaboration, and increased understanding of the scope of trafficking and modern-day slavery will go far in working to end trafficking and modern-day slavery. Perhaps one of the strongest directions that we can take is also the creation of transnational partnerships and legislation that have agreements, which allow for countries to work together in their anti-trafficking endeavors. Certainly, a clearer knowledge base around trafficking chains and patterns will be one way to trace where slavery exists as well as begin to hold various aspects of production, distribution, and business practices more accountable.

DISCUSSION QUESTIONS

1. What policies affect the agency you are working in?

2. What is the best method to inform your agency about different policies that affect the trafficking population?

3. Where are the gaps in policies and how can you bridge them?

4. How do we create policies that work in both sending and receiving countries? How would we operationalize them?

5. Imagine that you are able to create a "super anti-trafficking law" that every country in the world would have to follow. What would your legislation focus on? How would you implement and enforce it?

CHALLENGE

Find out what important anti-trafficking legislation is on the agenda in your city/state/country. Write to your local public official to demonstrate your support.

Supply Chain Transparency

When we arrived at the tour for a fair-trade coffee bean plantation in Tanzania, I realized that this "fair trade" plantation was probably the first of its kind. The guide spoke about previous farms he worked on and their deplorable conditions, often alluding to human trafficking and bonded servitude. This experience of seeing what a farm could look like when they chose to use ethical working conditions made me realize that there was another way to do business. People just had to make the decision to choose it. I wondered if it ever made a difference to me before, to know how things were produced, but touring that plantation, I knew without a doubt that it made a difference to those workers.

Eight years later, fair trade is a common term as are the words "transparency" and "accountability" when talking about supply chains. My brother, who understands supply chains from a management and financial perspective (as opposed to my perspective as a helping professional), said that it was a complex puzzle. The world wants things to be cheaper, he told me, and so if we have cheaper goods, we have to cut the cost of labor or the cost of the product. You can't make things without

(Continued)

(Continued)

people, so often it is the worker that made cheaper, even enslaved or put into hazardous working conditions. If places like that coffee plantation existed, why couldn't other industries or good follow suit? Was it that hard to be ethical and make a profit?

Since then, I've researched various policies and companies that are trying to make this difficult balance work. Even where there are transparency acts around the world, the laws and policies don't mandate things that would truly force a business to be more open to operating to eradicate slavery and trafficking. In fact, even the most progressive of policies don't call for surprise audits. If audits are even required, most audits are announced and can be planned for. I know that companies such as Starbucks, In-N-Out, and Costco like to point out how they audit their supply chain, but, most of their audits are done on an announced basis. While an announced audit helps streamline the process, it also allows for various unfavorable practices to be hidden and covered up. I know that this is a good beginning but I am impatient for it to be a good policy that really begins to make an impact when it comes to ending human trafficking and modern-day slavery.

Becoming more educated about trafficking and modern-day slavery and having the privilege to visit more places like this fair-trade coffee plantation has made me not only a better service provider but also a more conscientious consumer. I wear TOMS shoes and I shop at farmers' market collectives. I make sure that I buy sweatshop free and, if possible, from social enterprises that benefit other things. But, not everyone can shop this way. Some people cannot choose between cheaper or more ethical. The latter is a necessity, not a political statement. As long as this is the case and the more ethical something is, the higher its price tag, then driving down costs to the lowest denominator will always be prevalent. We have to have a better system because with every cent we drive things down, another person is exploited. People have to understand that consumer power is a real and that business as we know it is changing.

—Megan Healy

INTRODUCTION: LABOR TRAFFICKING OVERVIEW

Labor trafficking constitutes 78% of all trafficking and modern-day slavery in the world, according to the International Labor Organization (ILO) (ILO, 2012a). Depending on what statistics are used, this is means an estimated 21 million to 36 million people who are considered forced, indentured, or contract slave labor. In 2009, the U.S. Department of Labor's List of "goods produced by child or forced labor" included 58 countries with over 122 goods. By 2014, the number had grown to 74 countries with over 136 goods (Bayer, et al., 2015). Child labor is found primarily in the following areas: brick making, illegal fisheries, carpet making, and sex trafficking (mainly in child pornography) (DOL, 2016). Slavery and labor trafficking does not have one face. We see labor trafficking and modern-day slavery in almost every industry, appearing in different forms throughout the supply chains, especially when global businesses are operating under multiple legal and cultural value systems. There is even the rationalization that this modern-day slavery is justified because of such practices as inheriting slaves, the reciprocal exchange of feudal relationships, and the pragmatic course of receiving a pittance is still better than getting nothing. The ability to regulate and disclose what is going on is such supply chains may seem like the logical place to start, but it remains an almost impossible challenge. At least that is what some companies and big business would like us to believe. The assumption that supply chains are too complex to understand can be immobilizing. This is why it is important to understand the how supply chains work and the pivotal role they have in unmasking and hopefully ending labor trafficking and modern day slavery.

The Ghost Fleet

The Ghost Fleet is a documentary feature that uncovers the vast injustice of slavery in the Thai fishing industry through thrilling escape stories.

Thailand supplies a large portion of America's seafood, but Thailand's giant fishing fleet is chronically short tens of thousands of fishermen per year. Human traffickers have stepped in, selling captives from the region to the captains for a few hundred dollars each. Once at sea, the men may never return to land—unless they escape.

Slave ships, trafficking gangs, and heroic escapes behind the world's seafood.

The Ghost Fleet will introduce audiences this strange, watery underworld through several characters' eyes, bringing viewers deep into the lives of escaped slaves, corrupt officials, unlikely heroes and those working to end slavery on the sea.

Our project has begun production in Thailand, Malaysia, Borneo, and Cambodia, following several characters, locations, and storylines. At its core, this is the story of how a few men—a farmer, a motorcycle mechanic, and a construction worker—were lured onto boats, trapped at sea, and against all odds escaped to freedom.

One was on a boat for 7 years without seeing land before he escaped. Another was sold with his son and together they pulled off a hair-raising and miraculous escape. One man, Asorasak, escaped into the forests of Borneo before being taken in by a benevolent family of fisherman who sheltered him for 3 years before he could go home. We filmed his journey home and reconnected him to his family, capturing a truly rare and emotional moment.

We are following the man who runs a hotline for Burmese migrants, operated by Project Issara, 24 hours a day, from his cell phone and will connect his story to those on the other end of the line. We'll also work with everyday citizens in Thailand or Burma who go undercover to document and expose the trafficking gangs working in their area or embed with the police as they make arrests.

(Continued)

(Continued)

We will search the beaches where men swim to shore, check out the brothels where men are drugged before waking up on board, travel to villages in Myanmar (Burma) and Cambodia virtually empty of men and sail to remote islands where captains store men, sometimes in cages. We'll also provide an investigative through-line, tracing the roots of this issue up the chain of government command in Thailand and through the extremely murky fish supply chain back to supermarkets in the United States and Europe.

Our mission is to tell a captivating tale, full of incredible, real-time events and unforgettable characters that can catalyze change by shifting how we look at the fish on our plates. We believe a character-driven, widely accessible documentary film that lights up the American consciousness about fish could be *The Inconvenient Truth* or *Food Inc.* for the ocean. It would provide oceans advocates with a much-needed human face, add fire to the movement against forced labor and link environmental collapse with collateral economic damage.

There is no greater force on Earth than the promise of freedom.

The Gulf of Thailand, once teeming with life, is now barren. Decades ago, Thai boats plied rich waters and came home full after a few days or weeks. Now captains are out for years, chasing fish as far away as Ethiopia.

As Thailand's prosperity increases, fishermen are finding more family-friendly work and the enormous Thai fishing fleet—the second-biggest supplier of fish to the United States—is short tens of thousands of men per year.

Human trafficking gangs have stepped into the gap, luring men out of villages in Cambodia, Bangladesh, and Myanmar [Burma] with false promises of well-paying jobs in prosperous Thailand. Instead, they sell the men to captains for a few hundred dollars and the captives are held at sea, no land in sight, for years on end. Boats make perfect prisons.

Meanwhile, families at home wait for their men to return—elders plow fields, wives hold funerals after years of absence. Entire villages in Cambodia and Myanmar are eerily without men.

This flow of slaves from northern Asian nations to southern ones through the Thai fleet is estimated in the hundreds of thousands, though it has likely crossed the million-man mark. It's such a staggering problem that the U.S. ambassador in charge of investigating global human trafficking, Luis C. DeBaca, says the slave trade onto Thai boats knocks the entire economy of Southeast Asia off kilter. And, because Thailand is the second biggest supplier of fish to the United States, he believes our reliance on slave fish threatens American food security.

theghostfleet.com

UNDERSTANDING THE SUPPLY CHAIN

Quite simply, a "supply chain" is the series of processes (companies, services, people, resources, materials) that something must go through to produce a commodity (Simchi-Levi & Zhao, 2005). What makes supply chains complex is when you add more steps because of multinational, multilayered, and multipurpose companies. Coupled with the expanding globalization of companies as well as the development of more sophisticated information technology, facilitating faster communication and coordination, the complexity of supply chains and the management of them became a driver of profit and potential (Bayer, et al., 2015). In chapter 2, we discussed the roles of supply and demand within an economic perspective of trafficking and modern-day slavery. The move to reduce costs in production has resulted in justifications by some businesses that exploitative labor practices occur and are concealed in some part of the supply chain, but difficult to find (Datta & Bales, 2013). Supply chains are important to understand because the more complex a supply chain is, the harder it is to make transparent. Conversely, this is true as the more intricate a supply chain, the more internationally connected and highly outsourced they usually are, the easier it is to hide slave labor.

There are some areas of supply chains that are conceptually the same across the board. However, we cannot discount those things that are dependent on the type of industry they are connected to. It is important to be able to look at supply chains from both perspectives—the universal and the particular. For instance, this example of the supply chain is from the agricultural field, specifically the chocolate industry. While this supply chain focuses on chocolate production and distribution, many of the same elements, connections, and modes of transport are similar to most other supply chains. Understanding this example, helps provide you an idea of how complex and intersectional (i.e., nonlinear) supply chains can be.

Figure 10.1   Example of Supply Chain (Agriculture)

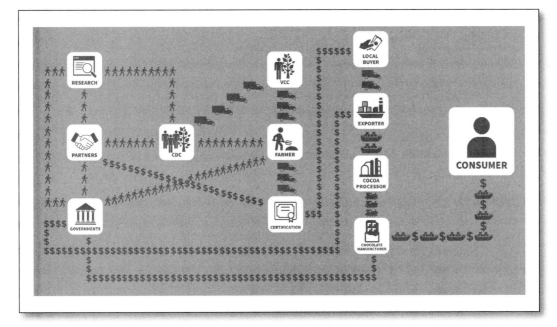

Source: Honey Imbo.

LAWS AROUND SUPPLY CHAIN TRANSPARENCY

Internationally, with the growth of globalization, the need for transparency and social responsibility came to the forefront in the 2000s with the crash of markets, protest of workers against current labor prices, and uneven conditions within multinational companies. Social media, websites, and applications such as Yelp, Amazon, and Trip Advisor put more power in the hands of users and consumers whose growing awareness on local, sustainable, human rights based, and moral practices was becoming more and more widespread. This "partnership" between workers and consumers, as well as some companies who were genuinely working to achieve corporate responsibility as more than just a tax break, began a movement toward more stringent codes of conduct and a culture of monitoring, transparency, and reporting (Gereffi & Mayer, 2004; Mayer & Pickles, 2010). Aligned with these actions, governments added their support through the creation of policies and legislation. In 2007, China attempted to put into place contract labor laws to create a more stable and higher base for workers (Lan & Pickles, 2011). In 2010, the European Union created a Forest Law Enforcement and Governance Act that made marketing of illegal timber prohibited. Still, it was not until laws were created to address conflict minerals that supply chains came into scrutiny and importance. Legislation such as the United States' 2010 Dodd-Franck Act and the 2011 UK Bribery Act required companies to disclose where conflict minerals originated from (Barraco, 2011).

The logic behind making supply chains for conflict minerals more transparent was mainly to dislodge areas where slave labor may be hiding. However, because of the intense work done in that area, it made sense that this could be applied in other industries. Admittedly, an executive at a major retailer explained that supply chains for minerals are much more complex and numerous than those for industries such as garments or other types of manufacturing. In other words, if we are able to find out where one single diamond has been mined, it should be even easier to do so for a sweater or a piece of technology (GAP Inc., personal communication, 2015). The key was persuading, influencing, or mandating companies to do so. Thus, the relationships between the public (consumers and citizen groups), stakeholders (including NGOs and advocacy organizations), companies/corporations, and government is an important one, with each one having differing motivations. Also, each actor has a different role, in part to expose slavery in supply chains. For example, for consumers, this may mean not purchasing slave-made or potentially slave-made products. For businesses, it may be being able to take an ethical stance toward production even if it cuts into profit.

CASE STUDY: BRAZIL, A NATIONAL PACT FOR THE ERADICATION OF SLAVE LABOR

Forced labor in Brazil is the largest form of trafficking in Brazil. Estimates are that there are over 25,000 men who are involved in slave labor (Gomes, 2010). They are primarily found in sugarcane plantations and cattle ranches. Ironically, the boom in "green sustainability" has exacerbated the trafficking problem in Brazil, which is one of the leading developers in sugarcane ethanol (marketed as "clean energy") (Fargione et. al., 2008). In 2009, 45% of those rescued by the Brazilian government came solely from sugarcane plantations. In

Figure 10.2   Corporate Social Responsibility

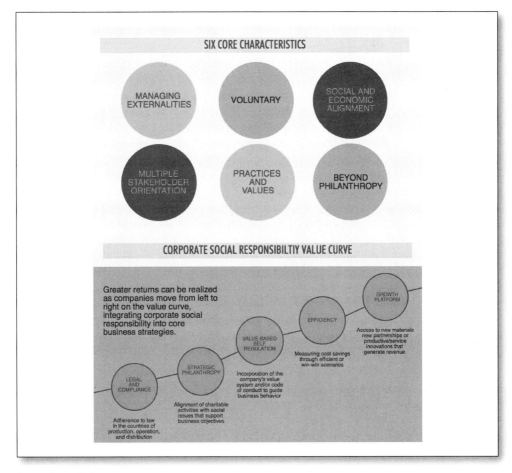

Source: Honey Imbo

addition to the heinous work conditions, the group Anti-Slavery International (2010) con-ducted research that revealed the average life expectancy for trafficked victims Honey Imbo enslaved on sugarcane plantations was 10 years from the time they were first enslaved. Similar to other labor trafficking schemes, most workers are recruited with promises of decent work conditions and the provision of food and lodging only to be charged with exor-bitant fees that are added to a never ending "debt" that they have to pay back to recruiters or subcontractors. Many of these settings are isolated and policed by "private security" or paramilitary-like professionals hired by the sugarcane landowners. Sex trafficking is also a growing problem, with about 500,000 children who are sexually exploited. Women are not included in this number because prostitution is legalized, so women who are sexually exploited are not counted. It is hard to get an exact number of those who are trafficked, although there is a recognized growth in child sex tourism due to the fact that it is "cheaper" for tourists to exploit children than adults (Hepburn & Simon, 2013). It is not so clear cut what the relationship is between sex and labor trafficking is in Brazil, though it does exist. In fact, as with other countries, there is often intersection, if not direct collusion between the two. For instance, often girls or women who are sex trafficked are used to lure or trick men into being labor trafficked (Andrade, 2013; Castillo, 2015).

In 2005, Brazil launched the National Pact for the Eradication of Slave Labor as part of its collaboration with the ILO. This is a voluntary multistakeholder initiative (MSI) and asks participating companies to cut ties with businesses that use slave labor. They also offer free training to those companies that want to know more about slave labor and supply chain transparency. This pact also supports Article 149 of Brazil's Penal Code, which prohibits working conditions that are "slave-like"; use of "malevolent persuasion" to move workers to remote work locations; impairment of labor rights via fraud or violence; and landowners from holding worker documents (Hall, 2004). In conjunction with this, the government's Ministry of Labor publishes what is called the "dirty list," (*lista suja*) which is basically a list of companies and individuals who are thought to be using slave labor. As of January 2012, the number of employers on the *lista suja* numbered 392. Those on this "dirty list" are subjected sanctions that include, but are not limited to, denial of financing by banks and other public institutions and also denial of credit (McGrath, 2013). The list is updated every 6 months and those companies who are on it for two years or more are not allowed to access any public funds (Anti-Slavery International, 2010). The only way to be removed from the list is to prove that the practice of slave labor within the company (and its supply chains) have ceased and any wages due to workers have been paid. If a company does not get off the list, then the Brazilian government and those companies who are signatories to Brazil's nonslavery commitment cease doing business together. This is a substantial loss to a company considering the number of signatories to the commitment.

The main challenges to these laws are both in implementation and enforceability mainly due to corruption of the system, which means that even in areas where implementation is occurring (and where legislation has outlined stiff penalties), consequences are not being leveled because of kickbacks to officials in the form of money or favors. One example is that companies who are known to violate the commitment are still allowed to sign on. Also, while the commitment and the penal code looks good on paper, it is not necessarily enforced per se. This not only undermines the agreement and the commitment itself but it sends the message that the government is not serious about holding companies accountable for irresponsible practices. To date, while there have been significant moves toward improving the system, especially around sugarcane plantations, there still must be more done to strengthen actual enforcement and sanctions. There has been major progress made with the passage of a constitutional amendment in 2012 to expropriate land used by companies that have been found to use slave labor (Looft, 2012). Additionally, Brazil has been an active partner with nations where Brazilians are trafficked and collaborates on international investigations. This kind of collaboration is detrimental and has resulted in a number of arrests. Brazil is an excellent example of how anti-trafficking legislation have developed in different country contexts and how one might address what is happening in their country as well as the more global impact.

THE ROAD TO TRANSPARENCY

Highlight: H2B Visas and Migration

The H2B visa program started in 1952 with the Immigration and Nationality Act for both agricultural (H2A) and nonagricultural (H2B) temporary workers. To be able to use this visa program and sponsor foreign nationals into the United States, an employer has to show they have searched and did not find enough U.S. workers who are qualified or willing to do the job. Also, they have to have paid in such a way that does not affect the wages of U.S. workers. The key here is the work must be temporary so there is a one-year limit. H2B visas are granted in the following industries: landscaping/grounds-keeping, forest and conservation, domestic labor, amusement and recreation, and construction.

The visas are awarded through the Department of Labor and the employer continues to sponsor the worker through paperwork filed with U.S. Citizenship and Immigration Services. There are only 68 countries where people are eligible to receive H2B visas and a cap of 66,000 visas issued annually. The visas can be renewed yearly for up to three years, and then the worker must return to their country of origin for at least three months before applying for another H2B visa.

The controversy around the H2B visa is that there are few safeguards for the workers in this program so that when they enter the country, they may be subject to any number of abuses. In a landmark case, a New Orleans company was found guilty of trafficking five Indian nationals in *David et al. v. Signal International, LLC*. They were fined $14 million dollars in damages, which is largest award in a labor trafficking case in the United States. It was found that the maritime construction company, a U.S. based immigration attorney, and an Indian-based labor recruiter conspired for labor trafficking, using the H2B program to bring hundreds of workers over. The nature of the visa allows for ambiguities of how the workers will be treated and room for extreme vulnerability, especially with these third-party recruiters who may misrepresent the nature and amount of work, raise debts, and build on the fear of deportation. The latter is especially salient because the workers are beholden to the employer's continued sponsorship.

migrationpolicy.org/article/recent-court-decisions-put-sharp-spotlight-us-h-2b-temporary-worker-visa-program

As early as the 1990s, there was a movement to address inconsistencies in legislation around supply chain transparency as well as the use and procurement of goods that may have been made with slave labor. In 2008, the CA–TISC was proposed by then Senate president Darrell Steinberg with the organization, Alliance to Stop Slavery and End Trafficking (ASSET) as the source and Coalition to Abolish Slavery and Trafficking (CAST) as the cosponsor (Gebauer, 2011a). The goals of these nonprofit organizations and advocacy groups were to create opportunities for companies to demonstrate "leadership" in the fight to eradicate slavery. This is notable, since before this, the main tactic of citizen groups centered around "shame and blame" tactics such as boycotts and public letters, and reports to the media. Despite the differences in tactics, the move to make California an example of what could be done with making supply chains transparent was a smart one. California is the largest state economy in the United States and the eighth largest economy in the world. In 2014, California's GDP was over $2.31 trillion (Bayer, et. al, 2015). With such deep resources, California was in the position it is always in—to leverage its economic power to serve as a model of the potential of such legislation. If California could make supply chain transparency work, then it could serve as a positive model to other states and eventually influence the federal stage. Tactically, this was a decisive step in getting anti-trafficking legislation passed.

Historically, California had experience with disclosure laws, albeit mainly within their interaction at the federal level. In the 1930s, what was referred to as the "Smoot-Hawley Tariff Act" (Tariff Act of 1930), California instituted that all goods produced by foreign prison labor would be banned from entry into the United States (Bayer, et. al., 2015). We see more modern law developing in 1986 with the Safe Drinking Water and Toxic Enforcement Act of 1986 (Proposition 65). This mandated companies to notify Californians if there were significant amounts of chemicals present in drinking water (Bayer, et. al, 2015). In 1999, Executive Order 13126, the "Prohibition of Acquisition of Products Produced from Forced or Indentured Child Labor," was signed by President Clinton, which made it illegal for U.S. federal agencies to procure goods made from forced or indentured child labor (Bayer, et. al., 2015). In 2001, part of the USA Patriot Act included the requirement for companies to "know your customer," which was tied to understanding the economic chain of money and whether or not any support was going into terrorist activities. This is key because it began to institutionalize independent audits and the underscored the necessity of creating internal compliance plans (Bayer, et. al., 2015). In 2008, the Trafficking Victims Protection Reauthorization Act was renewed and added the stipulation that the Department of Labor produce a list of goods and the countries they are produced in where they believe that this is being done via some form of slave labor (Bayer, et. al, 2015). These laws are the foundation of California businesses being exposed to the concept and relationship of transparency and disclosure. However, it is not until CA–TISC that there is legislation developed which directly addresses the issue of trafficking and slavery within supply chains.

CA–TISC was also founded on two other factors: that of business practices themselves and that of the consumer (market factors). First, the State of California emphasized that they had an ethical responsibility to ensure that goods and services were not being provided in any part by slave labor. Businesses had the right to learn how to manage their supply chains so that they were not inadvertently engaging in slave labor. Further, it was not just focal companies (the actual companies doing business) that were effected or should be considered stakeholders. Ancillary companies, financial investors, and other aspects of the business community had vested interests based on their ethical considerations around labor and slavery. CA–TISC would be able to provide that training and awareness. Second, and perhaps more importantly, consumers are taken into account as active agent who deserved the knowledge of where their goods were coming from and who was making them (Deloite, 2016). For both entities, CA–TISC asserts that companies and consumers have the right to not accidentally "sanction" forced, indentured, or slave labor.

When CA–TISC was being formulated, the media played their part in terms of raising awareness. More and more, the public was becoming aware of the multifaceted nature of trafficking and that when "trafficking" was discussed, it included more than just sex. According to labor trafficking abolitionist and founder of ASSET, Julia Ormand believes that the confluence of consumer shifts in buying, ethical business practice, and the work of the media to expose the shocking realities of slave labor were key in passing the legislation (Ormand, personal communication, 2016). As an example, she cites the campaign of the Coalition of Immokalee Workers' (CIW) Anti-Slavery Campaign and Fair Food Program as an example of the power of revealing the agricultural supply chain (Greenhouse, 2014). The CIW formed in 1993 from Immokalee, Florida, and exposed how slavery occurred within the supply chain of the $600 million tomato industry and its partners who were some of the major fast food chains in the world (Marosi, 2014).

CALIFORNIA TRANSPARENCY IN SUPPLY CHAINS ACT (CA–TISC)

CA–TISC was passed in 2010. It allowed two years for California businesses to prepare and transition to meet compliance. Starting in 2012, CA–TISC required that all companies who do business in California, have annual, worldwide gross receipts that exceed $100 million dollars, and are identified as manufacturers or retail sellers on their California tax returns (property or salaries in California exceed $50,000) fulfill compliance in five areas. These areas include, and are taken verbatim from the *California Transparency in Supply Chains Act: A Resource Guide* (Harris, 2015).

- **Verification**: at a minimum, disclose to what extent, if any, that the retail seller or manufacturer engages in verification of product supply chains to evaluate and address risks of human trafficking and slavery. The disclosure shall specify if the verification was not conducted by a third party.

- **Audits**: at a minimum, disclose to what extent, if any, that the retail seller or manufacturer conducts audits of suppliers to evaluate supplier compliance with company standards for trafficking and slavery in supply chains. The disclosure shall specify if the verification was not an independent, unannounced audit.

- **Certification**: at a minimum, disclose to what extent, if any, that the retail seller or manufacturer requires direct suppliers to certify that materials incorporated into the product comply with the laws regarding slavery and human trafficking of the country or countries in which they are doing business.

- **Internal Accountability**: at a minimum, disclose to what extent, if any, that the retail seller or manufacturer maintains internal accountability standards and procedures for employees or contractors failing to meet company standards regarding slavery and trafficking.

- **Training**: at a minimum, disclose to what extent, if any, that the retail seller or manufacturer provides company employees and management, who have direct responsibility for supply chain management, training on human trafficking and slavery, particularly with respect to mitigating risks within the supply chains of products.

The compliances must be posted on the company's websites in what the legislation calls a "conspicuous and easily understood link" on their homepage. If the company has no website, they have to give a written disclosure to consumers who request one. If a company is not doing any of these things, then they still have to disclose on their website or via written notice that they are not taking any actions related to the five areas of compliance (Harris, 2015).

A resource guide is provided by the California Attorney General's office and even offers examples of how companies should address each compliance point. The California Franchise Tax Board is responsible for collecting this information then send the list of CA–TISCA compliant companies to the California Attorney General's Office. Interestingly, the list is not released to the public nor is the list of eligible companies to begin with.

The law went into effect in 2010 and gave companies until 2012 to demonstrate compliance. Authority to enforce the law resides in the hands of the California attorney general's office, who has the power to file a civil action for an injunction, a type of legal remedy that provides a court order to cease a specified behavior. In spite of this, it was not until spring of 2015 that the California attorney general's office began sending out letters to companies who were not meeting compliance or who had not posted anything regarding their supply chains. These "warning letters" have been sent but it is not clear what the repercussions will be if compliance is not met. There is a strong potential for brand-damage, class action lawsuits, NGO and nonprofit organizational group "pressure," and even criminal prosecution.

Even before CA–TISCA was enacted, the issue of slavery in supply chains was of growing concern, particularly for retailers who required global compliances. Many of these companies had already started employing third party auditors and monitors (Galland, 2010). For example, GAP Inc. (clothing) created an actual human rights division. The formation of this division is to not only address labor trafficking and modern-day slavery but also other issues around sweat shops, quality of life, and poverty, especially in areas like Sumagali and India (GAP Inc., personal communication, 2015). Other companies such as Nordstrom (department store), Levi's (clothing), and Hanesbrands (clothing) also measured well because they had already passed the "expected minimums" and were engaging in improvement and collaboration at the expense of their own resources (Pickles & Zhu, 2013). To illustrate, as early as 2000, Hewlett Packard (HP) has ensured and verified the absence of forced or child labor in its supply chain not just in the areas covered by CA–TISCA, but also in the following: risk-based supplier assessments, supplier audits, supplier agreements, capacity building programs, and procurement training (HP, 2011).

In the first study of its kind, Dr. Chris Bayer led an in-depth study entitled "Corporate compliance with the California Transparency in Supply Chains Act of 2010." The study systematically evaluates not only corporate compliance but the *degree* to what they have disclosed (Bayer, et. al., 2015). Because the list of eligible companies is not released by the California attorney general's office, the study used a consulting database (Compustat North America), *Forbes'* list of private company rankings for 2015, and *Inc.*'s 5000 list of companies for 2015 to approximate eligibility using the $100 million annual revenue as a threshold and also whether or not companies were based in California. Finally, they conducted a general search using CA–TISCA as a search term to see if they could begin with companies who had already posted their disclosures on their websites. They then created an instrument based on a point system wherein companies were given a point for each compliance point of the legislation as well as what they called "affirmative points," which provides a point for the level of genuine change the company was engaging in (for example, even if the company reported not doing anything in the area, they could be currently involved in active planning or implementation of new measures). The study identified 2,126 companies that could "potentially qualify," which was more than the estimated 1,700 the California Franchise Tax Board said they identified. Out of the 2,126 companies, they found that 1,325 companies (62%) posted pertinent statements on their websites. Out of these, only 14% scored affirmative points on or above 70%.

There are also websites and applications being developed to help clarify which companies have been compliant with CA–TISCA. The site, KnowTheChain, a site led by Humanity United in 2013, was created to encourage greater corporate understanding of CA-TISC but has morphed into providing "practical resources to enable companies to comply with growing legal obligations." The website partners with *Verité,* who works with individual companies to help develop standards of performance and improve procurement and hiring practices. They also provide reports that look at labor trafficking and supply chain transparency. Resources for Responsible Recruitment is a web resource focused on recruitment and geared toward those recruiting and job seekers alike.

Though CA–TISCA is a step in the right direction but, though it takes place in the largest state economy of the United States, it is still just legislation in one state. Federal legislation was filed by Representative Carolyn Maloney (D–N.Y.) to the House of Representatives that would require all issuers to disclose (in their annual reports) what measures were being taken to identify and address conditions of slavery within their supply chains (Bayer, et al, 2015). However, as of 2014, the bill was referred to subcommittee. While the bill waits at the federal level, organizations who worked on CA–TISCA, such as ASSET gear up to replicate their work in other states, building momentum and support for nationwide legislation.

Highlight: Alliance to Stop Slavery and End Trafficking (ASSET)

ASSET Advancing Systemic Solutions to end Enslavement and Trafficking is an advocacy NGO dedicated to the eradication of enslavement and trafficking through amplifying the victim's voice and addressing the issues of trafficking and enslavement at the source of the problem, by identifying, incubating, advancing, and supporting solutions at the most effective points of engagement, to achieve measurable, impactful results. *"Enslavement is often hidden in the shadows, which makes it easy for governments, corporations and the public to ignore or be unaware of it despite its global scope. But slavery has a human face, and every slave is an individual whose life has meaning and value. Alliance to Stop Slavery and End Trafficking's acronym (ASSET) comes from our belief, hope, and aim that every survivor should find their place in the global work force as the true ASSET that is*

(Continued)

(Continued)

their human birthright and potential." Following her travels around California, Europe, Russia, Africa and Asia observing this issue and meeting with related entities involved in the movement; Institutional, Government, NGOs, Corporate, Philanthropists and Survivors, ASSET was founded by Julia Ormond to work on systemic solutions and align with the UNODC mandate of Prevention, prosecution and Protection. Julia is a former U.N. Goodwill Ambassador for the Office on Drugs and Crime on Trafficking and Slavery. ASSET is also a Clinton Global Initiative Commitment to Action (CTA). ASSET is dedicated to the eradication of slavery through amplifying the victims voice and supporting systemic solutions.

endslaverynow.org/alliance-to-stop-slavery-and-end-trafficking-asset

MODERN SLAVERY ACT—UK

In 2015, the United Kingdom ratified the Modern Slavery Act of 2015, which makes provisions to protect victims, calls for an Independent Anti-Slavery Commissioner, and just like CA–TISCA asks companies for disclosure. In general, the act is composed of seven parts. Specifically, part 6 of the Modern Slavery Act of 2015 requires "commercial organisations" to generate and issue a slavery and human-trafficking statement annually. According to the act, an organization is considered "commercial" if it "supplies good or services and had a total turnover of not less than the amount prescribed by regulations made by the Secretary of State." The annual slavery and human-trafficking statement includes a "statement of what steps are being taken during the financial year to ensure that slavery and human trafficking is not taking place (i) in any of its supply chains, and (ii) in any part of its own business" or "a statement that the organisation has taken no such steps." Furthermore, "commercial organisations" are incorporated, a partnership as outlined within the UK Partnership Act of 1890, and the business is done in any part in the United Kingdom. The statement may also include the following (taken verbatim from the Modern Slavery Act of 2015, Part 6):

(a) the organization's structure, its business, and its supply chains;
(b) its policies in relation to slavery and human trafficking;
(c) its due diligence processes in relation to slavery and human trafficking in its business and supply chains;
(d) the parts of its business and supply chains where there is a risk of slavery and human trafficking taking place, and the steps it has taken to assess and manage that risk;
(e) its effectiveness in ensuring that slavery and human trafficking is not taking place in its business or supply chains, measured against such performance indicators as it considers appropriate;
(f) the training about slavery and human trafficking available to its staff.

Once the statement is generated, it must be published on the website. Similar to the CA–TISCA, the link must not be hard to find and must be in "prominent" place on the homepage. Also, similar to CA–TISCA, if the organization does not have a website, they must provide a copy of their statement for anyone to makes a written request and do so within 30 days.

The writing of this act began in 2013, after the passage and the compliance deadlines of CA–TISC. It is clear in the overall act that legislators have been able to fold in lessons learned. Nonetheless, a glaring absence in the act is that there are no legally binding requirements to meet compliance and there are no criminal or financial penalties (Gebauer, 2011a). Nevertheless, the impact of this law is already far reaching. Consulting firm, Price Waterhouse Coopers has created an assessment tool designed to help companies examine their supply chains and identify vulnerabilities to trafficking (or areas where trafficking exists). These risk assessments use what they call "total impact measurement and management" that includes not only modern slavery but also sustainability, social issues, human rights, and labor rights (OECD, n.d.).

FEDERAL ACQUISITIONS REGULATION (FAR) (EXECUTIVE ORDER 13,627) AND THE TRADE FACILITATION ENFORCEMENT ACT OF 2015 (H.R. 644)

In 2012, President Barack Obama issued Executive Order 13,627, which mandated all federal contractors and subcontractors comply with actions to that disclose their actions to combat human trafficking (Funk, Oehler, & Breakstone, 2015). This portion of the Executive Order is known as the Federal Acquisition Regulation (FAR). This is a significant order considering that there are over 300,000 companies that do business with the federal government. The goal of FAR is to move closer to the government's zero tolerance objective. Contractors and subcontractors are required to

- take preventive steps to ensure employees to do not engage in trafficking related activities;
- cooperate with law enforcement agencies who are investigating compliance with anti-trafficking and forced labor laws;
- mandatory disclosure on receipt of any credible information from any source that alleges a contractor employee, subcontractor, or subcontractor employee has engaged in conduct that violates FAR provisions;
- develop and maintain a detailed compliance plan for contracts for supplies acquired outside the United States or services performed outside the United States with an estimated value exceeding $500,000; and
- file annual certifications exceeding $500,000 confirming that it has implicated its compliance plan, after due diligence, certifying that neither it nor its employees engage in any trafficking related activities (or remedial action was taken if transgressions were made).

For those contractors and subcontractors who are unable to comply, they face termination, disbarment, imprisonment, false claims act, class actions, consumer boycotts, and advocacy group pressure.

H.R. 644, or the Trade Facilitation and Trade Enforcement Act of 2015, was signed by President Obama in 2016. This act closed a loop in the 1930 Tariff Act, which still allowed good in from slave labor as long as American production could not meet the demand. It also provides more room to investigate companies that have been linked to forced or child labor and provides support to CA–TISCA. It also makes use of the "List of Goods Produced by Child Labor or Forced Labor," which is produced by the Department of Labor annually. This list will help with the identification of "trafficking hot spots" and also what products may carry the vulnerability of slavery in its supply chains. Trafficking advocates and the business world alike believe that the power of this act will be determined by the ability to enforce it, which will be dependent of obtaining solid, "actionable intelligence." The reporting requirement and the standard of proof will be difficult and would take coordinated efforts considering the tiers of suppliers and subcontractors that are involved (Booth, 2016).

CHALLENGES

Disclosure laws may not be new, but the focus of disclosure as it relates to supply chains and slavery is just beginning. The only template that we have to know this works is the work that has been done with exposing supply chains in conflict minerals. And, while templates are good starting points, the situation of human trafficking and modern-day slavery is much more complex and dealing with almost every industry, not focused on one. At this point, the legislation we currently have are in only a few areas, namely manufacturing and retail. Yet, the largest areas of profits generated by the presence of slave labor are (in this order) construction, manufacturing, mining, and agriculture, including forestry and fishing (Booth, 2016). In addition to only being focused on a small portion of industries, none of the legislation actually requires disclosure or plans for remediation to the public. In connection to this, companies do not have to actually become compliant, just be transparent about what they are doing to get closer to compliance. The biggest challenge is enforceability and legislation having actual power. There has only been one lawsuit in 2015 based on CA–TISCA (Bayer et al., 2015). Again, as of 2015, letters were just being sent out to companies from the California attorney general's office. Despite these challenges, this is a strong beginning to hold businesses accountable and it is an opportunity to concentrate of best practices of what we do know.

BEST PRACTICES

Just as with clinical interventions, there has not been a piece of legislation that has answered all aspects of labor trafficking. However, there are several "best practices" that seem to hold a lot of potential at creating impact. This list is by no means exclusive especially in light of the rapid changes that are occurring within the issue and in the movement to fight it. Notwithstanding the changing nature of things, they may serve as a starting point of what we know might work.

Consumers have untapped power: One of the main driving forces in this area that companies are recognizing is the growing power that consumers possess. In the past few years, consumer influence has grown especially in terms of retail and services. Consumer initiatives around "ethical" and "fair trade" products have grown from a small niche market into widespread lifestyle branding. Companies such as Toms Shoes' "One to One" program (where for every pair of shoes purchased, another is given to a child in need) and Patagonia clothing company mission to fair trade, clean supply chains, and focus on environment and climate change have made the public more aware than ever that their purchases do not just impact themselves but has the power to (literally) impact the world.

The popular website trendwatching.com reports that a common trend after 2010 is companies moving to more ethical or moral footprints in an effort to be an example of health, wellness, and holistic considerations of community (trending.com). Surveys, particularly of Millennials (the generation born after 1982), show that although this generation has become the largest share of the U.S. labor market (many occupying senior positions), the traditional driver of business—profit—is not what this generation is most concerned with. Indeed, a marked characteristic of this generation is that they prioritize their personal values over that of profit (Buckley, Viechnicki, & Baruahttp, 2016). The creation of "benefit corporations" exemplifies the importance of mission and vision over profits. Benefit corporations are created under corporate law to protect entrepreneur's social goals by mandating them along with a lower expectation of profit (Bend & King, 2014).

There is also the effect of social media and the "super connected" millennial or digital native who uses social media as a way to volunteer, donate, or campaign. This makes people feel like they are in different ways socially engaged, even if it is just virtually. This need, feeling, or self-efficacy to believe they can change the world through these vehicles make their expectations of business to behave in socially responsible ways part of how they examine and literally buy into business practices. Their participation does not always have to be paid either. While monetary benefits are considered the most important aspect of the millennial job decision, by contrast, they are also concerned with what the company allows them to dedicate their time to and the support of that. Salesforce, a leader in 2002, launched Salesforce Foundation that in part supports their charitable giving, corporate responsibility, and their employee volunteer program, wherein the company created it's philanthropic 1-1-1 model. This model dedicates 1% of Salesforces' equity, 1% of Salesforce's product, and 1% of Salesforce employees' time back to their communities via volunteering (Salesforce, 2016). When Salesforce Foundation saw that many of its employees were engaging in anti-trafficking work and that they also had clients that were interested, they launched a series of innovative initiatives with partners such as the Polaris Project (2014).

Best practices that focus on the power of harnessing the consumer's influence and to a certain extent the perspective of corporations themselves tend to work best in areas of the world that are more developed, where consumer awareness is established, and where socioeconomic status is higher. For instance, in some areas of the world, the choice is between being able to have enough to purchase food or not. In these cases, there is not a strong argument for actual choice because the "choice" is based only on cost and not the privilege of being able to select based on ethical standards. Even in areas where there might be a margin of choice, consumer awareness needs to exist to be able to discern that there are differences in the importance of what is purchased. The movement toward organic, locally sourced, and other food justice movements are an example of this.

Multisystem collaboration: Understanding supply chains is one way to root out slavery within company systems. A broader perspective to take is one through the ecological or ecosystems lens. For example, being able to take into account and start from the victim's perspective and build outward is a strong starting point that many practitioners often employ (Mace, 2015). To a much smaller extent, client ecosystem maps are similar to this best practice proposition. A top consulting and accounting firm, Deloitte has been working with organizations and companies to find common ground where they can really begin to have the discussion of how to end trafficking and slavery, beginning with their clients' companies and a group of nonprofit organizations. They propose the "Freedom Ecosystem," which takes into account those who have been trafficked (and their immediate circle), stakeholders, the usual organizations and institutions (both public and private), and organizations and institutions that have never even engaged in the issue. The inclusion of the latter does two things: first, it allows for fresh, new perspectives to the issue, and second, it emphasizes the main point of an ecosystem metaphor and that is that trafficking affects everyone regardless of industry, position, or geographic location. (See: Figure 2.2)

The idea of multisystem collaboration is not new to the anti-trafficking world. In fact, if you are ever at a conference, you will hear over and over again how collaboration is the key. Although we know this, the concrete reality is that there are issues of confidentiality, areas of jurisdiction, and also differing perspectives to contend with. All these things make it hard for collaboration to take place. Despite this challenge, because we do know multisystem collaboration is a necessity, many cities have set up human trafficking task forces and partnerships (Helton, 2016). More creative partnerships have also been started especially between the public and private sector.

Technical support for businesses: Just as awareness raising and training are utilized for health and human service practitioners, companies have the same needs. For example, disclosure laws are largely dependent on self-reporting and monitoring. Most companies agree with and want to make sure they are at least compliant, and even more so, want to take an active part at eradicating slavery but are unaware of how to capture the information, when, or who to report to. One basic example is the move by the California attorney general's office at generating and providing a handbook on CA–TISC, which is helpful and gives companies a starting point and overview of the legislation and their roles. However, we can be doing better; workshops, corporate consultants trained and specialized in trafficking, and even intensive "bootcamp"-like experiences may further help companies. Finally, another aspect that must be considered is that many companies also do not have the capacity or knowledge base to capture, organize, analyze, and distribute big data that is required to really understand the scope and depth of labor trafficking and modern-day slavery. In these cases, capacity building and collaboration would be optimal.

Case Vignette: Edward

Edward was born in Ghana to parents who already had three other children. His small village was a 2-day trip to Lake Volta, where he was sold into indentured servitude by his parents. His parents were poor, not being able to feed themselves or their children every day, much less three times a day. They thought it would be a good idea to send the children to work where they would at least get a chance to eat. However, Edward, at the age of seven, was sent to work for a fisherman who had purchased about 28 children under the age of 15. Although the fisherman said he did not like "employing" children, he admitted not knowing how he would earn a profit otherwise.

Edward joined other boys whose main jobs were to paddle the canoes, untangle fishing nets, and dive into the lake when the fishing nets were tangled. Lake Volta is actually a dam formed from the Akosombo Dam and is over 3,000 square miles. When it was created, the existing forests in the area were not bulldozed so there are whole areas where the sunken trees snarl and tangle fishing nets. The children are used to dive under the boats and untangle the nets. It is dangerous work and daily, several children are found drowned, washed up on the edge of the lake. It is estimated that as many as 10,000 "fishing boys" exist in this area. Edward is one of them now. He is given a place to sleep in a mud hut with other boys. An older boy "leads" his canoe. They all work over 100 hours a week and are often subjected to beatings by their masters who call them "bad boys." Edward says that he is always tired. He wakes up before the sun comes up and sometimes falls asleep while rowing.

"I'm afraid to get into the water," he admits, "I don't like it here. I'm afraid I'm going to die in the water." He doesn't remember home since he has been at the lake for over a year. He has seen other boys die at the lake and he has experienced two near-death experiences himself. He says that he dreams of drowning and wakes up in the middle of nightmares even though he is dead tired from the work he is forced to do. Edward was selected to be interviewed by the International Organization for Migration (IOM). During the interview, he stated that he did not have any friends. He said he did not even miss his family anymore because he did not remember them. He asked the interviewer why she thought his parents sold him like this. Edward says that he has never seen a doctor, nor has he ever gone to school. He did not have any free time so he there are no games he enjoys. However, Edward does say that the children are not mean to one another. They try to help each other. "We are all in the same suffering," he says, "but we all have no hope."

CALL TO ACTION: TRANSPARENCY TO FREEDOM

This chapter has demonstrated the importance of understanding supply chains to identify not only where trafficking and modern-day slavery may be occurring but also to show where points of vulnerability and risk may exist. Also, the more partnership and collaboration that occurs, the more transparent the processes. For example, in Guatemala, a major coffee company has partnered with a U.S. labor rights organization with support from the local government to promote transparency through their supply chain. The program includes improving communication between workers, corporate, and government actors that helps build capacity of all stakeholders but also to create instruments of monitoring and reporting, including the recruitment practices of those in the coffee sector (U.S. Department of State, 2016). The knowledge of certain pain points will allow providers to inform policy and advocacy but also to understand how clients may experience the continuum of trafficking and how to confront them more effectively. The policies highlighted in this chapter are only the beginning. The future will not only bring a growth in terms of more legislation being passed but also a widening of what such legislation covers. For example, current legislation does not comprehensively cover all industries where trafficking might exist. Future versions of existing legislation and new legislative measures will have to take into account both scale and scope.

DISCUSSION QUESTIONS

1. What can your organization do to implement the best practices for creating legislation that affects labor trafficking?

2. How can you make sure organizations are implementing the different policies in their respective country?

3. How can we partner with businesses and corporations to keep them accountable to legislation?

4. How would you create a "ranking" system for companies based on CA–TISC compliance points? Use the paradigm of how restaurants and food establishments are ranked. Do you think this ranking system would sway consumer opinions? In what ways?

5. Examining the Freedom Eco-System, what areas would you target? What would be the role of your organization?

CHALLENGE

Log onto the Slavery Footprint Survey from the organization Slavery Footprint (slaveryfootprint.org). Follow the survey to answer the question: "How many slaves work for you?" After taking the survey, take a moment to reflect on how you feel and what actions you might take. Take the challenge to the next level by taking action (however you define that) based on the results of your survey.

Advocacy, Activism, and Innovations

In the final section of this textbook, we return full circle to our intended goals based on the origins of the anti-trafficking movement as it was formed and built through the grass-roots women's movement. This perspective's goal is to guide change to prevent and end human trafficking and modern-day slavery. The role of the grassroots' women's movement was pivotal in the definition of trafficking and modern-day slavery as well as the ideological constructions that were created around it. It was not until after the turn of the 21st century that governments and mainstream organizations became involved in the issue in a widespread manner. By then, the grassroots women's movement had been pushing the commodification of women and children on agendas that ranged from the conflict of military bases from the 1940s and beyond, to the rise in mail-order brides in Southeast Asia and Eastern Europe that began in the late 1980s to the United Nations' Fourth World Conference on Women in Beijing in 1995, within a definite human rights framework.

With an ecosystems model as well as with an eye toward innovation, it is imperative that we understand the origin, context, and continuing trend of this issue. It is not enough to provide services that operate on a reactive level or policies that are responsive to what was happening when the legislation was drafted. There must be ways that we can get ahead of this issue, to begin to predict what we will need to stop it. Otherwise, we will always be playing catch up, always be ameliorating the situation instead of ending it. Often, practitioners may see the abolitionist and/or anti-trafficking work of advocacy and activism as beyond their purview because usually our concerns are immediate and compelled by crisis, or they are chronic and enduring. Either way, for most practitioners, we work in the trenches. Even when we can take a step back to see the big picture, it is difficult to imagine our caseloads with the additional responsibilities of advocacy and activism. However, as this section points out, it is exactly our voices and viewpoints that have to be added to the discussion. Most helping professions come from a tradition of social justice and empowerment; as we examine the roots of trafficking and modern day slavery, perhaps it is time to return to our own roots as well.

Chapter 11 will look at the evolution of the building of the anti-trafficking movement through coalitions of women's and human rights' groups. Constructs of advocacy and activism will be fully explained as well as the role that practitioners may take in these types of activities. A full description of what the human rights perspective entails versus the law enforcement (prosecution and protection) framework that became more prevalent once policies such as Palermo and TVPA was created. Best practices as developed by UNIFEM's work in gender violence through pilot trust funds have created best practices in advocacy and activism and can be related to anti-trafficking measures. The chapter concludes with tactics that practitioners can use in their own advocacy and activism efforts.

Chapter 12 continues to examine the construction of trafficking and modern-day slavery, through the perspective of religion and spirituality. This body of literature is included in this section because faith-based organizations were pivotal advocates for the passage of many anti-trafficking policies, mostly around sex trafficking. Moreover, faith-based organizations constitute a significant portion of service provision. For example, faith-based organizations run the most shelter services in the United States and in some countries, they are the only providers for trafficking victims. This chapter includes an overview of what faith-based organizations are and what makes them unique. Unlikely allies, religious doctrine, and values leading programs are some of the aspects that will be discussed. Faith-based organizations are key agents in the anti-trafficking movement in terms of prevention and intervention not just because of the programs they provide, but also because of the position that religion has in many people's lives as a strong protective factor. We will take a look at this from the micro to the macro perspective. Examples of U.S. based groups and international organizations are also included to provide examples of the extensive network and services such groups are providing to fill in the gaps of existing providers.

Chapter 13 pushes us into the area of prevention. Prevention is the main thrust of the Palermo Protocols and yet, it has taken the back burner to prosecution and protection. In part, this is due to the difficulty of measuring whether prevention programs are working or having any impact as opposed to prosecution and protection, which can have more quantitative measures. Root causes of poverty, globalization, migration, gender inequity, and demand are analyzed as ways in which prevention programs could target social issues that cause trafficking. Methods that have shown the most promise for prevention are also discussed such as social entrepreneurship to alleviate poverty, awareness raising campaigns, better education and training, and other prevention measures are included.

Chapter 14 presents the most cutting-edge innovations to fight trafficking and modern-day slavery. The biggest weapons we have on this front are the use of media, technology, and public awareness. This chapter will explain what social innovation is in depth and its various permutations. The components of social innovation such as design thinking, experimentation, prototyping, adaptation, and implementation are concepts that are also detailed in the chapter. We provide an overview of innovative programs and technologies that have been or are currently being developed in hopes of causing disruptions to the cycles of human trafficking and modern-day slavery. Briefly, we highlight some of the most promising innovations and technologies that are being developed.

Chapter 15 concludes with a discussion on current threats and trends in the field. As more perpetrators and traffickers find ways to further exploit men, women, and children, it is important that we are able to comprehend all the layers and areas in the ecosystem that they are operating in. Intersectionalities and multiple dimensions must be understood and incorporated into our practice knowledge. Though this is not an exhaustive list of trends, it is a starting point of what we know currently and hopefully leaves readers with ideas of the trajectories that trafficking is taking. The chapter focuses on a call to action for practitioners to join the fight against trafficking and modern-day slavery. As helping professions become further entrenched in anti-trafficking work, we will be asked to lead and take more crucial roles because we work on a number of levels where vulnerabilities of populations to trafficking must be attended to and championed. Thus, we need to maintain a critical eye on new technology, trends in interventions, and the political atmosphere in order maintain working knowledge that is up to date, relevant, and anticipatory of next steps.

GLOSSARY OF TERMS

Abolitionist—someone engaged in the movement to end slavery, whether formal or informal in action.

Activism—policy or action of using vigorous campaigning to bring about political or social change.

Advocacy—public support for or recommendation of a particular cause or policy.

Agency (personal)—action or intervention, especially such as to produce a particular effect.

Awareness Raising—form of activism, popularized by U.S. feminists in the late 1960s. It often takes the form of a group of people attempting to focus the attention of a wider group of people on some cause or condition.

Citizenship—status of a person recognized under the custom or law as being a member of a country.

Disruption—disturbance or problems that interrupt an event, activity, or process.

Ecosystem—community of interacting organisms and their physical environment.

Faith-Based Organizations—group of individuals united on the basis of religious or spiritual beliefs. Often, faith-based organizations work to promote their religious calls to action through various works of service and social justice movements.

Feminism—theories, concepts, and practices that share common goals of establishing, protecting, and enforcing the political, personal, and social equality and rights of women in society. Feminism is not unidimensional and as such, there are varying definitions and types of feminisms.

Innovation—a new method, idea, product, or intervention that causes impact and disruption to social problems.

Intersectionality—nature of social categorizations such as race, class, and gender as they apply to a given individual or group, regarded as creating overlapping and interdependent systems of discrimination or disadvantage.

Intervention—care provided to improve a situation. Often utilized by service providers and clinicians in order to better the lives of their clients.

Microfinance—source of financial services for entrepreneurs and small businesses lacking access to banking and related services. This has become popular in developing nations as a way to bring cash flow into building markets and businesses.

NGO—is a not-for-profit organization that is independent from states and international governmental organizations.

Prevention—the action of stopping something from happening or arising.

Prototyping—early approximation, sample, or model created to test a concept, process, or innovation.

Safe Space—A place (geographic, physical, or psychological) where anyone can relax and be fully self-expressed, without fear of being made to feel uncomfortable, unwelcome, or challenged.

Sex Tourism—the organization of vacations with the purpose of taking advantage of the lack of restrictions imposed on prostitution and other sexual activities by some foreign countries.

Social Enterprise—an organization that applies commercial strategies to maximize improvements in human and environmental well-being.

Superdiversity—used to refer to some current levels of population diversity that are significantly higher than before, coined by sociologist Steven Vertovec in 2007.

Underground Railroad—network of secret routes and safe houses used by 19th-century enslaved people of African descent in the United States in efforts to escape to free states and Canada with the aid of abolitionists and allies who were sympathetic to their cause.

UNIFEM—The United Nations Development Fund for Women. Since 1976, UNIFEM has been assisting innovative programs and implementing strategies that promote women's human rights, political participation, and economic security.

Wicked Problem—a circumstance or situation that is difficult or impossible to solve because of incomplete, contradictory, and changing requirements that are often difficult to recognize.

Grassroots Advocacy and Activism

She looks at me through rheumy eyes and her hands feel like thin vellum, blue-veined and fragile. But appearances could never be more deceiving, because she reaches across the way and clasps my hands in the strongest grip I've ever felt. Her spirit and her conviction are just as strong. Nanay Mameng, a mass leader for the urban poor communities of the Philippines, is so slight she does not reach my shoulder but as she speaks, her persona takes up the whole street where a thousand torches are lit and tens of thousands march in unison.

It is the first time I have come to the Philippines as an adult and as an activist. I have come as a Fulbright Fellow who is studying the grassroots women's response to domestic violence. While I would go on to investigate that topic and do the research, I was first baptized into the "fire" of action and

(Continued)

(Continued)

activism my second week there as workers took to the streets to demand the Philippine government protect their overseas contract workers abroad as well as their internal workers by not agreeing to the supposed free trade agreements crossing the globe like NAFTA (North American Free Trade Agreement) and APEC (Asian Pacific Economic Cooperation).

I watch in awe as Nanay Mameng rolls out statistic after statistic of the plight of the Filipino worker—the largest export of the Philippines, exported to over 168 countries in 1996. I march alongside a woman, her white t-shirt featuring the face of someone who is well known in the Philippines—Flor Contemplacion. She was the Philippine domestic who was executed in Singapore after wrongly being accused of a crime that was later proven she did not commit. She was the symbol of enslaved domestics from the Philippines. She could have become a cautionary tale, except most women could not afford to be scared from migrating to find better work. So, instead they pray not to end up like Flor and they come up with a mantra, "kainlangan mag trabaho, kailangan magtiis, kapit lang sa patalim: We have to work, we have to endure, to do so, hold onto the edge of the knife." The connotation is that work abroad may cause you to bleed, but it is necessary; it is seen as the only way.

—Annalisa Enrile

INTRODUCTION

In sections 2 and 3, we saw the largest challenges were not with the development of interventions but that of implementation, operationalization, and enforcement. To address this, we must examine the larger picture of how we continue to combat trafficking and modern-day slavery despite the continued barriers and struggles. One of the consistent features in anti-trafficking and antislavery work is the catalyst that helped expose the issue to begin with—the grassroots women's movement. It has done so by basing its work and focusing its ideologies on these three areas: removing stigma and silence; creating safe spaces to address the needs of individuals who have been trafficked; and reversing patriarchal practices (Brown, 2000).

Before there was Palermo or the TVPA, or even the acknowledgment that what was happening to women and children around the world was trafficking and modern-day slavery, these situations were treated as and struggled against as gender violence and then as human rights violations. Victims were overwhelmingly women and children because of the nature of sex trafficking. With other industries using slave labor, more men and boys were enslaved and truly broadened the definition of human rights. However, the funding that was available, especially the focus on sex trafficking, made the issues restricted to gender responses to violence. During the 1980s and 1990s, trafficking and modern-day slavery was not yet construed as a criminal justice issue, but a societal ill and was on the way to becoming a wicked problem (Lee, 2011). The universal call by activists and academics was not for trauma-informed treatment or visas to stay in receiving countries but for an end to the commodification of women's bodies, a toppling of the power structure, and to genuinely address the feminization of poverty and migration that were deemed root causes. In short, before we donned the label of "human trafficking," we simply referred to these situations as "human rights." In keeping with the ethics and values of many helping professions, a rights-based approach was the primary lens within which trafficking and modern-day slavery was viewed. Although it was eventually grassroots feminist movements, nationalist movements, and labor rights that "named" the issue as "trafficking and modern-day slavery," originally they did not start out combatting trafficking as an exclusive social issue in and of itself. On the contrary, groups such as these saw trafficking as one of the many effects of uneven power dynamics, political oppression, and cultural constraints. Because of this, activists and academics naturally take a multidimensional approach that includes many of the intersectionalities that people are located in.

Considering a "hierarchy" of vulnerabilities is dependent on understanding intersectional positioning, and therefore, impossible to ignore. For instance, those of lower socioeconomic backgrounds may experience widespread vulnerabilities. Similarly, workers who find themselves in contract slavery situations will also experience vulnerabilities. Though they are two different experiences, there are enough similarities to draw parallels, and enough departures to warrant trauma-specific understanding. European sociologist Vertovec (2007) recommends that we go a step further from just understanding intersectionality and take up a lens of what he calls superdiversity, which takes into account not just where there are intersections but also where there is privilege in hierarchy. Brown (2000) proposes that the most vulnerable to trafficking and slavery are at the bottom of different hierarchies which include gender (women), socioeconomics (poor families and communities), race (ethnic or indigenous), and religion (fundamentalists) to name a few. Men and boys are still a significant number of labor-trafficking victims and face their own unique vulnerabilities. In fact, there have been shifts in developing economies, which rely on their labor for development. This demographic begins to shift when countries themselves shift into a more service-oriented economy. Then, the demand is for service industry workers who are mainly women.

While it is true there are multiple intersections, the aspect of gender cannot be ignored, nor should it be minimized. The fact is that trafficking and slavery as well as its root causes—poverty, migration, and risk—are gendered (Hua, 2011). At its most basic, women experience types of vulnerabilities no matter what demographics (though there may be gradations). Often, we have heard the statement that "violence against women" cuts across all aspects of race, class, religion, and region. Whether or not this is true, what is notable is that women from all walks of life do report heightened awareness of the possibility of their safety being compromised. Once you start to get into the hierarchies of oppression, the gender issue becomes even more salient. For example, it is inarguable that there is a global feminization of migration and poverty. Women make up the majority of migrant workers and this has been the case since the shift for migrant labor has been in the service sector. For instance, even at the beginning of this growth in the late 1990s, Indonesian women constituted more than 90% of all Indonesian migrant workers (Lim, 1998). This pattern is replicated in various sectors, including domestic labor, caregiving, and nannies. Ito (1992) identified that this was gendered labor based on the lack of recognition of these duties as being "work" when carried out by women in familial roles. Since it is work that has been traditionally relegated into the private sphere of gender roles that women assume, it is an extension of these roles that women carry as wives and mothers. These patterns are also supported by governments and national economic policies, which also benefit from women's migration. Referred to as the "girl effect," is the premise that when women enter the work force, they delay marriage and child bearing (thereby reducing poverty) as well as providing economic support for their own and extended family members, helping grow the economy (Hickel, 2014). Similarly, trafficking is also a gendered issue, definitely for sex trafficking, and also for labor (depending on the demand of the market) where women constitute 98% of those sex trafficked and almost half of those labor trafficked (see http://www.equalitynow.org/traffickingFAQ). The grassroots women's movement grounds their analysis in root causes and overall contexts and so for many of these movements, gender is not just of import in specific issues, but that the overall international political economy is gendered (Cook & Roberts, 2000). In other words, by structure and intent, there is a gendered aspect that purposefully puts women in positions that leave them exploited and enslaved. Thus, women have led the movement, but out of necessity, it has to be a movement that benefits more than individual women's empowerment and extends to the benefit of the whole community.

(HUMAN) RIGHTS-BASED APPROACH

There are a number of different approaches for helping relationships. The three main perspectives are a charity-based approach, a needs-based approach, and a rights-based approach. Depending on your approach, the goals, accountability, process, target, emphasis, and interventions will be affected and will be different for each type. According to Gabel (2015), if you are adhering to a rights-based approach, then your goal is to meet someone's basic human rights in a way that will not only be empowering for them (as an individual) but will mean that overall there will be a shift in the allocation of resources and power so that it is more equitable for everyone involved. A rights-based approach is contingent on policy and legal maneuvers, so the burden of responsibility is placed squarely on the shoulders of governments to act. However, given the overall terrain of actors in this arena, governments (and government institutions), NGOs, nonprofit organizations, and even the private sector is accountable for helping attain the goals. This is achieved through authentic moves for change (not just lip service) through participation in the political process by marginalized and vulnerable populations. In Nepal, women's groups have been fighting against trafficking since 1987, but it took over 10 years to begin to convince the Nepali government to help. It wasn't until Indian police raided their own Bombay brothels and found more than 200 Nepali girls that the Nepali government stepped in, transforming the issue into one of national importance (Kaufman & Crawford, 2011a). Change, according to a rights-based approach, has to occur at a structural and systemic level or else everything else is just an alleviation of the symptoms.

The United Nations Development Fund for Women (UNIFEM) (2000) urged communities to "redraw" the human rights landscape to firmly house violence against women, of which trafficking was a growing issue, but one that had the danger of being framed in a more legalistic and criminal domain (which it eventually was). At the turn of the 21st century, UNIFEM called for the need to redirect to a more rights based framework rather than veer from it. Social justice work, defined by Nilsson, Schale, and Khamphakdy-Brown (2011), is the valuation of fairness and equity, usually in terms of resources, rights, treatments, and power for individuals and groups that are limited in these aspects. For example, access, information, self-determination, and participation are areas where social justice focuses (Crethar, Rivera, & Nash, 2008).

Berthold (2015) describes what a rights-based approach might look like at each level of practice. Of course, victims and survivors of trafficking should receive (micro) clinical treatment that is evidence based and part of a model of best practices. Identification and intervention is extremely important, but, from a rights-based approach, even with excellent interventions of wellness and healing, it is not enough. The rights-based approach demands that political opportunities are needed or else you are just dealing with a small portion of the issue on a person-to-person basis instead of creating real change, which will eventually end the practice of trafficking and modern-day slavery. Further, to gain these opportunities, victims and survivors must be given an active part to exercise their own agency. Their voices and their needs must be able to be expressed. Practitioner responses must span the micro-mezzo-macro and may include the facilitation or at least membership of multisystem coordinated teams. For instance, a practitioner may reach out to a victim or survivor through a direct service (micro), may facilitate further benefits to be accessed such as community supports (mezzo), and might use the case as an example or evidence for further use of an intervention or basis for a policy (macro). All of this could occur within the functioning of a multidisciplinary or multisystemic team. These teams are usually located in healthcare settings or wrap around service centers which include not only physical and mental health but also casework, legal issues, and cultural concerns.

From the first (and until now), there is no disputing the fact that trafficking and modern-day slavery falls under the definition of a violation of human rights. Fundamentally, those who are trafficked are by definition denied their basic human rights such as access to food, water, health care, as well as the lack of a safe environment. They are subjected to any number of physiological and psychological stressors.

ADVOCACY AND ACTIVISM

From the practitioner side, if we are to take a human rights or rights-based approach, then, it requires a different type of action that is neither objective or passive. This is the type of approach that requires the practitioner to take an active stance—to be more than just a provider of services but to be, at the least, an advocate and more often, an activist. Piper and Uhlin (2002) identify advocacy as "a way of organizing the strategic use of information to democratize the unequal power relations, particularly in transnational contexts" (p. 179). At its most basic, advocacy is a show of public support for a cause or a course of action. For most health and human services practitioners this means being able to advocate for our client, patient, or consumer rights. In almost every program of practice, students learn to advocate for rights that are tied to direct needs. This is the type of case advocacy wherein practitioners empower their clients to eventually become their own advocates and to learn to speak for themselves and their families to access much needed resources and/or meet their needs (Lee, Smith, & Henry, 2013). This is a starting point, but it is one that is located at the mostly individual level.

In the case of a rights-based framework, because victims and survivors of trafficking need more than just individual services and the aim is for empowerment, the definition of advocacy needs to be broader in scope and larger in scale. Advocacy in this sense can range from raising public awareness, mobilizing communities and groups, lobbying or supporting (or initiating) legislative change, to facilitating/helping have survivors' voices heard and counted. Additionally, there is the delineation of cause advocacy which asks practitioners to change a condition in society so that it is more just and equitable, as reflected in a rights-based approach (Crethar & Winterowd, 2012). In this sense, the practitioner becomes a "change agent" or an activist once they begin to note that the issues they and the populations they serve affect people in a larger arena.

A fine line beyond advocacy is an activist stance, which takes a more political and more forceful perspective requiring further actions that surpass awareness raising and discussion and are firmly entrenched in the more demonstrative and confrontational. The point of activism is to challenge the existing social structure and to fight for social justice to the extent that practitioners put themselves in the center of the fight. Often this is difficult because it requires not just the taking of a stance but literally to be willing and able to stand up to, defend, and fight for that stance. In other words, practitioners must not be risk averse because this requires choices and decisions where they may stand to lose a lot to do what they feel is right. Practitioners who are simultaneously activists need to be careful because they constantly walk the thin line between expressing their views, provoking power structures, and protecting the well-being of their clients or patients. Willingness to fight for social justice and transformation takes the form of direct action (Arrenondo & Perez, 2003). Direct action includes activities such as protests, civil disobedience, boycotting, petitions, sit-ins, strikes, and picketing (Sharp, 2010). These are all examples of the type of activist stances that we may be familiar with because they are stereotypical of what we might imagine when we hear the word "activist." However, in the past decade, there has been a shift in grassroots movements utilizing technology, social networking, and media in their activist efforts (Sharp, 2012). In the same ways that globalization and technology (especially in ease of transport and communication) has affected migration, it has also impacted activists and grassroots movements who must adapt and learn to use these new tools to organize communities.

Perhaps the most telling trend is that of moderation, collaboration, and wellness. The shift into these ways of practicing social change (in this case, those of the less confrontational type) have created more opportunities for people to participate and construct innovative and imaginative ways of expressing activism. It also allows for more participation by those who might be intimidated by more militant or confrontational methods. Conversely, social media also has the potential to make people feel more courageous in that there is a certain layer of protection and anonymity to say what you really think without any repercussions. Regardless of what form activism takes, there is a continuum that is contextualized in current circumstances. Some of the largest mobilizations of people have occurred through the use of social networking sites such as Facebook and Twitter. More importantly, organizations such as dosomething.org have been hugely successful at not just providing information but creating social action (Lublin & Ruderman, 2015). What is important is the ideology and motivation behind actions. Chiefly, this is the link between social justice and the wellness/healing of those that practitioners' serve.

One of the supplementary benefits of practitioners taking an advocate or activist stance is that it may contribute to their own self-care or at least mitigate feelings of helplessness that may arise. Many practitioners who work with individuals who have experienced trafficking express their own despair at addressing such a seemingly insurmountable issue. Further, they may experience their own levels of countertransference and perhaps even trigger their own retraumatization or experience secondary trauma (Basham, 2011). Numerous examples of the most inhumane acts against the most vulnerable populations are witnessed by practitioners. It is not surprising that by connecting to larger social movements or actions that are construed as working to end trafficking, feelings of efficacy and mastery lead to practitioners' own experiences of agency and capacity building. There are organizations such as are highlighted in this book where the activities construed as advocacy and activism are not only encouraged but necessitated within some organizations and agencies.

Highlight: UN Women

In July 2010, the United Nations General Assembly created UN Women, the United Nations Entity for Gender Equality and the Empowerment of Women. In doing so, UN Member States took an historic step in accelerating the Organization's goals on gender equality and the empowerment of women. The creation of UN Women came about as part of the UN reform agenda, bringing together resources and mandates for greater impact. It merges and builds on the important work of four previously distinct parts of the UN system, which focused exclusively on gender equality and women's empowerment:

- Division for the Advancement of Women (DAW)
- International Research and Training Institute for the Advancement of Women (INSTRAW)
- Office of the Special Adviser on Gender Issues and Advancement of Women (OSAGI)
- United Nations Development Fund for Women (UNIFEM)

(Continued)

(Continued)

The main roles of UN Women are

- to support intergovernmental bodies, such as the Commission on the Status of Women, in their formulation of policies, global standards and norms.

- to help Member States implement these standards, standing ready to provide suitable technical and financial support to those countries that request it, and to forge effective partnerships with civil society.

- to lead and coordinate the UN system's work on gender equality as well as promote accountability, including through regular monitoring of systemwide progress.

Meeting the Needs of the World's Women Over many decades, the UN has made significant progress in advancing gender equality, including through landmark agreements such as the Beijing Declaration and Platform for Action and the Convention on the Elimination of All Forms of Discrimination against Women (CEDAW). Gender equality is not only a basic human right but its achievement has enormous socioeconomic ramifications. Empowering women fuels thriving economies, spurring productivity and growth. Yet gender inequalities remain deeply entrenched in every society. Women lack access to decent work and face occupational segregation and gender wage gaps. They are too often denied access to basic education and health care. Women in all parts of the world suffer violence and discrimination. They are underrepresented in political and economic decision-making processes. For many years, the UN has faced serious challenges in its efforts to promote gender equality globally, including inadequate funding and no single recognized driver to direct UN activities on gender equality issues. UN Women was created to address such challenges. It will be a dynamic and strong champion for women and girls, providing them with a powerful voice at the global, regional and local levels. Grounded in the vision of equality enshrined in the UN Charter, UN Women, among other issues, works for the

- elimination of discrimination against women and girls;

- empowerment of women; and

- achievement of equality between women and men as partners and beneficiaries of development, human rights, humanitarian action and peace and security.

unwomen.org

FEMINIST MOVEMENT BUILDING

There is no one feminist movement just as there is no one distinct feminist ideology. Indeed, we have already discussed the differences in viewpoints that feminists hold regarding prostitution. For the purposes of this book, we base our discussions on the international, progressive women's movements that have strands of materialism, radicalism, identity politics, third world, and transnationalist feminist ideologies. According to Mohanty (2004), these feminist ideologies take into account the intersection of race, class, and other identities (for instance, sexuality, religion, ethnicity) as well as positions of nation, though the point is to understand where borders matter and where they don't. In a review of feminist ideologies, Saulnier (1996) identifies common elements shared between these ideologies as follows: the personal is political, shared analysis on patriarchy, the value that humans should not be treated as commodities, and social construction. Because of the global nature of trafficking and modern-day slavery, the international perspective must be the one that is taken when understanding this situation. The importance of internationalism took precedence in the 1990s as gender-based violence was analyzed as a human rights issue. This is reflected in the establishment of several commemorative events that spanned the globe and called for international women's solidarity, albeit occurring in different formations depending on the country. For example, in 1991, the 16 Days of Activism Against Gender Violence, which started on November 25th commemorating the assassination of the Dominican Republic's Mirabal sisters who helped topple the Trujillo regime, and ended on December 10th, International Human Rights Day, was launched. The coordination of the 16 days did more than create a space of time dedicated to actions against gender violence. According to Spindel, Levy, and Connor (2000), it "removed gender based violence out of its protective shell of culture and tradition and focused attention on state responsibility to work to eliminate it" (p. 13). It also allowed for women all over the world to take action at key dates, which provided opportunities for solidarity and joint activities (Maza, personal communication, 2015).

The human rights framework galvanized international women's organizations and intensified transnational networking efforts. After the United Nations Decade for Women (1975–1985), international women's organizations became more embedded in national and international structures (Piper & Uhlin, 2002). To support these organizations, international conferences were convened in mainstream venues such as the UN 1995 International Women's Conference in Beijing and in alternate arenas such as the NGO "parallel" conference held by those who were not included in the main proceedings. This is an example of the political opportunity for discussion, lobbying, and advocacy that grew during this period (Piper, 2001). Ancillary to this work is the funding that became available, although unevenly distributed. True grassroots organizations did not access funds as easily as more institutionalized groups, but it still provided resources within which to operate.

While international and transnational outlooks have been vital, we have to remember their expression in individual countries differ. Many countries have a long history of women's resistance to colonization, patriarchy, and antiwomen agendas in the public and private spheres of their lives. There are countless examples of how women's resistance has occurred. These examples are especially stark in countries that have experienced political repression, economic dislocations, and foreign domination. Not surprisingly, many of these countries are the same ones that are most vulnerable to and contain the largest numbers of women that are trafficked. For example, two international organizations, the Global Alliance Against Traffic in Women (GAATW) and the Coalition Against Trafficking in Women (CATW), operate globally, but have a focus in the Asia Pacific because of the high rates of labor and sex trafficking, also because of the region's strong resistance against trafficking (from antisex tour campaigns and antimilitarization campaigns). However, the ways in which this resistance has been expressed have varied according to individual countries. For instance, Indonesian women have not been able to organize as freely as Filipina women because of a concerted demolition of civic organizations by the Indonesian government. In Thailand, there is also a certain amount of openness but in Malaysia there is less because Malaysian groups are considered serious threats to the government (Gurowitz, 2000). Because of these gradations, things such as open protest may take various forms: civil disobedience, picketing, petitioning, workshops, media campaigns, and artistic collaborations.

Highlight: Coalition Against Trafficking Women

CATW is a nongovernmental organization that works to end human trafficking and the commercial sexual exploitation of women and children worldwide. CATW is the world's first organization to fight human trafficking internationally and is the world's leading abolitionist organization. A unique strength of CATW is that we engage in advocacy, education, victim services, and prevention programs for victims of trafficking and prostitution in Asia, Africa, Latin America, Europe, and North America, including in the United States.

Since 1988, CATW has provided widely recognized leadership on local, national, regional, and international levels, in promoting legislative, policy and educational measures to raise awareness about the root causes of human trafficking. CATW holds Special Status with the United Nations Economic and Social Council (ECOSOC) and was a key consultant at the UN Transnational Organized Crime Meeting from 1999–2000 the outcome of which is the Palermo Protocol, the world's most recognized legal instrument on human trafficking.

Human Rights–Based Solutions

Creating the legal, political, and social conditions that are inhospitable to human trafficking and affording women and children real economic alternatives is how we end human trafficking. We must oppose state policies and practices that channel women into conditions of sexual exploitation. Providing education and employment opportunities that promote women's equality diminishes women's vulnerability to human trafficking.

The most effective policies are ones that discourage the purchase of human beings for commercial sexual exploitation, and their strategic role in the chain of human trafficking. An effective fight against trafficking means taking legal action against the buyers and anyone who promotes sexual exploitation, particularly pimps, procurers and traffickers.

We must take a principled position against the legalization of prostitution and discourage the demand for commercial sex without penalizing the victims. The wrong people continue to be arrested; the prostituted should be decriminalized. The Nordic Model is the world's first to recognize prostitution as violence against women and a violation of human rights by criminalizing the purchase of sexual services and offering women and children an exit strategy. These laws are premised on the notion that women are human beings and therefore cannot be bought and sold.

The cultural acceptance and normalization of commercial sexual exploitation fuels the cycle of violence against women. It is essential that men make equality for women and ending all forms of violence against women their political priority. This is how we raise generations of boys to become men who will not exploit women and children.

catwinternational.org

GRASSROOTS INITIATIVES

In 1996, when trafficking was rising, UNIFEM created a Trust Fund in Support of Actions to Eliminate Violence Against Women, which was one of the first funding streams that exclusively provided resources for international demonstration projects that would help end violence and raise public awareness on the issues. Essentially, this was a small grants laboratory to explore successful strategies. The average grant was about $50,000. The programs began in Latin American and the Caribbean and were then replicated in Africa, Asia, and the Pacific. In keeping with the grassroots women's movement (removing stigma and silence; creating safe spaces; reversing patriarchal practices), these programs were focused in four areas:

a) Building community commitment
b) Forging institutional partnerships
c) Developing public and institutional support through research and advocacy
d) From the local to the global perspective

Although the programs did not focus solely on trafficking and modern-day slavery, many of the countries who launched projects were dealing with increasing numbers of trafficked women and children, who were included in their efforts. The following are promising practices that are related to gender violence overall, and can be explicitly applied to trafficking.

Building Community Commitment

As we stated earlier, there is a symbiotic relationship between state policies and the actual communities that are impacted. For instance, though laws and policies are needed, they cannot be correctly implemented or enforced if people do not understand or accept them. Similarly, if the stigma around an issue is too high, then no matter what kind of interventions you have, they will fail. Main lessons learned in successful community commitment and capacity building include:

- *Using shared values to reach the community*. While issues of women might be important to parts of the population, often, those working on the issue feel as if they are "singing to the choir" or working with people who already support and have knowledge about the issues. The challenge when building community commitment and capacity is to be able to create understanding, empathy, and knowledge in portions of the community that do not usually show any support because large portions of the community do not feel it is a relevant or pressing issue, shows of support are imperative. One of the ways that the projects did this was to identify common values that were part of the community culture already. In the case of one Honduran community, they were able to get support for women by concentrating on the value of peace instead of values of antiviolence. After decades of political instability, community members were interested in how to live in and practice peace. Large workshops were designed and the information on violence against women included.

- *Getting men and boys on board through sports*. Many times, men and boys will not participate in something that they feel is geared only to women and girls (i.e., "not my problem mentality"). It may also be that they do not see a problem exists or they are just not interested. At worst, they may feel justified that it is the status quo—with themselves as males dominating over females. Several projects used the opportunity of sports' participation to provide information or activities. The most effective workshops were held as part of sporting activity orientations or pre/post-practice and game sessions. Because the males wanted to participate in the activities or teams, they had to go through mandatory workshops. It was effective because you basically had a captured audience. Of course, this is not ideal because it does not assure buy-in or comprehension. But, it is a first step and their experiences demonstrated that if you are able to get people to listen, a majority will.

- *Replacing rituals with alternatives*. It is difficult to fight against cultural standards (as we discussed earlier), but it is not impossible. In Nigeria, the acts of female genital mutilation (FGM) and child brides was commonplace and culturally, a rite of passage. For the project in Nigeria, practitioners found that they were successful in halting these violent actions if they were able to replace them with something else as meaningful. For example, in Kenya, where FGM is also an important ritual, practitioners worked with communities to design an alternative ritual that would still be significant to them but eliminate the FGM portion of the rite. A celebration is held to signify the passage of girls into young adulthood, but there is no FGM component. Mothers and other women elders in the community oversee the celebration and in turn, support this "alternative" (DeCastro, personal communication, 2015). In Thailand, one organization works to end trafficking of the girls from hillside tribes such as the Kayan Lahwi tribe, who are known for their use of brass coils around their necks, giving them the nickname of "long neck tribe." Girls from these tribes are weighted down with the brass rings from the age of 5 years old. This cultural practice has opened them up to vulnerability for sex trafficking and tourism because they have become a tourist attraction. This organization creates a "trade" for the families where they give the material equivalent the brass rings are worth, while also re-creating the ritual. An international artist then takes the brass and creates rings (for their fingers) and bracelets for their arms, which they use to re-create similar rituals. This has helped minimize the use of the neck rings which cause the girls' collarbones to sink and shift as well as tourists to gawk (Herr, personal communication, 2015).

- *Identifying peer leaders in vocational groups.* This point is self-explanatory in that often peers may have more influence than outsiders, despite the fact that outsiders may be more trained and specialized. Women are willing to work with those they see are from their own circumstances or communities. This may be due to greater levels of trust, comfort, and identification. In Saipan, women who have been abused in slave-like situations in garment factories have little trust in the industry. When they are reintegrating into new jobs, they benefit when peers help them understand their rights and how to protect themselves much more than if so-called experts came in and conducted the trainings (Miranda, personal communication, 2013).

- *Helping women assert their rights: combining information and services.* Returning to Maslow's hierarchy of needs, this practice refers not only understanding women's needs but the pragmatic fact that though the goal might be empowerment, many individuals who have experienced the trauma of violence and/or trafficking have a multitude of needs that have to be met before they can become their own advocates. Those needs contain different levels of both information and services that are needed for the healing process. The best programs were those that accounted for both. For example, recall that the strongest survivor advocacy programs take into account the continuum of needs. Survivors cannot be effective advocates if they are worried about basic needs such as food and safety (Lloyd, personal communication, 2012).

- *Establishing support groups.* Along the lines of peer leaders in vocational groups, support groups that met regularly and provided a safe space for people in the community, especially women and former victims, were especially helpful in maintaining projects and keeping them consistent. In this sense, a "safe space" is not only one that is free from judgement and blame but also one that is literally safe from any type of violence or threat of violence. The use of support groups is a common tactic in activist culture because it provides a small group (micro-mezzo) space within which to discuss larger issues, campaign work, and overall political process. These groups can also reconstruct "family" situations that victims may miss or may never have had in the first place. If well facilitated, they can also be places to model good communication skills and relationship building (Bergstrom, personal communication, 2016).

FORGING INSTITUTIONAL PARTNERSHIPS

Once communities have gained more awareness (and even during this process), advocates and activists also need to return to institutions of government, private corporations, public agencies, nongovernmental organizations (NGOs), and civic groups. The need is to sensitize or raise awareness within these entities so that they become partners in antiviolence and anti-trafficking work. For instance, as we talked about in chapter 8, even with stricter, more enforceable laws against the commercial sexual exploitation of children (CSEC), if court officials are not trained in the issue, they can inadvertently (or purposefully) treat victims as if they are criminals and ones at fault. In fact, this continues to be one of the main challenges. In Cambodia, although there are laws to protect women, often the women are stigmatized to the point where they did not want to pursue prosecution due to ongoing victim blaming and shaming. For instance, even when a case is filed against perpetrators or traffickers, the women may be harassed and pressured into dropping suit or told that they should be "ashamed" at making their situations public, that they somehow brought on their own exploitation (Watanabe, personal communication, 2015). The following are best practices found in the creation of institutional partnerships that are truly advancing work because of these alliances.

Going Through the Right Channels

It is critical when you are attempting to create an institutional partnership that practitioners work with or bring a team together of people who have actual decision-making power in the situation, or at the least are able to influence the decision-making process. For example, those in leadership positions, in addition to being able to initiate and carry through projects, also have the bigger picture of their organization in mind. In other words, they are able to have an idea of what the overall strategic plans and goals are of their organization. They may be able to understand or see the strategic advantages of proposed work or partnerships in ways that those who are not leadership will not. Those in power will also be able to articulate what they are able and willing to do or not do. This is important as partnerships are created, maintained, and sustained. They can also mandate participation in partnerships from their entire organization as well as influence other leaders in their industries or areas (and beyond) to follow suit. The work that some companies are doing in terms of supply chain transparency follow this premise: They are striving to be templates of antislavery initiatives so that others may follow.

Practitioners need to become more adept at finding out what the motivations are for their institutional partners to participate. This will change depending on position or setting or values, but they will first begin by understanding the perspective of leadership within those settings. Each side will want to know what they will get out of a partnership and practitioners should also be aware that this will not always be the same motivation or goal for those included. Practically speaking as well, you want to always make sure that all sides understand exactly what might happen and to do that, you need to have an idea of what types of decisions those not in charge are able to make. While it is always good to speak to an ally who understands the issue and wants to do more work focusing on it, this is only beneficial if they are actually able to approve such partnerships and therefore allocate human and fiscal resources, and plans of action. Finally, it is very important that partnerships maintain a solid cocreation process so that power is not consciously or subconsciously placed in the power of the power of one party or another. This way, you can avoid any scenarios of "parachuting" help, or when the powerful party enters a situation taking control and dictating the parameters of the assistance without taking into account what is really needed or allowing their partners to have any real agency and input. The other vulnerability in these "parachute" cases is that once assistance is delivered, there is a tendency to disappear, leaving communities on their own in unsustainable situations.

Equality, Not Violence, as a Discourse

Similar to shared values, practitioners found that when they talked about violence, there was a lot of stigma, defensiveness, and outright denial of the topic, but when they talked about issues of equality, there was much more openness about it. This gave them an opportunity to discuss the issues of violence within the framework of access and equality. Practitioners found that they just needed the ability to start a conversation with institutions and that this ability was obtained by talking about something that the institution was already interested in. This way they were not starting at a zero-sum game but with some level of interest on both sides. This also had the value added of reframing the discussion so that practitioners themselves also looked at the issue from a fresh perspective.

Walking in Another Person's Shoes

This is a practice that makes sense to most practitioners. However, this is not just about experiencing things from another perspective; it is actually a more defined process of teaching active listening skills, role plays, survivor accounts/narratives, and empathy building. For most institutions, especially those in law enforcement, the contact that they had with survivors and hearing firsthand accounts were the most powerful activators of change. This practice is exemplary of the influence that these methodologies can hold in terms of catalyzing change through such partnerships.

Using Training to Get Commitment

Once the partnerships began, it proved to be a strong practice to be able to incorporate instances where a commitment to the group was made, especially in terms of next steps and planning. By providing a commitment, institutions address how the relationship will be structured and how partner entities will proceed in the future. For example, Sakshi in New Delhi, India, is a small, feminist NGO that focuses on women's rights and sexual violence that uses their role as trainers for local judges and other law enforcement to include what they call "action committees." These committees require further planning and goal setting to the basic training. This creates a situation where an organic relationship may occur because there is built in follow up and exchange as well as mutual interests developing over the course of goal setting. Another example of this practice is the Clinton Global

Initiative, where conference participants must fill out a "commitment to action," which is a plan for addressing what the initiative refers to as a "significant global challenge." The commitment must fill three criteria: it must be new (in idea or approach); it should be specific (and feasible); and it has to be measurable (which is monitored by an initiative "commitment monitor") (Clinton Foundation, n.d.).

DEVELOPING PUBLIC AND INSTITUTIONAL SUPPORT THROUGH RESEARCH AND ADVOCACY

The main goal of the UNIFEM Trust Fund was to break the silence and stigma around gender-based violence. Long-range change would only be possible through mechanisms that were well informed and that were able to be nimble enough to adapt to the shifting environments that violence occurred in. Almost all organizations and exploratory studies call for more research to base advocacy activities on. However, this is easier said than done because of limited resources. Even if there were more resources to support this avenue of research, there are difficulties that remain due to stigma, denial, or confidentiality, which make gender violence a consistently difficult area to conduct research. Still, we must keep pushing for more knowledge building in this area if we are going to construct relevant, responsive, and effective interventions. For example, the Red Thread Women's Development Organisation has a long history of women's resistance that focused on social and economic dislocation due to structural adjustment programs and divided political landscapes. Intimate partner violence, gender violence, and trafficking are issues that the group uses to demonstrate why national sovereignty is important. In addition to their advocacy and activism, Red Thread has conducted extensive research since 2001 through time-use surveys highlighting women's daily lives. They believe that women they surveyed were their own experts and all they needed to do was record their everyday lives to expose the inequalities and the oppression they faced. Their research hopes to blur the boundaries between those who are conducting the research and those who are the subjects and responders, giving the research a collective process and understanding (Trotz, 2007).

Combining Research with Advocacy

When one is trained to be a researcher in traditional scientific methodology, one is taught to be as impartial and objective as possible. Conversely to this logic, UNIFEM found that researchers who were distanced from their subjects and did not have any vested interest in what they were studying were ineffective. It was researchers who were also advocates or whose research purpose was a tool of advocacy that experienced the most cooperation and greatest results. Researchers, of course, should acknowledge their biases, but it was deemed important by communities that researchers understand that community members were not just specimens. Further, the community should understand how the research would be beneficial to the movement and/or how it would help create change. Methods that are included in this practice include: Changing perspectives to change women's lives (this includes reframing the issue to include voices from survivors' narratives), combining research with services (meeting client needs), building rapport, speaking in the language of that you wish to change (understanding and operating in norms), engaging sympathetic stakeholders and community members, and creating a safe space especially for victims.

Never Sacrifice the Individual for the Cause

This practice encompasses two related concepts: respect and confidentiality. First and foremost, researchers, practitioners, and advocates must have respect and empathy for what individuals who have experienced trauma and violence have gone through. This may mean that within the process of the research, subjects may decide not to disclose or they may stop providing information. Researchers must be able to understand these fluctuations in response and respect an individual's right to change their mind, their stance, or their decision not to join advocacy efforts. Similarly, there must be equal sensitivity in relation to strict levels of confidentiality. Because of their precarious positions, victims must remain protected from further harm from perpetrators. There is always the vulnerability of retraumatization and in the case of trafficking, of being trafficked again. Even when in the middle of a research or advocacy project, in the center of a campaign or case, it is imperative that practitioners always remember that there are real people that are in the center of that and therefore, must be willing to choose that individual's preference over the "cause."

OVERALL INSIGHTS: FROM THE LOCAL TO THE GLOBAL PERSPECTIVE

From the above lessons learned, several practices were found to be helpful across the board. These were:

Documenting Reality from Women's Perspectives

Women are gaining headway in terms of equity and access, but there is still a need to redefine women's rights as human rights so as not to silo them in the gender-only arena. This also serves to move the issue of gender rights outside the realm of the private sphere and into the public domain. This is done several ways, including the acceptance and encouragement of women's narratives to clarify quantitative research. We have to obtain a clearer understanding of prevalence and how many people are impacted before we can take conclusive and decisive action. Also, UNIFEM suggests that language needs to begin reflecting women's realities. Often, as we have seen especially within the issue of trafficking, we get into what is framed as a situation of semantics. However, this is to gloss over the concrete realities of a situation that demand we use a more precise language to understand the issue. It matters how one refers to the exploitation of sex or labor: as voluntary, or coerced, or as slavery. It especially matters if someone looks at the selling of children as a cultural foregone conclusion or as a human rights violation. Finally, it matters if you are using legal jargon and loopholes as a way to justify indentured servitude.

This is because, as we have stated throughout the book, there is power in language. As the popular lexicon shifts to include more sexualized and sexually exploitative language, it does have the power to shift perceptions, roles, and ideas as well. This could be either detrimental or mitigating to vulnerable populations (such as women) and their experience of violence and trafficking. Further, highlighting what language may be trying to hide serves to also remove any isolation from what exploited individuals are living through. Finally, whether you adhere to cultural sensitive language or language that is more frank and honest (in truth, it is a fine balance), practitioners need to understand how the language is being received and perceived from victims, stakeholders, other practitioners, and the community at large. Berthold (2015) even suggests a shift from cultural sensitivity and competence, to cultural humility, which indicates giving precedence to the practitioners' role to create bridges between differing perspectives to facilitate empowerment.

Creating Safe Spaces for Women to Take Action

As women and other vulnerable populations become aware of their situations and their rights, they will assert them and fight for them. This is a lesson that has played out numerous times in many countries. When this begins to happen, it is up to practitioners to ensure that they have a safe space to take action—not just to receive services. Remember, *safe spaces* refer to places where there is no judgment or victim blaming, but also where there is no actual violence or threat of violence. Studies have indicated that safe spaces are correlated with women's willingness to join or lead, and actual participation in social movements. For instance, women may not choose to participate if there is danger or a risk of backlash especially from communities they come from.

Having safe spaces is also tied to the types of action that are taking place. For this reason, as much as possible, the solutions that seem to work the best are those that come from their local communities. The efforts that are "close to home," so to speak, are those that are organic, grassroots, and respondent to local conditions. Those that operate at the community level have better response times and the ability to address concerns as they happen in real time.

Finally, creating safe spaces means that ultimately, governments will take responsibility for ensuring women's rights. This does not mean that any government has been able to be fully successful, but it does mean that women's rights as human rights becomes part of the political discourse. While this may take the main form of legislative agendas and law making, there are number of areas that are also important. These areas include government awareness raising campaigns, national hotlines, and mandated training for law enforcement and public officials. The work that occurs between community-based organizations, private corporations and governments is a trifecta that helps individuals feel as if the issue is being handled and championed from all sides.

Making Violence Everyone's Problem

Duska Andric-Ruzic, a grantee from Bosnia-Herzgovina stated, "To change it, everyone must feel that it is their problem" (Spindel, Levy, & Connor, 2000, p. 83). This has been a recurring theme in all of the different projects, but bears repeating since gender violence has only been formulized as a human rights issue since 1993. It was not long after this that trafficking moved from gender violence to a rights-based framework to currently being thought of as within the auspices of criminal justice. Interesting enough, anti-trafficking activists see that with the heavy emphasis on crime and discipline, there is a pendulum swing back to a rights-based framework, particularly justice (including restorative justice) when we see the upsurge of survivor advocacy and activism. This particular point of practice includes things we have already mentioned, such as being able to partner and access those in power who have the ability to impact the issue in the public and policy arenas. This does not always have to be individuals who have are leaders, or are famous, or who have mass influence but could also be those that can create the most change in individual's lives, such as a law enforcement officer who is trauma-informed and can help a victim access more power. Making connections with those who have influence is only one step in being able to gain a larger audience and raising public awareness, which is one of the key methods to making violence everyone's problem. For instance, in a partnership between a U.S.' child welfare office, Clear Channel Outdoor (a global outdoor advertising company), and several district attorney's offices, a billboard campaign was launched. The launch was led by law enforcement agencies but encompassed strong social service perspectives. The campaign featured nine billboards that raised awareness of child sex trafficking (Fernandez, 2014). Once awareness has become widespread, the next step is to be able to maintain support through commitment setting as we discussed in the previous section.

CHALLENGES

One of the biggest challenges in advocacy and activist work is that there is very little training for practitioners to engage in. Practitioners are not always trained or politically adept at working to shift power (Smith, Reynolds, & Rovnak, 2009). Haynes and Mickelson (2003) believe that practitioners can be trained to be advocates and activists but that they have to be purposive in this endeavor, because these roles require special skill sets. For instance, advocates and activists must have excellent written and communication skills (i.e., verbal, presentation, synthesizing, and facilitation) and be able to use these skills to address a variety of audiences from formal, legislative arenas to parents in the community. Other skills that can build capacity in this area are being able to analyze, initiate, and support policy, organize communities (especially communities where it is difficult and stigmatizing to speak out and/or fight back), participate in political campaigns, lobby, and understand politics overall. One of the most essential skills that one should learn to fulfill these roles is strategic thinking and planning. This type of way of understanding and defining problems and solution sets will help guide campaigns, programs, and also increase understanding of all the players involved. However, despite the need to hone these special skills, most practitioners can also rely on their foundational training, especially their micro, clinical skills, which can be used to build rapport in communities, actively listen to stakeholders, and help map out ecosystems to determine where change should be targeted.

There is also the overall challenge that has been raised for action-based research and activist academics, which has been a question of bias and subjectivity. The traditional role of practitioners is one where we are asked to be a helping professional that operates value free so as not to unduly influence those we are helping. But this has not always been the case. There are innumerable examples within the histories of helping professions where practitioners were at the front line as advocates and activists (Jansson, 2015). Also, a significant part of the second wave of feminism was to establish standpoint methodologies that included participant observation, grounded theory, and action-based research (Harding, 2004). There are some that would say it is the role of academics and practitioners to push the envelope and redefine our roles. In this case, it has been a very integrated process where advocacy, activism, knowledge building, and practitioner services have evolved.

CALL TO ACTION: ADVOCACY AND ACTIVISM TO END TRAFFICKING AND MODERN-DAY SLAVERY

As trafficking and modern-day slavery continue to grow and as the fight against them becomes more strident, those in the helping professions will be challenged to be advocates and activists. Whether this fits into the paradigm of your profession or your organization or just your own individual calling, there is the opportunity to expand your practice. The innovations in the field of trafficking and modern-day slavery support this; our endeavors to end this situation have included personal view points and political ideologies. We expect that it will continue to be this way.

DISCUSSION QUESTIONS

1. Which best practices from each focus area will work best in your work?

2. How can you incorporate cultural competency for each focus area when participating in grassroots initiatives?

3. How can we use technology to address the challenges of grassroots initiatives?

4. What are the differences between grassroots and "mainstream" responses?

5. How has grassroots movements changed over time?

CHALLENGE

Journalists Nicholas Kristof and Sheryl WuDunn (2009) wrote the landmark book, *Half the Sky: Turning Oppression into Opportunity for Women Worldwide*. The book, a series of stories of extraordinary women and their circumstances of modern-day slavery, became a movement fight against what authors call "our era's most pervasive human rights violation."

- Read the book or log onto their website: halftheskymovement.org.
- Select a story or a project.
- Answer the following: Does this story come from the grassroots? In what ways? What are those characteristics? If not, why not? How does the work of this group connect to others? What are some of its main successes and challenges?
- Then, Act: Share this story, host a screening, or volunteer with an organization in the name of *Half the Sky*.

CHAPTER 12

Faith-Based Organizations

Annalisa Enrile
with contributions from Melanie G. Ferrer-Vaughn, Gabrielle Aquino, and Megan Healy

Chapter Objectives

1. Readers will develop an understanding of what constitutes faith-based services and interventions.

2. Reader will illustrate how faith-based organizations have addressed trafficking and its influence for the overall anti-trafficking movement

3. Readers will critically analyze the unlikely partnerships that have been created between faith-based organizations and other entities.

4. Readers will perceive the different challenges faith-based organizations experience.

5. Readers will devise new solutions for the anti-trafficking movement based on practices learned from the faith-based perspective.

My faith has always been my source of hope. It helps me to believe in things that seem impossible and as a social worker, it's helped me have a truly strengths-based approach with the clients I work with. But the thing about faith in our line of work is that it is constantly tested in ways that never cease to surprise me.

I belong to a church that is very global in that we see the world as belonging to all of us, and therefore, the responsibility is ours, too. Because of this, every year, we send and support teams to partner with organizations doing human rights work. These trips are called "mission" trips because

(Continued)

(Continued)

you go with one mission—to spread love and justice. We hold the value that faith is equivalent to fighting for justice, especially for vulnerable populations like women and children living in poverty.

I had never gone on one of these mission trips but I felt compelled to respond to the need when the organization that asked us for help was Bridges to Nations, a nonprofit organization helping to prevent and provide services to trafficking victims in Thailand. The first part of the trip consisted of helping do prevention work in the form of helping set up a coffee shop that would have multiple purposes: a business that could train and hire, providing economic opportunities; a space for people to meet, including programs where English could be taught; and a hub for the community to receive information and other awareness-raising tactics. This part was easy because our work was the physical setting up of the coffee shop. Our church not only raised money to finance the building but our team worked with the local community to build it. Side by side, we spent days painting, decorating, and furnishing the shop. It was the sweetest cup of coffee I had ever had.

The second part of the trip was when my faith was truly tested. This part was actual field work where we did bar and beach outreach, trying to offer services and other opportunities for women or the ladyboys[1] that compose the bulk of the trafficked and commercially sexually exploited in Thailand. We did this nightly. I never got used to witnessing the seemingly casual way that (usually) male tourists would buy "sexual services" as carelessly as if they were ordering fast food. I never got used to the way that young, young girls would be led out of bars by the hand and return looking glassy-eyed and wrecked. My heart would break every time the brash, bold humor of a ladyboy would be tamped down and extinguished after doing a "trick."

Added to my emotional response was my intellectual and spiritual conflict. As a social worker, I had a certain set of beliefs around the dignity and rights of human beings. However, as a Christian, there were also moral codes and religious dogma that we are taught about what should be considered right and wrong. My church didn't use our teachings to exclude people, but I knew there were some religious institutions that did. It made me wonder whether or not I could be true to any side of it—the intellectual, the social worker, and the faithful.

Our partner in Thailand was a survivor herself. She seemed to have an indomitable spirit that never gave up. One night, she took me with her on her "rounds" of the beach, where she did outreach to homeless ladyboys. There were very few donations available for this type of work or for this population, so she usually only had the ability to provide food and water twice a week. When she didn't have anything to give, she just sat with them, held their hands, and listened to their stories. I wanted to believe that we were doing good work, but each night, facing these odds, change seemed futile. "No more use, they throw us away," she said in her makeshift English. "But, that is when we need people the most." She should know. She had contracted HIV on the street and she had struggled to get even

---

1. "Ladyboys" is the term used to describe transsexual men, many of whom are commercially, sexually exploited. This group has become an integral part of Thailand's sex tourism.

the most medical help. *"No one wants to help; that's why you are so important. Some groups think that ladyboys are dirty, that they are less. That they should be erased. We need see them."*

I knew she meant other faith-based organizations. It was something that we talked about, and it made me wonder how you can say you are spreading love and justice while making such moral judgments. It made me feel even more helpless, questioning our mission. When I shared my concerns with my team members, we talked a lot about what it meant to serve. We returned to a passage in the bible in Romans 13:10, "Love does no wrong to its neighbor. Therefore, love is the fulfillment of the Law." We recognized that not everyone shared our same beliefs but that part of our mission was to be accepting, to be open, and to recognize everyone's humanity. In other words, our mission goal remained the same—to love. It made me understand then that sometimes, even when you don't have the right medicine or enough of even the most basic things or even any sure answers, it is enough to simply sit and be someone's witness—to their pain, to their lives, to their survival. It was enough to have hope.

—Gabrielle Aquino

INTRODUCTION

Faith-based services, programs, and interventions have long supported the anti-trafficking movement. Namely, faith-based organizations have been able to fill in gaps in services which have been cause by a number of things such as stigma, fear, safety, and ignorance. Faith-based organizations are in a unique position because they are already a part of people's lives. At the very least, for a majority, faith-based organizations are familiar places or institutions. At a time when individuals who are exploited by trafficking are trying to run away or even if they are in the middle of the healing process, the ability to access a familiar institution not only brings them comfort but also provides them with some modicum of control. Over and above this, we cannot discount the power of someone's faith as a source of hope and strength. It is not uncommon for victims and survivors to report that their faith has helped them remain resilient in the face of adversity and trauma.

Faith-based organizations operate in the following manner: raising awareness of the issue; persuasion and exhortations that draw references from their spiritual texts; testimonies and sermons; and emotionally pitched calls to action, relating this to religious calling or purpose (Raimi, 2012). Supplementing these practices are religious beliefs that support actions to end trafficking or at the very least, condemn it. Christianity and Judaism liberally use their scriptures to refute trafficking and also as a way to mobilize their followers to work to end trafficking. The Jewish practice of mitzvah, which is a commandment that necessitates not just good deeds by their membership, but actual action to perform good deeds (National Council of Jewish Women, n.d.). Within Islam, faith-based organizations operate from the mandate of their religious text, the Qur'an, which does not consider slaves as chattel because of their humanity and abhors slaves being forced into prostitution, including the slavery and trafficking of girls (Raimi, 2012). Islam has received a lot of criticism because the religious sharia laws benefit men and deeply discriminate among women. Yet, if one were to reference the Qur'an, there would be countless references to the rights of slaves and to the overall condemnation of the practice to begin with. This is a good example of the contradictions that may exist in faith-based organizations in terms of what the beliefs are directed by, what public perception may be, and the many balances that must be maintained.

President Bush created the White House Office of Faith-based and Community Initiatives with the purpose of assisting "people of faith to help meet social objectives" (Farris, Nathan, & Wright, 2004). Much of the initial work revolved around anti-trafficking work especially with the release of millions of dollars of federal funds. Though the office was supposed to be a faith-based initiative for all faiths, there was an admittedly Christian bias. Specifically, there was an overwhelmingly biased representation of evangelical Christian groups, though the public officials involved denied that such a preference existed (Kuo, 2006). Despite denials, almost all the of grants were awarded to evangelical Christian groups. Because of this, they are overrepresented in the literature and this chapter will focus on what we know of best practices derived from the field. When possible, we have tried to include other faiths, but the dearth of literature continues to be a barrier.

FAITH-BASED SERVICES

A faith-based organization is typically characterized by the values and beliefs that are established and affiliated with a religious body and ideology (Ferris, 2005). In an organization's mission statement, there is often a reference to religious ethics and standards that are used as guiding principles. Their governing board may or may not consist of people who ascribe to the religion, but the decisions are made and directed by religious values. In some cases, the financial revenue may be donations from religious or private sources. The term "faith-based" supercedes "church-based" or "spirituality-based" because it allows for all types of congregations and worship (U.S. Department of Housing and Urban Development, 2001). Faith-based organizations and services do not just operate in the anti-trafficking arena but also have been working to bring awareness to other social justice issues such as genocide, immigration, and war/conflict zones. They do not just stop at awareness raising and services but began to actively advocate and lobby for various causes (Ferris, 2005).

Faith-based organizations can be categorized into three types: congregations, national networks, and freestanding religions organizations. Faith-based organizations have been widely involved in youth programs, food banks, hospice and illness support, and other human services. The U.S. Department of Housing and Urban Development goes on to stipulate that more than half of these organizations provide human services and community advocacy. They have invested between fifteen to twenty billion dollars annually in addition to millions of in-kind supports in volunteer hours (U.S. Department of Housing and Urban Development, 2001). For example, Safe Families for Children calls itself "faith in action" and is a volunteer initiative that is composed of host families that open up their homes to families who are experiencing crisis in the hope that children will remain safe and the family will not be involved in the foster care system. The host families practice what the call "biblical hospitality" based on scripture that requires them to care for "widows and orphans." The Safe Families process involves an in-depth training, background checks, intense application process, and ongoing education, all which is done on a volunteer basis (Olive Crest, 2015).

What defines organizations is that their values and belief systems are explicit. While there is a range in terms of how much of the actual religion they reference or incorporate, their religious beliefs are apparent. For Christians and Jews alike, Hebrew scriptures held themes and instructions for justice and caring for the poor and marginalized. Catholic entities established charities, hospitals, places for refuge and shelter, as well as other services to aid and offer support for those who have been disenfranchised. The value of service has been upheld with high regard for years in addition to valuing the human life as a whole by caring for others (Ferris, 2005). The Dalai Lama Center is an example of this, espousing respect for multiple beliefs in the spiritual umbrella of "human compassion" as they work to help victims as well as unite different faiths (Lama Tenzin, personal communication, 2016).

Some organizations focus primarily on assisting those of the same faith, but many adhere to a more global lens encompassing humanitarian work. They have been integral at providing substantial services in a number of areas. For instance, roughly one-third of all AIDS patients in the world are treated and assisted by faith-based services (Ferris, 2005). Faith-based services are often successful because they draw from a large community who share similar values and have a focus of helping others. There is no need to convince their members to help. This large volunteer pool is complemented with the ease at which most faith-based services are able to navigate sometimes politically difficult terrain. Often, governments, even those in conflict, assume that faith-based groups are not threatening or carrying their own agenda. This allows them to be able to get into community spaces and provide services in places where government offices might not be welcome or have overlooked them. Also, the power of faith in one's life is an important mechanism (as we stated earlier) and has come to symbolize or stand for safety, comfort, and trust for some. As such, individuals who have been trafficked may be more willing to disclose. Those representing faith-based organizations, more than law enforcement or secular practitioners, may have more access. For many since their faith is a source of strength, these interventions hold a lot of promise.

FAITH-BASED ABOLITIONIST MOVEMENTS

The confluence between religious values and doctrines and human trafficking and modern-day slavery is not as far-fetched as we might believe. There have definitely been negative roles that religious beliefs have played in facilitating or at least rationalizing trafficking. We include some examples to construct an understanding that, as with other social constructs we have discussed, faith and religion are also multilayered and not a dichotomous explanation of good or bad. Case in point, Buddhism believes that women are just as capable as men, but at the same time their teachings are that women are born women because of their bad karma (Brown, 2000). For example, in southern India and Nepal there is the practice of girls being given to the Hindu goddess Devi. Most of these women and girls are part of the Dalit caste, or the "outcaste" who are the poorest and lowest of the castes. They are known as *devadasis* ("servant of the diety"). The "giving" of their daughters to the temple is meant to appease the goddess from causing havoc in their families and when the daughters go, it is to "serve" and they are considered in a sacred marriage to the goddess. Because of this, they are not free to marry anyone else but are able to sexually be with men, mostly within brothels or in long-term sexual relationships. More than half of these devadasis are considered prostitutes or trafficked because of the young age at which they are given to the goddess as well as lack of any choice in the matter (Ramberg, 2011). Another example is the "juju vow" in parts of East Africa, including Nigeria, where traffickers make their slaves take the vow. The vow is a part of "Juju," which is a charm or fetish activity imbued with supernatural power, part of the religious witchcraft of voodoo practiced by in the region (Oviasuyi, Ajagun, & Isiraoje, 2011). Even if those who have been trafficked or enslaved manage to get free, they are feel that something harmful will befall them and their families by testifying against or telling anyone about their experiences (Friesch, personal communication, 2016). Another example are sects of the Church of Latter Day Saints (also known as the Morman Church) who practice polygamy. There are current trends in the literature that support similar tactics of polygamists and traffickers, particularly of young girls who are given to polygamist families and who will "marry" into them (Whitsett, personal communication, 2016).

In spite of the danger and role that religious doctrine may play on purpose or inadvertently in the proliferation of trafficking, many would argue that the role of faith is much more strengths based and involved in anti-trafficking or interventions to trafficking than the former. The stance of religions against trafficking, especially sex trafficking, has always been clear, mostly from the perspective of their antiprostitution and antipornography movements. In the United States, when President George W. Bush started to interject trafficking into the national discourse, he leaned heavily on moral convictions and outrage (Weitzer, 2007). He was building on the work of his predecessor, President Ronald Reagan, whose administration had already made advances to suppress the pornography industry. This work did not just rely on the support of the conservative right, but began to bring in the radical left through some sectors of the feminist movement. Their work together resulted in an increase in prosecutions and fines, and a decrease in sales during this time (but would change with the advent of the internet). It proved to be a strong collaboration that moved into anti-trafficking work and is often referred to as the "neoabolitionists."

Highlight: Hookers for Jesus (Domestic Organizational Highlight)

Hookers For Jesus was started by survivor Anne Lobart in 2005. She sincerely wanted to reach other victims of sex trafficking and those who had been severely abused by the system of the sex industry. What started as a simple outreach of love, support, and resources in 2005, eventually was founded into an official nonprofit 501c3 in 2007.

Why the name, "Hookers For Jesus"? The ministry work is based on the simple act of love of "fishing" for people who are looking for a way out of the dark waters they are drowning in of sex trafficking. Jesus said so himself:

"Follow me, and I will teach you how to fish for people."

Hookers for Jesus reaches out to ladies who are struggling with being abused by the system of the sex entertainment industry. They offer unconditional love, support, and resources through their core services:

- Destiny House—1-year residential program for sex trafficking victims and sex industry ladies

- Saturday Night Love—outreach on the Las Vegas strip to sex trafficking victims

- Ladies of Destiny—weekly educational and healing classes

- Grace Chicks—mentorship and resource program

- KISS—awareness and media education presentations

- Diamonds and Pearls—outreach to strip clubs

hookersforjesus.net

These neoabolitionists are certainly a case of strange bedfellows. The partnerships that have come together have not always been the most predictable. From the early stages of the anti-trafficking movement, the groups to come together were moral crusaders in the form of the Christian right and radical feminists. With sex trafficking and prostitution identified so closely to one another, the point of unity that the church and feminists found were that they were both staunchly antiprostitution. Organizations such as the Coalition Against Trafficking of Women (CAT–W) and Hookers for Jesus work on the same issues and provide similar services. More important, their extremely different ideologies seem to find intersection in their like goals. The stance of the church, which relies on morality and values based on religious texts and teaching, was misaligned with the agenda of radical feminists, but their goals were the same. When they first began anti-trafficking work, it was a surprising partnership, even to those involved (Mirkinson, personal communication, 2016). Radical feminists view prostitution and sex trafficking as a form of violence against women that is exploitative and degrading. This view also believes that women do not have a real choice so there is no differentiation between coercion or intentionality, since patriarchy, sexism, and capitalism have turned women into products to be sold. Christian groups and other faith-based organizations view prostitution and sex trafficking as deviant from traditional values, a moral wrong, and in the case of prostitution, a distortion of marriage vows (Chuang, 2010). They may have different reasons, but the outcome they wanted was the same: to abolish the commodification and sexual exploitation of women. That they share the same stance toward prostitution and trafficking is a testament to the wide continuum of the anti-trafficking movement.

The same partnership is occurring today. While there are divides with diverse views and they remain in different schools of thought regarding other issues, they agree and hold commonality when it comes to sexual exploitation (Weitzer, 2007). Feminists have commented and shared that they have valued the contributions and work of conservative and faith-based groups in campaigns. Others have also thought that they bring a fresh perspective in the ways they choose to combat trafficking and interpret their actions as a biblical mandate. In many ways, especially through policies, feminists admit to the partnerships with faith-based organizations has created more traction in the movement and international attention (Weitzer, 2007). This alliance has gained momentum together as they influenced policies such as the great impact on the creating and passing of the Trafficking Victims Protection Act (Bromfield & Capous-Desyllas, 2012).

Figure 12.1   Starting the Conversation on Combatting Human Trafficking

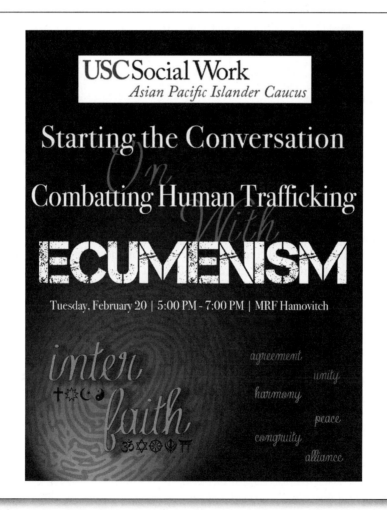

Source: Honey Imbo

FAITH-BASED SERVICES, PROGRAMS, AND PROJECTS

The best way to understand the scale and scope of faith-based organizations is to provide examples of the work. Many of these examples are focused on sex trafficking as opposed to labor trafficking. This make senses given what we know about the origin of such programming within faith-based organizations and their need to address sexuality, morals, and beliefs to serve those who are abused, exploited, and oppressed. Some faith-based organizations are more imposing about their faith and religious affiliations than others. Regardless of their expression, all are compelled and motivated by their religious beliefs and hope to make lasting change by that inspiration.

International Justice Mission—Washington, DC

International Justice Mission (IJM, n.d.) is a well-known faith-based organization that does tremendous work internationally. They have identified that there are broken justice systems that have not worked in the favor of the people, especially in developing countries. IJM believes that where the law is not enforced, violence becomes more likely and more of a norm for the culture. They identify that a justice system functions poorly when there is a lack of resources, training, accountability, and hope.

IJM's process to transforming the justice model works in four components: (1) rescue, (2) restore, (3) restrain, and (4) represent. *Rescue* works to identify children and adults who have been victimized into labor or sex trafficking, and IJM partners with law enforcement to conduct rescue operations. These rescue operations are also called "raids." Some are very dramatic, complete with guns, sirens, and chaos (Soderlund, 2005). IJM investigators try to rescue as many children as possible from the brothel. Once they are rescued, they are taken to shelters or safe houses to facilitate recovery. A key hallmark of faith-based organizations are the safe houses that have been set up specifically for child victims of trafficking. If you take into account that the Salvation Army is a faith-based organization, this sector has dominated in terms of shelter preparedness. This step then leads to *restore*. Restore aims to tailor treatment and healing for each survivor's need. This may mean long-term shelter, trauma counseling, job training, and so forth. *Restrain* works to keep survivors safe by supporting police in arresting and charging traffickers with crimes. IJM offers training and mentoring for law enforcement staff to help identify and collect the appropriate evidence and information for court cases. Last, they help survivors prepare testimonies and work with prosecutors to represent survivors and bring the perpetrator to justice.

IJM is well known and lauded for their work internationally but they have been criticized for including rescue and restoration in their model because this is a sensitive area. Rescues, raids, or *crusades,* as they are sometimes referred to, paired with restoration must be handled sensitively because victims will run away from safe houses and shelters post rescue. One of the reasons may be because they were not ready to leave their situations. They may even feel as if they are being punished by leaving their situations. Often, individuals who have been trafficked are not given the choice to be "rescued" and so there is the feeling that they are yet again being moved without any control. Though it might seem that no one would want to remain in a trafficked situation, there are complex psychological and physical considerations that might be in play. Also, to some of those "rescued," the shelter or safe house and a rehabilitation process may just be another form of imprisonment (Soderland, 2005).

Divided into two parts, IJM works to rescue victims and help them maneuver what can an intimidating and tricky justice system. Then, they work to repair the system that are failing the people it is meant to serve. As a faith-based organization, IJM shares they are inspired by God to love people and seek justice for the oppressed. They believe in serving and protecting all people.

Freedom Place—Houston, Texas

Freedom Place, a program under the auspices of Arrow Child and Family Ministries, is a confidentially located residential facility for child survivors of sex trafficking. Arrow Child and Family Ministries (n.d.a.) is a Christian service provider that focuses on child welfare. Residential services is just one area of programming. They also offer programs focusing on foster care, adoption, family services, and educational programs (Arrow Child and Family Ministries, n.d.c.). Freedom Place openly states that they are a Christ-centered recovery center for under-aged female victims of domestic sex trafficking.

This program launched in 2012 and is known to be one of the few residential facilities in the nation to target this population. The facility is stretched across 110 acres in Texas, and equipped with a living facility that comprises of two living-room areas, two kitchens, and many bedrooms and bathrooms, enough to house 30 girls (Arrow Child and Family Ministries, n.d.b.). They also have a school building, a volleyball court, basketball court, swimming pool, a lake for canoeing, and prayer garden. Included in the facilities is an on-site medical clinic, and mental health, substance abuse, and education professionals who work together to create an individualized plan to facilitate healing for each girl. One unique aspect of this program is that it includes spiritual components. Spiritual counselors are part of the treatment team for each individual. Spiritual counselors can assist residents to develop their faith and their beliefs, and provide them with opportunities on how to grow in their spiritual walks. Residents also have opportunities for their spirituality to develop. This could be through events such as studying the bible, meeting with counselors, and learning spiritual disciplines.

The length of the program for a girl typically lasts a year, at which point the girls may reunite with their family or relatives. Another option is having Arrow Child and Family Ministries facilitate a foster care placement within their network of Christian families. This is important because each family is prepared for the purpose of taking in a child who has been sexually exploited. There have been some arguments for specific trauma-informed care and this would fit that criteria. Some child welfare experts also state that a placement that houses a child who has suffered trafficking trauma needs to be placed by themselves—for their own healing and to keep them away from any other children in the system who may be trying to lure or procure them back into exploitative circumstances (De Los Reyes, personal communication, 2016). They also will help a child approaching the age of 18 prepare for independent living. Within Arrow Child and Family Ministries and Freedom Place, they believe that their spiritual component is what makes their work significant. Freedom Place assesses spiritual needs and will offer ways for the girls to engage in faith and maturing their spiritual journey.

Wellspring International

Wellspring International is the humanitarian arm of the Ravi Zacharias International Ministries (RZIM) where they identify and provide financial support to organizations, projects, and also individuals to support aid to women and children at risk. The individual scholarship supports education, health care, and basic living needs. They operate fully from private donations and 100% of the donations are distributed to their global projects. They fund several projects in the following areas: rescue (liberating people from what they term "destructive" environments); rehabilitation (treatment programs for health and mental health); restoration (respite, renewal); and re-entry (shelters, vocational training, and job opportunities). RZIM describes itself as "an apologetic ministry," which is a form of ministry that "defends" Christian beliefs. They believe their work is following the example of Jesus and meeting the world's needs with love. Although they lead with this strong ideology, they do not require their projects to share in these beliefs ("Wellspring international," n.d.a)

Highlight: Wellspring International

Wellspring International was established in 2004 by Ravi Zacharias International Ministries (RZIM). A humanitarian arm of the organization, Wellspring International is an extension of the central focus of RZIM, where we live out what we preach and defend. Through a process of due diligence, the vision of Wellspring is to identify and financially equip existing organizations aiding women and children at risk, as well as to provide individual scholarships to support education, healthcare, and basic living needs.

Wellspring International exists to empower you to impact the lives of women and children in need around the world. One hundred percent of donations designated for Wellspring are distributed to projects overseas that we have researched and vetted. Through a comprehensive process of due diligence, we research existing efforts so that our donors do not have to do so. Once a project is adopted, we enter into a contractual agreement with the organization to outline the details of the project and the specific management and use of funds. Throughout the project, Wellspring documents the progress and process on your behalf. You can be confident that with regular site visits, audit reports, and project management, Wellspring is looking out for your best interest and preserving the integrity of your contribution to a particular need. By connecting you to genuine need, together as partners we impact a world far beyond ourselves.

It is our privilege to aid organizations that embody four principle aspects we believe are vital to this effort: *Rescue*, liberating individuals from destructive environments; *rehabilitation*, offering programs that provide treatment, and healing for physical, and emotional needs; *restoration*, a period of respite, and renewal, that they may embrace a new hope, and freedom, claiming confidence, and independence; *re-entry*, providing homes, vocational training, and job opportunities.

(Continued)

(Continued)

Project Example: Word Made Flesh, Bolivia

Bolivia has one of the highest poverty rates in Latin America. It is the poorest country in South America. Seventy percent of its population lives on less than $3 USD per day. The city of El Alto sits on the fringe of the Bolivian Altiplano highlands high above its sister city of La Paz and hosts the largest indigenous population in Latin America, with over 1.2 million residents. Many of its inhabitants are transient farmers from the countryside, passing through the sprawling urban slum in search of work.

When unemployment disempowers and discrimination discourages them, many find themselves turning to drunkenness, violence, and the abundant brothels in the red-light district. Between 3,000–4,000 women are registered sex workers in El Alto. Many have been tricked into prostitution through promises of lucrative employment, the need to feed their children, or their debts have accumulated with no other foreseeable way to pay them off. Most are single mothers who hide their work from family and friends. Over 90% of women in prostitution were sexually, physically, emotionally, and mentally abused as children. CECASEN, the Center for Training and Services for Women, estimates there are over twenty illicit human trafficking rings in El Alto alone.

Word Made Flesh's Casa de Esperanza (House of Hope), in the red-light district of El Alto, will serve on average 120 women and children affected by prostitution each month. Through its two programs, Presence (Awaken) and Paso a Paso (Heal), Word Made Flesh seeks to practice and proclaim the Kingdom of God among persons affected by prostitution through relationship and opportunities for holistic transformation.

wellspringinternational.org

Word Made Flesh is one of their projects in El Alto, Bolivia. Bolivia has one of the highest poverty rates in Latin America with 70% of its population living on less than $three U.S. dollars per day. In El Alto, there are between three to four thousand registered "sex workers." In Bolivia, prostitution is legalized. In addition to these numbers, the Center for Training and Services for Women (CECASEN) in Bolivia estimate there are over twenty sex trafficking rings in El Alto. "Word Made Flesh" runs *Case de Esperanza* (House of Hope) right in the center of the red-light district. Every month, they serve 120 women and children through two programs, Presence and Paso a Paso (Heal). The programs use the scriptures and encourage those in prostitution or who are victims of trafficking to have a relationship with God. In their shelter, they feature a large dining room where they practice group and "family like" dinners. They also offer discipleship though bible study, workshops on topics such as crafts, health, and nutrition as well as life skills such as budgeting, cooking, and parenting, as well as rehabilitation counseling and therapy by licensed professionals. Their goal is to get women to leave brothels. Though there has not been extensive evaluation on Word Made Flesh, Wellspring International conducts extensive annual programmatic audits Wellspring International, n.d.-b).

Faith Alliance Against Slavery and Trafficking

Faith Alliance Against Slavery and Trafficking (FAAST) is an alliance of Christian organizations that are dedicated to fight trafficking. The existence of their alliance is rooted in the belief that there is a biblical mandate to serve and care for those who are poor and oppressed. FAAST believes that Christians must work together to address trafficking because as God's people they are able to offer change and restoration. FAAST is comprised of member organizations that unite on the basis that God is central to their work and believe they can utilize their resources and strengths to advance God's kingdom. As an alliance on a larger level, they meet on a monthly basis to determine and develop projects, research, training, and resource development. The organizations that participate then do work locally to participate in grassroots change. The member organizations of FAAST are Freedom's Promise, the Global Center for Women and Justice at Vanguard University, Nazarene Compassionate Ministries, Point Loma Nazarene University, Project Rescue, Rescue 1 Global, Rescue: Freedom, the Salvation Army, and World Relief.

DhammaMoli in Thailand

DhammaMoli is a Buddhist organization in Nepal that is run by Buddhist nuns. The two founding Buddhist nuns are Venerable DhammaVijaya and the Venerable Mulini. Both nuns have their doctorate degrees from a Buddhist university that studies Theravadan Buddhism. They felt compelled to start this organization because they believe that Buddha instructed them to help others in any capacity that they can. This inspired them to help girls of trafficking in their communities. Most of the girls that the DhammaMoli serve are elementary-aged. They are typically very young, shy, and quiet.

This organization seeks to provide shelter and education to young girls who are rescued from trafficking. This organization is located in Nepal, where Buddhism and Hinduism are both prominent in a coexisting way. What makes DhammaMoli a unique agency is that the nuns educate the young girls on Buddhist theory and practices to help facilitate with their healing journeys from trafficking. When the girls are first rescued, the Buddhist nuns educate the residents on the national language, Nepali, and Monsatic rules and regulations. The nuns then send the girls to schools where they receive an education in hopes of finding a better life for themselves. At school, the girls learn English and common school subjects, such as math, in hopes that education will lead them to better opportunities. Another aspect of this organization is that the nuns take the girls on field trips to local attractions during the holidays. When the girls do not have school, the nuns also educate them on Buddhist theory and spiritual practices. Spiritual practices include chants, mindfulness, and meditation. One spiritual practice that this organization values and uses daily is meditation. This form of mindfulness is embedded in their daily programming, usually happening twice a day in hopes to bring love, happiness, and healing to the girls. The nuns admit that they are not mothers themselves but they try their best to emulate the values of Buddhism, showing love and respect, to the young girls they serve.

Santa Marta Group

The Santa Marta Group is a transnational initiative that brings together law enforcement, nonprofit organizations, and Catholic bishops from around the world. This collaboration works with various communities to end modern-day slavery by combining resources for both prevention and intervention care (U.S. Department of State, 2016). The group was initiated out of the Catholic Bishops Conference for England and Wales and named after the hometown of Pope Francis. Over 30 countries have joined as have international law enforcement such as Interpol, Europol, U.S. Homeland Security, and forces from Ghana, India, Thailand, and Australia (Santa Marta Group, n.d.). The group has held three conferences in different parts of the world where they have created declarations, listened to testimony, launched research, and dedicated support to various helping groups.

CHALLENGES

There are several challenges for faith-based organizations. One of the main challenges is cultural competency. Faith-based organizations have specific values and beliefs based on their religious doctrines. Because of this, they view individuals from a certain lens or worldview that guides the interventions they should provide. This may limit their cultural competence or sensitivity because they may have certain perceptions of those who have been trafficked. For example, they may view women or young girls as needing to be protected and guided. This reinforces the patriarchal status quo that is a root cause of trafficking to begin with. Most faiths are heavily steeped in morality and this might be intimidating or overwhelming for victims of trafficking because it may trigger or add to existing traumas. The morality standpoint may also cultivate shame for those who have been trafficked, thus having adverse effects on his or her healing process.

Another challenge is that though faith-based organizations might mean well, they may not be equipped to handle needs of those who have been trafficked or enslaved. The credentials and training varies among different organizations and though there are some organizations that require credentials, it is not consistent, especially internationally, where there might be less of a separation between religions and governments. This is a challenge especially if there is a lack of training and understanding. For instance, we have seen how important a trauma-informed lens is in providing services. Also, best practices (cognitive behavioral therapies, intensive case management) should be enhanced by faith as a strengths-based or empowerment-based lens, not contrary to helping methods. One way to address this challenge would be for faith-based organizations to make sure they have licensed clinicians on staff (depending on what they deem the greatest needs are). This might change depending on context especially the country they are located in.

A possible vulnerability of faith-based organizations is that some may exhibit cult-like tendencies. For example, one faith-based organization may impose their beliefs on the individual because they "rescued" the victim. The rescued victim may feel obligated to immerse themselves in the religious values because it is "expected" or embedded in the programs themselves. This can create an increased vulnerability because the individual feels indebted or saved.

There is also limited communication and cooperation between faith-based organizations. The lack of cooperation may lower the efficiency to combat trafficking especially between agencies that seek to arrest and prosecute traffickers. There have been a lot of efforts to assemble multifaith coalitions, but how they have been able to operate has also been uneven. There have been some examples of strong alliances, especially when there is a project that they are working on or a common purpose. In these cases, shared decision making and ongoing dialogue have shown to be best practices for these groups to create successful working alliances.

Case Vignette: Fellowship Monrovia

Fellowship Monrovia is a Christian church in Southern California and their congregation of 600 felt compelled to respond to a need to end trafficking in Thailand after meeting with a local nonprofit organization. The church decided to support the programming of the nonprofit organization called Bridges to the Nations. All the programming falls into two categories: prevention work to help empower individuals so they do not enter the cycle of trafficking, and intervention work to disrupt this. The form of "support" was to create trips to Thailand to work with partners. They were named "mission trips" because participants would focus on one mission—to spread the love of Jesus Christ. The church believes that spreading love is equivalent to fighting for justice, especially for vulnerable populations such as women and children.

For the first year, 12 individuals—6 men and 6 women—were selected to help support the prevention and intervention work of the nonprofit. Two survivors who used to be sex slaves on Walking Street in Pattaya, Thailand, led the entire trip and team. The city of Pattaya is renowned for its tourism and has extensive red-light districts, much of them filled with underage girls. The proposed trip consisted of prevention work through the creation of a social enterprise. The project included working with survivors to set up, open, and begin running a coffee shop and bakery. Before leaving for the trip, the 12 members were provided with training on the country, culture, trafficking, and overall project goals. Next, funds were raised through private donations to support the project. Materials were purchased in the United States that were hard to find in Thailand, especially the equipment for a proper coffee shop such as espresso machines. Then, another partner was added, the Tamar Center, who taught English and provided other support services. With a team of three groups involved—The Monrovia Fellowship, Bridge to the Nations, and the Tamar Center—the group set out for Pattaya, Thailand.

The first portion of the trip was of the survivors providing a tour for the team, which now not only included the original 12 but also members from the other groups. After several sharings and discussions with the survivors, they were also taken to meet community members who hopefully would be using the coffee shop. Then, the team got to work by helping build the business through

(Continued)

(Continued)

things such as painting the building, designing and decorating the interior, and helping set up the actual business training of running a shop such as this one.

Part of the project was to also provide diversion services for youth in the neighborhood through the form of art classes and English lessons. The coffee shop is located near a bus stop in a rural village in Thailand, where most young girls are picked up and sent to Pattaya. They are sent to Pattaya from the nearby countryside because their families cannot to give them an education and instead, send them to find work to supplement the family income. The goal of the coffee shop is to create a space where young kids and their education are valued. The coffee shop will also bring funds for an afterschool program run by the nonprofit. This is where youth are taught English, equipped with vocational skills, and are given the opportunity to apply for scholarships so they can pay for their education. There is a year-round teacher that spearheads this program; however, when there are visiting missions teams, those individuals tend to work with the teacher and teach the students English as well. All these pieces are utilized to advance the goal of stopping young kids from entering the cycle of trafficking.

After working on the prevention aspect, the second portion of the trip was dedicated to bar outreach, where team members entered bars to speak with women and ladyboys who are trafficked. To do this, teams had to be discreet and make sure they did things that were of the norm such as ordering drinks as they spoke to those who had been trafficked. During the conversations, team members would inform them about the Bridge of Nations and the upcoming opening of the coffee shop. They would explain how the coffee shop was built and that there were other opportunities to start their own business like this one, and other ways that economic livings could be made outside of the bar. It is a difficult challenge because many of those in the clubs are homeless otherwise, and there is also a significant portion suffering from HIV who have no access to health care. The survivors would share their own stories and also talk about how their church saved them and provided them with resources. They also shared that the church was willing to help provide hospital care if they had immediate medical needs. Our church provided funds for medical bills. For those that are interested, the team walks them to the Bridge Center services.

CALL TO ACTION: BE THE LIGHT

Faith or religion is a strong protective factor for many individuals. Faith-based organizations are and will continue to create real change. Their unique position is not just their value base but also their extensive networks create a site to mobilize against trafficking as well as to raise resources for programs and projects. However, the power of faith-based organizations may be undercut by trends in religious extremism and public stigma. As practitioners begin to include more spiritual aspects into their treatment and advocacy these strengths and challenges will need to be addressed. Just as practitioners recognize the possibilities that exist within faith-based organizations to help prevent or intervene with trafficking and modern-day slavery, policy advisors and public officials should also recognize these organizations past their spiritual utility. Just as religion was used as a tool of colonization, conversely, it has the potential to be a method for development. For instance, there are many countries that do not have a clear distinction between church and state. Even countries that say there are clear boundaries between both may experience a blurring of lines (as exemplified by George W. Bush's presidency and disbursement of funds to churches). A more purposeful, guided partnership with faith-based organizations might yield stronger alliances and better interventions.

The examples of strong faith-based organizations and the work they are doing to fight trafficking seemingly outweigh those that have been questionable or even harmful. Overwhelmingly, faith-based organizations operate from a base of individuals who choose to come together to create good and impact change in the world. Similarly, there is a groundswell movement where faiths and congregations are uniting to have more influence. Faith-based organizations such as the Agape International Missions do transnational work to end trafficking through their spiritual word and action (Ridder, 2015). Covenant House and the Dream Center, both faith-based groups actively engage in programming, including outreach, prevention, and intervention. Coalition efforts are also being used with such groups such as Churches Against Trafficking, With Compassion, and Shared Hope International. Using basic principles of love, compassion, respect, community, and spirituality, faith-based organizations may be strong models for other groups working to end trafficking.

DISCUSSION QUESTIONS

1. Select a country of interest. What role does faith and religion have in that country? How would you use faith-based organizations to help mitigate trafficking in that country?

2. Faith-based organizations contain moral imperatives. What are strengths and challenges of this?

3. How would you incorporate faith-based organizations, practices, or even beliefs into secular spaces?

4. Faith-based organizations would benefit from partners and should be assisted to empower the poor who come to them. Who are some natural partners? Who are some untraditional partners? What would those alliances or partnerships look like? How do you imagine them working together?

5. There are a lot of contradictions in faith-based organizations such as the way that women are viewed and treated. Select a religion or faith and identify at least three of these contradictions. How do you as a practitioner work through them?

CHALLENGE

Many faith-based organizations have either established or are beginning to have programming, projects, or other types of work to stop trafficking. Select a faith-based organization and contact them. Interview one of their spiritual leadership on their antitracking work, paying special attention what they identify as barriers and challenges. Focus on one of these barriers or challenges. Create a list of 5–10 things (resources, knowledge, networks, or actions) that can help address or alleviate the barrier or challenge. Share your list with the organization and/or the person you interviewed.

CHAPTER 13

Prevention

Chapter Objectives

1. Readers will identify and understand the meaning of prevention methods.

2. Readers will discriminate between the different facets in the prevention methods of anti-trafficking work: awareness raising (for at-risk populations and the general public); addressing root causes (usually identified as poverty, gender inequity, and demand); providing adequate training; targeting key industries; and developing innovations.

3. Readers will survey different prevention methods as they relate to the use of media and technology.

4. Readers will debate the stance that prevention should target or prioritize (i.e., demand, supply, or both).

5. Readers will anticipate the challenges in prevention work when developing solutions.

There is a bit of a language difference, we think, or at the very least we are getting a little lost in translation. This is despite the fact the organization's executive director, whom we are meeting with, and us speak the exact same languages—English and anti-trafficking. We have been in a room for the last 12 hours trying to create a graduate student immersion on the topic of human trafficking and modern-day slavery in Thailand. In three short months, we would be facilitating a 12-day immersion experience for 25 students from the United States. We said to her again, "We have policy and prevention, but what about intervention practices?" She looked at me blankly and we went around the conversation. Then, she finally said, "Look, we don't worry about interventions. If we have strong enough prevention programs, then girls and women never get trafficked and exploited, then they never break, and we never have to take care of them and help them heal." We nod, comprehending her logic, and tell her, "We agree, but people are going to be trafficked. What interventions will help them?" She sighs and looks

(Continued)

(Continued)

wiser than her years as she takes our hands, then says definitively, "We concentrate on prevention. We operate on hope. We try to stop the selling of human beings. Let's do that for now."

—Annalisa Enrile and Wilhelmina De Castro

INTRODUCTION

Similar to the perspective of anti-trafficking activist and executive director of Daughters' Rising, Alexa Pham, this chapter will focus solely on prevention work. Prevention is one of the "four P's" of the Palermo Protocol and the Trafficking Victims Protection Act. Initially the main thrust of the legislative agendas, once policies were in place, it was quickly realized that protection and prosecution were much easier to operationalize, implement, and in some instances, measure. The challenge with prevention is, within a social problem where we can't even count the victims with any reasonable estimates because of the clandestine and criminal nature of trafficking and modern-day slavery, how could we begin to know if our efforts were lessening prevalence and impact? Further, just as challenges persisted in other areas such as policy and practice interventions, we could not be sure if our work in prevention was effective due to continued lack of evaluation research and overall knowledge-base building.

Pragmatically, as trafficking and modern-day slavery rose to epic proportions, practitioners scrambled to stem the tide. And, as with most of societies' wicked problems, we were doing triage on those who had already been injured, with very few reserves to try to prevent people from being trafficked in the first place. This is not to minimize the need for direct interventions and to service clients, but with a finite amount of resources, services, and practitioners, it was not surprising that prevention was either something we gave lip service to, did not really invest in, or pushed to the bottom of the agenda. This is often the case with prevention in other areas of health and human services, which also tend to be underfunded and underresearched. We learn to treat and not to avoid.

Prevention is conceptually built into almost every aspect of anti-trafficking work and has taken different theoretical stances. The 2016 TIP Report examined five elements of effective prevention: enhancing understanding through research, raising awareness to prevent recruitment and reduce demand, policies and programs that decrease risks or empower vulnerable groups, increasing collaboration between and within countries, and facilitating collaborative partnerships (U.S. Department of State, 2016). For our purposes, we will be examining prevention work through an ecosystems perspective, which begins with understanding the situation in the most comprehensive way possible by including social interactions and environmental contexts. Most of the prevention work has fallen into the following areas, which this chapter will detail:

- Addressing root causes (usually identified as poverty, gender inequity, and demand)
- Raising awareness (for at-risk populations and the general public)

- Providing adequate training
- Targeting key industries
- Developing innovations

There are also a number of different actors in addition to stakeholders that we should consider, namely, law enforcement, NGOs, corporations, the media, celebrities, and researchers to name a few. These different layers emphasize the need to view the issue of trafficking and modern-day slavery through an ecosystems perspective especially when doing prevention work. This chapter will highlight prevention work through an ecosystems lens and the patterns of what seem to be promising practices in this area.

ECOSYSTEMS LENS

The ecosystems model operates from a person in environment perspective that always allows us to start where our communities and individuals of focus are located. The placement of our focal point is imperative, because it will direct all course of action, and from a human rights paradigm, also make sure we do not lose sight the people and communities that prevention initiatives affect. The ecosystems model also provides practitioners with a logical starting point by mapping the terrain. Most ecosystems are complex, requiring that all components of the ecosystem be identified and the relationships of parts be understood before any activity should take place (Wolf-Branigin, Garza, & Smith, 2010, p. 428). Such mapping is used to understand prevalence and risk. Also, it could provide information on those who are trafficked and those who are doing the trafficking, building profiles for both. For example, within the ecosystem, are there already existing areas where prevention or resistance to trafficking and modern-day slavery are occurring? Where exactly is the community or organization in their knowledge base and what resources do they have? All these are salient inquiries that help uncover context and also launch the direction of prevention measures that would be the most relevant to decision making and planning.

ADDRESSING ROOT CAUSES

One of the first things to understand when using an ecosystems model is the root causes, identified as the reasons for a problem. By understanding and addressing root causes, practitioners are able to engage in prevention work that transforms systemic change. In the case of trafficking and modern-day slavery, root causes include poverty, globalization and migration, gender inequity, and demand.

Poverty

Poverty is the biggest reason that people are made vulnerable to trafficking and modern-day slavery. In chapter 3, we saw the effects that poverty could have on communities and individuals. Traffickers take advantage of the disparity between low wages and lack of opportunities in most developing countries. Indeed, traffickers both for sex and labor offer the promise of respite and a way out for people, especially those who are in dire situations and may have run out of options (Bales, 2005). Conversely, traffickers may also take advantage of situations that may benefit them even in areas where there is development and wealth. In these areas, pockets of abundant jobs and high wages such the so-called "emerging tiger economies" of East Asia. Where there are economic "booms" also experience a rise in development and usually this leads to a rise in labor trafficking (Kara, 2009).

Prevention programs that help alleviate or even deflect poverty do not have to focus or be specific to trafficking and modern-day slavery per se. Programs that support economic well-being would theoretically remove the main reason that people end up exploited and trafficked. By this rationale, formal social enterprises and less formal income-generating projects are strong prevention programs. Less formal income-generating projects may start from small programs that offer economic respite meant to fill in gaps that labor schemes such as contractualization have created. For instance, in Bangladesh, women who work for the garment industry are usually only employed for one-year contracts and then they are forced to wait several months before being employed again. This allows companies to be exempt from the cost of providing benefits since technically none of their workers are "regular employees." One group of women began to bring home scraps of material and create small personal items such as bags, wallets, and handkerchiefs to sell in the interim while they were waiting for work. Though this was an informal endeavor, it was one that helped the women generate income and a pattern that occurs in many communities of women and migrant workers (Balawan, personal communication, 2015). If the projects gain momentum—or as more often is the case, find a wealthy benefactor—they may evolve into a more formal social enterprise.

Social enterprises differ from traditional businesses in that they are designed to solve social problems through their business ventures (Smith, Gonin, & Besharov, 2013). While many may use traditional for-profit tactics, most of them are run by the passion and commitment to a particular issue. This mission is often more similar to a nonprofit organizational perspective and service orientation than a traditional business model. Social enterprises that are the most successful are those that are able to maintain the balance between running a business and remaining true to a mission. Some researchers and business analysts believe that this is an inherent tension that must be conquered, but is extremely difficult because of the contradictory nature—maintaining commitment to your social cause but also having the skill set and ability to turn a profit (Andre & Pache, 2013; Smith, Gonin, Besharoy., 2013). Moreover, because the social enterprises naturally bring in a variety of stakeholders (since the "business" is very process oriented as well as goal oriented toward social impact), this may also raise some tensions in terms of differing opinions of how the business should progress). In spite of these challenges built into the social enterprise model, the impact and promise of social enterprises to prevent trafficking is immense.

As of 2015, Cambodia was a Tier 2 country according to the TIP report. It is listed as a source, transition, and destination country and all provinces of the country are affected by both labor and sex trafficking. Particularly those who are poor are vulnerable to forced labor on fishing vessels, agriculture, construction, factories, or domestic servitude. Males are often forced into the illegal Thai fishing industry, where they are turned into slaves for years. Women and girls are stolen and trafficked into China for forced marriages, forced factory labor, and/or sex. Child sex tourism, though declining, is still a large issue, with the highest demand for child sex trafficking occurring within the country and also as a destination for foreigners. One of the ways that Cambodia has worked to prevent and also assist those who have been trafficked is through social entrepreneurial businesses. Many of these projects are actually started by foreigners who want to do work in the anti-trafficking field. For example, one of the most visible projects is branded with an "I (heart) Cambodia" logo and found everywhere is called the Kamonohashi Project and was started by three Japanese university students, Murata, Motoki, and Aoki, in 2002. While vacationing in Cambodia, they noticed the rampant poverty and the girls who were trafficked into massage parlors, karaoke bars, beer gardens, and other touristy areas. The project develops handicrafts through the traditional weaving that Cambodian women do. They use this production and their production sites as opportunities to provide workshops and classes for the nearby community. Kamonohashi operates from the perspective that they support communities and in doing so, help alleviate poverty and give women options. They are a purely preventative venture and do not provide services for those who have been trafficked. They feel that their work in prevention, which is composed of training, partnering with NGOs and law enforcement, and building entrepreneurial businesses, is important because it removes the necessity of interventions by safeguarding families from being vulnerable to trafficking in the first place. In 2006, they partnered with a local NGO and opened a factory near Angkor Wat in Siem Reap, Cambodia. In addition to providing classes such as literacy classes and computer training, the organization and social enterprise offer trainings on sex trafficking to law enforcement (Kamonohashi project, n.d.). They also make sure that those that work with them have work days that are only six-and-half hours long so that they can attend the workshops and classes. There is also child care on site, which helps the women because lack of childcare is one of the main impediments to work. They do outreach to nearby villages and target women who are poor based on concrete quality of life rather than other financial measures. For instance, one of their metrics is how many cows the family owns because this is a main resource in rural areas. If a family owns three cows or less, they are considered "poor" and can work for Kamonohashi (Watanabe, personal communication, 2015). As of 2015, they employed over 125 women, opened two stores, and were planning expansion into India, Bangladesh, and Kenya.

Social enterprise has several strengths. First, the process of creating this type of business requires a skill set, which those involved must learn. This supports education, from the managerial role to other areas that might be included, depending on the type of business. In addition to business considerations, there are a number of other aspects where people may learn a vocation or skill. For example, in Canada, a group of domestic helpers who were trafficked and waiting for their case to be prosecuted created a catering company. Not all the women knew how to cook and had to learn (Sayo, personal communication, 2014). Consumers also appreciate and support social enterprises. There is a whole genre of retail that is geared toward supporting businesses that stand for and/ or benefit a social cause. Bono and Bobby Shrivers' Product (RED) was launched to sell items that helped benefit the fight against AIDS (Moon, Norton, & Chen, 2008). On both the side of the consumer and those that are working for the social enterprise, there is a sense of agency; that there is choice and power to help one's self. While we are looking at this option as a prevention program, it can also be used for intervention for those who have been trafficked. If we assume that those who are trafficked have very little agency or were unable to retain anything but small traces of agency, then social entrepreneurism holds the promise of returning one's power to them (Wheaton, Schauer, & Galli, 2010). The real power that social entrepreneurship contains is the ability to be a tool that catalyzes actual systemic disruption. This is especially if the social enterprise is sustainable or can be brought to scale. Literally, a strong social entrepreneurial venture can stop the cycle of poverty in a family or even in a whole community. This, in turn, can be enough of a protective factor to shield individuals from being vulnerable to trafficking.

Microfinance is also another area that has shown great potential for the poorest of society. Research has shown these programs may counter human trafficking by creating jobs, saving strategies, training possibilities, and income (Getu, 2006). Microfinance programs were popularized with the Grameenn bank's efforts in Bangladesh, where clients are interviewed within their places of residence by bank officers (thereby providing more context to the bank than a regular application would and also eliminating the need for women to travel so far), and creating peer accountability to ensure that payments are made on time. Millions of loans have been made this way. Similar programs have occurred in countries such as Bolivia, Colombia, and even the United States (Campbell, 2010; Woodworth, 2000).

Unfortunately, as with every paradigm, there are pitfalls that were unforeseen, such as some small banks and loan sharks calling themselves "microfinancers" but really operating usury schemes where one missed loan payment pushes interest rates into exponential percentage increases (Marr, 2012). Also, there is some amount of criticism that this formula will not work for agricultural communities because of the fact that larger types of loans are needed for this industry. Further, other capacity barriers may also exist. For instance, even if people are able to gain capital and produce or implement their ideas, this does not mean they are able to harness communication, marketing, production, or distribution skills needed to help a business succeed (Marr, 2012). Finally, though the loans may help, if there is little infrastructure in their communities, it may be difficult or impossible to maintain the needed technology and equipment to foster success (Chahine & Tannir, 2010). Despite this, millions of people have been able to take advantage not just of loans to help alleviate the policy, but many programs have attempted to address these challenges by providing workshops and training, grouping collectives of borrowers together, and experimenting with new partnerships through the use of technology.

Globalization and Migration

Formerly a part of the discussion of poverty, globalization and migration have taken on a distinctive space of their own in the literature. This is a new trend of discourse in trafficking especially if we assert that most migration occurs within and because of coercive environments (Chang & Kim, 2007). Often, migration is targeted, with businesses having clear preferences for labor needs depending on area and industry. This is why there are clear trafficking patterns when it comes to certain types of labor and sexual exploitation. Young men and boys are often trafficked because they are needed to last for long hours working in labor-heavy industries, and "exotic"-looking women and girls are targeted for sexual exploitation. Depending on what part of the world their appearances are considered "exotic" such as yellow skinned females in the Caribbean being desired for prostitution, but white-skinned females in parts of Eastern Asia and China (Kempadoo, 2004; Bales, 2005). Employment needs also drive different industry trends such as the shift from construction workers to health care providers and caregivers in Israel (Kemp & Raijman, 2014). Employers and traffickers will not maintain migrant workers if the cost is too steep and it is easy to discard either workers who are trafficked or who are migrant. This viewpoint encompasses more than just migration for the sake of work, but takes the standpoint that countries are devastated by certain local and transnational economic policies coupled with unjust immigration and labor practices, thereby pushing workers out to migrate and finds jobs, maintaining cycles of exploitations. Moreover, this combination of the two work in conjunction to construct untenable situations where individuals, even those who initially chose to migrate, find themselves in slave like conditions. Unfortunately, it makes it difficult to discern what should be treated as trafficking and modern-day slavery, creating "gray zones" (Gee, 2014).

One of the ways to bypass these "gray areas" is to cease making these distinctions and define bad labor practices and conditions as trafficking and modern-day slavery. By doing so, we are able to focus on prevention programs that address labor practices in general though geared directly toward trafficking. Of course, this is easier said than done since for businesses, the "cheaper" the labor, the higher the profit. For instance, traffickers and exploitative employers will only provide the most minimal of well-being for victims, and even then, the conditions may be inhumane (Wheaton, Schauer, & Galli, 2010). Stories of sweatshop workers having to sleep in dorms where their beds were grass mats on the floor and women were stacked 10–15 to a room are common (Dimapilis, personal communication, 2015). Children who are cyber-trafficked and exploited in "cybersex" are in front of computer screens simulating and performing sex acts for 15 hours at a time in cubicle-like areas (Lagos, personal communication, 2014).

Prevention programs must be realistic in several factors: that people will naturally migrate if they think they have better economic opportunities abroad, migration is not going to end because of the current economic situations in most developing countries, and the process of migration is a clear opportunity to carry out prevention practices. People will always migrate because they believe that they will be able to earn higher wages abroad. They are willing to try and put up with oppressive situations because the promised pay is much higher in comparison to what they will earn in their home countries. Their thinking is also widely supported by their governments, making this a nationwide policy (and preference) because of the amount of remittance that overseas migrant workers send back. According to the World Bank (2012), overall global remittance was over $512 billion and rising. Thus, successful prevention programs are not those aimed at stopping or preventing migration, but those that prepare or educate workers who are contemplating migration or who are leaving the country.

The Project for the Prevention of Adolescent Trafficking in Latvia (PPAT–Latvia) is a prevention program that targets youth by providing education and information on the realities of the migration process. Again, the goal is not to halt their migration, but to make sure they have a realistic idea of what migration entails and enough information so that they can make more informed decisions about whether or not migration is the right choice for them. PPAT–Latvia incorporates a youth trafficking prevention curriculum that is used in youth centers. The curriculum is a series of modules that includes interactive activities and media, all focused on how to be safe when they work abroad. Those who are set to migrate are also given free pretravel consultations where important information such as what their rights are as workers are imbedded. Career workshops are also offered to youth and their families so that they understand the issues of trafficking and how to be safe during the migration process. In addition to these aspects, the government also launched a public media campaign that used public service announcements about trafficking and migration. The media campaign was used before popular youth television shows, in between trailers at movie cinemas, internet chat sites, and supplemented by posters, brochures, and magazine articles. Outcome evaluations indicated that there was a 37% increase in those who were exposed to the campaign versus those who were not. Those exposed reported they would take precautions and that they understood risks (Boak, Ciobanica, & Griffin, 2003; Rafferty, 2013).

Other preventative measures that have shown promise are increased government regulations on migration process. For instance, governments can monitor recruitment agencies more closely because of the crucial role these agencies have in creating debt peonage situations, considered a form of trafficking (Rafferty, 2013; Kemp & Raijman, 2014). Making brokerage or recruitment agencies more responsible for their role in migration through stricter regulations of practices such as exorbitant fees and the knowledge of possibly slave-like conditions is the one of the priority areas workers have identified as where government intervention is needed. Eliminating conditions that require workers to be tied either to their place of employment or their actual employer would also be a preventative measure against trafficking and exploitation. Often, migrant workers are threatened with either deportation or have their papers taken away. In fear, they stay in slave-like work conditions (Kemp & Raijman, 2014). In Canada, the Live-in Caregiver Program (LCP) meant that hundreds of (mainly) women who migrated for this work were forced to live with their employers and could not change employment for two years. This changed in 2014, allowing them to change employers, but the resident stipulation was not removed. The result continues to be that many domestics and caregivers are pressured or forced into servile marriages to their employers (Chang & Kim, 2007). Simple preventative and protective measures also include having materials on workers' rights available in native languages, having government agencies provide oversight to make sure employer-employee contracts are fair, and partnering with NGOs, nonprofit organizations, and other service agencies to provide assistance before and during the migration process.

Gender Inequity

Gender inequity, usually the product of patriarchal constructs, manifests itself in gender discrimination and exploitation across the continuum of trafficking. It is this type of inequity that underlies migratory flows as well as increased risk and vulnerability to trafficking. Added to this is what Chuang (2006) calls the "collusion of factors" that is exaggerated by trends such as globalization, which is reliant on export-oriented, import-dependent markets driven by multinational corporations (which operate mainly through a complex network of recruitment agencies and subcontractors) and ruled by structural adjustment policies. The presence of structural adjustment policies is crucial because it is through these types of economic policies that institutionalized supports traditionally used by women, such as social services, health care, and housing, are eroded or completely eliminated.

Figure 13.1 rights4girls

1 in 4 American girls will experience sexual violence by the age of 18

Girls are only 10% of the population in state-run facilities and 38% of the victims of staff on youth victimization.

"I raised up my voice, not so I can shout but so that those without a voice can be heard."
- Malala Yousafzai

Girls should never be criminalized for being victims of abuse and violence. Stop the abuse to prison pipeline.

In recent years 83% of sex trafficking victims in the United States were U.S. citizens

The rates of sexual abuse among justice-involved girls are 4X higher than among boys.

Girls in the juvenile justice system are nearly 2 times as likely as boys to report having experienced 5 or more forms of abuse and trauma.

73% of girls in the juvenile justice system have a history of sexual & physical abuse.

Of the child sex trafficking victims recovered in a nationwide raid, 60% came from foster care or group homes.

"Each time a woman stands up for herself, without knowing it possibly, without claiming it, she stands up for all women." - Maya Angelou

"The Nature of this flower is to bloom rebellious. Living. Against the elemental crush. A song of color blooming for deserving eyes. Blooming gloriously for its self." - Alice Walker

Many human trafficking victims have been sexually assaulted within hours or even minutes of their arrest but they are rarely screened for this trauma.

Girls account for 76% of all juvenile arrests for prostitution.

1,000 American children are arrested for prostitution each year in the U.S.

70-90% of commercially sexually exploited youth have histories of childhood sexual abuse.

"I am not free while any woman is unfree, even when her shackles are very different from my own." - Audre Lorde

It's not the oldest profession, it's the oldest oppression.

Native American girls are 5X more likely than white girls to be confined to a detention facility

15% of sexual assault and rape victims in America are under the age of 12.

It is 4X more likely than others that girls aged 16-19 will be victims of rape, attempted rape, or sexual assault

66% of incarcerated girls are girls of color, despite accounting for only 22% of the general youth population.

"We are not charity cases; We are strong young ladies." - Jessica, Survivor

73% of girls in the juvenile justice system have a history of sexual & physical abuse.

80% of justice-involved girls meet the criteria for at least one mental health disorder.

There should be no difference between abusing a child and paying to abuse a child. But there is. #NoSuchThing

rights4girls

Source: rights4girls © 2016.

Gender inequity also expresses itself in the type of work women find available to them. Often it is exploitation that emphasizes or is derived from defined gender roles such as sex, caregiving, or domestic duties. This is true both in formal sectors or at worst, formal sectors that have morphed into informal circumstances because of the nature of the work. Again, a fitting example would be the shift from domestic or care-giver role to servile wife that many migrant women in Canada find themselves (Rafferty, 2013). Ironically, though women are treated in this inhumane fashion, whole nations look to and depend on their women to migrate out so that they will send money back. Entire countries are literally dependent on these women (and men) for their economic survival. For example, in the Philippines, almost $25 billion in remittances are derived every year from the work of overseas contract workers (Anjaiah, 2013). The women are referred to by the Philippine government as "heroes" but are not provided any protections.

Gender inequity is perhaps the most difficult of root causes to address because it is one that is located not only in the economic and political fabric of nations but in the very heart of the familial, spiritual, social, and cultural beliefs. Because of this, there is the reality of public and private spheres, with abuse often taking place in the private sphere, which is also the location of the exploitation or labor of women and girls. Even in countries where there have been significant public gains for gender equality, those gains have not been extended into the private sphere and, in fact, may become worse (WHO, 2009; Mirkinson, personal communication, 2016). Given these circumstances, the most successfully demonstrated prevention against gender inequity is education. UNIFEM (2011) found that educating girls through to secondary and higher levels was a protective factor against gender-based violence and mitigating risk for trafficking. Practitioners can help increase protective factors by partnering with schools or launching their own educational programs that address not only academic subjects but also issues on gender, human rights, trafficking, and violence. Modules or workshops could be created. Also, life skills and capacity building should be included in education. This would encompass topics such as problem solving, conflict resolution, communication skills, negotiation, self-awareness, interpersonal relationships, empathy, and coping with changing stress and emotions. Specifically for children, social development and independent living skills are also important (Rafferty, 2013). The outcome of strong educational programs and keeping girls in school is a convincing one.

Demand

The topic of demand has been prevalent in the discussion of sex trafficking, but less so in the area of labor trafficking. The United Nations Office of Drugs and Crime (UNODC) identifies demand occurring in three levels: employer demand; consumer demand; and third parties who benefit from the trafficking (IPU & UNODC, 2009). This identification can be applied to labor and sex trafficking though originally created exclusively for understanding sex trafficking. However, as we saw in the previous section, employer demands and needs have the power to dictate migration patterns as does consumer demand. Finally, as we also saw with the use of subcontractors, resellers, and other entities, trafficking is a networked activity benefitting a number of entities we may not see or assume benefit.

Most of the literature on demand has centered around sex trafficking and this is also where most of the prevention programs have been focused on. Although male demand has been identified as the root cause of sex trafficking, it cannot be the sole consideration. There are other demands that fuel sexual exploitation. Case in point, there is an intersection between sex and labor trafficking that has not been thoroughly explored. This is where sex trafficking is used either as a lure into labor trafficking or as a form of "compensation" for those who are labor trafficked. For instance, men who are labor trafficked into the slave shrimping industry are often tricked by women who are sexually trafficked—usually by being drugged and then kidnapped onto a boat. Also, there have been reported cases where agricultural workers who were trafficked reported that they were given sex slaves (Franzblau, personal communication, 2007). The 2016 TIP Report stresses that this interaction is often found in more isolated industries where there are large numbers of male workers such as within the mining industry. For instance, Bolivian and Peruvian girls are found sex trafficked in Peruvian logging areas and near the gold mines of Suriname and Guyana (U.S. Department of State, 2016).

Several prevention programs have been created to target demand. Not all the programs are designed to address sex trafficking specifically. Actually, most are targeted to alleviating participation of the overall areas of sexual exploitation, including prostitution. Although not targeted to sex trafficking, reducing demand in these areas will affect/impact demand for trafficking. Though not fully understood, there is a definite connection between sex trafficking and prostitution. For example, in countries such as Germany where prostitution has been legalized, the influx of trafficking has also increased (Cho, Dreher, Neumayer, 2012). Further, as practitioners, we have taken the perspective of reducing male demand by ending male consumerism. However, a more active role can also be taken and encouraged. Instead of men just being told not to purchase sex, they could become proactive in the effort to end the sale of women. For instance, the U.S. military is starting to provide trainings that encompass more than just information but also ways that soldiers can identify sex trafficking and how to report these incidences (De Los Reyes, personal communication, 2016).

The Coalition Against the Trafficking of Women (CAT–W) has run several camps in the Asia Pacific Region, starting in the Philippines since 2004. Each of the camps are geared toward the issue of demand and preventing young men from sexually exploiting women. The premise of the camps is to target men who are student leaders on college campuses (ages 17 to 21) in the hopes that others will emulate their actions. The camps include educational trainings on gender role socialization, patriarchy, social institution's messaging, and the role and impact of pop culture. In South Korea, CAT–W reports the need for such camps to address the cultural explosions around Korean dramas, which reflect patriarchy and masculinity (Enriquez, n.d.). Programs such as these have demonstrated changes in the notion of gender issues and shifts in perception. However, it is not clear that shifts in perception are enough to slow or stop demand (Van der Laan, Smit, Busschers, & Aarten, 2011).

EXAMPLES OF BEST PRACTICES

Awareness Raising

For many, prevention begins with raising awareness about the issue. Similar to what we discussed in chapter 11, the need for the general population to acknowledge and understand what is really happening is the first phase of their anti-trafficking work. This was certainly true with the women's movement as they attempted to legitimize the issue. In much the same way, this is how practitioners, organizations, institutions, and other groups approach their work. There are two types of awareness raising that generally occurs: one is directed toward the general public and the other is more targeted to populations at most risk of being trafficked. Bales (2007) recognizes that the two major tools for fighting trafficking are resources and awareness. This makes sense in that providing awareness and knowledge means that you should also provide avenues for assistance or options other than those things that lead to more vulnerability to trafficking. For example, in one study of emergency room nurses, only 42% were able to identify minor trafficking victims, and 68% said they never received training to understand the population and the issue more thoroughly (Beck et. al., 2015).

Successful awareness raising campaigns are somewhat constrained by the limitations of their campaign media and materials. For example, the use of posters, print ads, billboards, and the like usually mean that one or two images must be dominant with minimal text. This cannot accurately convey the complexities of trafficking, so this necessitates the use of the most effective way to reach the public as well as at-risk populations and those who are have been trafficked. One of the best practices around awareness raising campaigns has been to create stories. Research shows that successful campaigns are those that favor descriptive terms of victims and their situations as a "set of experiences" as opposed to dry, legalistic definitions (O'Brien, 2013). For instance, the Body Shop's Stop Campaign is an example of highlighting stories of survivors and trafficking as a whole. "The Ugly Truth" is an education campaign from End Demand Illinois that was created from the "Voices and Faces Project." Posters, billboards, and brochures are used, but the campaign has been expanded to include mp3 and radio ads to increase access (see World Without Exploitation Campaign: https://www.worldwithoutexploitation.org). The campaign is provocative and shifts the discussion of blame and shame from the victims of trafficking to traffickers, the "johns," and others who sexually exploit (Voices and Faces Project, 2017). This awareness raising campaign brings together many perspectives from law enforcement, nonprofit organizations, service providers, academics, women's centers, justice centers, coalitions against sexual assault, and businesses. A professional media company, Kinectic Worldwide volunteered their services and their extensive networks to the campaign, which has meant a sweeping release to an audience of over 76 million people. The campaign has been so successful, it has evolved into "World Without Exploitation," a collaboration and community of anti-trafficking entities (organizations, activists, policy makers, academics, survivors, etc.) that engages people in the conversation around commodification and slavery.

The Polaris Project oversees the National Human Trafficking Resource Center, which is the United States' hotline and resource center that serves victims and survivors of trafficking. The hotline is toll free and can answer calls 24 hours a day/7 days a week, in over 200 languages. To popularize the hotline and raise awareness of its existence, providers and practitioners can log onto their website and download outreach materials in almost 20 languages. There are also other materials that can be sent to them. Outreach for this program is done through widespread partnership from all areas of services who may come into contact with victims. They have also developed a widget for organizations to use on their websites that include not only the hotline information but also materials and resources (National Human Trafficking Resource Center, n.d.-b). Though this is not part of a prevention program (as presumably those who are calling are in need of help), the more popularized it becomes, it will serve as a way to distribute information and materials.

Figure 13.2 The Ugly Truth ("Choices")

Source: The Voices and Faces Project.

Figure 13.3 The Ugly Truth (Sex Trafficking)

Source: The Voices and Faces Project.

ADEQUATE TRAINING

As we have seen time and again, strong policies and interventions are only as good as the people who are trained to implement them. One of the main impediments is that there is very little training, especially training that is provided to multidisciplinary teams. Most trainings are developed for singular fields and institutional specificity, which although it is something, it is not comprehensive, nor does it offer a multisystem, much less a global view. Unfortunately, the state of trainings is very similar to the state of clinical interventions in that the ones that have been developed in large part have been in reaction to need and not because they are well tested, rigorous, or evidence based. Even though this is the case, for practical reasons, trainings still must be developed and given. We cannot wait for research and evaluation to catch up, especially for first responders such as child welfare, law enforcement, and health care providers. This is also true for fields that we might consider ancillary to the area of trafficking, but who might actually be quite salient, such as Transportation Security Administration (TSA) officers and school teachers who might be able to identify and therefore intervene in trafficking situations. TSA officers, in fact, who received even basic awareness level training on identification of human trafficking demonstrated the greatest capacity building than any other groups who did not receive any training (Wolf-Branigin, Garza, & Smith, 2010).

In Illinois, a rescue and restore collation was established with the Department of Health and Human Services, with 115 member organizations composed of 96 nonprofit agencies; 2 for-profit groups; and 17 public agencies. The public agencies included the FBI, 5 major state departments, and 11 local government agencies. They found that though 40% were aware of trafficking, most of it was focused on domestic matters. Further, the participants also assumed that the public knew more about trafficking than they actually did (19% versus 7%). Even if people knew about trafficking, it did not mean that they knew about laws, policies, or practices (Hounmenou, 2012). Only half of the coalition received training, but of those that had, there was a high correlation between receiving training and having practitioners who felt that they had raised awareness enough to participate in identification of trafficking victims. The biggest challenges for this coalition was being able to work with foreign nationals because of language as well as a lack of resources for more interagency cooperation. Ideally, if there were resources available, the coalition could move from an agency-by-agency training model into an interagency training model. Such models demonstrate increased identification in service areas, less duplication of services, and smoother operations between agencies. The goal is to maximize the identification of at risk populations so that prevention services (and intervention) could be targeted toward them.

Internationally, the Wyndham Hotel Chain joined in anti-trafficking efforts by creating extensive training and defined procedures for its staff. They did this in response to stories on gang-led child trafficking in the United States and in general sexual exploitation occurring globally (Martinez, 2011). Wyndham had already been doing work in this area with Ending Child Prostitution and Trafficking (ECPAT) and the Polaris Project. Wyndham is one of the largest hotel and hospitality chains with over 7,000 hotels. Through these joint projects, they will provide training to their staff on how to spot traffickers and the how to report it (CBIS, n.d.). There are also plans for the hotel chain to even begin working with their vendors to make sure their supply chains are clear of trafficking (Wyndham Worldwide, 2014). Internationally, they have also signed onto the Code for the Protection of Children in Travel and Tourism initiated by UNICEF. In addition to the training of staff to identify and report trafficking, the code also includes having materials on trafficking within the hotel, security such as room key elevator access, and the even providing emergency shelter for victims (Hetter, 2012). Targeting multinational chains and companies who are well trained can help combat and prevent trafficking and slavery from occurring. There are always some type of warning signs and patterns; professionals, practitioners, and the public just have to know what they are looking for and have viable methods for reporting them.

CORPORATE SOCIAL RESPONSIBILITY AND SUPPLY CHAIN MANAGEMENT

Human trafficking is just now gaining the attention of the corporate business world. When considering trafficking prevention, let's ask ourselves how much could we mitigate just by maintaining decent labor practices? In an attempt to do just that, corporate social responsibility programs (CSRs) and transparent supply chain management have been emphasized as two ways in which prevention efforts to end labor trafficking and slave like conditions are housed. CSR policies and practices are the responsibilities that a company has to society as a whole (not just their own stockholders). It has evolved to include aspects that are more than economic, but ethical considerations of business practices, legal issues, and philanthropic projects as well (Carroll, 2010).

In the United States in 2013, of the Fortune 500 companies, only 31% addressed trafficking in any preventative measures. These 155 companies were comprised of 106 in manufacturing, 29 in retail, and 20 in service. It is important to note that these are not large numbers or representative of smaller, less influential companies. Given this cross section of business, it may seem that there is far to go in the fight against trafficking, but there are some promising trends. For example, the Ford Motor Company provides regular employee trainings in human rights and global working conditions (including trafficking) as part of its code of corporate responsibility. This includes regular audits of its factories to make sure they are compliant. Furthermore, if there are any violations found, those in violation must fix and remedy the situation, which is unique for a company since at this point, most companies are at the point of identification not remediation (Ford, 2013). Coca Cola provides knowledge about its supply chain to identify where there are areas of vulnerability for human trafficking and its policies reflect ways to prevent risk (O'Neill, 2013). Microsoft is working on different technology to make it difficult for traffickers to use their products (Smith & Betts, 2014).

In Singapore, the Prevention of Human Trafficking Act (PHTA) created an interagency task force who hopes to target specific industries to reduce gray zones of trafficking and slave-like migrant worker conditions. In addition to making its supply chains more transparent, the PHTA also supports what they call "security of presence" that allows workers to transfer to new employers, which they were unable to do before the PHTA. Also, the task force requires "in principle approvals," which are employment contracts or memorandum of agreements between workers and companies, to be written in workers' native language, because they are currently written in Mandarin or English. The PHTA also hopes to institute other practices such as the enforcement of the "passports act," which makes it illegal for employers to take workers' passports, and also create itemized bills where workers can understand the debts they are incurring, hoping to lessen the levels of debt peonage (Gee, 2014).

Best practices include the need for top management to be committed enough to support programs, create policies, and invest resources for creating strong CSR programs and to work on making supply chains transparent, if applicable. The Deming Wheel outlines four activities that help make strong programs possible (Swink, Melynk, Cooper, & Hartley, 2011). The first step is to plan which would include how supply chains will be made transparent, what supplier standards are (including cost, quality, delivery, etc.), and what areas of the supply chain need to be made more explicit. The second step is for implementation that focuses on building partnerships with like-minded companies who have similar stances on trafficking and human rights; seeking multiple suppliers so that they are incentivized to support anti-trafficking measures; leveraging purchases for higher business volume but based on the compliance with shared standards and expectations; and requiring all suppliers to have minimum levels of standards that they comply with. Step three is that once these codes of conduct are agreed to, companies should require audits to all parts of the supply chain. The power of the audit is a basic element, but there are differing degrees of audits, from in-house audits that the company conducts itself to audits that are conducted by third parties. Frequency of audits can also be variable and depends on the degree of risk to the industry, country, and company culture. Finally, the last step is to act on the information that an audit reveals. For example, the company would implement remedies that would be put into place if there are risks to trafficking or actual trafficking found within their supply chains. Other suggestions include the creation of a supplier scorecard, developing reward/penalty systems, and participation in the Global Business Coalition Against Human Trafficking (gBCAT). gBCAT is a coalition of companies that provides training and education around supply chain transparency, sex trafficking, and communication and outreach (gBCAT, n.d.).

CHALLENGES

Prevention work is extremely challenged within anti-trafficking work, although it is often referred to as the "answer" to ending trafficking (literally) before it begins. Practitioners who find themselves in this work are usually in the areas of wellness, education, and training. While it may make intrinsic sense to focus on prevention programs, many countries have not engaged in this work in a manner that has included proper evaluation as previously discussed. However, there are also a few other barriers. For instance, there are some countries that may not feel there is a trafficking problem. This could be a form of public denial. But, more often than not, this may be a combination of how trafficking is defined as well as cultural and societal context. Earlier, we discussed how China and other countries only consider sexual exploitation as a form of trafficking. Another example is that there are countries and populations that believe that child brides are part of their cultural ritual, and so for them, this would not be interpreted as trafficking. There are also those who believe that if people agree to slave-like wages, then they are making the choice to work in those conditions and therefore, it should not be considered trafficking or modern-day slavery.

In many of these examples, the logic is that there is either greater needs for intervention or no need for prevention, and so the resources must be given to the former. Of course, we know this is not true, and unlike advocacy and activism, the realm of prevention is one that practitioners are very comfortable with as most helping professions begin with prevention at one end of our service continuum. Chuang (2006) advocates for a prevention model, emphasizing that meaningful victim protection, laws, and policies are only temporary measures if we do not find a way to end the phenomenon. Although the challenges presented to prevention are great, this does not mean that groups do not prioritize this kind of work, such as the organization in our opening vignette. In fact, many organizations, institutions, and services focus on how to get in front of the issue so that it doesn't occur in the first place.

CALL TO ACTION: ADDRESS "COMPLETE RANGE OF VULNERABILITIES" FOR EFFECTIVE PREVENTION

Effective prevention measures would require moving from an issue, based perspective into efforts that either dismantle oppressive mechanisms or build healthy systems. Rafferty (2013) refers to this as addressing the "complete range of vulnerabilities" that may put people at risk. This echoes the ecosystems model, which examines, layer by layer, the issue of trafficking, paying special attention to the intersections that are present. One should consider trafficking in broad socioeconomic contexts to address root causes (Chuang, 2006). For example, while it is important for companies to take an active anti-trafficking stance and understand its role in trafficking, more and more companies are making these decisions with consumers in mind. The power of consumers is stronger than ever. The presence of social media and crowd sourcing means that allegations of trafficking can ruin a company's reputation and hurt their profits. Consumers and stakeholders are voicing their preferences for companies that are "good corporate citizens" (Smith, Smith, & Wang, 2010). As with other prevention models, the ecosystems perspective relies on stakeholders as well as accountability. The challenge in the issue of trafficking is that it is difficult to discern where accountability begins and ends as well as where we assign blame for who is responsible for exploitation. With a multitude of intersections and hierarchies, it is difficult to answer these questions and essential to understand the overall environment and people's positionality within that environment as we move forward in prevention work.

Anti-trafficking and modern-day slavery prevention is an area where there is still minimal commitment to resources—material and otherwise. With more mindfulness and partnership, prevention programs are being designed with the purpose of ending trafficking and not just stemming the tide. This is going to make a difference as we are already seeing the immense creativity and innovation that is emerging from a variety of sources and disciplines. Prevention is no longer just the siren call of nonprofit organizations, social services, health providers, and policy makers. It is fast becoming the adage of stakeholders and communities who are dedicated to ending the selling of human beings.

DISCUSSION QUESTIONS

1. What media campaigns would be effective on college campuses?

2. How early should prevention work be addressed in schools? How can prevention work be addressed in elementary schools?

3. What are other modalities to help secure funding for prevention work?

4. Microloan and financing is controversial. Examine existing models of microfinancing such as Kiva and crowdfunding. What are some pros and cons to these adaptations of this model? If possible, apply to a real project; how would it work (or not)?

CHALLENGE

Partner with someone in your class, your organization, or your life. Think about the concepts that you learned about social enterprise. If you could, what kind of social enterprise would you design? What type of product or products would you include/design/manufacture? What current market exists for your proposed enterprise? What makes your proposal unique? Who would you partner with (i.e., NGOs, communities, institutions, companies)? What would it take to make your idea a reality?

CHAPTER 14

Social Innovations in Human Trafficking: Solutions to a Wicked Problem

Annalisa Enrile and Renée Smith-Maddox

Chapter Objectives

1. Readers will show understanding of wicked problems.

2. Readers will construct design thinking and innovation as a way to disrupt human trafficking and modern-day slavery.

3. Readers will focus on different social innovations in the fight against human trafficking.

4. Readers will develop criteria for how to best use technology in designing innovations against human trafficking and modern-day slavery.

5. Readers will experiment with various innovation techniques and methods such as social innovation labs to addresses human trafficking and modern-day slavery.

My marker is smooth as it scrawls across the dry erase board. "Here are examples of a few wicked problems," I am saying as I write my list:

- *How do you end human trafficking?*
- *What should our mission statement be?*
- *What resources are needed?*

(Continued)

(Continued)

- *What to do when resources run out?*
- *What features should be in our new anti-trafficking social innovation?*

As expected, many hands were raised immediately. Almost everyone had an answer—and so quickly. Students offered a range of responses from helping the victims to putting traffickers in jail. "But, what makes these ideas innovative?" I ask. The students are clearly taken aback by my response to what they think is cutting-edge thinking.

A student replies, "No one sees the problem like us."

"Okay, given your perspective, what does it mean to help the victims?" I pushed.

Another student responds, "We meet the clients where they are and give them access to the resources they need."

I still push. Students are stubbornly loyal to their professional identity. They need to be kicked out of the box. "All right, what are the resources that trafficked victims need and how do they access them? Think about it. And before you answer this question," I go on emphatically, "what do you know about human trafficking?" I continue to challenge them to unpack the problem and recognize its dynamics. Understanding the problem is the starting point.

As an educator, I aim to arm my students with the critical-thinking skills to be advocates for and designers of social change. Each teaching experience has reinforced what I've always known instinctively: that with an ongoing and transdisciplinary approach to inquiry, change happens. This is what I try to impart to my students. Witnessing the most profound social, environmental, and political challenges of our time, I challenged them to ponder over the sequence of events that have led to the current state of affairs. They offer another smattering of responses.

Undeterred, I ask, "Yes, but what does all that do to actually dismantle human trafficking?"

Frustrated, a student blurts out, "What can be done to actually stop it? You want us to stop it? The whole thing?" She looks incredulous.

I smile. They finally understand. I respond, "Yes, that's why we are here . . . to find solutions to this wicked problem."

—Renée Smith-Maddox

INTRODUCTION

In the 1800s, the Underground Railroad was a vast network of meeting places, secret routes, passageways, safe houses, and abolitionists (such as Harriet Tubman) who helped fugitive slaves in the United States escape from slave holding states to the North and Canada. It was a tool of resistance for slaves to escape bondage. It was also a way to address slavery subversively, becoming an urban legend to slave owners and slaves alike that there was a literal way to break the chains of slavery. In this sense, it was also the genesis of disruptive innovations that led to subsequent breakthroughs. These breakthroughs adapted to different contexts and the entrenched nature of slavery. In the current iteration of modern-day slavery, we are in need of new type of Underground Railroad, literally and figuratively. To obtain either, we have to look critically at the scale and complexity of the problem and identify the trends and barriers to systemic change. As a response, key areas of social change have emerged. A paradigm shift has taken place where technological innovations, funding initiatives, victim-centered policies, and collaborative ventures represent the new efforts for dismantling the complex ecosystem of recruitment, transporting, harboring, and enslavement of people.

Unfortunately, the promise of freedom still eludes millions of women, men, and children who are labor and/or sex trafficked. Hundreds of girls are kidnapped and sold as child brides by the Boka Haram in Nigeria. In China, there are orphanages dedicated for girls who are "thrown away" just for being born female. Trafficking rings from Asia to Africa to Europe and the United States have transported countless women, girls, and boys in human trade. Victims are recruited with false promises of a sizable yearly wage but when they arrive in the country, the traffickers force them to work for nothing by confiscating their passport, keeping them under close surveillance, and threatening to kill them or their family members if they disobey orders. As we can see from the challenges identified here and those discussed throughout this book, the scale and scope of human trafficking is a serious global threat. To abolish the strong ties of human trafficking networks and to help survivors rebuild their lives, it is imperative to draw on existing efforts and blend some of the traditional interventions with broad sector coordination that simultaneously deploy innovative ways to dismantle all forms of modern slavery.

For the most part, the challenges we face are well understood but the solutions remain elusive. There are several emerging challenges to the eradication of modern slavery, including the growing and evolving nature of local and transnational gangs, the use of technology by traffickers to contact and recruit their victims, and the increasing profit yield of the sex and labor trafficking. These challenges bring into focus the need to develop and align current anti-trafficking efforts. Given the insidious nature of human trafficking and the challenges it presents, there are unprecedented opportunities for social innovation—new ideas, leadership, policies, and practices to eradicate this crime against humanity.

Social innovation is a response to the strategic priority for addressing human trafficking worldwide. The power of innovative ideas is evident in victim-centered approaches that ensure victims have access to the road to freedom. Thus, the modern-day Underground Railroad must focus on (1) distributing knowledge, services, and products that radically change the human condition in a positive way; (2) bringing a diverse array of specialists and interests together; and (3) figuring out how to do a better job dismantling human trafficking.

Anti-trafficking networks have enlisted new partners to thwart recruitment efforts, find and recover victims, and raise the public awareness on the grave acts of labor and commercial sexual exploitation in the United States and around the world. People are working to combat every phase of trafficking (including global supply chains) by analyzing trafficking activities, identifying cross-sector partnerships, and developing new policies and practices. This chapter will detail the work that is being done in the anti-trafficking movement, including how corporations, activists, everyday people, artists, and victims have joined forces and shared resources to diffuse social innovations designed to address human trafficking.

This chapter will also examine some of these social innovations, which respond to growing social, environmental, and demographic challenges—often called "wicked" problems because they are complex, multifaceted, and are by nature, almost impossible to solve.

WICKED PROBLEMS

Human trafficking is a multifaceted problem that requires creative solutions. It is a special type of issue that can be called a wicked problem. According to urban planners Rittel and Weber (1973), "wicked problems" are ill-defined, ambiguous, and messy. They represent issues that are extremely difficult and seemingly impossible to solve because of the complex and ever-changing environments in which they exist (Conklin, 2005). Rittel and Weber (1973) outlined ten criteria for a problem to be deemed as "wicked." They include:

1. There is no definite formulation of a wicked problem.

2. Wicked problems have no stopping rules. In other words, there is no "final solution."

3. Solutions to wicked problems are not true or false, but better or worse.

4. There is no immediate and no ultimate test of a solution to a wicked problem.

5. Every solution to a wicked problem is a "one-shot operation;" because there is no opportunity to learn by trial and error, every attempt counts significantly.

6. Wicked problems do not have an enumerable (or exhaustively describable) set of potential solutions, nor is there a well described set of permissible operations that may be incorporated into the plan.

7. Every wicked problem is essentially unique.

8. Every wicked problem can be considered to be a symptom of anther (wicked) problem.

9. The causes of wicked problems can be explained in numerous ways. The choice explanation determines the nature of the problem's resolution.

10. [With wicked problems,] the planner has no right to be wrong.[1]

Levin, Cashore, Bernstein, and Auld (2012) expand the definition to include what they called "super wicked problems." They add the following four features of a problem:

1. Time is running out.

2. Those who cause the problem also seek to provide a solution.

---

1. These ten criteria are taken directly from: Ritchey, 2013, p. 4–5.

3. The central authority needed to address it is weak or nonexistent.

4. Policy responses discount the future irrationally.

The importance of being able to define the issue as a wicked problem is that in doing so, it also defines the solution space. With super wicked problems, it is difficult to use the same types of predictive factors that help shape solutions (Bernstein, Lebow, Stein, & Weber, 2000). This is in part because the nature of such problems is that they occur in open, nonlinear systems, where how people act may be completely unpredictable as they try to gain purchase and control (Patomaki, 2006). In other words, the way in which human trafficking has been defined has determined the number, quality, and types of proposed solutions. Although we know that the problem exists, the crime of human trafficking continues to evolve. The perpetrators have become more sophisticated and organized, which requires an equally sophisticated set of responses to disrupt and dismantle their networks. Among the emerging trends is the adoption of new technologies by traffickers such as social media to recruit victims, facilitate their crimes, and evade law enforcement. As a wicked problem, or even super wicked problem, the criteria for social innovation is even more challenging and therefore, as practitioners, we must identify solutions when others can't and have hope when others don't.

GROWING INNOVATION IN THE ANTI-TRAFFICKING MOVEMENT

Social Innovations represent the evolving landscape for how we address and solve problems such as human trafficking. It is a widespread and powerful approach that often involves risks, new funding opportunities, and novel adaptations of existing ideas and/or their application to new areas. Inherently, it is a mechanism for systemic change that is geared toward social practices and structures (Howaldt & Schwarz, 2010). Social innovations that are successful can be measured as such when there is a shift or change in attitudes, behavior, or perceptions that result in a change of practice or structure (Neumeier, 2012). While some social innovations can be predicated on already proposed solutions or previously launched projects, for the most part, what makes something a social innovation is that it is fundamentally different from anything that has been established before. This does not mean that it has to incorporate the newest and brightest piece of technology or trend. On the contrary, social innovations may take on more of a nonmaterial basis especially if it is a social practice or policy, which will become institutionalized, but not necessarily monetized (or creates some type of artifact or product).

Social innovation practice contributes to transformation, developing when different ways of thinking and behavior begin to emerge and impact our existing ways of thinking, perhaps to the point of changing them (Cajaiba-Santana, 2014). It draws on diverse perspectives and strategically employs a variety of methods, activities, and tools that are part of comprehensive process of change. There is a body of evidence as to the growing importance of social innovation with regard to human trafficking.

BEST PRACTICES IN SOCIAL INNOVATION

To develop a social innovation practice, you have to be willing to explore the many dimensions of the problem and experiment with a portfolio of different types of solutions. For instance, in the human trafficking field, this requires a full understanding of victims' needs and problems as well as of the larger patterns and trends, similar to the ecosystems lens. As with other areas, there are no well-researched methods demonstrating effectiveness in trafficking specifically, but there do exist best practices in social innovation such as design thinking, adaptive practice, audacious problem definition, innovation dynamics, social innovation labs, and technological intervention that may be applied. Design thinking is an approach to innovation. It gives practitioners, social innovators, and activists a way to reconceptualize the problem and discover possible solutions in the form of new products, services, and strategies that could ultimately have a positive impact.

Design Thinking

Perhaps the largest component of social innovation is that a new way of thinking is necessary. The way of processing information—design thinking—is not a method or way that many human service practitioners are not used to working in. Design thinking is quite simply a set of strategies and approaches to understanding problems. It is a set of principles that allow one to develop more creative, flexible responses. Design thinking can play a significant role in curating social innovations addressing human trafficking. According to Tim Brown and Roger Martin (2015), design centric principles have been applied to make things work better. Although design thinking has been an integral part of the design, engineering, technology, and business fields, it is new the field of human and social services. While this may be the case, design thinking actually fits well into human and social services because it relies on creative thinking in generating solutions that many of us engage in every day. We include it here as best practices for activating innovative processes.

The design thinking process has a unique benefit to creating social change. It is a series of activities that guides the social innovation process, but should not be thought of as a set of predetermined steps. Design thinking is an iterative process. It can define the way an initiative functions at the most basic level—how it relates to victims, how it prototypes products, and how it assesses risk. Design thinking includes:

- Challenge (Inspiration). This is where the problem is analyzed and thought of. Mainly, the driving force here is determining what the problem is. How do people think about it? Who is most affected by it? What are the stories around it? How can technology help? One key activity here is to bring together people from different fields so that you can get different viewpoints. This information should be organized before you move into the next phase of problem solving. This is a period of discovery and defining, where you are understanding the issue and also coming to agreements over important aspects such as identifying key people who can share valuable information with you, sharing your observations with each other, and building an understanding of the complexity of the issue.

- Ideation. Ideation is the process of generating, developing, and testing your ideas. Hopefully these ideas are those that will lead to solutions. In this space, you should be telling more stories and seeing how they fit together (i.e., integrative thinking, creation out of chaos) and also building your first prototypes of the solution. The communication here is with your internal teams so that no one is working in silos. Instead, this is a period of intense discussion, trading ideas, and rethinking the problem. Brainstorming and reframing of the problem helps you identify opportunities for new products and services where there is a gap in the market.

- Implementation/Prototyping. Implementation is when the solution can "go to market" or be put into practice. One of the significant activities during this time is prototyping. Prototyping is when you build a representation of your idea to share with others. This doesn't have to be an actual example of what you are suggesting, but it is something that people can interact with such as a storyboard or blue prints. It is this prototype that you test to see how people react and what works or will have to be changed. This is when communication must occur to the outside world, especially in terms of popularizing your solution. Steps after this may have your moving onto your next project or building your solution to scale, replicating it in different locales or with varying populations.

These steps are deceptively simple. Actually, a lot happens in each phase that drives the innovation. The way that the process works is by finding a logical starting point so that you can "begin at the beginning," which means to start before any direction or solutions have been suggested. This is important because you do not want to have your ideas shaped by solutions that have already been suggested or that only address a portion of the problem. The next is to take a human-centered approach, which should be where we are most comfortable as practitioners as many of our helping professions urge us to start where the clients, patients, consumers are at. This means to eschew judgment and listen carefully. But this also means to understand the problem from a human point of view; for instance, how does human behavior play into this issue? What are human needs and preferences? There is no point in developing innovations that people don't use, and one of the strengths of design thinking is to follow a course of action all the way to how people will interact with it. It is also essential that your process include "trying early and often," which is the idea of quick experimentation and prototyping so that you know what doesn't work as much as you know what does. It's alright to fail within the paradigm of design thinking (Brown, 2008). While this may seem antithetical to most of our professions because people's lives are affected and sometimes on the line, we have to recalibrate our thinking around this as not all failures are detrimental or life threatening. Building a more robust attitude toward failure will allow us to not be stunned or immobilized when something doesn't work, especially in the face of such super wicked problems.

Further, design thinking is more closely in line with our values and viewpoints than we may think. Five personality traits that are present in design thinking include the following:

- Empathic. Being able to imagine a world from a different person's and cultural perspectives. This allows you to understand at a fundamental level what people are experiencing and how they may experience your solutions. Empathy is different from sympathy or sensitivity as the latter is about being able to commiserate with people and empathy is actually being able to put yourself in their place and understanding those implications. This also allows us to understand things at a micro level, paying attention to what is important to people but may be overlooked without this layer of understanding or connection.

- Integrative Thinker. This moves us from just using scientific, rational, or analytic thinking processes and includes thinking through things on a number of other levels: emotional, spiritual, cognitive, behavioral, and so forth. For instance, integral psychology incorporates an in-depth inclusion of different types of consciousness, Eastern and Western ways of thinking and practice, internal and external thought, spirituality, biological processes, and evolutionary context to name a few (Wilber, 2000). This type of thinking allows us to go beyond traditional methodologies and broaden our understanding of what is possible.

- Optimistic. This is the outlook that no matter how difficult the situation, there is a solution and that you gear yourself toward discovering it. In empowerment practices, this can also be interpreted as a "strengths-based" model. There is an answer and a solution; we just have to develop it.

- Open to Change (Experimental). Some aspects of the experimental method means that we are taking educated guesses that are not always comfortable or our "natural" path. This makes it important for us to be open to changes that may be large departures form our comfort zones. They may seem like great leaps so we need to brace ourselves, be open, and flexible. This is a constant move into new directions and goes along with the "try early and often" process.

- Collaborator. We have already agreed and defined the types of problems we are dealing with as super wicked or wicked so it is no surprise that they are complex and multifaceted. The best way to really understand them is to bring in as many perspectives as you can in genuine partnership. Even better would be if practitioner's own multidisciplinary lens could be developed so that you can come from more than one perspective.

Designers for social change create intentional outcomes and are constantly relying on their creativity. They have an awareness of the context that might be impacted by the work. Moreover, they create a path for stakeholders who want to work at a leadership level or the micro level (i.e., programmers) in social innovation. When it comes to the human trafficking ecosystem, the problem of integrating a new response to combat it is challenging. For example, the successful rollout of anti-trafficking initiatives require policymakers; technology providers; city, national, and worldwide governments; service providers; and victims to collaborate in new ways and engage in new behaviors. This sounds like an easy endeavor but the politics, scramble for meager resources, shifting alliances, and constantly developing best practices may be difficult to maneuver around.

Adaptive Practice

There is something extremely ambiguous about social innovation work. For one, you are operating with no "rule book" per se. The only parameters are the ones that you place on the problem itself. Again, this is contrary to what we usually experience in the helping professions, which for the most part (when possible), may be extremely formulaic. In the case of innovations, we have to be adaptive and responsive on several fronts, the two most important being: responsive to the problem, as it is always changing, and then responsive to the solution set—trying and failing, or trying and succeeding. In the case of the former, we then have to be able to adapt, either by making changes (or scrapping the idea all together) to our innovations or by targeting another area of the problem. This requires a type of pivoting and flexibility that we have to exercise as we would any of our physical muscles. Too often, the problem is that we get attached to a solution prematurely and limit exploring a family of solutions.

Similarly, because the problem changes so quickly and is so different from other problems we have encountered or dealt with, we have to be willing to let go of former, and perhaps basic ways of thinking about the problem and possible solutions. A child welfare practitioner, working with a team who is developing a mobile application for sharing information between counties, said, "I know that we are all worried about confidentiality. Everyone is. But, we have to let that go. The thing is that the traffickers are able to find out where these kids are, that's not going to change if we share information or not. We can do the best we can, but we aren't living in the same world as we did when it was easier to maintain confidentiality. If a kid has a smartphone, which most of them do, the predators can find them. We have to rethink the way we act and that may mean redefining something as basic as confidentiality" (Morgan, personal communication, 2016).

Audacious/Transformative Idea Generation

A rule of thumb of innovation is to think big! This also helps us get out of the ways of thinking and doing that we might be used to. Particularly practitioners who are operating in small nonprofits or NGOs may think that they are constrained by resources. However, if we decouple our resources from what we are able to do, then we can begin to engage in some "blue sky thinking" or visioning. The idea is to create in large and audacious ways in an attempt to transform, not remediate. This should allow you to free your mind. There is enough time to bring ideas "down to size," which is easier than having to think big once you have fixated on one area.

For example, Greenhouse is a social impact venture that creates, designs, and develops proprietary technology and products to solve complex social problems (Blackie, 2017). They begin their process by posing large questions about changing the world, not one small part of the issue. Some of these questions to get you thinking audaciously include the following:

- Pretend for a moment you were trying to make your problem worse, not better. How would you do it?

- Beyond the people you're trying to help and the people who give you resources, there are additional groups in society who you must understand to solve your problem. Who are they?

- Imagine an obstacle course between you and the change you're trying to make in the world. What are three of the obstacles?

- What if someone just invented the essential piece of technology to solve your problem forever. What would that technology do?

- Let's say there is some other problem in the world that, if solved, would make your problem go away completely. What would it be?

These questions are based on the premise that no matter what kind of problem we confront, there are properties that are universal which compose the dynamics of a problem. These questions are part of a subset of problem dynamics known as "innovation dynamics" that help us understand problems in novel ways, and unlock insights and possibly even solutions. There are six proposed universal properties that innovation dynamics encompass: actors, limits, configuration, parthood, history, and future. Each are present in every problem that has a social nature (Benedict-Nelson, 2016). Innovation dynamics are important because the defining factor of wicked problems are that they are social, built on human relationship and circumstance and innovation dynamics are concerned with human behavior and social norms. Beginning to define and understand these problems will be crucial to the next step: formulating possible solutions.

GreenHouse

GreenHouse, a social innovation organization, proposes that social innovation is a "systemic disruption of social norms to effect social change" and as such one must understand social norms, the deviance to those norms, and then diffuse the deviance to cause such disruption. The ability to do this is aided by what they call "innovation dynamics," a way of *seeing* social norms that are for the most part invisible and informal. Further, the innovation dynamics allow us to understand the problem and more importantly, begin to define the solution space.

Innovation dynamics operates on the context and premise of social norms so it is important to understand this concept first. Social norms are the way we behave, a type of informal code that influences and regulates how one behaves in social settings. The best way to understand them is to maintain a value free attitude because then, their identification is not clouded by moral judgements. They are primarily determined by your referent groups or networks, empirical and normative expectations, conditional preferences, and sanctions and rewards. Conversely, once you understand social norms, you can identify the deviances to those norms—both good and bad. Another way of thinking about deviance is that these are cases of outliers and nonnormative approaches. Leitner (personal communication, March 23, 2016), a GreenHouse funder states, "Deviance is behavior with the potential to subvert social norms." Specifically, for trafficking, where many behaviors are incomprehensible, understanding the norms and the deviances are critical.

There are a total of six innovation dynamics. They are as follows:

- Actors—people who are related to the problem. This may be obvious relationships to the problem or more ambiguous connections. For instance, in relation to trafficking, obvious actors are the trafficker and victim. Less obvious actors may be the consumers at the end of a supply chain or the communities where trafficking is widespread.

- History—the origin stories of why a problem exists. Note that this is the "story" of how a problem came into being or understood as a problem, not necessarily the real or root causes of that problem. The type of myth making or storytelling is crucial to understanding how people have come to understand the problem and the issue in general.

- Limits—formal constraints of the problem or solution. Many people chafe at the thought of limits, especially when they are being asked to innovate and be creative. But, actually, the opposite is true. Knowing your limits provides you with your parameters, the edges of the problem, if you will, and shows you clearly what area you should focus on.

- Future—your expectations on how the problem may evolve over time. It is important to note that these are not based on predictions but rather on presumptions based on our current expectations.

- Configuration—the grouping or labeling of elements within the problem. We tend or organize what we know about a problem into categories that are driven by social norms but if investigated more closely, are mostly arbitrary. The deconstruction of current configurations may unlock a way of seeing the problem.

- Parthood—the problems roll within larger problems. Parthood returns us to our ecosystems perspective and helps clarify the other areas connected to our problem, the layers and interconnections of other problems (usually bigger) to ours.

Social Innovation Labs

Social innovation labs are being used more and more to address complex social problems. These "labs" are curated spaces that bring together groups of people to discuss social, political, and environmental challenges. Some of the labs are part of larger NGOs, think tanks, or institutions such as UNICEF Innovation Labs or Stanford ChangeLabs.

Others are independent entities whose existence is to hold labs for their clients. This is a growing phenomenon in richer countries, mainly in North American and parts of Europe, but it is gaining ground. Most labs are currently used to drive and test new solutions, but using them to mobilize stakeholders to move solutions is a close second (Bridgespan, 2014). The Rockefeller Foundation's Social Innovation Labs project held a lab of their own where they identified three common features of successful labs (Bliss, 2014). These features were

1. **Diverse perspectives:** Successful labs draw from different perspectives within the systems they are studying and also across. In some instances, the people brought together to a lab did not have anything to do with the issue at all. However, in both examples, experts, public officials, professionals, and the general public can provide insights into the problem are and of course, the solution set.

2. **Innovation mind-set**: Many of the traits that we have discussed in terms of design thinking are what you want the group of people in your innovation lab to involve themselves in. This is because labs that are moved to think and process in this way will not just talk, discuss, and brainstorm, but they will actually begin to map out and possibly storyboard or blueprint ideas. This way, they can also give insight into how implementation might take place in "real world" circumstances. This is not to simplify their solutions, but to give a broad overview of what those solutions might look like. It also may increase levels of confidence and optimism for those involved who are searching for a doable solution.

3. **Unique processes, approaches, and tools**: Labs that use more than one method, include interactive exercises, have an ecosystems view, and use constructs of collaborative problem solving tend to be successful. People in the lab have to be interested, open-minded, enthusiastic, and curious about what they are trying to solve for. Labs that use alternative approaches keep a high level of energy up that is needed for dynamic discussions.

These three features underscore the necessity for curating a strong social lab experience. From the physical place, to the agenda, to the guest list of participants—all these are crucial aspects to how to set up a lab. Once there, exercises, questions to facilitate discussion, and the type of facilitation will feel chaotic, especially to anyone experiencing it for the first time. Currently the use of labs has not been well evaluated, receiving mostly anecdotal evidence, but their growth within the nonprofit arena into for-profit and government institutions and the move from North America and Europe into Asia signal that it is perceived as a useful tool.

Technology Innovations

Highlight: LaborVoices

LaborVoices is a technology that addresses what they feel are two global issues: transparent supply chains for corporate brands as well as being an outlet for global workers. Specifically, they provide a space for workers to provide direct feedback about their work conditions and experiences in a way that allows them to then create early warning signs for supply chain vulnerabilities, safety standard violations, or general working conditions through an integrated platform of services that companies pay into and request. Workers are able to anonymously "report" what is happening in their company through text or voice mail. Calls and texts are screened and then passed onto the right people to address the issues. Conversely, management is able to send out polls to their workers asking about specific conditions. This allows for real- time information gathering. Information such as worker's rights and quality standards are also able to be "pushed" much like notifications on a phone. With 70% of the working population with access to a smartphone, LaborVoices is a viable technology for both workers and administrators. LaborVoices also provides impact assessment and change monitoring for their clients. Currently, this technology is being used in 11 countries and over 100 companies around the world, including Bangladesh and Turkey.

Social innovations do not automatically mean that they will incorporate technology, but this is an area that is being heavily pursued by anti-trafficking innovators. In a landmark study by Latonero (2011), the role of technologies as viable anti-trafficking measures were examined. The following five principles for technological interventions and innovations were proposed as best practices in this arena:

1. The ultimate beneficiaries of any technological intervention should be the victims and survivors of human trafficking. This is in keeping with a human-centered model of innovation. Specifically, Latonero recommends that all technology innovations operate with the guiding question: How will technology maximize the benefit and minimize the harm to victims and survivors of trafficking? Any risks, especially to security, should be considered.

2. Successful implementation of anti-trafficking technologies requires cooperation among actors across government, nongovernmental, and private sectors, sharing information and communicating in a coordinated manner. This type of coordination will minimize inefficiency and redundancies.

3. Private-sector technology firms should recognize that their services and networks are being exploited by traffickers and take steps to innovate and develop anti-trafficking initiatives through their technologies and policies. This is particularly true with social networking sites and online classified sites. It should be a company's social responsibility to take an active role.

4. Continuous involvement is necessary to ensure that tools are use-centric and refined over time to most effectively respond to shifts in technology and trafficking. Hopefully, this will help improve usability by focusing on concrete needs of users. Depending on practitioners' roles—social services, health care, law enforcement, and so forth—they would have specific needs. Also, all technological innovations should be sustainable and this requires involvement and updates when needed.

5. Technological interventions should account for the range of human rights potentially impacted by the use of advanced technologies. Issues of privacy, security, and freedom of expression must be treated seriously to minimize any reckless encroachment. For example, information that is collected should be have a purpose.

Technological innovations are able to reach areas that were formerly isolated due to location, stigma, or cultural barriers. Also, there is the potential for connection and coalition of different actors that did not exist or would be quite costly without the vehicle that technology provides. Current technology is able to use data mining, web crawling, computational linguistics, and mapping to support anti-trafficking efforts. Globalization and technology have been used by traffickers to expand their exploitation, so it is time for the anti-trafficking side to harness the usages of technology, beginning with using it to understand prevalence and other rates of trafficking and what they might be related to. Some of the promising technologies include creations of information sharing platforms (globally this is would help provide information on trafficked persons no matter what country they are coming from or going to); hotline data gathering; survivor connections; and various mobile applications.

Highlight: TraffickCam

TraffickCam is a mobile application developed by Exchange Initiative, a social action organization and researchers from Washington University in St. Louis, providing "real resources" to end sex trafficking. TraffickCam utilizes smartphone technology (both iOS and Android platforms) that allows anyone to anonymously photograph hotel rooms and upload these photos to the app. The photos are then added to a national database. On the side of law enforcement, federal, state, and local law enforcement can securely upload photos of victims who are posed in hotel rooms. Then, the software matches features such as patterns in the carpeting, furniture, accessories, and any other identifying features. The app is 85% accurate at identifying where the photo has been taken. These photos can help them locate victims and their pimps because a study by the National Human Trafficking

Resource Center found that hotels/motels had the second highest cases for sex trafficking (after commercial brothels). This is a desirable location for traffickers because they can pay for rooms in cash and change locations often. Traffickers will often take photos of their victims in these rooms as a "promotion" or "ad." The app is only a year old (as of 2016) and already has a database of 1.5 million photos from more than 145,000 American hotels. There are also confidentiality safe guards. For example, information that is uploaded with any personally identifying information (other than the phone's GPS) are disregarded and photos with any images are not posted. The app also partners with hotels and event spaces through the company, Nix Conference and Meeting Management, who launched a conference "IGNITE: Sparking Action Against Sex Trafficking" (see: exchangeinitiative.com/902) with ECPAT–USA (End Child Prostitution and Trafficking), addressed child trafficking with hotel and conference managers. They have adopted this app in their company. Law enforcement sees this as another technological tool to reach victims in a quicker, more proficient manner. The longest it has taken to find a victim once a match has been made was three days and founders feel that this is still too long. The app is constantly being improved in real time (changes are made as challenges are encountered).

About Exchange Initiative

Exchange Initiative provides resources, information and networking solutions to combat sex trafficking in the United States. For more information, call Molly Hackett at (314) 645-1455 or visit ExchangeInitiative.com, facebook.com/exchangeinitiative, and twitter.com/TheEXInitiative. Nix Conference & Meeting Management manages meetings, conferences and trade shows in the United States and internationally. Nix leads the charge among meeting planners to end sex trafficking in hotels. For more information, call (314) 645-1455 or visit nixassoc.com.

itunes.apple.com/us/app/traffickcam/id1067713017?mt=8
exchangeinitiative.com/
prweb.com/releases/2016/06/prweb13497362.htm

In the anti-trafficking movement, technology is the catalyst for promoting a culture of innovation in a widespread, cost-effective manner and provides compelling models for combating human trafficking. Technology has created a steady flow of social innovations that are durable and disruptive. Most technology falls into these categories: technology that disrupts behaviors that are the root causes of trafficking and modern-day slavery; technology that increase cooperation; and technology that creates public awareness or provides support for victims and survivors. Some of the most innovative examples include:

- The Defense Advanced Research Projects Agency (DARPA)'s Memex program, which was launched in 2014 to combat human trafficking through an advanced search engine. Although this tool is not widely available, DARPA has fostered research that focuses on revolutionizing technology in the anti-trafficking space.

- The National Human Trafficking Resource Center (NHTRC), operated by Polaris. This toll-free hotline assists victims and community members 24 hours a day, 7 days a week in over 200 languages. The hotline services can also be accessed via e-mail and an online tip reporting form. Polaris's Global Hotline Program also supports other countries looking to set up hotlines similar to NHRTC in the United States.

- Microsoft'sPhotoDNA, which aids in identifying images of children who are sexually exploited online. The PhotoDNA Cloud Service is available free of charge to qualifying organizations and has made monitoring illicit online ads more manageable for law enforcement.

- The CyberTipline, which is operated by the National Center for Missing and Exploited Children (NCMEC). This serves as a mechanism for community members to report suspected exploitation of children. Since 1998, the tipline has received over 4.3 million tips.

- In 2013, Polaris and Thorn partnered with Twilio and Salesforce Foundation to develop the NHTRC SMS-based textline; victims can text the shortcode "BeFree" for a discreet and time-efficient way to access the hotline.

We have selected seven social innovations addressing human trafficking. The innovations featured here met the following criteria: they are adaptive, provide a new and different product offering, are a new and different way of doing things, and create a new or different organizational structure or resource allocation. They also provide an in-depth understanding of the problem (such as supply chain identification), new victim-centered solutions or innovative opportunities for healing and wellness, increased empowerment, and improved social services with a greater likelihood of scale (more victims reached). Conversely, the anti-trafficking movement and society at large should also begin to see how social innovation plays a role in creating a positive impact.

CHALLENGES

Many of the challenges with social innovation is not just limited to anti-trafficking efforts alone but to the entire field of innovation. As with anything new, it is difficult to create widespread buy in. Some of what is proposed requires a "leap of faith," but this is the case with virtually every intervention and prevention program. As the innovation field expands, we anticipate this will change. More technological companies and private for-profit firms are expanding to develop these innovations. In doing so, there is always the challenge that they will not understand the scope of the issue from a multidisciplinary perspective. Also, for every innovation created, there is the possibility that it will be used by the traffickers. Vigilance against that kind of harm would have to be something monitored or regulated.

There are countless logistical, legal, and moral discussions around the creation of innovation, but we are at a point where the urgency to address this super wicked problem demands developing alternatives and trying anything that might work—even those things

Table 14.1   Social Innovations in the Anti-Human Trafficking Field

Typology of Anti-trafficking Social Innovations	Examples
Products	**Thorn** wearethorn.org/child-sexual-exploitation-and-technology The Spotlight tool was introduced by Thorn: Digital Defenders in Spring 2014. Spotlight is available to law enforcement across the nation and is designed to aggregate data from online commercial sex advertisements. Law enforcement agencies using Spotlight have seen a 43% reduction in their investigation time. This agency partners across the tech industry, government, and NGOs and leverages technology to combat predatory behavior, rescue victims, and protect vulnerable children. Their strategies include research, victim identification, and disrupting platforms to deter predators. They also operate The Thorn Technology Task Force comprised of more than 20 technology companies that lend their knowledge, time, and resources to the work. Thorn runs "challenges" through their innovation lab that intersect intelligence, cybersecurity and social media. Thorn's work illustrates how social innovation occurs between sectors. The structure and goals of Spotlight consist of the Core Elements of Social Innovation (WeAreThorn, 2017), including • **Novelty.** It is a new innovation for the anti-trafficking field that turns data into an asset for law enforcement. It adapts technology to adjust to the emerging needs of law enforcement and victims of trafficking. • **From ideas to implementation**. Drawing on design thinking, 880+ SPOTLIGHT assisted investigations, and 49 states are using SPOTLIGHT. • **Meets a social need.** It addresses the needs of law enforcement to sift through escort ads to identify vulnerable victims. • **Effectiveness.** 330+ trafficking victims identified and connected to resources. • **Enhances society's capacity to act.** Spotlight is free of charge to law enforcement. It changes the way law enforcement investigates sex trafficking.

(Continued)

Table 14.1 (Continued)

Typology of Anti-trafficking Social Innovations	Examples
Policy	**Dear John Letters—Oakland** scpr.org/news/2013/10/21/39938/could-dear-john-letters-help-deter-prostitution-in An example of a policy where letters that are mailed from the Oakland Police department's vice unit to the registered owners of vehicles (in some cases they are company vehicles so the employer gets the letter) that are seen in a high-prostitution areas in the Easy Bay of northern California. The letter writing campaign is a partnership between the community and the Oakland Police Department. Community volunteers are trained to spot prostitution activity and type of information police need such as vehicle's license plate number, a description of the car, and the time and location of the suspicious activity.
Markets	**Polaris** polarisproject.org Operates the National Human Trafficking Resources Center (NHTRC) hotline and has trained over 72,000 individuals in law enforcement, social services, education, the health-care field, the military, the courts and bar associations, private industry, and communities throughout the United States and around the world. The National Human Trafficking Resource Center (NHTRC) is a national, toll-free hotline, available to answer calls from anywhere in the United States, 24 hours a day, 7 days a week, in more than 200 languages. Polaris works with Salesforce, the largest Customer Relationship Management (CRM) solution provider, who helps manage not only the data base but the operations of the hotline. With their partnership, Polaris is able to identify over 200 variables and track them so that this information can be used to implement specialized responses to specific cases, connect providers globally, and analyze data from other organizations as well as their own.
Platforms/Digital Social Innovation	**Phones4Freedom** phones4freedom.org Advance anti-trafficking networks using mobile technology. Polaris and Thorn partnered with Twilio and Salesforce Foundation to develop the NHTRC SMSbased textline; victims can text the shortcode "BeFree" for a discreet and time-efficient way to access the hotline.

Typology of Anti-trafficking Social Innovations	Examples
Organization Structure for Advocacy	**Truckers Against Trafficking (TAT)** truckersagainsttrafficking.org TAT seeks to make the TAT training DVD, wallet cards, (and other materials a regular part of training/orientation for members of the trucking industry so that when they suspect human trafficking is taking place they can call the National Human Trafficking Resource Center (NHTRC). The website details personal accounts, numbers of persons rescued, as well as calls to NHTRC. The TAT program operates the Freedom Drivers Project, which is a mobile exhibit educating audiences about the realities of domestic sex trafficking as well as what they can do to combat it. Truckers have made over 1,300 calls to NHTRC and identified 415 likely cases of trafficking involving 723 victims (including 241 minors). Since 2009 over 181,000 people have been TAT trained.
Innovative Funding & Partnership	**Partnership for Freedom** is a coalition of funders in partnership with the federal government to identify and fund new models for "innovative and sustainable social services for human trafficking survivors." This partnership has curated a public funding challenge that asks social entrepreneurs to propose new solutions for helping victims of human trafficking in the United States. That challenge has a prize of up to $1.8M over two years to fund the big ideas and measure their impact. **2016 Challenge Winners for Rethinking the Global Supply Chain** Sustainability Incubator and Trace Register teamed up to develop the winning solution to help companies uncover and address the risks of trafficking. The team will receive a $250,000 grant to support the Labor Safe Digital Certificate, a digital risk assessment tool that will help seafood suppliers and major retailers better screen for risks of forced labor and address high-risk zones within their supply chains. Good World Solutions was named the runner-up winner and will receive a $50,000 grant to advance Laborlink Trafficking Module, its mobile technology for improving visibility of trafficked workers by capturing and analyzing worker feedback.

(Continued)

Table 14.1 (Continued)

Typology of Anti-trafficking Social Innovations	Examples
Cross-enterprise	Organizations such as the Thomson Reuters Foundation use their intellectual capital, technology, and human expertise to cultivate social innovation. Their cross-enterprise efforts include • Thomson Reuters Special Services, which partner with the U.S. intelligence services and other government agencies to investigate human trafficking and other deviant behavior at large events. At Super Bowl XLVIII, their investigative capabilities led to the recovery of nine victims. • The Thomson Reuters Foundation trains and provides a forum for journalists to report stories of human trafficking worldwide. Through events such as Trust Women and programs such as TrustLaw, the Foundation empowers a network of people to deliver innovative solutions. • Data Innovation Labs, which show the power of data and computer science to empower real answers. Through events such as in #HackTrafficking4Good with Demand Abolition or Science Against Slavery Hackathon with Open Data Science, or encouraging other people to join the effort through presentations about Using Data to Combat Sex Trafficking at Ignite Data—Boston/the power of innovation have taken off worldwide. • Thomson Reuters Third Party Risk Proposition, a preeminent leader in the third party risk space, will lead the development of the first global platform on slavery in the supply chain. It will expand and connect internal and external datasets on slavery, leveraging existing technology capabilities, to better address human trafficking risks.

that seem fantastical out of our realm of practice. Questions to ask ourselves are as follows: Which trends and technologies have augmented the work of those fighting slavery? What are the challenges that we consider as solvable or difficult to overcome? How can we strategize effective solutions to this wicked problem? These questions and similar inquiries will become more salient as more technology is created, but also they will become of more importance once social innovation labs are widely developed and accepted as the space for rapid knowledge sharing and production.

Figure 14.1 Word Cloud

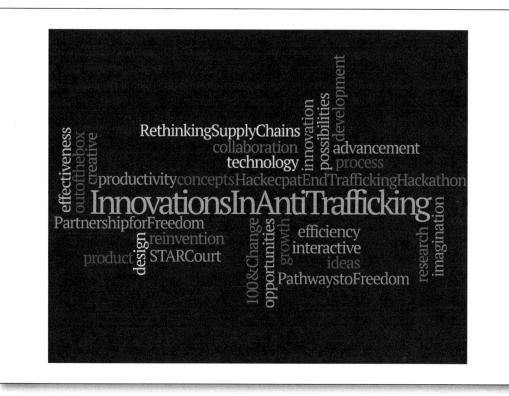

Source: Honey Imbo.

Case Vignette: The Mariposa Center

The Mariposa Center is an organization based in Seattle, Washington, that works with women in seven different countries: Philippines, Malaysia, Mexico, Canada, United States, Spain, and Italy. They have chapters in each of the countries, and they have programs with local, grassroots organizations whose purpose is to encourage women to become active in local government roles, as well as influence and advocate for policy and legislation. They have been an organization that has relied on private donations since their founding three years ago. This year, the board of directors of Mariposa has set the goal of joint legislation and cooperation, hopefully in the future even creating uniform legislative

(Continued)

(Continued)

policies. This means that they will have to also build their own internal capacity and forge new relationships and coalitions. The only way to do this is to increase their development work and garner more material support. Since they have an international scope, they believe they should look for funding that can be used for their global work. They convene their supporters and form a development committee to help look for funding. The committee believes that the UN Trust Fund will be an avenue of support.

The United Nations created Trust Fund to End Violence Against Women in 1996. It is administered by UN Women and is the only "global, multilateral, grant-making mechanism that is dedicated exclusively to addressing all forms of violence against women and girls." There are over 110 organizations in 76 countries that are supported through the UN Trust Fund. Over 1 million people benefitted through outreach and awareness. Almost 200,000 women and girls were helped directly. Based on their strategic plan, one of the areas of focus will be on "Strengthening the implementation of laws, policies, and national action plans."

While this may have been a good opportunity, the Mariposa Center had never applied to this type of funding before but they knew that they had good ideas that fit the same goals of the UN Trust Fund. The board of directors and the center's administration thought that the next step was to hold an innovation "sprint" to clarify their ideas and settle on one to create into a full project proposal for the fund. Since they had never done anything like this, they decided to work with a local software development company to help them begin to organize their task. They felt that the easiest format to follow was a version popularized by Google Ventures (Knapp, 2016). According to this format, the sprint would take five days, which would include

1. Mapping/defining the problem

2. Sketching solutions

3. Deciding/storyboarding

4. Prototyping

5. Testing

Seven people were selected, including the executive director of the Mariposa Center, who was made the "decider" of the process. This role is set up to make sure that there is someone who has the power to sign off on ideas, to break any stalemates, and also to just step in and make a decision to move the process along. The other six people were stakeholders from the organization, including a representative from each of their geographical regions (Asia, North America, and Europe). During the first day, experts were also invited to present on different aspects of their anti-trafficking work. By the end of the day, they decided that the problem they would focus on was migrant labor practices that left domestic helpers vulnerable to being trafficked or enslaved and that the solution should be one that was transnational. The next few days were dedicated to narrowing down the solutions and developing one or two of the key ideas. Though the process was difficult, it was not only productive but creative. They created a reporting mechanism for the anti-trafficking legislation that specifically targeted unscrupulous recruiters who often charged usurious fees, making it easy for domestic workers to end up in debt bondage. This mechanism would be an app created for mobile devices since many migrant workers invested in a smartphone to communicate with families they left back home. The app would report directly to local government units and allow those reporting to remain anonymous. Prototypes of the "mock-app" were set up and tested locally in each of the regions. This was an expanded version of the "test" stage but they felt that it was needed because of the vastly different contexts of each of the regions where they would launch it. This added a couple of days to the sprint but the group felt it was worth it. Once they received the results from the test, they could see where the gaps in their thinking were and revised their plans to address each.

After this process, the center was able to bring together the right groups and people to write a strong proposal for a UN Trust Fund that included not only their ideas but preliminary data collected from their prototype testing sessions.

CALL TO ACTION: IMPACT AND DISRUPTION AS THE ROAD TO ENDING TRAFFICKING

Mechanisms of social innovation are shaped by trends. Social innovation in human trafficking contribute to the growing portfolio of innovative solutions that disrupt the supply chain for human trafficking, help victims rebuild their lives, and help bring their traffickers to justice. Strong innovative solutions will adapt to the context in which human trafficking exists and formulate interventions that are relevant. For example, when developing an innovative solution, a policy context that consists of international human rights law, bilateral agreements, and domestic law is important to know. Similarly, being open to new partnerships that spawn effective strategies to attack trafficking is also helpful in addressing the issue in new and nontraditional ways. Combatting trafficking and modern-day slavery is not going to be successful if we stick to traditional ways of practitioners and their service areas. We must work faster if we are going to stop this phenomenon. When Harriet Tubman and others suggested the creation of an Underground Railroad, it must have been met with skepticism, fear, and the unknown. With all these trepidations, imagine the first group of slaves who first made their way to freedom, and the astonishment of everyone when it worked. That is the nature of social innovations; you have get past the fear of the unknown and test your idea because it may fail and you may have to try again. On the other hand, it may succeed, and you will have changed the world. The modern Underground Railroad needs to continuously evolve through a cross-pollination of new methods, approaches, and perspectives to abolish human slavery. The way to begin a new chapter in antihuman trafficking movement is to be ruthless and diligent of what works—letting go of things that fall short and moving forward with those innovations that show promise.

GUIDING QUESTIONS FOR SOCIAL LABS

1. Identify something you feel is an innovation for individuals who have been trafficked or enslaved. What is the innovation? Where is it being used? Who developed it? What makes it innovative? Is it effective? How do you know?

2. Think about your favorite innovation or piece of technology (in any area). How would you adapt the principles or framework of that innovation to address anti-trafficking efforts? What would it look like?

3. If you could invite any group of people to a social innovation lab you are curating for trafficking and modern-day slavery, who would you invite and why? Be as specific as possible.

4. If you had unlimited resources, what type of innovation would you propose to end the labor trafficking? Where would you pilot the innovation? How would you bring it to scale?

5. This chapter talked about Underground Railroads during the 1800s. Are there modern versions of the Underground Railroad? If so, describe and discuss.

CHALLENGE

Hackathons are events that are being held in different sectors that can range from a whole day to lasting several days where a large gathering of people come together to tackle a problem. Form a group from your class, organization, or community and host a "stop trafficking hackathon" or day of innovation. Post the events and results of the day using social media and the hashtag #freedomsjourney.

Ending Trafficking and Modern-Day Slavery

1. Readers will conceptualize the evolving trends in combatting trafficking locally and globally.

2. Readers will highlight the continuum of activities anti-trafficking advocates, activists, and practitioners.

3. Readers will hypothesize on current trends and patterns that will affect human trafficking and modern-day slavery.

4. Readers will elaborate on their knowledge in the following 3 P's: *preparation, partnership,* and *promise* as it relates to trends in human trafficking and modern-day slavery.

5. Readers will be called to action for advocacy and change.

I take a step backward and come into contact with the podium, letting myself lean for a moment as I take in the view. Hundreds of women and girls crowd together in the largest lecture hall of the university. Some are wearing their native garb, colorful materials that are hand woven, painted by shells, and embellished with bells that chime with every step. Some are in worn jeans and feminist t-shirts declaring political stances unapologetically. There are little girls in batik dresses running up and down the aisles, older women with white hair held back from their faces, large hoop earrings dancing at their ears, and teens whose sneakers and high heels create a staccato rhythm. All of them wear a small, geometrically shaped purple rose. It is in their hair as an adornment, or on their lapel, or made into a pendant. As I move forward to pick up the microphone again, a group of women has come up to the stage to triumphantly unfurl a banner mirroring the purple rose, its satin petals written with the names of survivors and victims.

(Continued)

(Continued)

In 2005, grassroots women's groups came together to make a commitment in sisterhood and solidarity to fight against the commodification and sale of women and children through sex and labor trafficking. Women leaders from all over the world, survivors from different regions, and girls from right down the street gathered because it was time their voices were heard. One voice rose above the rest, and in her characteristic New York inflection, her speech reached its crescendo, declaring, "We cannot afford to vacillate, we cannot afford to hesitate, we cannot—because women are dying, girls are dying. It is time to fight, now more than ever." The rallying cry of Philippine author Ninotchka Rosca brought the audience to their feet as she raised her fist to the chants of "Makibaka, Huwag Matakot," the chant of Philippine feminists meaning, "Struggle On, Do Not Fear."

Ten years later, in a classroom of social work graduate students and my fellow anti-trafficking warriors, I watch again. The students confer, they diagram elaborate plans on dry erase walls, they debate, and they create. They are in the middle of a social innovation lab where, as professors and advisors, we direct them to tackle society's wicked problems, challenge them to think outside of the box, to partner, and to dream about how to put their plans into action. It is a tall order for 15 weeks of class especially for some students who have never engaged past their textbooks and hypothetical cases. But, they rise to the challenge and they do not vacillate, they do not hesitate, because people are still dying and it is still time to fight.

—Annalisa Enrile

WHAT WE HAVE LEARNED SO FAR

This book was designed as an overview of human trafficking, modern-day slavery, and anti-trafficking initiatives. While we have tried to be as comprehensive as possible, by now, you know how fast the issues in this area shift and change. Also, though we have attempted to take a global perspective, there are many unique details and systems for every country, that those we have included should only serve as exemplars when applicable to the context, content, and materials. While there are many variables, there are basic areas of knowledge that every practitioner should be aware of as they provide services, advocate, research, or create policy for these issues, survivors, and/or victims. These basic areas include understanding the root causes and antecedents of trafficking, especially those factors that make people more vulnerable and at risk. We have identified root causes as poverty, patriarchy, militarism, colonialism, imperialism, and demand. The only way to understand the full and continuing consequences is to understand the historical and structural basis of how these causes continue to aid in the proliferation of trafficking and modern-day slavery.

The book has also used the lens of transnational feminist theory. Our transnational feminist perspective necessitates the position that we believe that all sexual and labor exploitation should cease. Though that has not been the pattern of belief in the mainstream discourse, we feel that we should be clear that we think that the sale of human beings is not an inevitability. Thus, we dispute anything that has to do with this type of commodification and abuse. Feminist Andrea Dworkin worked to eradicate prostitution and in doing so, stated that this was the only way to simultaneously end sex trafficking since both situations were predicated on the same premise of exploitation. Dwokin states, "The girls and women who are bought and sold for sex and *equality for those women* cannot exist simultaneously" (Hoffer, 2010, p.1832). While we maintain the utmost respect for perspectives that champion sex work and liberal standpoints of regulating sex work, our position is to end exploitation all together. Likewise, we do not equivocate semantics over the nuances of language that have created loopholes or excused some types of abusive labor situations as not being "exactly" trafficking or modern-day slavery. To the broadest extent possible, we label labor trafficking and modern-day slavery to the spirit of the definitions as outlined by the United Nations, with more leeway toward examining the actual circumstances that people live in. For the most part, we view "slave-like conditions" and slavery as the same thing, even when they do not fit legal definitions.

This book has also utilized an ecosystems lens throughout, paying close attention to the totality of systems involved and the person in environment model, which centers individuals within their contexts. This same model can also be used for focus areas that are larger such as communities, groups, and organizations. We believe that there is no way to be truly exhaustive but that an ecosystems lens does offer the most promise in terms of being able to at least map out the literal and figurative territory where situations of trafficking or modern-day slavery are occurring. An ecosystems lens also fits appropriately within the paradigm of collective impact models to address social issues that have been resistant to change. Collective impact requires the involvement of a number of different actors, including stakeholders, service providers, businesses, survivors, victims, companies, and government entities, to name a few, from varying parts of the systems involved. The "freedom ecosystem" that business consulting firm Deloitte proposes is aimed at the whole configuration of trafficking, even though current examples of successful collective impact projects have only been aimed at single portions of problems such as the cocoa industry and conflict diamonds. The ambitiousness of the freedom ecosystem is the next step in the process, bringing to scale what we know works.

Built on the conceptual and political foundations of what is presented are what we hope have been practical applications. While it is important to understand how the situation is defined and continues to be conceptualized, it is imperative that practitioners are able to provide actual services in the areas of clinical intervention, policy formation, and implementation, as well as advocacy and activism. When possible, we have pooled our experiences and presented them here, representing over a quarter century of work in all aspects of the anti-trafficking and abolitionist fields. At the same time, we do recognize that there have not been any rigorous studies that would constitute evidence-based practices, but what is being used that demonstrates promise we have included as "best practices" or "promising practices." In a review conducted by the Campbell Collaboration, it was discovered that out of 19,398 citations related to sex trafficking, only 20 studies contained empirical research that was relevant for their review. Of the 20, only 4 of them were actual evaluations. None of them met a score of 3 or higher in the Maryland Scientific Methods

Scale, which is widely recognized as a strong scale to assess strength of evidence (Farrington, Gottfredson, Sherman, & Welsh, 2002). The purpose of the review was to establish best practices in approaching cross-border sex trafficking, but because there were no studies that fit the criteria, there are no conclusions on what we should consider best practices. However, there was also nothing that refuted any of the work that is currently being done (van Der Laan, Smit, Busschers, & Aarten, 2011). Currently, there has not been a systematic review of the literature for labor trafficking. In the absence of such research and evaluations, we can only rely on anecdotal evidence and practical experience, both of which we have tried to include in this book.

EVOLVING TRENDS

Trafficking and modern-day slavery has not remained a static phenomenon. On the contrary, at times it seems as if it has picked up momentum, grown exponentially, especially in areas of conflict, economic depression, and disasters, all of which make certain populations (poor, rural, women, etc.) more susceptible to trafficking. As this example illustrates, there are new threats that intersect with and exacerbate trafficking. Transnational criminal syndicates such as the Yakuza in Japan and the Mexican cartels have become templates for business for localized, regional street gangs. San Diego, California, at the border of the United States and Mexico, has witnessed the shift from gangs trafficking in drugs to gangs trafficking primarily in sex. One gang member said, "It's better business. You can use a girl over and over. You can even trade her with your homie when you are done with her and keep your inventory fresh" (De Los Reyes, personal communication, 2014). In one of the first studies of its kind, the National Institute of Justice found that in the San Diego area alone, over 110 gangs were involved in sex trafficking with 85% of the pimps/traffickers that were interviewed being gang affiliated (Carpenter & Gates, 2015).

Natural disasters also represent a growing threat, leaving children exposed to trafficking, especially the selling of babies through sham adoptions. This predicament came to light after the 2010 earthquake in Haiti. Soon after the earthquake, hundreds of children were taken out of the country, supposedly to be "adopted." With such widespread devastation, the paperwork, certificates, agreements, and contracts of adoption were difficult to substantiate. There were also thousands of children who were left orphaned when their parents were lost or killed. Seemingly out of nowhere, couples asserted that they were in the middle of the adoption process and demanded their children. While this might have been true, traffickers used the circumstances as a guise to get large groups of children out of the country and sell them for sex and labor. Because of the case of Haiti, UNICEF began to recommend that after a natural disaster all foreign adoptions be put on hold for at least a year while the country rebuilds and recovers.

Conflicts and other forms of unnatural disasters also leave communities at risk to trafficking. Conflicts such as civil wars create situations of dire impoverishment, displacement, loss of national identity, and disruption of family systems. For example, the Syrian conflict since 2011 has resulted in millions of Syrian refugees outside of the country and internally dislocated. Three out of four Syrians lived in poverty by the end of 2013 along with the added burdens of high inflation rates for basic market goods and inaccessibility of services. The level of vulnerability to trafficking is extremely high in these humanitarian situations where there is a lack of migration policies or refugee resettlement services. Syrian cases of trafficking have been reported in labor exploitation, domestic servitude, conscription in armed conflict, forced marriage, and sexual exploitation (Healy, 2015). The political and social situation is aggravated by cultural and religious mores, which do not protect women and girls. Da'ish militants in Syria have also been reported as kidnapping boys into the armed conflict as child soldiers and abducting thousands of girls for forced marriages and sexual slavery. This is only one example of conflict occurring in a world where there are over 20 identified significant or critical conflicts (Council on Foreign Relations, n.d.).

An ongoing threat is also the trafficking of organs, which is on the rise. Organ transplants began in 1954 with the first transplant, but even in the 1980s, they were considered risky procedures and the proliferation of such transplants did not become a standard medical procedure until the development of immunosuppressive drugs, or a practice in over 90 countries until the turn of the 21st century (Shimazono, 2007). However, as early as the 1980s stories of the black-market organ trade from Brazil and India started to surface in light of limited legitimate sources of organ procurement (Scheper-Hughes, 2001; Salahudeen et al., 1990). The most common organ trafficking is the live kidney trade (Shimazono, 2007). By the 21st century there were more verified cases of people selling their kidneys in what has been dubbed as "medical tourism" and the trafficking trade of organs between donor exporting countries (Egypt, China, India, Pakistan, and the Philippines) and demand countries (the United States, Canada, Israel, the United Kingdom, and various European countries). Countries such as the United States, Israel, and South Africa were also included as places where operations were taking place. In some places, such as South Korea, the Philippines, and South Africa, hospitals are built as five-star hotels, catering to the first world not just for organ trafficking but for other types of "medical tourism" such as plastic surgery and fertility treatments (Kelly, 2013). Organ trafficking constitutes almost 1.2 billion dollars in illegal profits per year (Ambagtsheer, Zaitch, & Weimar, 2013) even though it is prohibited worldwide and protected under the Palermo Protocols.

Developments and threats in trafficking further stress the need to expand trends in response such as multidisciplinary teams working to tackle the grand challenge of ending trafficking and modern-day slavery for good. We have discussed how this might look at the macro level, using ecosystems approaches that bring together crucial actors who may influence transformative structural change. However, this type of multidisciplinary team approach begins at the micro levels of prevention and intervention. Public health and human services have demonstrated the power of having various perspectives handle cases by providing a holistic view of wellness so that all things are considered in a strengths-based approach as opposed to one based on deficit and illness. HEAL Trafficking, an independent, interdisciplinary network of health professionals working to combat trafficking, created a public health tool kit. This tool kit includes information on identification, resources, and how to respond in a health care setting, especially emergency rooms (Stoklosa, Personal Communication, 2017). Similarly, intensive case managers who focus on those who have been trafficked or enslaved count on being able to bring in different practitioners and providers to the case to ensure that nothing that the victim or survivor needs is missed. These actions can expand because we know the promise that new ideas and outlooks bring to the solution set. Because trafficking and modern-day slavery affects everyone, it then follows, that we begin to include everyone in the conversation and the solution. For example, celebrities have played prominent roles in social change movements, using their public following to influence and access spaces of change. Celebrities have included Julia Ormond, Demi Moore, Ashton Kutcher, Kathy Ireland, and Mira Sorvino who have used their status and fame to help raise awareness. In the most scenarios, celebrities can amplify awareness raising campaigns and bring these issues to the forefront, but celebrity can also bring together and curate networks to fight trafficking especially in the areas of policy and advocacy (Haynes, 2014). For example, actress Julia Ormond not only used her fame to bring to the public forefront trafficking issues such as the illegal fishing trade, agricultural trafficking, and other labor trafficking situations, but she also helped write and pass the California Transparency in Supply Chains Act (Asset, 2014).

Another trend in confronting trafficking and modern-day slavery is the overall move to innovative methods. While the previous chapter focused on programs and projects that are targeted to specific areas, the move toward social innovation in every area of trafficking is already happening. International grants and U.S.-based initiatives and resources have increasingly prioritized redefining how anti-trafficking work is being carried out. For instance, one of the persistent challenges is in estimating prevalence rates and identifying trafficking victims due to a number of reasons. Partnerships from all fields are working to reconceptualize how we use traditional methods and develop more "untraditional approaches." Predictive analytics is currently being employed as a way to crunch big data into something usable that will help shed light on trafficking in ways that will actually help foresee incidences before they can occur (Heimpel, 2014). The time to stubbornly hold onto ways of practice that we are used to because they have been long standing operating procedures is at an end. Practitioners on the front line and those with decision-making powers are seeing that we need new tools, even those that seem far out of the box, or that reinvent the box entirely.

CHANGING ROLE OF SURVIVOR ADVOCATES AND/OR ACTIVISTS

The biggest changes in the fight against trafficking have been within the population of survivors. Formerly, the voices of the trafficked, the survivors themselves have been subsumed under concerns of retraumatization, confidentiality, and other considerations of protection. While these are still concerns, they are not enough to keep survivor voices from the forefront of anti-trafficking efforts. This is more than a tactic or strategy; it is a true shift in movement building. In a collection of survivor narratives, Murphy (2014) provides a showcase of trafficking through the eyes of those most affected. The collection begins with "an open letter to the anti-trafficking movement" penned by Minh Dang, a survivor of sexual exploitation. It is this missive that outlines, from the perspective of survivors, principles for the anti-trafficking movement and the changing relationship with survivors. To honor her words and her agency, we have used her narrative verbatim, followed by our commentary (Murphy, 2014, p. x111–xxii).

1. *Principle Number 1: Rehumanize Survivors.* As we incorporate survivors into the anti-trafficking movement and encourage them to be at its forefront, we need to recognize their humanity. Find a way to relate with survivors. You do not need to have gone through what they went through to imagine what they might experience. Also, share your own story. When asking survivors to share their story, publicly, pay attention to how this process may contribute to their continued dehumanization

2. *Principle Number 2: Get Out of the Box.* I invite our movement to join me in breaking down the boxes that we live in. I invite us to challenge the restrictions we put on our ways of being and thinking. Let's think outside of the box about how we do our work. What is *not* being said? Whose story is *not* being told?

3. *Principle Number 3: Sing a New Song.* It is time for us to sing a new song—to raise our voices in unison and drown out the old verses. In the "doings" of our movement, we now have our own recycled song—that of the three P's: *prevention, protection,* and *prosecution.* Although I do not minimize the importance of these three P's, I suggest that we transition to embracing three additional P's: *preparation, partnership,* and *promise.*

    a. *Preparation.* Prevention efforts include training of law enforcement and service providers, but I also argue that preparation goes beyond learning statistics and warning signs. Preparation must include a self-reflective and emotional component. How prepared are people to hold the horrors of human trafficking? How informed are people of their motivations? What stereotypes are we reinforcing? I am adamant about training and supporting those who serve in communities and those who work for social justice. How will we sustain this movement for the long term? How will we ensure that those who do work do not succumb to their despair but find ways to embrace it, share it, and move on?

    b. *Partnership.* I urge all of you to continue to partner with survivors—to ask survivors not just about their stories but also about their policy recommendations, their ideas for improved intervention, as well as their hopes and concerns for the movement. I also ask that members of our movement do not seek to divide and separate survivors by focusing only on sex trafficking or on labor trafficking or to overemphasize international survivors or domestic survivors; rather, I ask that you face the complexities of this issue, refrain from reducing diverse experiences into a neat package, and portray both the similarities and differences in the survivor experience. Partnership is defined as having joint interest; I ask that you build relationships with survivors and find joint interests with them.

    c. *Promise.* I speak not of contract or agreement that one makes with another but rather of *potential.* Prevention, prosecution, and protection do not address much about the future for survivors of human trafficking. What about their hopes and dreams and their potential to live life beyond their years of slavery? They must consider long term support and services to ensure (re)acclimation to freedom. We must consider the potential for thriving, not just surviving.

4. *Principle Number 4: Address Emotional Poverty and Profits.* I argue that we are at a time of extreme *emotional poverty* and that traffickers receive *emotional profits* from their deeds. Emotional poverty does not just happen; it is developed over many years. Financial gratification is only temporary. Money doesn't buy happiness, so a trafficker may seek to earn more and more money, hoping that it will fill that emotional hole. And while they are on an impossible quest to extinguish their feelings of emptiness by using other people as objects of gratification, many people's basic human rights are robbed, spit on, and disrespected.

5. *Principle Number 5: Peace is in the Pain.* Grieving for my losses will help me pursue goals that are possible rather than goals that are impossible (like making up lost time). Grieving frees me of the pain and burden I've carried for so many years and opens up space for new adventures and joy. Grieving brings me true peace with what I have suffered and where I am now. In our movement, how do we sit with the grief of survivors? Or do we even sit at all? Are we too eager to "take action" that we forget sitting and listening are actions? Grieving is not just for survivors. Grieving is for all of us. We live in a world where violence pervades our everyday ways of relating with each other. We have experienced violence, and we have enacted violence—whether big or small. What losses does the anti-trafficking movement need to recognize? What sorrows are we avoiding?

6. *Principle Number 6: Survivor Stories Are Not Enough to Sustain This Movement.* I am adamant that any pursuit of social justice must coincide with our own pursuit of personal justice. Individual healing and community healing must go hand in hand. My story is not enough to sustain this movement. It is surely not enough to sustain you. In the words of aboriginal activist Lilla Watson, "If you have come here to help me, you are wasting your time, but if you have come here because your liberation is bound up with mine, then let us work together."

The salient points that Minh Dang raises should be used as a guideline to construct work within the anti-trafficking movement. The principles fit many of our trauma-informed protocols as well as provide insight into the ways in which survivors can and wish to take part and take leadership. Particularly important is the emphasis that she places on the ability to connect not just as survivors to nonsurvivors but within the entire context of intersectionalities, which exist and play a part in our progress against trafficking. Dang also highlights those areas that we do not often deal with because they are somewhat "slippery" and difficult to initiate into practice. While these are certain challenges, she also is able to clearly articulate her unique perspective as a survivor who has an acute understanding of having to maintain her own healing daily as well as carry on the message of the overall movement. This is something that all practitioners should pay attention to as the chances of retraumatization and triggering mechanisms are high and not fully understood. What is also very clear is that survivor participation needs to move beyond the mere sharing of narratives and to leadership and advisement on their own experiences and recommendations based on those experiences. While we are in the pursuit of evidence based interventions and actions, we cannot ignore the experiences and opinions of those who have lived through and survived trafficking and modern-day slavery.

Case Vignette: Women's Rights Defenders

Tina was born in Jakarta, Indonesia. She was the oldest child of a family that would grow to seven children. Tina's mother worked in a garment factory as a contractual laborer. When she was off contract or they did not have work for her, she would take in laundry or piecework. Tina would often help her mother with these duties as well as watch the younger children. Her father was a taxi driver and often worked long hours, so the family rarely saw him except for when they went to temple together, which was not often. Her parents were originally from Bali and had come to Jakarta to find work. They practiced Hinduism, which was difficult because Jakarta is mainly Muslim. Still, Tina's parents attempted to keep as much of their spiritual beliefs and pass them onto their children as they could.

Tina grew up in an urban poor neighborhood. Although it was difficult to grow up with very little, and often the children had to find work to contribute to the family, they were happy together. Tina was even able to go to school off and on, but was not able to graduate because her mother became ill. When Tina was 14, her mother passed away. They never had enough money to go to the doctor's so they were not sure what she died of. Tina's father worked harder for the family. Tina lied about her age and got a job as a laundress in a rich household. If the family was having a party, they would let her work as a waitress or kitchen staff. Tina did not mind because the money helped her brothers and sisters go to school. However, she was uncomfortable on the nights when they asked her to stay late. The master of the house often hosted his friends and she was uneasy about being around so many men. One night, they asked her to stay until very late and one of the men offered to drive her home. She insisted on walking, but her boss became angry what he viewed as her ungratefulness and insisted she ride with his friend. On the way to her home, he pulled the car over and raped Tina. Bleeding and injured, Tina went home. She cleaned herself up and never told her father or her siblings.

Tina returned to work because she needed the money, but she also looked for work elsewhere. She was very despondent and depressed. She had trouble sleeping, but it was difficult for her to get up every day and do everything she needed to do for the family. One day her younger sister invited her to go to a program at her school. Tina usually didn't do this because she always tried to work as much as possible, but she thought it would make her feel better. The program was sponsored by a local nonprofit who offered different social services and classes. Tina picked up a brochure for a women's group. It was interesting to her and she thought she might try doing something to help her move on.

(Continued)

(Continued)

Tina attended a women's meeting one evening after work. The meeting was in a small office and when she got there, she realized it was a workers' union. At the meeting, the facilitator introduced the group as being one where "women gave other women support." It was that general. They sat in a circle and were invited to talk about their lives. As the women shared, they talked about their problems with money and also with work. One woman talked about how she was working in a factory when the foreman pulled her off the line and raped her in his office. She did not cry as she spoke, but Tina started to. She found herself telling the women about her experience. They comforted her and then the facilitator told Tina that she had legal rights. She explained what her rights were and that it was hard because she worked in a private home. There was no union for domestic workers as there was for factory workers. Tina did not say much because she was scared. Everyone knew that it was dangerous to organize in Jakarta; the government went out of their way to break up union activities and other people's organizations. She went home thinking she would not return, but soon found herself going to meetings at least once every other week.

At the end of March, the women's group started planning for a big protest rally to be held May 1st for International Workers Day. She said that she did not think she could attend. However, two weeks later, two of her sisters were unfairly dismissed from work. They were accused of stealing from the factory, but they were only removing remnants of the fabric, which they were told to do by their supervisor. They had no one who would believe them. Tina felt this was unjust and decided that one way she could feel like she was doing something for her sisters was to help for the worker's day march. On the day of the march, Tina carried a sign that she made with the slogan "Worker's Rights are Human Rights." Afterward, she told the other women that she "felt like she was taking her power back."

Soon Tina worked with the group every spare moment she had. She was especially good at working with women who had been trafficked, mainly for labor but also for sex. It was not easy work for her. Often, she would find herself very angry when other women shared their experiences, particularly if they had to do with sexual assault, and it would make her work harder. Pretty soon, Tina was not only organizing and participate in rallies, she was also speaking at them. Her father was unhappy about her work because he was scared for her. "It's not good, the government will see you as a rebel," he told her. She dismissed his worries and started to work with the group full time. They paid her a modest allowance and she also made money from speaking engagements and donations. Tina still helped provide for the family but her brothers and sisters were older and could help out more. Tina became an outspoken activist and was often on television and radio. She worked tirelessly and was often fatigued, but she never complained.

One night, her father's fears were realized when their home was stormed by police who were looking for Tina. She was accused of destroying property at one of the factories whose picket line she was demonstrating at. Tina protested saying that she was not even there on the day in question, but they still took her into custody. Her family was not told where she was detained. Three days later, her father was informed that she was moved to another facility because on an "altercation with another detainee." Her father went to her women's organization, who demanded that the police tell them what happened to Tina. Eight weeks later, Tina's family was told she was at a local military facility and given a pass to visit her. Tina's father was accompanied by a human rights' attorney who volunteered for her women's organization. When they visited her, she looked very thin and her hands would shake. She told them that she was being treated well and that she was fine. When the guard wasn't looking, Tina slipped the lawyer a carefully folded piece of paper that read, "I have been raped and beaten. Please get me out of here." By this time, Tina faced trumped-up charges for vandalism, theft, assault, and attempted murder. Later, the lawyer explained to her father that the accusations were fabricated; that Tina was becoming a strong voice for workers in the country and the government wanted her silenced. Because of the power of the government, the women's organization decided that they needed help for Tina that was beyond their reach. They contacted Women Human Rights Defenders International Coalition (WHRDIC), a network that supports and protects women human rights defenders as they fight for others. WHRDIC supports women activists, but also men who are defending women's rights. They help with building international solidarity, provide resources and tools, and urgent responses to cases such as Tina's.

CALL TO ACTION: END TRAFFICKING AND MODERN-DAY SLAVERY NOW!

There are some skills that can't be manualized and formulated. For instance, we are just beginning to understand how to integrate restorative and transformative justice models into the domain of trafficking and modern-day slavery or how to apply faith-based notions of compassion. We are just beginning to see the promise in cutting-edge technologies such as global positioning systems (GPS) and artificial intelligence (AI). We are challenged to operationalize sweeping concepts such as social justice, transformation, and even love. Of course, there are and will continue to be prevention and intervention methods evolve in our different practice areas. If we are smart and forward thinking, these areas will begin to intersect with one another by necessity and not just because we contrive them so. Eventually these skills that are currently difficult to operationalize and put into practice will become part of our vernacular. Twenty years ago, no one operated with a trauma-informed lens. Fifteen years ago, empathy was not considered a skill-set. Five years ago, we did not recognize transcendental meditation as part of a treatment plan. But, leaps in neurobiology, insights into attachment, sociological expansions in defining culture and ritual, and a growing reliance on multidisciplinary approaches have created a new site for us to experiment with, and refine, our praxis. As practitioners, we must not only be flexible to change as more knowledge is built and more avenues to healing are discovered and formulated, but we must also rise to the challenges presented to us.

There is no doubt that the list of challenges is a mile long when it comes to how to fight trafficking and modern-day slavery. We have mentioned many throughout this book and there are probably ten more for every one that we have included. Many of the challenges are not unique to trafficking and modern-day slavery, but encompass overall social problems that our world experiences. We could eradicate trafficking if we lived in a world where the basic human rights of people were not denied. We could rid ourselves of modern-day slavery if we created just labor and work environments. If society ceased to put price tags on everything or construct everyone as a commodity, we would stop believing there was monetary value and a profit to be made on human lives. We are challenged to create a slave-free world, but this cannot be done without focusing on the deep complexities and web of intersections that protect, and in fact, thrive off its existence.

One of the first things that we must do is to supplement and continue to build our knowledge about trafficking and modern-day slavery. As we discussed earlier, there are virtually no studies that constitute strong evidence based methodology so this must be remedied. Another area where we can do better would be in how we define and perceive the issue. We can return to a human rights framework without losing the need for enforcement or protection. It does not have to be an either/or proposition. This is one of the reasons that multidisciplinary teams are so important. This type of work also includes better coordination, sharing of information, communication, training, and of course, innovations. Finally, one of the most concrete ways that impacts our work is the issue of funding. We have to begin to shift funding into areas that are underserved, but underfunded. Most of the money and research in the trafficking field has been focused on direct assistance to victims and not on development, equality, or human rights (Chuang, 2006). In general, the priority given by the U.S. government to trafficking is woefully underfunded—roughly $150 million annually compared to the $30.5 billion spent on the "war on drugs" (Krulak, 2016). Increased funding that goes toward research, organizations, community efforts, policy advocacy, support for new ideas, and ongoing training will make the biggest differences.

We are working in areas where we see and hear about the worst that humanity can do to one another. This is the part of the book where we can talk about self-care and secondary trauma, but let's go one step beyond that and talk about purpose. Why do we insist on doing this work? Why do we elevate it to proportions that are much more than clinician and client, than practitioner and patient? Wouldn't it be easier to treat these situations as we would any other population that needs our help—with objectivity and clinical detachment? But, it is impossible. There is no way that you can do an assessment of someone who has been trafficked and not feel a continuum of emotions. We are not advocating a blurring of boundaries or an enmeshing of relationship. Indeed, we are well aware and fully endorse that all professional ethics and standards be followed. But, we are suggesting being honest about our realities; that there is something qualitatively different about working with individuals who have been trafficked because it connects with our own lives and perhaps even to the basic calling to the work that we do. This is why we have to talk about purpose—what brings us to this work and how we remain mindful of that. This may leave us vulnerable as practitioners because it takes vulnerability to hear the present tense of people's trauma and to share in that. However, in doing so, practitioners are able to craft a shared space that is about connection and transformation (Brown, 2012).

There is no prescriptive plan of action that is the answer, just as there is not one practice methodology that has proven to work in all instances. If that were the case, our job would be easier. Because of this, our approach should be broad and open, but consistent, multidisciplinary, and best practice driven. Trafficking and modern-day slavery is an incredibly complex, monster of a problem. Our attempts to bring it down to size, to make it simpler and more manageable have failed. We need to let it be as big as it is, as wicked or grand as it currently is. That is the only way that we will understand the sheer expanse that our practice needs to cover. It is important to sharpen our ability to map the edges of this phenomenon because that is the place our practice is most effective—at the edges,

Figure 15.1   Wish List

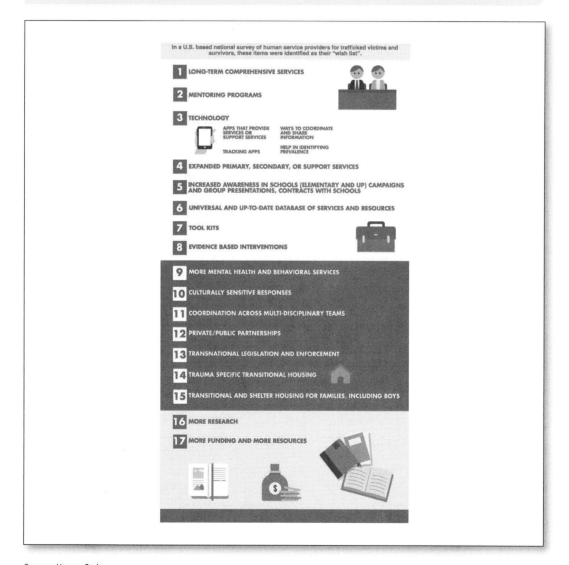

Source: Honey Imbo.

fighting to control its expansion, seeing the full scope so that we can stop it all together. When and where does our work begin and end? It is different for all of us as our entry points are defined by our job descriptions, our professional and theoretical approach, and the positionality of our industry in this area. Our work doesn't end until trafficking ends. This is why we have to focus and fight for absolute eradication, because anything less than that is remediation and temporary band-aids.

A child slave who escaped and eventually founded Challenging Heights, an organization that helps child slaves, James Kofi Annan states, "There are many children who are in the same situation, suffering similar abuses and enduring the same conditions, and I stand privileged to do something for them." We are privileged to be in the position to do something for those who are trafficked and enslaved. We are also privileged to be in the position to prevent and stop this horrific trade. But to do so, we must practice a certain amount of bravery within our fields, recognizing each opportunity as not just one of service, but of advocacy and change.

Survivor Statements: In Our Own Words . . .

Over the course of writing this book and over the years of working with this issue, we have had the privilege and honor of speaking to countless survivors. We believe there are no words that we can say that are more powerful than their articulation of this complex wicked problem, interpretation of their experiences, and what prioritize as the most important for solutions and the future as whole. Though we cannot include a transcript of all the words we have been gifted, we would like to share some with you:

"We were kept in the refugee camps. I don't know what was worse, the war where we came from or not being able to leave this refugee camp. We all thought it would be better but there is no work and no learning. We are all trapped here like animals because that is how they see us—animals. I hear them sometimes at night; they take the girls, especially the pretty ones and we never see them again. We can't look for them because if we leave, then anything can happen to us and no one will be responsible. But, how can we keep existing like this? We have a right to move on and heal. We have a right to freedom."

—**Wai**, age 14, Burmese refugee, Chaing Mai, Thailand

"We never knew when we would get food and it was never enough. Sometimes the older women would give us more, but I always thought maybe they needed it more. When it was the harvest it was the worst because we worked almost 24 hours a day. It was strange you know- spending all day picking food, but never knowing when you were going to get to eat."

—**John**, age 16, agriculture labor trafficking, Cambodia

"I have a daughter. She is only 3. I have to provide for her. I don't want to have to do this, but I don't have a better choice. So, I dance, and I force myself to sleep with men I don't know who make do things I never do. I don't want my daughter not to have any choices like me. This is all I can give her. There are 8 of us. We had to live together because our trafficker took our passports. Always, we were scared of being deported. I did it for five years because I kept thinking it was my only choice, but it wasn't really my choice you know? No one chooses this—to be a slave for sex, for my body. But, I had a daughter to raise. I wanted to make it better for her than I had."

—**Kat**, age 22, Philippines, sex trafficked to Singapore

"There were 18 to us in one room. Imagine that? Eighteen of us and we slept in bunk beds and on the floor. We barely had anything, but anything we had was always shoved near our sleeping area. We carried all our belongings because at first we didn't know each other. We were so tired from work that we did not care that there were so many people in the room. We just fell asleep until we had to go back to work. We worked sometimes for 16 or 18 hours a day. It was hard for me because my job was dangerous and I used to think that I could fall or cause an accident. I had to concentrate to make sure I stayed alive. I never thought of leaving because we needed the money, but I also didn't want to admit that I got myself trapped. Even after the police raided us and caught our traffickers, I kept thinking, I mean wishing, I still had work even if it was very hard."

—**Ahmed**, age 26, Indian construction worker, modern-day slavery, Saudi Arabia

"He threw me around like I was a toy. He hit me, too. He told me, *I can do what I want. I paid for you. I own you for tonight.* I thought, how could someone own me? How can this be true? Sometimes I still dream of that. No one should ever be *owned.*"

—**Toni**, age 32, Dutch sex trafficking survivor, Amsterdam, Netherlands

"There were whispers that we should run away, but everyone was too scared. One day I decided I was more tired of being scared than I was even of the abuse. I kept thinking, *I don't want to die like this. I need to see my family again. I have to try. If I get caught, death cannot be worse than this.* So, I tried and we got away. I'm not saying that everyone can do it, but for us, we had enough. We had to try."

—**Tricia**, age 34, sweatshop labor trafficking, Mexico

"I forgot what the rest of the world looked like. We would go into the mines when it was still dark outside and come back as the sun was setting. My world was only dirt and digging and tunnels and darkness. They would put us on buses and take us away from everything except the mines. When we were saved, I couldn't believe it. The lawyers, they told us not to talk

(Continued)

(Continued)

about it, but we have to. I want everyone to know what happened to us because if we hide it we are as bad as the slavers."

—**Mariano**, age 41, mining labor trafficking, Brazil

"I wanted to make my parents proud, go to school, and be a doctor. But, we never had any money for school and I barely graduated before I had to work to help the family. I thought going abroad to work would be the best thing. But, I was locked up and made to work hours and hours every day. I was so scared because my boss said that he would call immigration to deport me if I ran away or complained and then my family would starve. I was so scared I believed it. I only ran away because one night he beat me so badly I could not walk. I thought then, I have to fight to live. My family needs that more."

—**Jeanette**, age 49, Haitian migrant worker, New York City

"I want to play in the sunshine and forget all the bad men. Someday, I want to fly free like a kite."

—**Chynna**, age 8, Nepalese sex trafficking victim, Kathmandu, Nepal

DISCUSSION QUESTIONS

1. What are ways you can increase funding for researching in the anti-trafficking movement?

2. What are ways you can reconceptualize the shifts in perspectives of survivor advocates?

3. After learning about the evolving trends in the movement, what tools do you need to stay up to date?

4. How can you advocate for survivors of trafficking in your respective fields? What supports or resources would you need to do this?

5. Imagine it is 2030. How has the issue of trafficking and modern-day slavery changed? How would we respond to the issue differently at that time?

CHALLENGE

Think about all the ways in which you can take action to fight human trafficking and modern-day slavery. Make a list of 12 things you can do. During the next year, try to do at least one thing from your list every month. You are one your way to being an anti-trafficking warrior—fight on!

Glossary

SECTION 1

Amerasian—the term used to commonly refer to a person born of a U.S. military father and an Asian mother (particularly, this term colloquially refers to the phenomenon of the Asian women who are prostituted). Often this person is the subject of discrimination based on their parentage.

APEC—the Asia-Pacific Economic Cooperation was created in 19 89. Twenty-one countries make up this forum. The United States is one of the members of the economic community.

Caste—system of dividing society into hereditary classes. Some groups inherit specific privileges, while others experience deprivations all because of parentage.

Chattel Slavery—often referred to as "traditional slavery" because of the person being owned as personal property.

Contractualization—replacing of regular workers with temporary workers who receive lower wages with no or lesser benefits.

Deregulation—reduction or elimination of government power in a particular industry in favor of privatization. Deregulation is usually enacted to create more competition within the industry.

EU—the European Union, formerly known as the European Economic Community, was begun in the aftermath of World War II, but formalized into the organization in 1993. 28 countries make up this union. The EU abolished formal "borders" between countries, allowing citizens to travel throughout the participating countries to access better jobs and living conditions. In 2016, the United Kingdom exited from the EU, opting to be independent, which caused economic instability in the region.

Export Processing Zone—areas within developing countries that offer incentives and a barrier-free environment to promote economic growth by attracting foreign investment for export-oriented production.

GDP—Gross Domestic Product is the monetary value of all the finished goods and services produced within a country's borders in a specific time period.

Globalization—the development of an increasingly integrated global economy marked especially by free trade, free flow of capital, and the tapping of cheaper foreign labor markets.

Human Rights—legal, ethical, or social principles sometimes expressed as policies or legislation that describe and/or protect rights that are understood to be inalienable, fundamental, and inherent to all human beings regardless of their status. Human rights are considered to be universal invariants such as the right to life, health and well-being, food, and shelter. Further, rights such as education, freedom from enslavement, and political freedom are also considered by many (though not all) to be human rights.

IMF—according to the website, the International Monetary Fund is an organization of 189 countries, working to foster global monetary cooperation, secure financial stability, facilitate international trade, promote high employment and sustainable economic growth, and reduce poverty around the world.

Labor Migration—the movement of people for the purpose of employment, often in the informal sector or sectors vulnerable to abuse and exploitation.

Liberalization—process of relaxing government restrictions. These relaxations of policies can be in social, political, or economic forums.

Mail-Order Brides—a woman brought from another country to be married, usually in return for a payment to a company that makes such arrangements.

Militarization—the process by which a society organizes itself for military conflict and violence.

Military-Industrial Complex—network of individuals and institutions involved in the production of weapons and military technologies. The military-industrial complex in a country typically attempts to marshal political support for continued or increased military spending by the national government.

Modern-Day Slavery—refers to the current phenomena of slavery after the 20th century.

Multinational Corporation—a company that is operating in several different countries, but is usually manages in one "home" country. The corporation usually makes a large amount of its profits from business in various outside countries.

NAFTA—North American Free Trade Agreement refers to the trade agreement between the United States, Mexico, and Canada signed on January 1, 1994.

Nonpersonage—no longer having qualities that would define a human being.

Patriarchy— system of government, society, and culture where men hold all power and decision making (and women are largely excluded). The ideology that men inherently should hold all the power. In patriarchal cultures, familial lines are traced through the male line.

Price Elasticity of Demand—the measure of the change in demand of a product because of the change in price.

Push and Pull factors—socioeconomic, political, cultural, or other forces that force people to migrate to a new location. Push factors are those that drive people to leave their homelands (usually conflict, poverty, natural disaster, etc.). Pull factors are those that attract people to a new location (such as job opportunities, education, quality of living).

ROI—return on investment is a ratio designed to understand the profitability of a commodity.

Social determinants—conditions and contexts into which people live, such as where they are born, grow, live, health, class, culture, religion. Social determinants may shape situations and affect distribution or access to resources.

Structural Adjustment Loan—type of loan provided to developing countries. This loan often creates dependency of developing nations on developed nations and has been widely criticized as creating more poverty instead of alleviating poverty.

Structural Adjustment Program—loans provided by the IMF and the World Bank to countries and regions that are experiencing economic crisis.

Supply and Demand—the amount of a commodity, product, or service available and the desire of buyers for it, considered as factors regulating its price.

Supply Chain—a network between a company and its suppliers to produce and distribute a specific product, and the supply chain represents the steps it takes to get the product or service to the customer.

TIP Report—The Trafficking in Persons (TIP) Report is the U.S. Government's principal diplomatic tool to engage foreign governments on human trafficking.

Trafficking (ensure understanding of no "grab and go" or moving locations)—the recruitment, transportation, transfer, harboring or receipt of persons, by means of the threat or use of force or other forms of coercion, of abduction, of fraud, of deception, of the abuse of power or of a position of vulnerability or of the giving or receiving of payments or benefits to achieve the consent of a person having control over another person, for the purpose of exploitation. Exploitation shall include, at a minimum, the exploitation of the prostitution of others or other forms of sexual exploitation, forced labor or services, slavery or practices similar to slavery, servitude or the removal of organs.

Transnational (Corporations)—operating in or involving more than one country. Unlike other companies that operate in multiple countries, a transnational corporation does not identify any one country as its home base.

Transnational Social Movements—a group of organizations or single organization in multiple countries that are united in fighting for a similar goal or cause.

Transnational social movements are characterized by mobilization of people in a sustained manner for the promotion of social and political change objectives. However, transnational social movements are distinctive in that either or both their activities and their objectives cross national boundaries. Transnational social movements include the work of a subcategory of international nongovernmental organizations—those concerned with political and social transformation, known as "transnational social movement organizations." They also include the work of broader coalitions of transnational social movement organizations, as well as more loosely arranged networks of people promoting political and social transformations beyond the confines of individual states. The range of objectives promoted by transnational social movements is diverse, including democracy, environmentalism, feminism, human rights, labor standards, peace, and religious goals, among others. Academic literature on the topic sheds light on the ways in which social movements organize transnationally, disseminate ideas across borders, shape understandings of global issues, and wield influence in intergovernmental and transnational arenas. Each of these aspects is covered in this bibliography, which focuses specifically on the transnational dimension, since domestic social movements are covered in other *Oxford Bibliographies* articles. While much of the literature on transnational social movements consists of single case analyses, this bibliography pays particular attention to works with wider significance, and to the contrasting perspectives on each of these aspects.

World Bank—international financing group that works to promote developing nations. The organization offers loans to developing countries to promote the goal of ending extreme poverty.

SECTION 2

ABC—Antecedent behavior consequence is a behavioral analysis measuring tool commonly found in the CBT therapy model. ABC measures the events that happen before a behavior and the consequences that follow in an effort to identify behavioral patterns.

Best Practice—commercial or professional procedures that are accepted or prescribed as being correct or most effective.

Biopsychosocial Assessment—The biopsychosocial assessment approach systematically considers biological, psychological, and social factors and their complex interactions in understanding health, illness, and health-care delivery.

Case Management—collaborative process of assessment, planning, facilitation, care coordination, evaluation, and advocacy for options and services to meet an individual's and family's comprehensive health needs through communication and available resources to promote quality, cost-effective outcomes.

CBT—Cognitive behavioral therapy is a psychosocial intervention that is the most widely used evidence-based practice for treating mental disorders.

Collective Impact—framework to tackle deeply entrenched and complex social problems. It is an innovative and structured approach to making collaboration work across government, business, philanthropy, nonprofit organizations, and citizens to achieve significant and lasting social change.

Compassion Fatigue—The emotional residue or strain of exposure to working with those suffering from the consequences of traumatic events. Often referred to as secondary trauma.

CSEC—Commercial sexual exploitation of children is defined as criminal practices that demean, degrade, and threaten the physical and psychosocial integrity of children. There are three primary forms of commercial sexual exploitation of children: prostitution, pornography, and trafficking for sexual purposes.

Cultural Competency—awareness, understanding, and reacting to a variety of cultural variances. It is important in a client/patient relationship.

Cultural Humility—encourages an individual to recognize their biases when working with those from other cultures and backgrounds. It acknowledges that balance of power between individuals to more effectively interact and engage with other cultures and communities.

Cultural Sensitivity—awareness that cultural differences and similarities between people exist without assigning them a value—positive or negative, better or worse, right or wrong.

DST—Domestic sex trafficking (sometimes referred to as CSEC—commercial sexual exploitation of children)

EMDR—Eye movement desensitization and reprocessing is an evidence-based therapy commonly utilized for PTSD. The therapy utilizes various sensory inputs, such as side-to-side eye movements or rapidly flashing lights.

Empowerment Model—theory of human behavior based on the ideology that people have inherent strengths and should build on those strengths. The empowerment model is concerned with awareness raising, building individual and community capacity, and the ability to increase self-efficacy and mastery to create change.

Evidence-Based Practices—is the integration of the best available research with clinical expertise in the context of patient characteristics, culture, and preferences.

Maslow's Hierarchy of Needs—This five-stage model can be divided into basic and psychological needs, which ensure survival (e.g., physiological, safety, love, and esteem) and growth needs (self-actualization). This model has been utilized by traffickers to best manipulate their victims.

Mindfulness—maintaining a moment-by-moment awareness of one's thoughts, feelings, bodily sensations, and surrounding environment.

PTSD—Post-traumatic stress disorder is a disorder that develops in some people who have experienced a shocking, scary, or dangerous event. The disorder can manifest via disrupting thoughts, vivid dreams, feelings, or physical reactions. These symptoms will last for more than a month after the traumatic event.

SAMHSA—The Substance Abuse and Mental Health Services Administration is a branch of the U.S. Department of Health and Human Services.

Self-Care—activities that an individual engages in to relax or attain emotional well-being, such as exercise, meditating, or other enjoyable activities. This is especially important within the context of trauma or secondary trauma.

Strengths Based/Strengths Perspective—social work practice theory that emphasizes people's self-determination and strengths. It is a philosophy and a way of viewing clients as resourceful and resilient in the face of adversity.

Survivor—a person who continues to function or prosper, in spite of opposition, danger, trauma, hardship, or setbacks.

TF–CBT—is an evidence-based treatment for children and adolescents impacted by trauma and their parents or caregivers. Research shows that TF–CBT successfully resolves a broad array of emotional and behavioral difficulties associated with single, multiple, and complex trauma experiences.

Victim—a person harmed, injured, or killed as a result of a crime, accident, or other event or action.

SECTION 3

Act—a formal decision, law, or the like, by a legislature, ruler, court, or other authority; decree or edict; statute; judgment, resolve, or award.

Audit—an official inspection of an individual's or organization's accounts, typically by an independent body.

Bill—a draft of a law presented to a legislature for consideration.

Certification—the confirmation of certain characteristics of an object, person, or organization. This confirmation is often, but not always, provided by some form of external review, education, assessment, or audit.

H1B Visa—a nonimmigrant visa that allows U.S. companies to employ foreign workers in specialty occupations that require theoretical or technical expertise in specialized fields such as in architecture, engineering, mathematics, science, and medicine.

H2B Visa—is a temporary work visa for foreign workers with a job offer for seasonal, non-agricultural work in the United States.

Law—a rule made by the government of a town, state, country, and so forth.

Multisystem Collaboration—group of organizations that are committed to meeting the same goal. Often collaborations are formed between law enforcement, child welfare, and community-based organizations to better serve and meet the needs of the population.

Palermo Protocol—Three protocols that were adopted by the United Nations to supplement the 2000 Convention against Transnational Organized Crime (the Palermo Convention). They are as follows: the Protocol to Prevent, Suppress, and Punish Trafficking in Persons, especially Women and Children the Protocol Against the Smuggling of Migrants by Land, Sea, and Air; and the Protocol Against the Illicit Manufacturing of and Trafficking in Firearms, their Parts and Components, and Ammunition. The convention marks great strides toward fighting transnational crime and identifies those member states in the United Nations who acknowledge the gravity of such crimes.

Policy—a course or principle of action adopted or proposed by a government, party, business, or individual.

Procurement—act of acquiring or buying goods, services, or works from an external source, often via a tendering or bid process.

Safe Harbor Laws—Safe harbor laws were developed by states to address inconsistencies with how children who are exploited for commercial sex are treated. Safe harbor laws are intended to address the inconsistent treatment of children and ensure that these victims are provided with services.

Sanction—a threatened penalty for disobeying a law or rule.

Supply Chain Transparency—The extent to which a company has the information on their suppliers and sourcing locations available and understandable to the public.

T Visa—a visa for those who are or have been victims of human trafficking, which protects victims of human trafficking and allows victims to remain in the United States to assist in an investigation or prosecution of human trafficking.

TVPA—The TVPA, and its reauthorizations in 2003, 2005, and 2008, define a human trafficking victim as a person induced to perform labor or a commercial sex act through force, fraud, or coercion.

U Visa—is a nonimmigrant visa, which is set aside for victims of crimes (and their immediate family members) who have suffered substantial mental or physical abuse and are willing to assist law enforcement and government officials in the investigation or prosecution of the criminal activity.

UNTOC—The United Nations Convention against Transnational Organized Crime is a United Nations–sponsored multilateral treaty against transnational organized crime. The Convention was adopted by a resolution of the United Nations General Assembly on 15 November 2000.

Verification—the establishment by empirical means of the validity of a proposition.

SECTION 4

Abolitionist—someone engaged in the movement to end slavery, whether formal or informal in action.

Activism—the policy or action of using vigorous campaigning to bring about political or social change.

Advocacy—public support for or recommendation of a particular cause or policy.

Agency—action or intervention, especially such as to produce a particular effect.

Awareness Raising—is a form of activism, popularized by U.S. feminists in the late 1960s. It often takes the form of a group of people attempting to focus the attention of a wider group of people on some cause or condition.

Citizenship—the status of a person recognized under the custom or law as being a member of a country.

Disruption—disturbance or problems that interrupt an event, activity, or process.

Ecosystem—community of interacting organisms and their physical environment.

Faith-Based Organizations—a group of individuals united on the basis of religious or spiritual beliefs. Often, faith-based organizations work to promote their religious calls to action through various works of service and social justice movements.

Feminism—theories, concepts, and practices that share common goals of establishing, protecting, and enforcing the political, personal, and social equality and rights of women in society. Feminism is not unidimensional and as such, there are varying definitions and types of feminisms.

Innovation—a new method, idea, product, or intervention that causes impact and disruption to social causes.

Intersectionality—the interconnected nature of social categorizations such as race, class, and gender as they apply to a given individual or group, regarded as creating overlapping and interdependent systems of discrimination or disadvantage.

Intervention—care provided to improve a situation. Often utilized by service providers and clinicians in order to better the lives of their clients.

Microfinance—is a source of financial services for entrepreneurs and small businesses lacking access to banking and related services. This has become popular in developing nations as a way to bring cash flow into building markets and businesses.

NGO—is a not-for-profit organization that is independent from states and international governmental organizations

Prevention—the action of stopping something from happening or arising.

Prototyping—early approximation, sample, or model created to test a concept, process, or innovation.

Safe Space—A place where anyone can relax and be fully self-expressed, without fear of being made to feel uncomfortable, unwelcome, or challenged.

Sex Tourism—the organization of vacations with the purpose of taking advantage of the lack of restrictions imposed on prostitution and other sexual activities by some foreign countries.

Social Enterprise—an organization that applies commercial strategies to maximize improvements in human and environmental well-being.

Superdiversity—used to refer to some current levels of population diversity that are significantly higher than before, coined by sociologist Steven Vertovec in 2007.

Underground Railroad—a network of secret routes and safe houses used by 19th-century enslaved people of African descent in the United States in efforts to escape to free states and Canada with the aid of abolitionists and allies who were sympathetic to their cause.

UNIFEM—The United Nations Development Fund for Women. Since 1976, UNIFEM has been assisting innovative programs and implementing strategies that promote women's human rights, political participation, and economic security.

Wicked Problem—a circumstance or situation that is difficult or impossible to solve because of incomplete, contradictory, and changing requirements that are often difficult to recognize.

References

Abas, M., Ostrovschi, N. V., Prince, M., Gorceag, V. I., Trigub, C., & Oram, S. (2013). Risk factors for mental disorders in women survivors of human trafficking: A historical cohort study. *BMC Psychiatry*, *13*(1), 1.

The Advocates for Human Rights. (n.d.). Sex trafficking, exploitation, and safe harbor training. Retrieved from http://www.theadvocatesforhumanrights.org/safe_harbor_resource_pack

Agence France-Presse. (2015). Isis slave markets sell girls for "as little as a pack of cigarettes," UN envoy says. Retrieved March 10, 2015, from http://www.theguardian.com/world/2015/jun/09/isis-slave-markets-sell-girls-for-as-little-as-a-pack-of-cigarettes-un-envoy-says

Agustín, L. M. (2005). New research directions: the cultural study of commercial sex. *Sexualities*, *8*(5), 618–631.

Albanese, J. (2013). Commercial sexual exploitation of children: What do we know and what do we do about it? Retrieved from https://www.amazon.com/Commercial-Sexual-Exploitation-Children-About/dp/1288843259

Allness, D. J., & Knoedler, W. H. (2003). *A manual for ACT start-up: Based on the PACT model of community treatment for persons with severe and persistent mental illnesses*. Arlington, VA: National Alliance for the Mentally Ill, (NAMI).

Alphabet Profit Margin (Quarterly). (2016). Retrieved February 1, 2016, from https://ycharts.com/companies/GOOG/profit_margin

Alvarez, M. B., & Alessi, E. J. (2012). Human trafficking is more than sex trafficking and prostitution implications for social work. *Affilia*, *27*(2), 142–152.

Amahazion, F. (2015). Human trafficking: The need for human rights and government effectiveness in enforcing anti-trafficking. *Global Crime*, *16*(3), 167–196.

Ambagtsheer, F., Zaitch, D., & Weimar, W. (2013). The battle for human organs: Organ trafficking and transplant tourism in a global context. *Global Crime*, *14*(1), 1–26.

American Psychological Association. (2013). *Post-traumatic stress disorder*. Retrieved from http://www.apa.org/topics/ptsd/

Anda, R.F., Bremner, J.D., Dube, S.R., Felitti, V.J., Giles, W.H., Perry, B.D., Whitfield, C. (2006). The enduring effects of abuse and related adverse experience in childhood: A convergence of evidence from neurobiology and epidemiology. *European Archives of Psychiatry and Clinical Neuroscience, 256*(3), 174–186.

Anderson, B. (2007). *Motherhood, apple pie, and slavery: Reflections on trafficking debates*. Center on Migration, Policy, and Society (Working Paper No. 48). Oxford: University of Oxford.

Andrade, S. (2013). Violence and women in Brazil: What happens indoors stays indoors. Retrieved from http://www.independent.co.uk/voices/comment/violence-and-women-in-brazil-what-happens-indoors-stays-indoors-8809947.html

André, K., & Pache, A. C. (2013). From caring entrepreneur to caring enterprise: Addressing the ethical challenges of scaling up social enterprises. *J Bus Ethics*, 133(4):1–17.

Anjaiah, V. (2013). RI ranks third on SE Asia remittance list. Retrieved from http://www.thejakartapost.com/news/2013/04/29/ri-ranks-third-se-asia-remittance-list.html

Anti-Slavery International. (2010, February 3). Shell makes deal with Cosan in Brazil despite slave labour claims (Press release). Retrieved from www.antislavery.org/english/press_and_news/

news_and_press_releases_2009/030210_shell_makes_deal_with_cosan_despite_slave_labour_claims.aspx

Arciniega, G. M., Anderson, T. C., Tovar-Blank, Z. G., & Tracey, T. J. (2008). Toward a fuller conception of Machismo: Development of a traditional Machismo and Caballerismo Scale. *Journal of Counseling Psychology, 55*(1), 19.

Arredondo, P., & Perez, P. (2003). Expanding multicultural competence through social justice leadership. *The Counseling Psychologist, 31*(3), 282–289.

Arrow Child and Family Ministries. (n.d.-a). Child sex trafficking recovery/freedom place. Retrieved March 31, 2016, from http://www.arrow.org/services-programs/residential-services/freedom-place/

Arrow Child and Family Ministries. (n.d.-b). Child sex trafficking recovery/freedom place: Campus. Retrieved March 31, 2016, from http://www.arrow.org/services-programs/residential-services/freedom-place/campus/

Arrow Child and Family Ministries. (n.d.-c). Child sex trafficking recovery/freedom place: Program. Retrieved March 31, 2016, from http://www.arrow.org/services-programs/residential-services/freedom-place/program/

Asquith, S., & Turner, E. (2008). Recovery and reintegration of children from the effects of sexual exploitation and related trafficking. Geneva: Oak Foundation.

Assembly, U. G. (1948). Universal declaration of human rights. *UN General Assembly*. Retrieved from http://www.un.org/en/universal-declaration-human-rights/

Asset. (2014). Transparency in supply chain act (TISC). Retrieved from https://www.assetcampaign.org/ca-tisc/

Bach, J. M., & Guse, T. (2015). The effect of contemplation and meditation on "great compassion" on the psychological well-being of adolescents. *Journal of Positive Psychology, 10*(4), 359–369.

Baker, M. (1981). *Nam: The Vietnam war in the words of the men and women who fought there*. New York: Morrow.

Bales, K. (1999). *Disposable people: New slavery in a global economy*. Berkeley, CA: University of California Press.

Bales, K. (2000). Expendable people: Slavery in the age of globalization. *Journal of International Affairs, 53*(2); 461.

Bales, K. (2005). *Understanding global slavery: A reader*. Berkeley and Los Angeles: University of California Press.

Bales, K. (2007). *Ending slavery: How we free today's slaves*. Berkeley and Los Angeles: University of California Press.

Barraco, G. (2011). *The impact of new social compliance regulations on U.S. retailers and manufacturers*. Retrieved from www.techexchange.com/library/The%20Impact%20of%20New%20Social%20Compliance%20Regulations%20on%20US%20Retailers%20and%20Manufacturers.pdf

Barrientos, S. (2008). Contract labour: The "Achilles heel" of corporate codes in commercial value chains. *Development and Change, 39*(6), 997–990.

Barrientos, S. (2011). Beyond fair trade: Why are mainstream chocolate companies pursuing social and economic sustainability in cocoa Sourcing. In *Paper to ILO/IFC Better Work Conference*.

Barry, K. (1995). *The prostitution of sexuality: The global exploitation of women*. New York: New York University Press.

Basham, K. (2011). Trauma theories and disorders. In J. Berzoff and L. Flangan (Eds.). *Inside out and outside in: Psychodynamic clinical theory and psychopathology in contemporary multicultural contexts* (p. 440–474). Maryland: Roman and Littlefield Publishing Group, Inc.

Bayer, C., Ball, M., McCoy, M., Reed, S., Trautsch, J., & Xu., J. (2015). Corporate compliance with the California transparency in supply chains act of 2010. Retrieved from www.development international.org

Beber, B., Gilligan, M. J., Guardado, J., & Karim, S. (2015). U.N. peacekeeping and transactional sex. *The Washington Post*. Retrieved from www.washingtonpost.com/news/monkey-cage/wp/2015/06/16/u-n-peacekeeping-and-transactional-sex/

Beck, M. E., Lineer, M. M., Melzer-Lange, M., Simpson, P., Nugent, M., & Rabbitt, A. (2015). Medical providers' understanding of sex trafficking and their experience with at-risk patients. *Pediatrics*, *135*(4), e895–e902.

Bend, D., & King, A. (2014, May 30). Why consider a benefit corporation. *Forbes*. Retrieved from https://www.forbes.com/sites/theyec/2014/05/30/why-consider-a-benefit-corporation/#6549636865e9

Benedict-Nelson, A., Leitner, J., Malham, H., Huang, L.S. (2017). Innovation dynamics: Quick-start guide & online course. [map].

Benedict-Nelson, A. (2016). Problem dynamics teaching guide.

Berg, K. K. (2013). *Cultural factors in the treatment of battered women with privilege: Domestic violence in the lives of white European American, middle-class, heterosexual women*. Los Angeles, CA: SAGE Publications. doi:10.1177/0886109913516448

Bernstein, S., Lebow, R. N., Stein, J. G., & Weber, S. (2000). God gave physics the easy problems: Adapting social science to an unpredictable world. *European Journal of International Relations*, *6*(1), 43–76.

Berthold, S. M. (2015). Rights-based approach to working with torture survivors. In *Human Rights-Based Approaches to Clinical Social Work* (pp. 31–61). Springer International Publishing.

Bhanji, Z. (2008). Transnational corporations in education: filling the governance gap through new social norms and market multilateralism? *Globalisation, Societies and Education*, *6*(1), 55–73.

Bishop, R. A., Morgan, C. V., & Erickson, L. (2013). Public awareness of human trafficking in Europe: How concerned are European citizens? *Journal of Immigrant & Refugee Studies*, *11*(2), 113–135.

Blackie, S. (2017). SBP + greenhouse. Retrieved from https://www.spbovariancancerfoundation.org/Greenhouse.aspx

Bliss, A. (2014). How social innovation labs contribute to transformative change. Retrieved from https://www.rockefellerfoundation.org/blog/how-social-innovation-labs-contribute/

Blue Blindfold. (2012). *Services for victims of child trafficking*. 40. Dublin, Ireland: Department of Justice and Equality.

Boak, A., Ciobanica, L., & Griffin, K. W. (2003). Preventing youth trafficking: Developing an effective information campaign. In A. Boak, A. Boldosser, & O. Biu (Eds.). *Smooth flight: A guide to preventing youth trafficking*. 40–49. Brooklyn: International Organization for Adolescents.

Booth, B. (2016). The world's biggest risk: The victims of the 21st-century slave trade. Retrieved from http://www.cnbc.com/2016/03/03/hr644-bill-passed-to-end-the-150-billion-global-slave-trade.html.

Borjas, G. (2008). *Labor economics*. Boston: McGraw-Hill Irwin.

Bridgespan. (2014). 2014 innovation labs survey. Retrieved from http://www.bridgespan.org/getmedia/d9f734ae-c4f8-4f36-a842-c03b75e4f668/Innovation-Labs-Survey-Data-Summary-2014.pdf.aspx

Bromfield, N. F., & Capous-Desyllas, M. (2012). Underlying motives, moral agendas and unlikely partnerships: The formulation of the U.S. Trafficking in Victims Protection Act through the data and voices of key policy players. *Advances in Social Work*, *13*(2), 243–261.

Briggs, E.C., Brymer, M.J., Gully, K.J., Ippen, C.G., Kim, S., Otrowski, S.A., Steinberg, A.M., (2013). Psychometic properties of the UCLA PTSD reaction index: Part I. *Journal of Traumatic Stress*, *26*(1), 1–9.

Brown, B. (2012). *Daring greatly: How the courage to be vulnerable transforms the way we live, love, parent, and lead*. New York: Gotham Books.

Brown, N. M., Green, J. C., Desai, M. M., Weitzman, C. C., & Rosenthal, M. S. (2014). Need and unmet need for care coordination among children with mental health conditions. *Pediatrics, 133*(3), e530.

Brown, T. L. (2000). *Sex slaves: The trafficking of women in Asia*. London: Virago.

Brown, T. (2008). Design thinking. *Harvard Business Review*, *86*(6), 84.

Brown, T., & Martin, R. (2015, September). Design for Action. *Harvard Business Review, 55–64.*

Brusca, C. (2011). Palermo Protocol: The first ten years after adoption. *Global Security Studies, 2*(3), 1–20.

Buckley, P., Viechnicki, P., & Baruahttp, A. (2016). *A new understanding of millennials: generational differences reexamined.* Deloit University Press. Retrieved from https://dupress.deloitte.com/dup-us-en/economy/issues-by-the-numbers/understanding-millennials-generational-differences.html

Cahill, S.P., & Rauch, S. A. (2003). Treatment and prevention of posttraumatic stress disorder. *Primary Psychiatry, 10*(8), 60–65.

Cain, M., & Howe, A. (Eds.). (2008). *Women, crime and social harm: Towards a criminology for the global age.* Oxford: Hart.

Cajaiba-Santana, G. (2014). Social innovation: Moving the field forward. A conceptual framework. *Technological Forecasting and Social Change, 82,* 42–51.

California Child Welfare Council. (2013). *Ending the commercial sexual exploitation of children: A call for multi-system collaboration in California.* Sacramento, California. Retrieved from http://www.ojjdp.gov/mpg/litreviews/CSECSexTrafficking.pdf

California Legislative Information. Safe Drinking Water and Toxic Enforcement Act of 1986 (Proposition 65). Retrieved from http://leginfo.legislature.ca.gov/faces/codes_displayText.xhtml?lawCode = HSC&division = 20.&title = &part = &chapter = 6.6.&article

Cambodian Women's Association. (1996). *Selling noodles, the traffic in women and children in Cambodia.* Phnom Penh: Cambodian Women's Association.

Campbell, G. (2010). Microfinancing the Developing World: How small loans empower local economies and catalyse neoliberalism's endgame. *Third World Quarterly, 31*(7), 1081–1090.

Campbell, R., Patterson, D., & Lichty, L. F. (2005). The effectiveness of sexual assault nurse examiner (SANE) programs a review of psychological, medical, legal, and community outcomes. *Trauma, Violence, & Abuse, 6*(4), 313–329.

Cardoso, J.B., & Fong, R. (2010). Child human trafficking victims: Challenges for the child welfare system. *Evaluation and Program Planning, 33*(3), 311–316.

Carpenter, A., & Gates, J. (2015). Measuring the nature and extent of gang involvement in sex trafficking in San Diego, executive summary. Retrieved from https://www.ncjrs.gov/App/AbstractDB/AbstractDBDetails.aspx?id = 271387

Carroll, A. B. (2010). Corporate social responsibility. In W. Visser, D. Matten, M. Pohl, & N. Tolhurst (Eds.). *The A-Z of corporate social responsibility*, p. 106–113. West Sussex, England: Wiley. Retrieved from http://www.doleta.gov/agworker/report9/naws_rpt9.pdf

Carroll, D., Samardick, R. M., Bernard, S., Gabbard, S., & Hernández, T. (2005). Findings from the National Agricultural Workers Survey (NAWS) 2001–2002: A demographic and employment profile of United States farm workers. Washington, DC: U.S. Department of Labor.

Cave, D. (2011). Mexico's drug war, feminized. *The New York Times.* Retrieved from http://www.nytimes.com/2011/08/14/sunday-review/mexicos-drug-war-draws-in-women.html?_r = 4

CBIS. (n.d.). *Wyndham creates tools and training to counter child exploitation.* Retrieved from http://cbisonline.com/us/news/wyndham-creates-tools-training-counter-child-exploitation-cbis-continues-fight-human-trafficking/

Center for Missing and Exploited Children. (n.d.). Retrieved May 30, 2016, from http://www.missingkids.org/home

Chahine, S., & Tannir, L. (2010). On the social and financial effects of the transformation of microfinance NGOs. *Voluntas: International Journal of Voluntary and Nonprofit Organizations, 21*(3), 440–461.

Chang, G., & Kim, K. (2007). Reconceptualizing approaches to human trafficking: New directions and perspectives from the field(s). *Stanford Journal of Civil Rights and Civil Liberties, 3*(2).

Chant, S. (2006). *Re-visiting the "feminization of poverty" and the UNDP gender indices: What case for gendered poverty index?* Gender Institute, London School of Economics (Working Paper Issue 18). Retrieved from www.lsc.ac.uk/collections/genderinstitute

Chapkis, W. (1981). *Loaded questions: Women in the military.* Amsterdam: Transnational Institute.

Chemtob, C. M., & Carlson, J. G. (2004). Psychological effects of domestic violence on children and their mothers. *International Journal of Stress Management, 11*(3), 209.

Chicago Alliance Against Sexual Exploitation | Prevention. (n.d.). Retrieved from http://caase.org/prevention

ChildTrauma Academy. (n.d.). *Childtrauma.* Retrieved from http://www.childtrauma.org/

Cho, S. Y., Dreher, A., & Neumayer, E. (2013). Does legalized prostitution increase human trafficking? *World Development, 41,* 67–82.

Chuang, J. (2006). Beyond a snapshot: Preventing human trafficking in the global economy. *Indiana Journal of Global Legal Studies, 13*(1), 137–163.

Chuang, J. (2010). Rescuing trafficking from ideological capture: prostitution reform and anti-trafficking law and policy. *University of Pennsylvania Law Review, 158*(6), 1655–728.

Chuang, J. (2014). Chains of debt: Labor trafficking as a career in China as a construction industry. *Human Trafficking Reconsidered: Rethinking the Problem, Envisioning New Solutions,* 58–68.

Clawson, H. J., & Dutch, N. (2008). *Case management and the victim of human trafficking: A critical service for client success.* Washington, DC: U.S. Department of Health and Human Service, Office of the Assistant Secretary for Planning and Evaluation.

Clawson, H. J., Dutch, N., Solomon, A., & Grace, L. G. (2009). *Human trafficking into and within the United States: A review of the literature.* Washington, DC: Office of the Assistant Secretary for Planning and Evaluation, US Department of Human and Health Services. Retrieved from hhtp://aspe.hhs.gov/hsp/07/HumanTrafficking/LitRev/

Clawson, H. J., & Goldblatt Grace, L. (2007). Finding a path to recovery: Residential facilities for minor victims of domestic sex trafficking. *Human Trafficking: Data and Documents,* 10.

Clawson, H.J., Grace, L.G., & Salomon, A. (2008). *Treating the hidden wounds: Trauma treatment and mental health recovery for victims of human trafficking.* Retrieved from: https://aspe.hhs.gov/basic-report/treating-hidden-wounds-trauma-treatment-and-mental-health-recovery-victims-human-trafficking

Clinton, H. R. (1995). Retrieved February 8, 2016, from http://www.un.org/esa/gopher data/conf/fwcw/conf/gov/950905175653.txt

Clinton Foundation. (n.d.). Commitments to action. Retrieved from https://www.clintonfoundation.org/clinton-global-initiative/about-us/commitments-action

Cloitre, M., Stolbach, B. C., Herman, J. L., Kolk, B.V.D., Pynoos, R., Wang, J., & Petkova, E. (2009). A developmental approach to complex PTSD: Childhood and adult cumulative trauma as predictors of symptom complexity. *J. Traum. Stress, 22*: 399–408. doi:10.1002/jts.20444. Retrieved from http://onlinelibrary.wiley.com/doi/10.1002/jts.20444/abstract;jsessionid = DC127344EF467D124 5E3A0E4F6533EADB.f02t03

Coalition to Abolish Slavery and Trafficking in Los Angeles. (n.d.). *About us.* Retrieved from: http://www.castla.org/training

Cohen, J.A., Kliethermes, M., Mannarino, A.P., & Murray, L.A. (2012). Trauma-focused CBT for youth with complex trauma. *Child Abuse and Neglect, 35*(8), 637–646.

Cohen, J. A., Mannarino, A. P., & Deblinger, E. (2006). *Treating trauma and traumatic grief in children and adolescents.* New York: Guilford Press.

Congressional Research Service (CRS). (2000). Trafficking in women and children: The U.S. and international response. 7. Washington, DC.

Conklin, J. (2005). *Dialogue mapping: Building shared understanding of wicked problems.* Hoboken, NJ: John Wiley & Sons, Inc.

Connecticut Department of Children and Families. (2012). *A child welfare response to domestic minor sex trafficking.* Retrieved from http ://www.ct.gov/dcf/lib/dcf/humantrafficking/pdf/response_to_domestic_minot_sex_trafficking.pdf

Connell, N. M., Jennings, W. G., Barbieri, N., & Reingle Gonzalez, J. M. (2015). Arrest as a way out: Understanding the needs of women sex trafficking victims identified by law enforcement. *Journal of Crime and Justice, 38*(3), 351–10. doi:10.1080/0735648X.2015.1007614.

Cook, J., & Roberts, J. (2000). *Towards a gendered political economy*. UK: Palgrave Macmillan.

Council on Foreign Relations. (n.d.). *Global conflict tracker*. Retrieved from http://www.cfr.org/global/global-conflict-tracker/p32137#!/

Courtois, C.A. (2004). Complex trauma, complex reactions: Assessment and treatment. *Psychotherapy: Theory, research, practice, training, 41*, 412–425.

Cozolino, L. (2010). The neurobiology of attachment. In *The neuroscience of psychotherapy* (2nd ed., p. 213–358). New York: W.W. Norton.

Craig, G. (2013). Sexual trafficking: Modern slavery in the UK. In V. Mishra (Ed.), *Human trafficking: The stakeholders' perspective* (p. 186–197). New Delhi, India: SAGE.

Crane, A. (2013). Modern slavery as a management practice: Exploring the conditions and capabilities for human exploitation. *Academy of Management Review, 38*(1), 49–69.

Creeden, R., Drotar, D., Flannery, D.J., Friedman, S., & Spilsbury, J.C. (2008). Profiles of behavioral problems in children who witness domestic violence. *Violence and Victims, 23*(1), 3–17.

Crethar, H. C., Rivera, E. T., & Nash, S. (2008). In search of common threads: Linking multicultural, feminist, and social justice counseling paradigms. *Journal of Counseling & Development, 86*(3), 269–278.

Crethar, H. C., & Winterowd, C. L. (2012). Values and social justice in counseling. *Counseling and Values, 57*(1), 3–9.

Crossette, B. (1996). When peacekeepers turn into troublemakers. *The New York Times, 7*, 6.

Datta, M. N., & Bales, K. (2012). Slavery is bad for business: Analyzing the impact of slavery on national economies. *Brown J. World Aff., 19*, 205.

David et al. v. Signal International, LLC, 08–1220 (E.D. La, 2008).

Davidson, J. O. C. (2003). British sex tourists in Thailand. *Heterosexual politics*, 42–64.

Davis, K. (2016). Violent gang guilty in racketeering case. *The San Diego Union-Tribune*. Retrieved from http://www.sandiegouniontribune.com/news/2016/mar/11/west-coast-crips-babiez-guilty-rico/

de Chesnay, M. (2013). Sex trafficking as a new pandemic. *Sex trafficking: A clinical guide for nurses*, 3–21.

Deloitte. (2015). The freedom ecosystem: How the power of partnership can help stop modern slavery. Retrieved from http://dupress.com/articles/freedom-ecosystem-stop-modern-slavery/?id = us:2el:3dc:aht:awa:cons:102315

Deloitte. (2016). *The 2016 deloitte millennial survey: Winning over the next generation of leaders*. Retrieved from http://www2.deloitte.com/content/dam/Deloitte/global/Documents/About-Deloitte/gx-millenial-survey-2016-exec-summary.pdf

DeNavas-Walt, C., & Proctor, B. (2015). *Income and poverty in the United States: 2014*. Retrieved February 8, 2016, from https://www.census.gov/content/dam/Census/library/publications/2015/demo/p60-252.pdf

Deshpande, A. (2000). Does caste still define disparity? A look at inequality in Kerala, India. *The American Economic Review, 90*(2), 322–325.

Deshpande, N. A., & Nour, N. M. (2013). Sex Trafficking of Women and Girls. *Reviews in Obstetrics and Gynecology, 6*(1), e22–e27.

Di Nitto, D.M. (1987). *Social welfare: Politics and public policy*. Englewood Cliffs, NJ: Prentice-Hall, Inc.

Dkhar, U. (2015). Devadasi: A Sex Trafficking. Available at SSRN 2696871.

Durchslag, R., & Goswami, S. (2008). Deconstructing the demand for prostitution: Preliminary insights from interviews with Chicago men who purchase sex. *Chicago Alliance Against Sexual Exploitation, 33*.

Durso, L. E., & Gates, G. J. (2012). Serving our youth: Findings from a national survey of services providers working with lesbian, gay, bisexual and transgender youth who are homeless or at risk of becoming homeless. Retrieved from http://escholarship.org/uc/item/80x75033

The Economist. (2016). *Foreign lives: Migrant labour brings enormous economic benefit, and wrenching heartache*. Retrieved from http://www.economist.com/news/asia/21700460-migrant-labour -brings-enormous-economic-benefits-and-wrenching-heartache-foreign-lives

Enloe, C. (2000). *Maneuvers: The international politics of militarizing women's lives*. Berkeley and Los Angeles: University of California Press.

Enrile, A., &. De Castro, W. (2015). Trafficking and modern-day slavery: A case study of the Philippines. In E. Weiss and E. Schott (Eds.), *Transformative Social Work Practice* (p. 437–452). Thousand Oaks, CA: Sage.

Enriquez, J. (n.d.). *The demand side of trafficking and sexual exploitation in the Philippines: Focus on the role of Korean men*. Retrieved from https://catwap.wordpress.com/resources/speeches-papers/the-demand -side-of-trafficking-and-sexual-exploitation-in-the-philippines-focus-on-the-role-of-korean-men/

Errington-Evans, N. (2012). Acupuncture for anxiety. *CNS Neuroscience & Therapeutics, 18*(4), 277–284.

Executive Order No. 13387, 70 FR 60697 (2005).

Fargione, J., Hill, J., Tilman, D., Polasky, S., & Hawthorne, P. (2008). Land clearing and the biofuel carbon debt. *Science, 319*(5867), 1235–1238. doi:10.1126/science.1152747

Farley, M. (2003). Prostitution, trafficking and traumatic stress. *Psychology Press, 2*(3–4).

Farrington, D. P., Gottfredson, D. C., Sherman, L. W., & Welsh, B. C. (2002). The Maryland scientific methods scale. *Evidence-based crime prevention*, 13–21.

Farris, A., Nathan, R. P., & Wright, D. J. (2004). *The expanding administrative presidency: George W. Bush and the faith-based initiative*. Roundtable on Religion and Social Welfare Policy.

Feingold, D. A. (2005). Human trafficking. *Foreign Policy*, 26–32.

Felitti, V. J., & Anda, R. F. (1997). *The Adverse Childhood Experiences (ACE) Study*. Centers for Disease Control and Prevention. Retrieved from http://www.cdc.gov/ace/index.htm.

Fernandez, S. (2014). *San Diego launches anti-trafficking billboard campaign*. Retrieved from http:// www.humanrightsfirst.org/blog/san-diego-launches-anti-trafficking-billboard-campaign

Ferris, E. (2005). Faith-based and secular humanitarian organizations. *International Review of the Red Cross, 87*(858), 311–325.

Figley, C. R. (2013). *Compassion fatigue: Coping with secondary traumatic stress disorder in those who treat the traumatized*. New York: Routledge.

Findlay, M. (2008). *Governing through globalized crime*. Cullompton: Willan.

Frederick, J. (2005). *Guidelines for the operation of care facilities for victims of trafficking and violence against women and girls*. 50. Kathmandu, Nepal: Planete Enfants.

Free the Slaves. (n.d.). Retrieved January 28, 2016, from http://www.freetheslaves.net/about-us/ mission-vision-history/

Freire, P. (2000). *Pedagogy of the oppressed*. New York: Bloomsbury Publishing.

Fry, D. (2007). *How S.A.F.E. is NYC? Sexual assault services in emergency departments*. New York: New York City Alliance Against Sexual Assault.

Fong, R., & Cardoso, J. B. (2010). Child human trafficking victims: Challenges for the child welfare system. *Evaluation and program planning, 33*(3), 311–316.

Fong, R., & Furuto, S. M. (Eds.). (2001). *Culturally competent practice: Skills, interventions, and evaluations*. NJ: Pearson College Division.

Ford. (2013). Forced labor and human trafficking in supply chains. Retrieved from http://corporate .ford.com/microsites/sustainability-report-2012-13/supply-materials-trafficking.html

Friedman, S.A. (2013). ECPAT USA and boys too: Am ECPAT-USA discussion paper about the lack of recognition of the commercial sexual exploitation of boys in the United States. Retrieved from https:// traffickingresourcecenter.org/sites/default/files/And%20Boys%20Too%20-%20ECPAT%20USA.pdf

Funk, M., Oehler, R., & Breakstone, E. (2015). The day government contractor compliance changed: Federal acquisition regulations on human trafficking released. Bloomberg BNA: Federal Contracts Report.

Gallagher, A. (2001a). Human rights and the new UN protocols on trafficking and migrant smuggling: A preliminary analysis. *Human Rights Quarterly, 23*(4), 975–1004.

Gallagher, A. T. (2012). Abuse of a Position of Vulnerability within the International Legal Definition of Trafficking. United Nations Office of Drugs and Crime. Retrieved from http://works.bepress.com/anne_gallagher/47/

Galland, A. (2010). *Toward a safe, just workplace: Apparel supply chain compliance programs*. San Francisco: As You Sow.

gBCAT. (n.d.). *About gBCAT*. Retrieved from http://www.gbcat.org/#about

Gearing, R.E., Hoagwood, K.E., Lee, R., & Schwalbe, C.S.J. (2013). The effectiveness of booster sessions in CBT treatment for child and adolescent mood and anxiety disorders. *Depression and Anxiety, 30*(9), 800–808.

Gebauer, S. (2011a). *Complying with the California transparency in supply chains act 2010*. Corporate Compliance and Ethics Professional, White Paper. Minneapolis, MN: Society of Corporate Compliance and Ethics.

Gee, J. (2014). *The Anti-Trafficking Act: Looking ahead*. Retrieved https://stoptrafficking.sg/2014/11/17/the-anti-trafficking-act-looking-ahead/

Gereffi, G., & Mayer, F. W. (2004). *The demand for global governance*. Terry Sanford Institute of Public Policy Working Paper, Duke University.

Getu, M. (2006). Human trafficking and development: The role of microfinance. *Transformation*, 142–156.

Gibson-Graham, J.K. (2006). *The end of capitalism (as we knew it): A feminist critique of political economy*. With a new introduction. Minneapolis: University of Minnesota Press.

Gilligan, C. (1982). *In a different voice: Psychological theory and women's development*. Cambridge: Harvard University Press.

Giri, V. (1999). *Kanya: Exploitation of little angels*. New Delhi: Gyan.

Girls Educational and Mentoring Services. (n.d.). *Training curriculum*. Retrieved from http://www.gems-girls.org/get-trained/training-curriculum

Girls Not Brides. (n.d.). *Child marriages around the world*. Retrieved from http://www.girlsnotbrides.org/where-does-it-happen/

Goldblatt Grace, L. (2009). Understanding the commercial sexual exploitation of children. *The Link: Connecting Juvenile Justice and Child Welfare, 7,* 1–13.

Gomes, M. (2010, May 19). Clean development mechanism "endorses" expansion of sugarcane. *Reporter Brasil*. Retrieved from www.reporterbrasil.org.br/biofuel/exibe.php?id? = 129

Gozdziak, E. M., & Collett, E. A. (2005). Research on human trafficking in North America: A review of literature. *International Migration, 43*(1–2), 99–128.

Grace, L. G., Starck, M., Potenza, J., Kenney, P. A., & Sheetz, A. H. (2012). Commercial sexual exploitation of children and the school nurse. *The Journal of School Nursing, 28*(6), 410–417.

Greenberg, J., Reiner, K., & Meiran, N. (2012). "Mind the trap": mindfulness practice reduces cognitive rigidity. *PloS one, 7*(5), e36206.

Greenhouse, S. (2014). In Florida tomato fields, a penny buys progress. *The New York Times*. Retrieved from http://www.nytimes.com/2014/04/25/business/in-florida-tomato-fields-a-penny-buys-progress.html?_r = 1

Grewcock, M. (2007). Shooting the passenger: Australia's war on illicit migrants. *Human trafficking*, 178–200.

Gurowitz, A. (2000). Migrant rights and activism in Malaysia: Opportunities and constraints. *The Journal of Asian Studies, 59*(04), 863–888.

H2B temporary worker visa program. (n.d.). Retrieved from http://www.migrationpolicy.org/article/recent-court-decisions-put-sharp-spotlight-us-h-2b-temporary-worker-visa-program

Hall, K. G. (2004). Slavery exists out of sight in Brazil. *Knight Ridder Tribune Business News*, 5.

Harding, S. G. (2004). *The feminist standpoint theory reader: Intellectual and political controversies*. UK: Psychology Press.

Harris, K. (2015). *The California transparency in supply chains act: A resource guide.* Retrieved from http://oag.ca.gov/sites/all/files/agweb/pdfs/sb657/resource-guide.pdf

Harris, M. E., & Fallot, R. D. (2001). *Using trauma theory to design service systems.* New York: Jossey-Bass.

Hassan, S., Miller, D., Phelps, C., & Thomas, R. (n.d.). *Ending the game.* Retrieved from http://ending thegame.com/etg/.

Hayashi, H. (2008). Disputes in Japan over the Japanese military "comfort women" system and its perception in history. *The ANNALS of the American Academy of Political and Social Science, 617*(1), 123–132.

Haynes, K. S., & Mickelson, J. S. (2003). *Affecting change: Social workers in the political arena.* Boston: Allyn & Bacon.

Haynes, D. F. (2014). The celebritization of human trafficking. *The ANNALS of the American Academy of Political and Social Science, 653*(1), 25–45.

Healy, C. (2015). *Targeting vulnerabilities: The impact of the Syrian war and refugee situation on trafficking in persons.* Vienna: ICMPD.

Heffernan, K., & Blythe, B. (2014). Evidence-based practice: Developing a trauma-informed lens to case management for victims of human trafficking. *Global Social Welfare, 1*(4), 169–177.

Heimpel, D. (2014). *Preventive analytics.* Retrieved from https://chronicleofsocialchange.org/featured/preventive-analytics/8384

Heinrich, K. H. (2010). Ten years after the Palermo Protocol: Where are protections for human trafficking? *Human Rights Brief, 18*(1), 1.

Helton, M. (2016). Human trafficking: How a joint task force between health care providers and law enforcement can assist with identifying victims and prosecuting traffickers. *Health Matrix: The Journal of Law-Medicine, 26*, 1.

Hepburn, S., & Simon, R. J. (2013). *Human trafficking around the world: Hidden in plain sight.* NY: Columbia University Press.

Hepworth, D. H., Rooney, R. H., Rooney, G. D., & Strom-Gottfried, K. (2012). Developing resources, organizing, planning, and advocacy as intervention strategies. In *Direct social work practice: Theory and skills* (pp. 439–470). Belmont, CA: Brooks/Cole, Cengage Learning.

Herman, J. L. (2003). Hidden in plain sight: Clinical observations on prostitution. In M. Farley (Ed.), *Prostituion, trafficking, and traumatic stress* (p. 1–16). Binghamton, NY: The Hawthorne Maltreatment and Trauma Press.

Hetter, K. (2012). *Fighting sex trafficking in hotels, one room at a time.* Retrieved from http://www.cnn.com/2012/02/29/travel/hotel-sex-trafficking/

Hewlett Packard (HP). (2011). *California Transparency in Supply Chains Act of 2010: Supply chain responsibility.* Retrieved from www.hp.com/hpinfo/globalcitizenship/society/california-transparency-in-supply-chains-act-of-2010

Hickel, J. (2014). The "girl effect": liberalism, empowerment and the contradictions of development. *Third World Quarterly, 35*(8), 1355–1373.

History World. (n.d.). *Timelines.* Retrieved from http://www.historyworld.net/timesearch/default.asp?conid = timeline&getyear = 0&keywords = %20%20%20Slavery

Hodge, D. R. (2014). Assisting victims of human trafficking: Strategies to facilitate identification, exit from trafficking, and the restoration of wellness. *Social Work, 59*(2), 111-118. doi:10.1093/sw/swu002.

Hoffer, K. M. (2010). A response to sex trafficking Chicago style: Follow the sisters, speak out. *University of Pennsylvania Law Review, 158*(6), 1831–1848.

Hom, K. A., & Woods, S. J. (2013). Trauma and its aftermath for commercially sexually exploited women as told by front-line service providers. *Issues in Mental Health Nursing, 34*(2), 75–81.

Horning, A., Thomas, C., Henninger, A. M., & Marcus, A. (2014). The Trafficking in Persons Report: A game of risk. *International Journal of Comparative and Applied Criminal Justice, 38*(3), 257–280.

Hosseini-Divkolaye, N.S. (2009). *Iran: Migrant smuggling and trafficking in persons*. Refugee Studies Centre of the Oxford Department of International Development, University of Oxford. Retrieved from www.fmreview.org/FMRpdfs/FMR32/66-67.pdf

Hounmenou, C. (2012). Human services professionals' awareness of human trafficking. *Journal of Policy Practice, 11*(3), 192–206.

Howaldt, J., & Schwarz, M. (2010). Social Innovation: Concepts, research fields and international trends. In K. Henning, & F. Hees (Eds.), *Studies for innovation in a modern working environment: International monitoring* (vol. 5). Germany: IMA/ZLW.

Hua, J. (2011). *Trafficking women's human rights*. Minneapolis: University of Minnesota Press.

Hughes, D. M. (2000). The" Natasha" trade: The transnational shadow market of trafficking in women. *Journal of International Affairs*, 625–651.

Hur, M.H. (2006). Empowerment in terms of theoretical perspectives: Exploring a typology of the process and components across disciplines. *Journal of Community Psychology, 34*(5), 523–540.

Hutchinson, E.D. (2013a). Early childhood. In L.W. Charlesworth, & E.D. Hutchinson (Eds.), *Essentials of human behavior: Integrating person, environment, and the life course* (p. 461–500). Thousand Oaks, CA: Sage.

Hutchison, E.D. (2013b). Essentials of human behavior: Integrating person, environment, and the life course (p.17–23). Thousand Oaks, CA: Sage.

Hvistendahl, M. (2011). *Unnatural selection: Choosing boys over girls, and the consequences of a world full of men*. New York: Public Affairs.

ILO (n.d). *Statistics and indicators on forced labour and trafficking*. Retrieved from http://www.ilo.org/global/topics/forced-labour/policy-areas/statistics/lang—en/index.htm

ILO. (2004). *Eliminating the worst forms of child labor*. Jakarta, Indonesia: International Labor Organization.

ILO. (2006). *Child-friendly standards & guidelines for the recovery and integration of trafficked children*. Bangkok, Thailand: ILO.

ILO. (2012a). *Global estimate of forced labour*. Retrieved from www.ilo.org/washington/areas/elimination-of-forced-labor/WCMS_182004/lang-en/index.htm

ILO. (2013). *Domestic workers across the world: Global and regional statistics and the extent of legal protection. Genova*. Retrieved from http://www.ilo.org/wcmsp5/groups/public/—-dgreports/—dcomm/—-publ/documents/publication/wcms_173363.pdf

ILO. (2014). Profits and poverty: The economics of forced labour. Retrieved from http://www.ilo.org/wcmsp5/groups/public/—-ed_norm/—-declaration/documents/publication/wcms_243391.pdf

Institute for Trafficked, Exploited & Missing Persons (ITEMP). (n.d.). Poverty causes human trafficking, new analysis proves. Retrieved February 1, 2016 from http://www.itemp.org/

Interdepartmental Committee on Human Trafficking and Slavery. (2015). *Trafficking in Persons: The Australian Government's Response 1 July 2014–30 June 2015*. Retrieved from https://www.ag.gov.au/CrimeAndCorruption/HumanTrafficking/Documents/Report-Interdepartmental-Committee-Human-Trafficking-Slavery-July-2014-June-2015.PDF

International Justice Mission. (n.d.). How we work. Retrieved March 30, 2016 from https://www.ijm.org/how-we-work

International Society for the Study of Trauma and Dissociation. (2009). Dissociation and Trauma. Retrieved May 30, 2016, from http://www.isst-d.org/

Inter-Parliamentary Union (IPU), & United Nations Office of Drugs and Crime (UNODC). (2009). *Combatting trafficking in persons: A handbook for parliamentarians*. Vienna, Austria. Retrieved from http://www.unodc.org/documents/human-trafficking/UN_Handbook_engl_core_low.pdf

Ito, R. (1992). Japayuki-san Genshoo Saikoo. Re-examination of the Japayuki-san Phenomenon. In T. Iyotani and T. Kajita (Eds.). Global approach, theories on foreign migrant workers. Tokyo: Kobundo. pp. 293–332.

Jackson, S. H. (2007). Marriages of convenience: International marriage brokers, "mail-order brides," and domestic servitude. *University of Toledo Law Review*, *38*(895).

Jamison, E., M. P. H., Herndon, K., Bui, A. G., & Bol, K. (2014). Suicide among first responders in Colorado, 2004-2014: A Summary from the Colorado Violent Death Reporting System.

Jani, N., & Anstadt, S. P. (2013). Contributing factors in trafficking from South Asia. *Journal of Human Behavior in the Social Environment*, *23*(3), 298–311.

Jansson, B. S. (2015). *Social Welfare Policy and Advocacy: Advancing Social Justice through 8 Policy Sectors.* Thousand Oaks, CA: Sage.

Jena, A. K., & Pandey, T. (2012, December). Overview on human trafficking: Snaps of shame. In *National symposia on human trafficking: A violation of human rights–an universal issue.*

Johnson, B.C. (2012). Afterare for survivors of human trafficking. *Social Work and Christianity, 39*(4), 370–389.

Jones, P. (n.d.). The U.S. military and the growth of prostitution in Southeast Asia. Retrieved from http://www.jbu.edu/assets/faculty/resource/file/faculty_profiles/preston_jones/navy_and_asia.pdf

Kabeer, N. (2008). Marriage, motherhood and masculinity in the global economy. *Asia Insights*, (1), 6.

Kamonohashi Project. (n.d.). *About us.* Retrieved from http://www.kamonohashi-project.net/english/about/

Kara, S. (2009). *Sex trafficking: Inside the business of modern slavery. New York*: Columbia University Press.

Kaufman, M. R., & Crawford, M. (2011a). Research and activism review: Sex trafficking in Nepal: A review of intervention and prevention programs. *Violence Against Women*, *17*(5), 651–665.

Kelly, E. (2013). International organ trafficking crisis: solutions addressing the heart of the matter. *BCL Rev.*, *54*, 1317.

Kelly, U. (2010). Intimate partner violence, physical health, posttraumatic stress disorder, depression, and quality of life in Latinas. *Western Journal of Emergency Medicine, 11*(3), 247–251.

Kemp, A., & Raijman, R. (2014). Bringing in state regulations, private brokers, and local employers: A meso-level analysis of labor trafficking in Israel. *International Migration Review*, *48*(3), 604–642.

Kempadoo, K. (2004). *Sexing the Caribbean: gender, race, and sexual labor*. Psychology Press.

Kim, K. (2007). Psychological coercion in the context of modern-day involuntary labor: Revisiting United States v. Kozminski and understanding human trafficking. *University of Toledo Law Review*, *38*(3).

Korićanac, I. (2013). Human trafficking, trauma and psychotherapy. *Human Trafficking Trauma and Psychotherapy Collection of paper*, 13.

Kotiswaran, P. (2011). *Sex work* (p. 11–62). New Delhi: Women Unlimited.

Kristof, N., & WuDunn, S. (2009). *Half the sky: Turning oppression into opportunity for women worldwide. New York*: Random House.

Krulak, C. C. (2016). A call to the next president: "It's time to make human trafficking a top priority." Retrieved from http://www.cnn.com/2016/04/27/opinions/human-trafficking-generation-freedom-krulak/index.html

Kumagai, N. (2014). Asia women's fund revisited. *Asia-Pacific Review, 21*(2), 117-148. doi:10.1080/13439006.2014.978986

Kuo, D. (2006). *Tempting faith: An inside story of political seduction. New York*: Simon and Schuster.

Lan, T., & Pickles, J. (2011). *China's new labour contract law: State regulation and worker rights in global production networks.* Retrieved from https://papers.ssrn.com/sol3/papers.cfm?abstract_id = 1987685

Largoza-Maza, L. (1995). The medium-term Philippine development plan toward the year 2000: Filipino women's issues and perspectives. *Women's rights human rights: International feminist perspectives*, 62–66.

Latonero, M. (2011). Human trafficking online: The role of social networking sites and online classifieds. *Available at SSRN 2045851*. Retrieved from https://papers.ssrn.com/sol3/papers.cfm?abstract_id = 2045851

Lawson, J. E. (1989). "'She's a pretty woman . . . for a gook": The misogyny of the Vietnam War. *Journal of American Culture, 12*(3), 55–65.

Lee, C., Crawford, C., Wallerstedt, D., York, A., Duncan, A., Smith, J., & Jonas, W. (2012). The effectiveness of acupuncture research across components of the trauma spectrum response (tsr): A systematic review of reviews. *Systematic reviews, 1*(1), 1.

Lee, J. K., & Orsillo, S. M. (2014). Investigating cognitive flexibility as a potential mechanism of mindfulness in generalized anxiety disorder. *Journal of Behavior Therapy and Experimental Psychiatry, 45*(1), 208–216.

Lee, M. (2011). *Trafficking and global crime control.* Los Angeles: SAGE.

Lee, M. A., Smith, T. J., & Henry, R. G. (2013). Power politics: Advocacy to activism in social justice counseling. *Journal for Social Action in Counseling and Psychology, 5*(3), 70.

Leung, J. C., & Xu, Y. (2015). *China's social welfare: The third turning point.* NJ: John Wiley & Sons.

Levin, K., Cashore, B., Bernstein, S., & Auld, G. (2012). Overcoming the tragedy of super wicked problems: constraining our future selves to ameliorate global climate change. *Policy Sciences, 45*(2), 123–152.

Levy, A. (2006). *Female chauvinist pigs: Women and the rise of raunch culture.* NY: Simon and Schuster.

Lim, L. L. (Ed.). (1998). *The sex sector: The economic and social bases of prostitution in Southeast Asia.* Geneva: International Labour Organization.

Lloyd, R. (2011). *Girls like us: Fighting for a world where girls are not for sale, an activist finds her calling and heals herself. New York*: HarperCollins.

Long, L. D. (2002). Trafficking in women and children as a security challenge in Southeast Europe. *Southeast European and Black Sea Studies, 2*(2), 53–68.

Looft, C. (2012). After decade of struggle, Brazil Anti-Slave Labor Law moves forward. Sight Crime. Retrieved from InSightCrime—Organized me in the Americas: www.insightcrime.org/news-analysis/after-decade-of-struggle-brazil-anti-slave-labor-law-moves-forward.

Lublin, N., & Ruderman, A. (2015). *The xyz factor: The dosomething.org guide to creating a culture of impact.* Dallas, TX: BenBella Books.

Mace, S. L. (2015). Child trafficking and child welfare: Implications for policy and practice. *Journal of Trafficking, Organized Crime and Security, 1*(2), 47.

Macy, R. J., & Graham, L. M. (2012). Identifying domestic and international sex-trafficking victims during human service provision. *Trauma, Violence, & Abuse, 13*(2), 59–76.

Macy, R. J., & Johns, N. (2010). Aftercare services for international sex trafficking survivors: Informing U.S. service and program development in an emerging practice area. *Trauma, Violence, & Abuse, 12,* 87–98.

Madigan, S. (2011). *Narrative therapy.* Worcester, MA: American Psychological Association.

Manzo, K. (2005). Modern slavery, global capitalism and deproletarianisation in West Africa. *Review of African Political Economy, 32*(106), 521–534.

Marosi, R. (2014). Desperate workers on a Mexican mega-farm: "They treated us like slaves." *Los Angeles Times.* Retrieved from http://graphics.latimes.com/product-of-mexico-labor/

Marr, A. (2012). Effectiveness of rural microfinance: what we know and what we need to know. *Journal of Agrarian Change, 12*(4), 555–563.

Martin, R. J. (2009). *How to be a pimp using Maslow's hierarchy of human needs to make the most money.* Retrieved from www.associatedcontent.com/article/75184/how_to_be_a_pimp_using_maslows_hierarchy.html?cat = 7.

Martin, R. J. (Richard J.), & Sterry, D.(2009). *Hos, hookers, call girls, and rent boys: Professionals writing on life, love, money, and sex.* Brooklyn :[S.l.]: Soft Skull Press ;Distributed by Publishers Group West.

Martinez, M. (2011). *Hotel chain boosts staff training to fight child prostitution.* Retrieved from http://thecnnfreedomproject.blogs.cnn.com/2011/08/01/hotel-chain-boosts-staff-training-to-fight-child-prostitution/

Martinez, O., & Kelle, G. (2013). Sex trafficking of LGBT individuals: A call for service provision, research, and action. *The International Law News, 42*(4).

Mayer, F., & Pickles, J. (2009). *Governance and implications for decent work in apparel global value chains.* Geneva: Institute for International Labor Studies, International Labor Organisation (ILO).

McClain, N. M., & Garrity, S. E. (2011). Sex trafficking and the exploitation of adolescents. *Journal of Obstetric, Gynecologic, & Neonatal Nursing, 40*(2), 243–252.

McCurry, J. (2009). Japan's yakuza gangsters swot up on the law. *The Guardian*, 26.

McGrath, S. (2013). Fuelling global production networks with slave labour: Migrant sugar cane workers in the Brazilian ethanol GPN. *Geoforum, 44*, 32–43.

Merriam-Webster. (n.d.). *Work.* Retrieved from http://www.merriam- webster.com/dictionary/work

Meyer, L. D. (1996). *Creating GI Jane: Sexuality and power in the women's army corps during World War II.* New York: Columbia University Press.

Mezzacappa, E., Kindlon, D., & Earls, F. (2001). Child abuse and performance task assessments of executive functions in boys. *Journal of Child Psychology & Psychiatry & Allied Disciplines, 42*, 1041–1048.

Mill, J.S. (2004). *Principles of political economy.* Amherst, NY: Prometheus Books.

Mishra, V. (2013). Introduction: Perspective, cause, and effect of human trafficking. In V. Mishra (Ed.), *Human trafficking: The stakeholders' perspective* (p. 1–22). New Delhi, India: SAGE Publications.

Modi, M. N., Palmer, S., & Armstrong, A. (2014). The role of Violence Against Women Act in addressing intimate partner violence: A public health issue. *Journal of Women's Health, 23*(3), 253–259.

Mohanty, C. (2004). Cartographies of struggle: Third World women and the politics of feminism. In *Feminism without borders: Decolonizing theory, practicing solidarity* (pp. 43–84). Durham: Duke University Press.

Moon, Y. E., Norton, M. I., & Chen, D. (2008). (PRODUCT) RED (A). Harvard Business School Supplement, 509–014.

Moran, B. (2015). Sex abuse scandals cast shadow over UN peacekeeping summit. Retrieved February 8, 2016, from http://america.aljazeera.com/articles/2015/9/28/sex-abuse-scandals-cast-shadow-over-un-peacekeeping-summit.html

Moser, K. (2012). Prevention, prosecution, and protection: A look at the United States' Trafficking Victims Protection Act. *International Journal of Business and Social Science, 3*(6).

Munro, V. E. (2008). Of rights and rhetoric: Discourses of degradation and exploitation in the context of sex trafficking. *Journal of Law and Society, 35*(2), 240–264.

Muraya, D. N., & Fry, D. (2016). Aftercare services for child victims of sex trafficking: A systematic review of policy and practice. *Trauma, Violence, & Abuse, 17*(2), 204–220. doi:10.1177/1524838015584356.

Murphy, L. (2014). *Survivors of slavery: Modern-day slave narratives.* New York: Columbia University Press.

Najavits, L. M. (1993). Seeking safety: A new psychotherapy for posttraumatic stress disorder and substance use disorder. In P. Ouimette & P. Brown (Eds.), *Trauma and Substance Abuse: Causes, Consequences, and Treatment of Comorbid Disorders.* Washington, DC: Americal Psychological Association Press.

Najavits, L. M. (2002). *Seeking safety: A treatment manual for PTSD and substance abuse.* NY: Guilford Press.

National Alliance on Mental Illness. (2012). *Cognitive behavior therapy.* Retrieved from: http://www2.nami.org/Content/NavigationMenu/Inform_Yourself/About_Mental_Illness/About_Treatments_and_Supports/Cognitive_Behavioral_Therapy1.html

National Child Traumatic Stress Network. (2003). *Complex trauma in children and adolescents.* Retrieved from http://www.nctsnet.org/sites/default/files/assets/pdfs/ComplexTrauma_All.pdf

National Congress on State Legislature. (2014). Human trafficking crimes against children: States respond. Retrieved from http://www.ncsl.org/documents/summit/summit2014/onlineresources/ Human_trafficking_document_Summit_Handout.pdf

National Council of Jewish Women. (n.d.). *Exodus: NCJW's anti-sex trafficking initiative*. Retrieved from http://www.ncjw.org/trafficking/

National Human Trafficking Resource Center. (n.d.-b). *Outreach and awareness*. Retrieved from https:// traffickingresourcecenter.org/get-involved/outreach-and-awareness

National Survivor Network. (2011). Retrieved from http://nationalsurvivornetwork.org/

National Survivor Network. (2017). National survivor network: Background. Retrieved from http:// nationalsurvivornetwork.org/

Nawyn, S. J., & Birdal, N. B. K. (2014). Counter-trafficking policy and immigrant rights in Turkey. *Insight Turkey*, *16*(4), 77.

Neumeier, S. (2012). Why do social innovations in rural development matter and should they be considered more seriously in rural development research? Proposal for a stronger focus on social innovations in rural development research. *Sociologia Ruralis*, *52*(1), 48–69.

Newell, J. M., & MacNeil, G. A. (2010). Professional burnout, vicarious trauma, secondary traumatic stress, and compassion fatigue. *Best Practices in Mental Health*, *6*(2), 57–68.

Nghiem, A. (2013). *Singapore bus death triggers riot*. Retrieved from http://www.bbc.com/news/world -asia-25294918

Niemi, J. (2010). What we talk about when we talk about buying sex. *Violence Against Women*, *16*(2), 159–172.

Nilsson, J. E., Schale, C. L., & Khamphakdy-Brown, S. (2011). Facilitating trainees' multicultural development and social justice advocacy through a refugee/immigrant mental health program. *Journal of Counseling and Development: JCD*, *89*(4), 413.

Nitto, D.M. (2011). *Social welfare: Politics and public policy* (7th ed.). Boston: Allyn & Bacon.

Norcross, J. C., Krebs, P. M., & Prochaska, J. O. (2011). Stages of change. *Journal of Clinical Psychology*, *67*(2), 143–154.

Norton-Hawk, M. (2002). The lifecourse of prostitution. *Women, Girls & Criminal Justice*, *3*(1), 7–9.

O'Brien, E. (2013). Ideal victims in trafficking awareness campaigns. In *Crime, Justice and Social Democracy* (pp. 315–326). UK: Palgrave Macmillan.

OECD. (n.d.). OECD Guidelines for Multinational Enterprises: Responsible business conduct matters. Retrieved from https://mneguidelines.oecd.org/mneguidelines_rbcmatters.pdf

Office of High Commissioner for Human Rights (OHCHR). (2009). *2009 Report on activities and results*. Retrieved from http://www.ohchr.org/Documents/Publications/I_OHCHR_Rep_2009_complete_ final.pdf

Oko, J. (2006). Evaluating alternative approaches to social work: A critical review of the strengths perspective. *Families in Society*, *87*(4), 601–611.

Olive Crest. (2015). Safe families for children. Retrieved March 29, 2016 from http://www.olivecrest .org/safe-families/

O'Neill, D. Human trafficking: The global issue in your backyard. Retrieved from: http://www.coca -colacompany.com/stories/human-trafficking-the-global-issue-in-your-backyard

Oppliger, P. A. (2008). *GIRLS GONE SKANK: The sexualization of girls in American culture*. North Carolina: McFarland & Company.

Orlans, M., & Levy, T. M. (2014). *Attachment, trauma, and healing: Understanding and treating attachment disorder in children, families and adults*. London: Jessica Kingsley Publishers.

Organization for Security and Co-Operation in Europe. (2010). *Unprotected work, invisible exploitation: Trafficking for the purpose of domestic servitude*. Research paper on trafficking in human beings for domestic servitude in the OSCE Region: Analysis and Challenges, Vienna: OSCE Office of the

Special Representative and Coordinator for Combating Trafficking in Human Beings. Retrieved from http://ftsblog.net/wp-content/uploads/2011/02/Unprotected-Work-Invisible-Epxplitation.pdf

Ottaviani, C., Watson, D. R., Meeten, F., Makovac, E., Garfinkel, S. N., & Critchley, H. D. (2016). Neurobiological substrates of cognitive rigidity and autonomic inflexibility in generalized anxiety disorder. *Biological Psychology, 119*, 31–41.

Outshoorn, J. (2001). Debating prostitution in Parliament: A feminist analysis. *European Journal of Women's Studies, 8*(4), 472–490.

Outshoorn, J. (2012). Policy change in prostitution in the Netherlands: from legalization to strict control. *Sexuality Research and Social Policy, 9*(3), 233–243.

Overs, C. (2009, March 12–14). "Ain't I a woman"—A global dialogue between sex workers' rights movement and the stop the violence against women movement Bangkok, Thailand." Melbourne: The Paulo Longo Research Initiative, Department of Epidemeology and Preventative Medicine Monash University, Aifred Hospital Campus.

Oviasuyi, P. O., Ajagun, S. O., & Isiraoje, L. (2011). Fetish Oath Taking in Nigerian Politics and Administration: Bane of Development." *Journal of Social Science, 27(3)*, 193–200.

Padgett, T. & Ghosh, B. (2010). Human predators stalk Haiti's vulnerable kids. *Time.* Retrieved from http://content.time.com/time/specials/packages/article/0,28804,1953379_1953494_1957160,00.html

Panchal, T. J. (2013). Immoral women or victims? Prostitution in India. In V. Mishra (Ed.), *Human trafficking: The stakeholders' perspective*. New Delhi, India: SAGE Publications.

Passas, N. (2000). Global anomie, dysnomie, and economic crime: Hidden consequences of neoliberalism and globalization in Russia and around the world, *Social Justice,* 27(2): 16–45

Patkar, P. (2013). Civil society initiative of a decade against human trafficking. In V. Mishra (Ed.). Human trafficking: *The stakeholders' perspective* (p. 25–53). New Delhi, India: SAGE Publications.

Patomäki, H. (2006). Realist ontology for futures studies. *Journal of Critical Realism, 5*(1), 1–31.

Pearce, J., Hynes, P., & Bovarnick, S. (2009). *Breaking the wall of silence*. London: NSPCC.

Pearlman, L. A., & Courtois, C. A. (2005). Clinical applications of the attachment framework: Relational treatment of complex trauma. *Journal of Traumatic Stress, 18*(5), 449–459.

Perry, B. D. (2007). *Maltreated children: Experience, brain development and the next generation*. New York: W. W. Norton & Co.

Perry, B. D., Pollard, R. A., Blakley, T. L., Baker, W. L., & Vigilante, D. (1995). Childhood trauma, the neurobiology of adaptation, and use-dependent development of the brain: How states become traits. *Infant Mental Health Journal, 16*(4), 271–291.

Perry, K. M., & McEwing, L. (2013). How do social determinants affect human trafficking in Southeast Asia, and what can we do about it? A systematic review. *Health Hum Rights, 15*(2), 138–59.

Pickles, J., & Zhu, S. (2013). The California transparency in supply chains act. Retrieved from https://poseidon01.ssrn.com/delivery.php?ID = 7771190810901141161260011230690790291170460250680040100661171070280061081041021211190290350550090080440051040961171270280101251060710600230141270681030651060920800280310520511130661181000251110210990660920971191250641000080000930640720830020880840200948&EXT = pdf

Piper, N. (n.d.). Migrant labor in southeast Asia. *Country study: Singapore*. Singapore: Asia Research Institute. Retrieved from http://www.fes.de/aktuell/focus_interkulturelles/focus_1/documents/8_000.pdf

Piper, N. (2001). Transnational women's activism in Japan and Korea: the unresolved issue of military sexual slavery. *Global Networks, 1*(2), 155–170.

Piper, N., & Uhlin, A. (2002). Transnational advocacy networks, female labor migration and trafficking in East and Southeast Asia: A gendered analysis of opportunities and obstacles. *Asian and Pacific Migration Journal, 11*(2), 171–195.

Pitts, M.K., Smith, A.M.A., Grierson, J., O'Brien, M., & Misson, S. (2004, August). Who pays for sex and why? An analysis of social and motivational factors associated with male clients of sex workers. *Arch Sex Behav (2004) 33:353. doi: 10.1023/B:ASEB.0000028888.48796.4f*

Plan International. (2005). *Growing up in Asia: Plan's strategic framework for fighting child poverty in Asia*. Bankok: Plan International.

Plant, R. (2008). Forced labor: Critical issues for U.S. business leaders. In Background paper prepared for conference on Engaging Business: Addressing Forced Labor, Atlanta, Georgia.

Polaris Project. (2014). *Child trafficking and the child welfare system*. Retrieved from https://polaris project.org/sites/default/files/Child%20Welfare%20Fact%20Sheet.pdf

Polaris Project (2015a). *Current Federal Laws*. Retrieved from http://www.polarisproject.org/what -we-do/policy-advocacy/national-policy/current-federal-laws

Polaris. (2015b). *Recognize the signs*. Retrieved from https://polarisproject.org/recognize-signs

Poston, B. (2009). An exercise in persons: Maslow's hierarchy of needs. *The Surgical Technologist* 347–353. Retrieved from http://www.ast.org/pdf/308.pdf

Prabhakaran, P. (2013). Globalization, sexuality, and human trafficking. *Human Trafficking: The Stakeholders' Perspective*, 67.

Rafferty, Y. (2013). Child trafficking and commercial sexual exploitation: A review of promising prevention policies and programs. *American Journal of Orthopsychiatry*, *83*(4), 559–575.

Raimi, L. (2012). Faith-based advocacy as a tool for mitigating human trafficking in Nigeria. *Humanomics*, *28*(4), 297–310.

Ramberg, L. (2011). When the devil is your husband: Sacred marriage and sexual economy in South India. *Feminist Studies*, *37*(1), 28–60.

Rank, M. R. (2004). *One nation, underprivileged: Why American poverty affects us all*. UK: Oxford University Press.

Raphael, D. (2006). Social determinants of health: present status, unanswered questions, and future directions. *International Journal of Health Services*, *36*(4), 651–677.

Raphael, J. (2004). *Listening to Olivia: Violence, poverty, and prostitution*. Boston, MA: Northeastern University Press.

Rashid, T. (2015). Positive psychotherapy: A strength-based approach. *The Journal of Positive Psychology*, *10*(1), 25–40.

Ray, N. (2007). Wither childhood? Child trafficking in India. *Social Development Issues*, *29*(3), 72–83.

Raymond, J. G. (2002). The new UN trafficking protocol. *Women's Studies International Forum*, *25*(5), 491–502.

Raymond, J. G. (2004). Prostitution on demand legalizing the buyers as sexual consumers. *Violence Against Women*, *10*(10), 1156–1186.

Reauthorization, V.P. (2008). William Wilberforce Trafficking Victims Protection Reauthorization Act of 2008. *Public law*, *110*, 457.

Refugee Camps. (n.d.). Retrieved February 1, 2016, from http://www.burmalink.org/background/ thailand-burma-border/displaced-in-thailand/refugee-camps/

Richard, A. O. (1999). *International trafficking in women to the United States: A contemporary manifestation of slavery and organized crime*. Washington, DC: Bureau of Intelligence and Research.

Ridder, K. (2015). 7 Christian groups working to end human trafficking, *Newsmax*. Retrieved from http:// www.newsmax.com/FastFeatures/christians-human-trafficking-humanitarian-organizations/ 2015/10/27/id/634700/.

Rigby, P., Malloch, M., & Hamilton-Smith, N. (2012). A report on child trafficking and care provision: Towards better survivor care. *Love, 146*.

Ritchey, T. (2013). Wicked problems: Modelling social messes with morphological analysis. *Acta Morphologica Generalis*, *2*(1), 1–8.

Rittel, H. W., & Webber, M. M. (1973). Dilemmas in a general theory of planning. *Policy Sciences*, *4*(2), 155–169.

Roe-Sepowitz, D. E., Hickle, K. E., Dahlstedt, J., & Gallagher, J. (2014). Victim or whore: The similarities and differences between victim's experiences of domestic violence and sex trafficking. *Journal of Human Behavior in the Social Environment*, *24*(8), 883–898.

Royal Thai Government. (2008). Thailand Anti-Trafficking in Persons Act B.E. 2551. Retrieved from http://www.refworld.org/docid/4a546ab42.html

RT. (2016). *Okinawans protest murder by ex-marine ahead of Obama's Japan visit*. Retrieved from https://www.rt.com/usa/344133-okinawa-rape-protest-american/

Ryan, C., & Jethá, C. (2012). *Sex at dawn: How we mate, why we stray, and what it means for modern relationships*. New York: Harper Collins.

Sachs, J. D. (2006). *The end of poverty: Economic possibilities for our time*. London: Penguin.

Safe Families for Children. (n.d.-a). *About*. Retrieved from http://safe-families.org/about/

Salahudeen, A. K., Woods, H. F., Pingle, A., Suleyman, M. N. E. H., Shakuntala, K., Nandakumar, M., . . . & Daar, A. S. (1990). High mortality among recipients of bought living-unrelated donor kidneys. *The Lancet*, *336*(8717), 725–728.

Salesforce. (2016). *About*. Retrieved from http://www.salesforce.org/about-us/

SAMHSA. (2014). *Preventing Suicide: Following up after the crisis*. Retrieved from http://www.samhsa .gov/samhsaNewsLetter/Volume_22_Number_2/index.html

Samuels, G. M., & Ross-Sheriff, F. (2008). Identity, oppression, and power: Feminisms and intersectionality theory. *Affilia*, *23*(1), 5–9. doi:10.1177/0886109907310475.

Sanghera, J. (2005). Unpacking the trafficking discourse. In K. Kempadoo (Ed.), *Trafficking and prostitution reconsidered: New perspectives on migration, sex work, and human rights* (p. 3–24). Boulder, CO: Paradigm.

Santa Marta Group. (n.d). *About*. Retrieved from http://santamartagroup.com/about-santa-marta-group/

Satyarthi, K. (2013). Trafficking of children: Causes and possible solutions. In V. Mishra (Ed.), *Human trafficking: The stakeholders' perspective* (p. 101–113). New Delhi, India: SAGE Publications.

Saulnier, C.F. (1996). *Feminist theories and social work: Approaches and applications*. Haworth Press.

Scheper-Hughes, N. (2001). Commodity fetishism in organs trafficking. *Body & Society*, *7*(2–3), 31–62. doi:10.1177/1357034X0100700203

Schott, E., & Weiss, E. (2016). *Transformative social work practice*. Thousand Oaks, California: SAGE.

Sharma, N. (2003). Travel agency: A critique of anti-trafficking campaigns. *Refuge: Canada's Journal on Refugees*, *21*(3).

Sharp, G. (2012). *From dictatorship to democracy: A conceptual framework for liberation*. New York: The New Press.

Sheldon-Sherman, J. A. (2012). Missing p: Prosecution, prevention, protection, and partnership in the Trafficking Victims Protection Act. *Penn State Law Review*, *117*(443).

Shelley, L., Picarelli, J., & Corpora, C. (2003). Global crime Inc. In M.C. Love (Eds.), *Beyond sovereignty: Issues for a global agenda* (pp. 143–166). Wadsworth. Retrieved from http://traccc.gmu.edu/pdfs/ publications/transnational_crime_publications/shelle72.pdf.

Shigekane, R. (2007). Rehabilitation and community integration of trafficking survivors in the United States. *Human Rights Quarterly*, *29*(1), 112–136. doi: 10.1353/hrq.2007.0011

Shimazono, Y. (2007). The state of the international organ trade: a provisional picture based on integration of available information. *Bulletin of the World Health Organization*, *85*(12), 955–962.

Simchi-Levi, D., & Zhao, Y. (2005). Safety stock positioning in supply chains with stochastic lead times. *Manufacturing & Service Operations Management*, *7*(4), 295–318. doi:10.1287/msom.1050.0087

Skinner, E. B. (2008). *A crime so monstrous: Face-to-face with modern-day slavery*. New York: Simon and Schuster.

Smith, K. T., Smith, M., & Wang, K. (2010). Does brand management of corporate reputation translate into higher market value? *Journal of Strategic Marketing, 18*(3), 201–221.

Smith, S. D., Reynolds, C. A., & Rovnak, A. (2009). A critical analysis of the social advocacy movement in counseling. *Journal of Counseling and Development: JCD, 87*(4), 483.

Smith, W. K., Gonin, M., & Besharov, M. L. (2013). Managing social-business tensions: A review and research agenda for social enterprise. *Business Ethics Quarterly, 23*(03), 407–442.

Soderlund, G. (2005). Running from the rescuers: New U.S. crusades against sex trafficking and the rhetoric of abolition. *NWSA Journal, 17*(3), 64–87.

Spindel, C., Levy, E., & Connor, M. (2000). With an end in sight. Strategies from the UNIFEM Trust Fund to Eliminate Violence Against Women. Washington, DC: United Nations development fund for women.

Steinberg, A.M., Brymer, M.J., Kim, S., Briggs, E.C., Ippen, C.G., . . . Pynoos, R.S. (2013). Psychometric properties of the UCLA PTSD reaction index: Part I. *Journal of Traumatic Stress, 26*(1), 1–9.

Sterry, D. (2009). In R. J. Martin (Ed.), *Hos, hookers, call girls, and rent boys: Professionals writing on life, love, money, and sex* (p. 27–32). Brooklyn, NY: Soft Skulls Press.

Stromquist, N. P., & Monkman, K. (2014). Defining globalization and assessing its implications for knowledge and education, revisited. In N. P. Stromquist & K. Monkman (Eds.) *Globalization and education: Integration and contestation across cultures* (pp.1–38). Lanham, MD: R&L Education.

Sturdevant, S. P., & Stoltzfus, B. (1992). *Let the good times roll: Prostitution and the U.S. military in Asia.* New York: New Press.

Summers, N. (2015). *Fundamentals of case management practice: Skills for the human services.* Toronto: Nelson Education.

Sutter, J.D. (2012). Slavery's last stronghold. Retrieved from http://edition.cnn.com/interactive/2012/03/world/mauritania.slaverys.last.stronghold/.

Swart, D. (2011). Problems surrounding the combating of women and child trafficking in Southern and South Africa. *South African Professional Society on the Abuse of Children Child Abuse Research: A South African Journal, 12*(1), 26–37.

Swart, D. (2012). Human trafficking and the exploitation of women and children in a Southern and South African context. *Child Abuse Research in South Africa, 13*(1), 62–73.

Swink, M., Melnyk, S. A., Cooper, M. B., & Hartley, J. L. (2011). *Managing operations across the supply chain.* New York: McGraw-Hill Irwin.

Sykiotou, A. (2013). *Cybercrime and human trafficking.* Retrieved from http://www.vidc.org/index .php?id = 1745&L = 1&id = 1745

Thorat, S., & Neuman, K. S. (2012). *Blocked by caste: economic discrimination in modern India.* UK: Oxford University Press.

Todres, J. (1999). Prosecuting sex tour operators in U.S. Courts in an effort to reduce the sexual exploitation of children globally. *Boston University Public Interest Law Journal, 9*, 1–23.

Trafficking and Violence Protection Act of 2000, Public Law No. 106–386 (2000).

Trauma-Informed Care. (n.d.). Retrieved from http://www.ahrq.gov/professionals/prevention-chronic -care/healthier-pregnancy/preventive/trauma.html

Trotz, A. (2007). Red Thread: the politics of hope in Guyana. *Race & Class, 49*(2), 71–79.

Turner, S. G., & Maschi, T. M. (2015). Feminist and empowerment theory and social work practice. *Journal of Social Work Practice, 29*(2), 151–162.

Twigg, N. M. (2012). A description of services provided by U.S. rehabilitation centers for domestic sex trafficking survivors (Doctoral dissertation, University of St. Francis).

Ugarte, M. B., Zarate, L., & Farley, M. (2004). Prostitution and trafficking of women and children from Mexico to the United States. *Journal of Trauma Practice, 2*(3–4), 147–165.

UNIAP. (2008). *The trafficking situation in China.* Retrieved from the United Nations Inter-Agency Project on Human Trafficking: www.no-trafficking.org/china.html

UNICEF. (2005). *The true extent of child trafficking*. London: UNICEF.

UNICEF. (2001). *Profiting from abuse: An investigation into the sexual exploitation of our children*. New York: UNICEF.

UNICEF. (2012). *The state of the world's children*. New York: UNICEF.

United Nations Development Fund for Women (UNIFEM). (2000). *Progress of the world's women 2000*. UNIFEM Biennial Report. Retrieved from http://iknowpolitics.org/sites/default/files/progress_of_the_world_s_women_2000.pdf

United Nations Development Fund for Women (UNIFEM). (2011). *Investing in gender equality: Ending violence against women and girls*. Retrieved from http://www.endvawnow.org/uploads/browser/files/genderequality_vaw_leaflet_en_web.pdf

United Nations Development Program (UNDP). (2005) *Human development report*. New York: UNDP.

United Nations Entity for Gender Equality and the Empowerment of Women (UNEGEEW). (2009). *Convention on the elimination of all forms of discrimination against women*. Retrieved February 8, 2016, from http://www.un.org/womenwatch/daw/cedaw/

United Nations Fourth World Conference on Women Secretariat. (1995). Proceedings from U.N. Fourth World Conference on Women '95: *First Lady Hillary Rodham Clinton Remarks for the United Nations Fourth World Conference on Women*. Beijing, China

United Nations of Human Rights Office of the High Commissioner. (2017). *Conventions on the rights of the child*: Adopted and opened for signature, ratification and accession by general assembly resolution 44/25 of 20 November 1989, entry into force 2 September 1990, in accordance with article 49. Retrieved from http://www.ohchr.org/EN/ProfessionalInterest/Pages/CRC.aspx

United Nations of Human Rights Office of the High Commissioner. (2017). *International covenant on civil and political rights*: Adopted and open for signature, ratification and accession by general assembly resolution 2200A (XXI) of 16 December 1966 entry into force 23 March 1976, in accordance with article 49. Retrieved from http://www.ohchr.org/EN/ProfessionalInterest/Pages/CCPR.aspx

United Nations Office of the High Commissioner. (n.d.). Special Rapporteur on trafficking in persons, especially women and children. Retrieved from http://www.ohchr.org/EN/Issues/Trafficking/Pages/TraffickingIndex.aspx

United Nations Office on Drugs and Crime (UNODC). (2004). *United nations convention against transnational organized crime and the protocols thereto*. New York: UNODC. Retrieved from http://www.unodc.org/documents/treaties/UNTOC/Publications/TOC%20Convention/TOCebook-e.pdf

United Nations Office on Drugs and Crime (UNODC). (2009). *Global Report on Trafficking in persons*. Retrieved from http://www.unodc.org/documents/Global_Report_on_TIP.pdf

United Nations Office of Drugs and Crime (UNODC). (2010). *Toolkit to combat smuggling of migrants: Understanding the smuggling of migrants*. 1. New York: United Nations. https://www.unodc.org/documents/human-trafficking/SOM_Toolkit_E-book_english_Combined.pdf

United Nations Office on Drugs and Crime (UNODC). (2012). *Global report on trafficking in persons*. Vienna, Austria: UNODC.

United Nations Office on Drugs and Crime (UNODC). (2014). *Global report of trafficking in persons*. Vienna. Retrieved from https://www.unodc.org/documents/data-and-analysis/glotip/GLOTIP_2014_full_report.pdf

United Nations Office on Drugs and Crime. (UNODC). (2015). *The role of recruitment fees and abusive and fraudulent practices of recruitment agencies in trafficking in persons*. Vienna: UNODC. Retrieved from http://www.unodc.org/documents/human-trafficking/2015/Recruitment_Fees_Report-Final-22_June_2015_AG_Final.pdf

United Nations Office on Drugs and Crime (UNODC). (2015). *Trafficking in persons for the purpose of organ removal*. Vienna: UNODC. Retrieved from https://www.unodc.org/documents/human-trafficking/2015/UNODC_Assessment_Toolkit_TIP_for_the_Purpose_of_Organ_Removal.pdf

U.S. Department of Health and Human Services. (2014). *Treatment improved protocol (TIP) no. 57: trauma informed care in behavioral health services*. Rockville, MD. Retrieved from https://store .samhsa.gov/shin/content/SMA14-4816/SMA14-4816.pdf

U.S. Department of Health and Human Services. (2013). Guidance to states and services on addressing human trafficking of children and youth in the United States. Retrieved from https://www.acf .hhs.gov/sites/default/files/cb/acyf_human_trafficking_guidance.pdf

U.S. Department of Homeland Security. (n.d.). Retrieved from https://www.dhs.gov/blue-campaign/ about-blue-campaign.

U.S. Department of Homeland Security. (2009a). *Improving the process for victims of human trafficking and certain criminal activity: The T and U Visa*. U.S. Department of Homeland Security, Office of the Citizenship and Immigration Services Ombudsman. Retrieved from: www.dhs.gov/xlibrary/ assets/cisomb_tandu_visa_reccomendation _2009-01-26.pdf

U.S. Department of Homeland Security. (2009b). *I-914, application for T nonimmigrant status*. U.S. Department of Homeland Security, U.S. Citizenship and Immigration Services. Retrieved from: www.uscis.gov/files/form/1-914.pdf

U.S. Department of Housing and Urban Development. (2001). *Faith-based organizations in community development*. Retrieved from https://www.huduser.gov/portal/publications/faithbased.pdf

U.S. Department of State. (2008b). *Major forms of trafficking in persons*. Retrieved from http://www .state.gov/j/tip/rls/tiprpt/2008/105377.htm

U.S. Department of State. (2009). Trafficking in persons report. Retrieved from http://www.state.gov/ documents/organization/123357.pdf

U.S. Department of State. (2010b). *Trafficking in Persons Report*. Department of State publication. Retrieved from www.state.gov/documents/organization.142979.pdf

U.S. Department of State. (2010c). *California SB 657- Transparency in Supply Chains Act of 2010*. Retrieved from http://www.state.gov/documents/organization/164934.pdf

U.S. Department of State. (2011). *Trafficking in persons report*. Retrieved from www.state.gov/j/tip/rls/ tiprpt/2011/

U.S. Department of State. (2012). *Trafficking in persons report*. Retrieved from http://www.state.gov/j/ tip/rls/tiprpt/2012/

U.S. Department of State. (2013). *Trafficking Victims Protection Reauthorization Act of 2013*. Retrieved from http://www.gpo.gov/fdsys/pkg/PLAW-113publ4.htm

U.S. Department of State. (2015). Trafficking in Persons (TIP) Report: July 2015. Retrieved from https:// www.state.gov/documents/organization/245365.pdf

U.S. Department of State. (2016). *Trafficking in persons report*. Retrieved from http://www.state.gov/ documents/organization/258876.pdf

Vandenberg, M. (1997). The invisible woman. *The Moscow Times*, 8.

Van Der Laan, P., Smit, M., Busschers, I., & Aarten, P. (2011). Cross-border trafficking in human beings: Prevention and intervention strategies for reducing sexual exploitation: A Systematic Review. *Campbell Systematic Reviews*, 7(9).

Vanguard University, Global Center for Women and Justice. (2013). Summary findings from the 2013 frontline summit to combat child sexual exploitation. Retrieved from http://www.vanguard.edu/ gcwj/wp-content/uploads/2014/04/2013-Frontline-Summit-Findings-web.pdf

Vertovec, S. (2007). Super-diversity and its implications. *Ethnic and Racial Studies*, 30(6), 1024–1054.

Vieira, C. (2010). Paramilitaries don't want to take the blame alone. Retrieved from Inter Press: http:// ipsnews.net/news.asp?idnews = 52115

Voices and Faces Project. (2017). *About us*. Retrieved from http://www.voicesandfaces.org/mission.html

Wellspring International. (n.d.-a). *About us*. Retrieved from http://wellspringinternational.org/about/

Wellspring International. (n.d.-b). *Word made flesh*. Retrieved from http://wellspringinternational.org/ project/word-made-flesh/

Weitzer, R. (2007). The social construction of sex trafficking: Ideology and institutionalization of a moral crusade. *Politics & Society*, *35*(3), 447–475.

WestCoast Children's Clinic (2012). Research to Action: Sexually Exploited Minors (SEM) Needs and Strengths. Oakland, CA: WestCoast Children's Clinic. Retrieved from http://www.westcoastcc.org/wp-content/uploads/2012/05/WCC_SEM_Needs-and-Strengths_FINAL1.pdf.

Whaley, A. L., & Davis, K. E. (2007). Cultural competence and evidence-based practice in mental health services: a complementary perspective. *American Psychologist*, *62*(6), 563.

Wheaton, E. M., Schauer, E. J., & Galli, T. V. (2010). Economics of human trafficking. *International Migration*, *48*(4), 114–141.

White, S., & Lloyd, R. (2014). *The survivor's guide to leaving*. New York: Girls Educational and Mentoring Services (GEMS).

Wilber, K. (2000). *Integral psychology: Consciousness, spirit, psychology, therapy*. Boulder, CO: Shambhala Publications.

Williams, D., & Goldblatt Grace, L. (n.d.). *My life my choice*. Retrieved from http://www.fighting exploitation.org/

Williams, O. J., Oliver, W., & Pope, M. (2008). Domestic violence in the African American community. *Journal of Aggression, Maltreatment & Trauma*, *16*(3), 229–237.

Williamson, C. & Cluse-Tolar, T. (2002). Pimp-controlled prostitution: Still an integral part of street life. *Violence Against Women*, *8*(9), 1074–1092.

Wirsing, E.K. (2012). Outreach, collaboration and services to survivors of human trafficking. *Social Work & Christianity, 39,* 466–480.

Wolf-Branigin, M., Garza, S., & Smith, M. A. (2010). Reducing demand for human trafficking: A non-linear approach for developing capacity. *Social Work and Christianity*, *37*(4), 424.

Women's Media Center. (n.d.). *Women under siege. Conflict profiles*. Mexico: Women's Media Center. Retrieved from http://www.womenundersiegeproject.org/conflicts/profile/mexico

Woodtich, A. (2011). The efficacy of the trafficking in persons report: A review of the evidence. *Criminal Justice Policy Review*, 22(4), 471-493.

Wooditch A., DuPont-Morales M. A., Hummer D. (2009). Traffick jam: A policy review of the united states' trafficking victims protection act of 2000. *Trends in Organized Crime*, 12, 235-250.

World Bank. (2016). Remittances to developing countries edge slightly up in 2015. Retrieved from http://www.worldbank.org/en/news/press-release/2016/04/13/remittances-to-developing-countries -edge-up-slightly-in-2015

World Health Organization (WHO). (2009). *Violence prevention: The evidence: Promoting gender equality to prevent violence against women*. Geneva, Switzerland: WHO. Retrieved from http://www .who.int/violence_injury_prevention/violence/gender.pdf

Wyler, L. S. (2010). *Trafficking in persons: U.S. policy and issues for Congress*. 7(5700). Darby, PA: DIANE Publishing.

Wyndham Worldwide. (2014). *Wyndham hotel group partners with Polaris to help prevent human trafficking*. Retrieved from http://www.wyndhamworldwide.com/news-media/press-releases/wyndham -hotel-group-partners-polaris-help-prevent-human-trafficking

Xin, C. (2012). Equality urged for migrant workers. *China Daily.* Retrieved from http://usa.chinadaily .com.cn/business/2012-09/13/content_157544560.htm

Zimmerman, C., Hossain, M., Yun, K., Gajdadziev, V., Guzun, N., Tchomarova, M., & Motus, M. N. (2008). The health of trafficked women: a survey of women entering posttrafficking services in Europe. *American Journal of Public Health*, *98*(1), 55–59.

Index